The Smell of Water

The Smell of Water

a twelve-year-old soldier's
escape from the Khmer Rouge army

As the long line of soldiers picked up its pace,
my comrade casually turned to me again.
"Don't worry. I can get us home."

and his determination to stay alive

Lang & Cornelia Srey

previous page –
foot soldiers carved into the wall of a gallery in Angkor Wat,
nearly nine hundred years ago

To all the children who never made it home...

...and the mothers who wait for them still

Our most heartfelt thanks to:

Preah Maha Vimaladhamma Pin-Sem Sirisuvanno
Mr. Vanny Hin
Mr. Retthy Reach
Mr. Chun Pel
Mr. Pho Nau
Mrs. Naum Tang

the survivors who so patiently answered our questions

the Vietnamese veteran of the 1979 invasion of Cambodia

now a life-long friend

Francis Smith

for his instruction in Khmer,
without which we would never have found Pong Tuk

all the staff at Google Earth and Google Maps

without their satellite photographs we could not
have traced the two boys' route, because we would not
have been able to see the terrain that forced their decisions

Dr. David P. Chandler

for making Cambodian history come alive

Former-President Bill Clinton

for releasing the Air Force data
on the American bombing of Indo-China

Dr. Ben Kiernan & Dr. Taylor Owen

for their research on the American bombing of Cambodia

Andy Martin, Leslie Hoover, David Shi,
Michael Szmania, Peony Tang & Frederick Granados

for their encouragement, and review of the text

The Story Behind
The Smell of Water

I undertook the task of writing down this story because it was the best story I'd ever heard in my life. The beginning – the escape itself, and how *two children* engineered it – incredible. And the ending? *Unbelievable.* But it was *true*.

Lang wanted to tell his story, but for a different reason. He wanted people to understand what happens when human civilization collapses completely. And how *quickly* it can happen – the Khmer Rouge and their Communist allies destroyed two thousand years of Cambodian civilization in less time than it takes a child to learn to read. He wanted to take you into the world he knew, so you would see the world we live in now through his eyes. Because what happened in Cambodia can happen again – anywhere.

His story begins with two boys, conscripted from labor camps as soon as they were tall enough to shoulder an AK-47 without the butt dragging on the ground. They were able to escape from their unit when it was routed by invading Vietnamese infantry. The older boy immediately took charge, designating himself their navigator and Lang their reconnaissance – their plan was to get back to whatever remained of their families. But all the territory they'd have to traverse to do so was unknown to them, and there was nothing from which they could get information – it was as though they'd escaped to some lost planet. The older boy navigated by the sun and the rivers, and relied on Lang to tell him what – and who – lay directly ahead of them. Lang did this by climbing the tallest trees he could find and surveying the landscape around them. So I just did what he did – but I did it with Google Earth. I inched my way across the Cambodian landscape with my laptop, and was able to zoom in so close that I could see the current in the Mekong.

But, in the beginning, we didn't know where he went. We knew where he'd *ended up* – but not where he and the other boy had started. The army had withheld their location, and had marched them at night so they couldn't figure it out. And Lang didn't know what year it was, or even how old he was, because the Khmer Rouge had abolished the calendar when he was eight. So how was I going to write the story?

Well, I thought, surely I can find out *something* – if not the whole story. I began with the historical record, and narrowed the time of the escape to December of 1978 or January of 1979 – the Vietnamese blitzkrieg invasion of Cambodia. Most of the combat had been in Southeastern Cambodia, in the two provinces nearest to Saigon. Lang had said that he remembered two things very clearly. There had been heavy artillery fire the day he escaped, and two days after – but none the *day* after. And his commanding officer had ordered their platoon to retreat up a mountain. So I started looking for mountains in Svay Rieng and Prey Veng provinces – and found none.

Then I got incredibly, miraculously, unbelievably lucky. We knew only one person from that area, and asked if he might know something that would help us.

He told us his brother had been in the same battle that Lang was describing. And that there's only one tiny cluster of mountains in the two provinces – Ba Phnom. Easy to miss, if you don't know it's there. He said Lang couldn't have been anywhere else.

I then went back to the historical record. There had been heavy artillery fire on January 5th, 1979, when the Vietnamese had routed the Khmer Rouge troops in the area of Ba Phnom, and more artillery fire on January 7th. But there had been *no artillery fire on January 6th* (I've explained in the back of the book what happened). This established the day of Lang's escape as January 5th, 1979. By then I'd located someone who knew with certainty when he'd turned up again, after his escape. Mid January, 1979. The pieces fit, and we were eventually able to determine where he was when he escaped within an eight-kilometer radius.

Then I got unbelievably lucky again. I needed to talk to someone who'd fought on the Vietnamese side, but most veterans of the Cambodia takeover still live in Vietnam.* Under the same Communist government that perpetrated the takeover – I didn't think any of them would want to talk to me. So I resigned myself to learning what I could from American Vietnamese. I knew that many returned home every few years to visit relatives – maybe I could find someone who knew *something*. But the only Vietnamese I knew were the young ladies in my local nail salon. Well, I thought, I'll just go in and ask – all they can do is think I'm crazy. The *first person I spoke to* told me her husband had been sent into Cambodia in 1979 – and had later escaped from the Vietnamese army! Conscripted, as Lang had been, he'd been assigned to a reconnaissance and "clean-up" unit – if he'd found the two boys, he might have had to shoot them. He still jokes with Lang that he was happy to have met him in another place and time.

This was an incredibly difficult book to write simply *because* the story was true. Oh, it was easy to figure out the route the boys took – at every turn, there was only one way they could go. But if they had to cross an insurmountable obstacle, I couldn't write them around it. And Lang couldn't always remember how they did it. When I asked him how they got across a body of water that was three kilometers across, he didn't even have to think about it. But when I saw what lay ahead of them on the other side, and he told me why it would have been impossible to get across any of it, we both drew a complete blank. I started tossing and turning at night around two in the morning – not awake, and not asleep, but in some other state of consciousness – with my brain *grinding* away at the problem. This went on for two weeks. Then, one morning, I woke up knowing just what they must have done.

If these two boys seem to you to be superhuman – they were. They had survived all four years of one of the worst genocides in human history. Alone after their families had been shattered, they had survived labor camps as bad as the Nazi camps of World War II – only to be conscripted to fight until they were killed. They were the *last* of the survivors – the smartest, the toughest, the most adaptable, the most educated. And their luck never completely ran out.

The references to what they'd learned in school by the ages of eight and ten, when their schools were closed, are as accurate as I could make them. Lang was put in the second half of the eighth grade when he came to the United States, although he hadn't yet learned English. And he had to work part time to help support the family. But he passed all his subjects, except English. I asked him how this was possible – he should have been five years behind. He said he'd already had everything in Cambodia before the end of the third grade, including elementary geometry, algebra and physics. In public school. I started asking about the teaching methods used. He said that students were given a short recess every two hours, during which they played outside. They walked home for lunch, ate with their families, and then walked back to school again. He said that every time he came back into the classroom he was ready to learn again, and attributes the amount he was able to absorb to these two regimens. But he and his classmates were learning in three very different ways – the "French way", the method employed by their teachers, where the material is presented to the child; the "Cambodian way", the way they learned at home, where the material is not presented, but the child is encouraged to observe and ask questions; and perpetual memorization, also employed by their teachers, a method of learning that may have come to Cambodia from India. Being able to employ all three techniques must have been of great advantage in a curriculum that followed the French model, heavy in science and math. As it turned out, things the two boys learned in school later saved their lives.

But Lang had another advantage. He was raised by an exceptionally wise and learned man – an expert in traditional medicine and astronomy, horticulture and the ways of animals. His grandfather. The old man took Lang with him wherever he went – out to his fields, to the Mekong, to their Buddhist temple to talk to the monks, to his patients' houses, and to the homes of his friends. Most Cambodian children are dismissed from adult conversation – Lang was not. By the time he was seven he knew how to bring down a fever, treat dehydration, and keep a minor wound from becoming infected. He could find food where the land had been completely burned over, and preserve it so that he could eat again tomorrow. And he could project the darkest hours of the night by when he knew the moon would rise; critical, when he would have to steal food in the work camps to stay alive.

His country education came to an end the year before the Khmer Rouge seized control, when his family was forced into the capital by the military skirmishes in their village. He and his grandfather, not quite knowing what to do without their farm around them, began to watch television. Foreign television. This was just twenty-one years after Cambodia had gained its independence from France, and Phnom Penh was very cosmopolitan – all the embassies were still open, the American military was there to shore up the Lon Nol regime, and the port was still in operation. Lang's favorite shows were the ones he and his grandfather could understand without having to read subtitles, like *The Road Runner*. And movies whose plots were easy to follow, like *The African Queen*. He watched Clint Eastwood and John Wayne westerns and saw for the first time "the *American* way of doing things". Television became his window on the world, and enabled him to join in the conversations of his new, more cosmopolitan classmates. Their school was closed when the Khmer Rouge began their final assault on Phnom Penh; it is now known as S-21, the worst of the killing facilities.

Lang told me he had nightmares about the Khmer Rouge for twenty-two years after his escape from his unit. When we started the book I said that if he began to have them again, we should abandon the project. He had one nightmare after that, but asked me to continue. He didn't have another.

I wrote most of this book on top of a demanding full-time job. I never got enough sleep, and began to have nightmares myself. I'm a technical writer by profession and so managed the historical research** with no difficulty, but had a great deal of trouble writing dialogue for boys twelve and fourteen. And the sand kept shifting – a fragment of a memory would suddenly come back to Lang, and I would have to go back and rewrite chapter after chapter after chapter. Then, when we finally got to the end of his memories, we found ourselves left with gaps in his story; this is the simple reality of survivors of years of war. I filled the gaps in, and wrote an epilogue to explain what I'd done. In the end it took us six years to record a journey of less than a fortnight.

We had to interview many survivors to recreate Lang's journey. They all helped us selflessly, and smiled. But after such a war as the one that they went through – the American carpet bombing, the Khmer Rouge insurgency, and the genocide that followed – you are never the same.

Cornelia Srey

*The invasion was four years after the fall of Saigon, and the exodus of refugees to the United States had slowed dramatically.

**There is a tremendous amount of confusion in war, and there was more in Cambodia than is usual because the Khmer Rouge withheld so *much* information from the general populace. In addition, conditions differed widely by administrative region. For these reasons historical accounts of this period differ from one another, and some are overly-simplified, vague or imprecise. We synchronized our text with the writings of historian Dr. David Chandler, except in one case where Lang's family's experience was different.

"You cannot understand Cambodia until you know her seasons."

Tonle Sap River reverses to flow north

monsoon starts

rice is planted at a different time in each geographical region

76 to 89 F
June
6″ rain

76 to 88 F
July
6″ rain

76 to 91 F
May
6″ rain

76 to 88 F
August
6″ rain

MONSOON SEASON

New Year

74 to 93 F
April
3″ rain

76 to 88 F
September
9″ rain

74 to 91 F
March
1.5″ rain

76 to 86 F
October
10″ rain

Northeast Trades blow southwest year round

72 to 89 F
February
.4″ rain

74 to 86 F
November
5.5″ rain

DRY SEASON

70 to 89 F
January
.4″ rain

70 to 86 F
December
1.6″ rain

monsoon ends, Tonle Sap River reverses to flow south

rice is harvested, winter crops are planted

2012 information, Phnom Penh (18 kilometers from Prai Anchaan).
Temperatures were cooler in 1979.

Rainfall		Temperature	
Inches	Centimeters	Fahrenheit	Centigrade
.4	1.0	70	21.1
1.5	3.8	72	22.2
1.6	4.0	74	23.3
3.0	7.6	76	24.4
5.5	14.0	86	30.0
6.0	15.3	88	31.1
9.0	23.0	89	31.7
10.0	25.5	91	32.8
		93	33.9

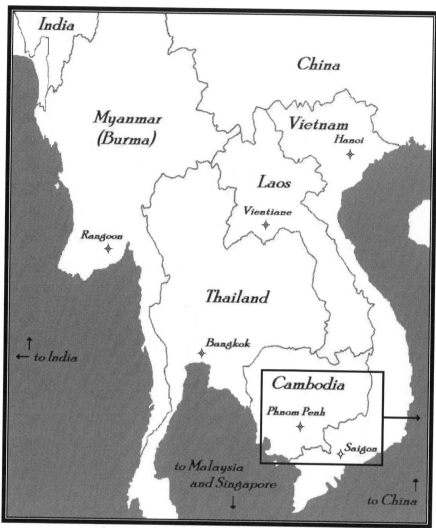

◄ *1700 kilometers (1056 miles)* ►

Indo-China

Cambodia, Laos, Malaysia,
Myanmar, Singapore, Thailand and Vietnam

French Indo-China

Cambodia, Laos, Vietnam

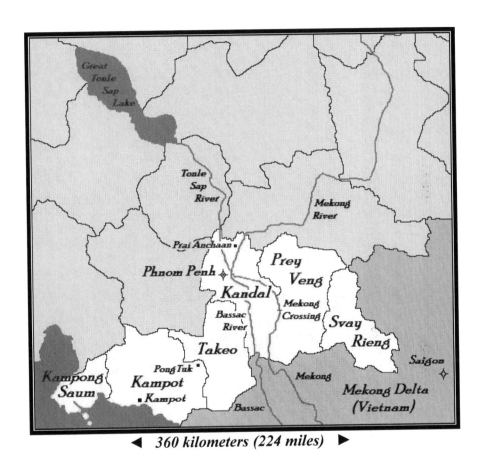

◀ *360 kilometers (224 miles)* ▶

Southern Cambodia

Svay Rieng, Prey Veng, Kandal, Takeo,
Kampot and Kampong Saum Provinces

Mekong, Bassac and Tonle Sap Rivers

Gulf of Thailand

Southern Cambodia

Svay Rieng Province	"Khait Svay REE-ung"
Prey Veng Province	"Khait Prey VEng"
Mekong River	"TōnlEY Mey-kOng"
Kandal Province	"Khait KaandAAl"
Prai Anchaan village	"Phoom Prai AnchAAn"
Phnom Penh	"PnAUm Pĭn"
Bassac River	"TōnlEY BasAA"
Takeo Province	"Khait TakAAo"
Kampot Province	"Khait KaampOUt"
Pong Tuk village	"Phoom Pōng Tŭk"
Kampong Saum Province	"Khait Kaampong SAUm"

Prai Anchaan is Lang's ancestral village, and the village in which he grew up.

Useful Notes

The **Khmer** are the majority ethnic group in Cambodia. In English, "Khmer" is pronounced as it's spelled (the "e" like the "e" in "pet"). Note that there's only one syllable and one vowel. In the Khmer language, "Khmer" is pronounced, "Khmai" (rhymes with "try").

The **Khmer Kraum** (also called "Khmer Vietnamese") are ethnic Khmer who became Vietnamese by nationality when Vietnam annexed the Mekong Delta early in the 18th century. Most speak both Khmer and Vietnamese.

The **Cham** (pronounced, "Chaam") are an ethnic minority whose homeland was along the south-central coast of what is now Vietnam. They speak Cham, a language in the same family as Malay. The Cham who live in Cambodia today are Muslim, and most speak both Cham and Khmer.

"Puamaak" is pronounced, "PuaMAAK", the first "a" pronounced like the "uh" in the American expression, "Uh oh!".

A **Bodhi tree** is a banyan started from the tree under which the Buddha reached enlightenment in Bodhgaya, India.

The Smell of Water

Book One - The War Zone

Book Two - The Water Glass

Book Three ~ *Takeo*

What Really Happened (and How we Figured it Out)

A Word from Lang

The Water Dragon ~ *Is... It... <u>Real?</u>*

Bibliography and Recommended Reading

Book One ~ *The War Zone*

Out!

It was almost dark. And it was cold, for Cambodia – we were in the mountains.

We could still hear them below us – a relentless *boom... boom... pssssssssss... BOOM!* It was almost dark, and they were still shelling. We didn't know how long we'd been running – we just ran.

We'd thought only of getting away, getting home. We hadn't thought about our chances. Neither of us had any food or water, or way to look for it without giving our position away. We had no blankets, either, or warm clothing of any kind. We had no matches, no medicine, no maps, no compass, no radio... we didn't even know where we were.

But these were the little problems – we had a much bigger one. By getting ourselves away from our unit, and then from the Vietnamese when they'd started shelling, we'd put ourselves right in between the two of them.

I was eleven, or twelve, I didn't know for sure. My comrade was fourteen or so, from the same village as me. "OK..." he gasped, watching the jungle around us, "OK... *get out of your uniform as quick as you can.* Put on the farm clothes you had in the work camp, before you got drafted." We each pulled out a faded Mao shirt and a pair of shredded shorts, half rotted from years spent working the paddies.

"Here's the plan," he choked, still trying to whisper, "If *our* unit catches us, our story is that we couldn't keep up, got lost, and ran the wrong way. Nyah, let me do the talking. I've kissed up to our commanding officer so long he'll actually think I'm telling the truth." He closed his eyes for a moment, then opened them again. "They'll be missing us right about now, as they try to regroup. Our squad leader will be looking for *you.* And when he doesn't find you, he'll start looking for *me. If they catch us* they'll ask us why we're not in uniform. We tell them we changed into our work clothes so the Vietnamese would think we're just farm kids – not Khmer Rouge. That's why I ditched my AK-47."

I just stood there and looked at him, waiting to hear the rest of the plan.

"OK," he continued, his lungs still trying to catch up with him, "If another unit catches us, they'll shoot us if they think we're deserters. Or worse, if they don't want to waste their bullets on a couple of kids. Our story is that we got separated from our unit and are just trying to catch back up. We're lost – *lost,* that's all. You do the talking then, 'cause you're smaller than I am. They'd believe you before they'd believe me. And I'll just *shut up* and pass myself off as younger than I am. I can do it, without my gun."

Oh, I was small all right. My aunts had abandoned my real name before I was even old enough to ride around the farm on my grandfather's shoulders – I was so skinny, they'd said all they could see was eyes. I'd been "Nyah" ever since, to everyone who knew me. Just Nyah. "Little Gecko". I'd survived the succession of tropical diseases that had made me so thin as a child, but now, after four years of work camps and the army, my knees were bigger than my head.

Puamaak was finally beginning to catch his breath. "OK. If the Vietnamese find us ... I don't want to think about that. Hey, we can't get caught with these uniforms – ditch 'em!" We each pushed our army clothes – a cap, a shirt, and a pair of long pants – under a tangle of vines. "Shoes, too," he said. He saw my face, and shook his head. "Army issue. Dead giveaway."

We sat down to rest underneath the old banyan that spread over us. "If the Vietnamese find us," he said, "let's try talking to them in Khmer. If they're Khmer Vietnamese they'll be able to understand us. If that doesn't work, well, neither one of us speaks Vietnamese, so we just gotta *look* lost." He sighed. "We need to start rehearsing all this. Hey, which side of the border do you think we're on?"

I leaned back against the tree and just shook my head.

So we started rehearsing. All three scenarios. If our unit found us we were just lost, and *so* happy they'd found us. If another unit found us we were *really* lost, and *so* grateful for a little food and water so we could help them continue to fight. If the Vietnamese found us we were just plain *lost*. A couple of hungry farm kids, separated from their families and left behind in the chaos of evacuation.

The more we rehearsed, the more it became clear to us that the most dangerous scenario was the second one – if another unit found us and figured out how far we were from ours, they'd know we were deserters and kill us for sure. But there was yet another possibility. The Khmer Rouge just loved to shoot, if they could come up with a good-enough excuse. So if their unit had a quarrel with our unit, they'd use us for human target practice.

Well, we'd have to pass for farm boys. Local boys. We'd have to look like we were *from* where we *were*. But where *were* we? We'd been marching at night for about a month now, and as we'd passed country villages we could see the lights of their oil lamps, but couldn't tell if they were Cambodian or Vietnamese.

Let me tell you, we hadn't planned to escape – we hadn't planned to escape at all. This afternoon had been just like any other. We were just... hanging around, waiting for the scout to come in to tell us where to march that night. Suddenly, with no explanation, our commanding officer had ordered all of us – an entire platoon – to march straight up into the mountains. And that could mean only one thing.

As our unit had turned around, my comrade and I had been marching side by side. We'd turned to look at each other, and then, slowly, straight ahead again – he'd said that was the only way we could whisper to one another without arousing suspicion. "If we don't separate ourselves from our unit before the Vietnamese find them," he said, "we'll die with them. And the Vietnamese *will* find them. It won't be long."

As the long line of soldiers had picked up its pace, he'd casually turned to me again. "Don't worry. I can get us home."

Now, as we leaned against the tree, we began to realize that the most dangerous scenario was also the most likely one – that we'd be found by another Khmer Rouge unit, and couldn't explain what we were doing there. So we rehearsed, and rehearsed, and rehearsed again, knowing our lives would depend upon our ability to lie.

He was *good* at it. He had two years' experience on me. You *had* to lie, to stay alive in Khmer Rouge Cambodia. But I'd always feared my big eyes would give me away, and had gotten someone else to do my lying for me. Too late to start practicing now.

Then it hit us. Our best chance of survival would be to look *too insignificant* for any soldier, on either side, to bother with. That way, they'd never stop and question us.

You must understand that we had grown up with war – the first years of our childhoods must have been just a lucky respite. We knew the North Vietnamese and the South Vietnamese had been fighting since the '50s; forever, as far as we were concerned. And that the French had been mixed up in it somehow. Then the Russians had joined in, and then the Americans. With *their* allies. Our neighbors' war had become ours when the Americans began carpet-bombing Cambodia, the year before I was born. And then our civil war had started. We'd thought the whole world must be fighting, round and round in a death spiral, year after year after year. Phnom Penh fell to the Khmer Rouge in April of 1975. OK, we thought, now all the fighting's over – in our country, at least. But then the Khmer Rouge declared war on *us* – the urban, the educated, the well-off. We didn't understand any of it.

For Puamaak and me it had all started in March of 1970. When I was only three. One morning, when my grandfather and I were walking out to his fields, we saw a comet. Coming from the east.From Vietnam. He pointed to it as it flew through the sky and explained to me, "War always comes from the direction of the comet's tail."

A week before Prince Norodom Sihanouk had been deposed by his prime minister, Lon Nol. The Americans had immediately stepped up their carpet bombing of Vietnamese Communist base camps in Cambodia. From Vietnam.

So you see, my grandfather knew that comet would come – he was looking for it. And he knew it would come from Vietnam.

Sihanouk threw his support behind the Communist Khmer Rouge, and civil war broke out between the Khmer Rouge and the Lon Nol regime. The Vietnamese Communists had thrown their support behind the Khmer Rouge and had sent troops into Cambodia; the Americans, with the South Vietnamese, quickly invaded our country to try to flush the Vietnamese Communists out. This pulled all of Cambodia into the Indo-China war.

The American carpet bombing reached my village in 1973, when I was six. Underground in a homemade bomb shelter, my family tried to make sense of it. There were no Vietnamese Communist base camps in our area – we were eighteen kilometers outside of Phnom Penh. With every bomb that hit I thought I was going to die. But I didn't, and the Americans began to pull out of Vietnam later that same year.

But one enemy was quickly replaced by another – which is just how it is in war. The Khmer Rouge, as they fought their way across the countryside, finally reached my village. My family moved into Phnom Penh, trying to get out of the way.

But we couldn't. The Khmer Rouge won the civil war in 1975, and within days force-marched us out of Phnom Penh. They resettled us in a commune a hundred and forty kilometers away, then took me away from my family and put me in a work camp. I was nine, I think. That's when I started losing track of time...

I thought I'd die in the work camp – but I didn't. The Khmer Rouge eventually turned on their Vietnamese allies, and my comrade and I were drafted as soon as we were tall enough to shoulder an AK-47 without the butt dragging on the ground. Like all the other boys in our unit. They gave us a few weeks' military training and started marching us east, toward the Vietnamese border – we were Border Patrol. Then, yesterday, our squad leader had come to my friend and told him he'd be sent into combat in a couple of days.

But we'd escaped, and here we were. Now, we were just displaced civilians again. No food, no shoes, no nothing.

"I think we're in *great* shape," said Puamaak, desperately trying to whisper despite his excitement. "Best shape since the Khmer Rouge took over. We're away from our unit, we're not in a work camp, and we're on our way home!"

I knew he wasn't just trying to rally me, I knew that what he said was true. Yes, we were caught between two armies with no weapons and no supplies, but our chances of survival were suddenly the best they'd been in four years. *If* we could make it back to our families.

"Can you believe it?" he said. "So simple, how we escaped, but no one thought of it but us. OK. The most important thing is that no one stops us. Because if no one stops us, no one questions us. Practice looking *too little* for anyone to bother with. Practice looking... insignificant."

He suddenly stopped and looked at me, all four and a half feet of me, swimming in a Mao shirt that had fit three years before. A wild-looking boy with black, matted hair that hadn't been cut since the day he'd been drafted. "Never mind, Nyah. OK, let's go through all of this again..."

So we rehearsed our lines in case we got caught, over and over and over. 'We lost you guys when you headed up the mountain.' 'Sergeant! We're trying to find our families, sir!' 'Older Brother, Older Brother, look – we have no gun! Do you speak Khmer? We're trying to find our families. Please, may we have some food?'

It never occurred to us – not even for a moment – that we *were* what we were *rehearsing* to be. Just two kids, caught up in someone else's war, lost, alone, starving.

Older, seasoned soldiers would have made a pact in that moment, to survive by bravado and grit. They would have pooled their information, poured out all their ideas, and devised a master plan. They would have been able to see how each move could be built upon the last, because they would have been able to envision the future. And, in the end, they wouldn't have hesitated to kill. They would have believed they had license to.

But our story doesn't go like that. It doesn't go like that at all.

We didn't know what courage was – we were just trying to stay alive. And grit? We'd survived the work camps by our good karma. And luck.

We didn't know how to devise a master plan – we'd never heard of one. We knew we had to go *west*, and we knew we couldn't get *caught*. That was *it*. That was *our* master plan.

And as for information, we'd never been 'Border Patrol'. We'd been brought in as backup for regular troops. When the Vietnamese had launched a full-scale invasion *two weeks* before we'd been shelled, we hadn't even been told. Suddenly we weren't Border Patrol *or* backup – we were *it*.

But the first of our Buddhist precepts forbade us to kill. Anything. We were more afraid of killing than we were of being killed. We didn't have a gun anyway. It was lying on the forest floor somewhere, about a kilometer behind us.

And we'd lost any concept of future, because 'now' was always the same – we were hungry, and we wanted to go home. When 'now' never changes, when tomorrow is never different, the future… disappears. It was the past that loomed ahead of us. We questioned only that we could make it home – not what we'd find when we got there. Our families might have been killed years ago. And we would not have known.

As we rested under the banyan tree we contemplated our chances. And suddenly, it was dark.

Life Before the Escape, 1966 to 1978

July 1966-7	1968	1969	1970	1971-2	1973	1974	1975	1976	1977-8
Lang is born & is quickly nicknamed "Nyah"	Nyah doesn't die	Nyah still doesn't die	Lon Nol overthrows Sihanouk, Sihanouk backs Khmer Rouge	civil war continues	U.S. steps up carpet-bombing & Nyah gets caught in it	civil war reaches Nyah's village & his school is closed	Khmer Rouge overthrows Lon Nol	Nyah & Puamaak are moved from camp to camp, & find themselves in the same camp for a brief period of time	Puamaak is drafted
U.S. carpet-bombing, begun in 1965, continues	U.S. carpet-bombing continues	U.S. carpet-bombing continues	civil war breaks out between Lon Nol regime & Khmer Rouge	Vietnamese Communist, U.S. & South Vietnamese forces withdraw from Cambodia, but U.S. carpet-bombing continues	U.S. begins to pull out of Vietnam	UXO accident	Nyah's family & Puamaak's are caught up in the march out of Phnom Penh		Nyah is drafted nine months later, spots Puamaak at muster, & they 'buddy up' for protection
Nyah contracts several tropical diseases & is taken from the hospital by his mother's father to die at home			U.S. invades Cambodia with U.S. & South Vietnamese troops			Nyah's family moves into Phnom Penh for safety	Saigon falls to the Communist Vietnamese		
							Nyah & Puamaak are put in separate work camps		

Day One ~ *Alive*

"Nyah… are you awake?"

"Yes."

"We're still alive."

"I guess so. I'm hungry… You're not hungry if you're dead, are you?"

"No, Nyah, you're not hungry if you're dead."

We'd awakened as we'd fallen asleep – sitting up, still propped against the tree. It was not quite light yet.

I was so *cold.* "Are you *sure* we're not dead? How do you *know?*"

My friend didn't answer, and I put my hand on his arm. He was just as cold as I was, but he certainly wasn't dead. Which meant that I wasn't, either.

"Are you OK?" I asked, still whispering.

"Yeah… just *cold."*

"I know. I am too. But don't worry, tonight we can sleep in our hammocks. And I know just how to fix them up to keep us warm."

He didn't answer again – it was as though he hadn't heard me. "You sure you're OK?" I asked.

He was looking around in the half light, at the jungle all around us. "Nyah, this was not our plan. This was not our plan at *all.*" He straightened up, as he remembered. "We were going to keep walking all night. But when we sat down to rest for a minute, we just… blacked out." He shook his head. "Not a good start."

He leaned back into the tree, stared straight ahead, and exhaled very slowly – as though finishing a cigarette. But I knew he didn't smoke.

Suddenly he sat up again, and shook his head like a dog getting out of the water. "OK. Help me think. We've got to figure out where *we* are in relation to everyone else. Then we'll know what we have to do – get out of here quickly, or stay where we are until dark."

"The easiest position to figure out is that of our platoon." I rolled my eyes backward. "Right above us."

"Yeah. And other retreating units would have either gone west, or up the mountain with ours... That's another reason I wanted us to split off, Nyah – there won't be enough food up there for everyone, even if the Vietnamese *don't* get them."

He turned to watch the woods again. "Any unit that stood its ground yesterday will still be down in the plains. And from the sound of the artillery fire after we took off, dead. OK, that accounts for our army. As for theirs..."

He stopped, and turned to me again. He had this really funny look on his face. Then he tilted his head up – as though he were listening for something. But he didn't *say* anything.

"What's wrong?" I whispered. *"I don't hear anything."*

"That's what's wrong." He put his ear to the ground, sat up again and shook his head.

The morning mist had begun to rise, and I suddenly felt even colder. "The shelling. We haven't heard it since we fell asleep last night... *That's why we didn't wake up.*"

He nodded. "That's why we didn't wake up."

Now his eyes panned the jungle around us like those of a nervous cat. "I don't like it, Nyah. I don't like it at all. If our troops are in retreat the Vietnamese should be shelling the hell out of them. Chasing the last of the retreating units below us, and finishing off the ones above us." He looked up to where he thought our platoon should be, and then away again. "It just doesn't make any *sense.*"

"Nothing makes sense in war. Don't expect it to."

He turned and looked at me as though he'd never seen me before. He started to say something, thought better of it, and looked away again. "Well the Vietnamese can't see where to fire, that's for sure. They can't see any better than we can. So maybe it does make sense that everything's quiet. But as soon as the sun's up..."

"Oh, the darkness wouldn't stop them – they'd just use parachuting flares. Or tracers. Or blindly lob mortars onto the mountain."

"Nyah – how would you know *that?* You just got drafted. You've only been *in* three months. You haven't even been in combat yet."

"Not in this war. In the last one. When the Khmer Rouge insurgents set their guerillas on the Lon Nol troops. There was heavy fighting in my village. When I was seven. We thought the Khmer Rouge would be defeated quickly – we just stayed in the house all the time, to be sure we were out of the way. But when the fighting dragged on, day after day, we just... moved. But I still remember looking out my window at night, to watch the tracers."

"I guess I was just lucky there was none of that where I was. I guess my village just... wasn't that important." He paused, still trying to make sense of the silence, but knowing we had no time. "Nyah, what do *you* think is going on?"

"After yesterday, the Vietnamese know they have the advantage. So they're just taking their time. They're down in the plains – somewhere."

"OK... Well if they're 'just taking their time', that buys us a little. But I'm sure they know where our platoon is just as well as we do. They would have seen them turn and run for the mountain yesterday."

"Ha!" I rolled my eyes backward again. "Driving them up there was probably their plan. Like a big, growling dog trying to tree a cat. The cat keeps climbing higher and higher, until there's nowhere left to go."

"I wonder how many other units went up there with ours?"

I shrugged my shoulders. "As many as the Vietnamese wanted to tree."

He looked up at the mountain again, then turned back to me. "Little brother, I can't believe we got *away*. We wouldn't have, if it weren't right after harvest season. It was the extra rations throughout December that gave us the strength to run like that. And the cooler weather. Just lucky the Vietnamese didn't attack us in monsoon season – we wouldn't have made it, Nyah."

He looked up again, but couldn't see in the half light. He looked down toward the plains, but couldn't see through the thick of the jungle. *"Damn* it. The Vietnamese are just *sitting* there, waiting to pick us all off." He shook his head again. "I can't believe we fell asleep like that. We could've been out of here by now. Instead we may have to find a place to hide, and just... dig in. We may not even be able to look for food."

"We're still alive, and that's all that really matters." The difference in our ages made my view of things far less complicated than his. "And they may be sitting down there, but there's no one up here. Look at this place..." I stretched my hand out in front of me. "Thick underbrush, banyans a hundred years old, and vines running along the ground like tripwires. And it's *dead* silent – everything would have been hunted out right after the takeover, when people first got short of food. Believe me, no one could make a move up here without being heard. Not even Viet Cong. If it stays quiet, I think we should look for food. Because we won't get far without it."

He sighed. "Well we can't find anything until we can see..." He turned to watch the jungle again, and leaned back against the tree.

"We can put our hammocks over us while we're waiting for the sun to come up," I said, reaching for my pack. I pulled out a thin, dark green sheet of nylon and wrapped it around myself.

Puamaak reached into his pack and pulled out a hammock just like mine – a slice of an old parachute left over from some other war. "So, how do you make these things warmer?"

"You find some banana leaves. The biggest ones you can get. Then you roast them by passing them over hot coals. That makes them flexible, so they won't tear."

"Oh, yeah. I used to watch my mother do it. She'd roast the leaves, cut them into strips, then fold each strip around a ball of sticky rice filled with coconut and palm sugar. To make a little packet. Then she'd steam all the packets, and set them on the windowsill to cool. She used to make extra on festival days so we could take some to the temple... So here we are surrounded, and all I can talk about is my mother's cooking. What's wrong with me?"

"Same thing that's always wrong with us, Puamaak. No food."

"Yeah. No water, either, since lunchtime yesterday." He shook his head like a dog again, then smoothed back his matted hair. "So after you roast the banana leaves, what do you do?"

"You put some in the bottom of your hammock and line the sides with the rest. Then you just get in and wrap yourself up, like a caterpillar in a cocoon. The leaves keep you warm even after they've cooled off, and they keep the mosquitoes from biting through the fabric."

"It really works?" he asked.

"Oh yeah. It's a trick I learned in my first work camp. From one of the older boys."

"Sure wish I still had my ammo vest, though – I'd be a *little* warmer. Had to ditch it with my AK-47. Hey. Your porter's vest. They always had you carrying dried fish and rice. You didn't think to save some of the fish before you ditched the vest, did you?"

"That's not what they had me carrying yesterday."

"No?" He adjusted his hammock, turned and looked at me. "So what was in the vest?"

"Clips."

Puamaak looked as though his heart had stopped. *"What?"*

"Clips. Just like yours. And a couple of grenades."

He blinked. "So if you'd been hit..."

I nodded. "Detonated."

"Nyah, we wouldn't even have been able to find your body."

"Yours either – you were right next to me. Oh, yeah, I ditched that vest before you even ditched yours. You didn't see me do it because I'd already fallen in behind you. I mean, you didn't have time to explain how we were going to escape – you just said, 'Follow me!' So I did. You know, I think I ditched that vest before we were even out of sight."

"Nyah, if they switched you over from carrying food to carrying ammo, they knew yesterday morning that the Vietnamese were close." He shuddered, and pulled his hammock up closer around him.

And that's when he figured it out. *They were going to send him into combat with me,* he thought. *But why didn't our squad leader tell him? Well, neither one of us will have to go in now – so there's no point in me telling him anything.*

"You know," I said, "we've had no food or water since yesterday, but I feel better than I did when we got up here last night. Stronger, somehow. Yeah, nothing makes sense any more."

"Oh, it makes perfect sense. We got almost twelve hours of sleep last night. How many did you get in the work camps? And in the army? You didn't figure out what they were doing? They kept us sleep-deprived so they could control us, so we wouldn't try to escape. And they did it for *four years.* You feel stronger now because you got a full night's sleep, that's all."

"Well we must have been a lot less sleep-deprived than everyone else, because we were the only ones who got away."

He shook his head. "I can't believe the other guys in our section of the line didn't figure out what we were doing. I mean, I know they were brainwashed years ago, but... they have eyes."

"Puamaak, they have eyes, but they don't see."

I looked up at the mountain and remembered the chaos of the day before. The chaos that had given us that tiny window of escape. It had taken my friend a split second to make his decision, but if I'd known they were going to put me into combat, I would have beaten him to it. And I don't think he *asked* me if I wanted to escape. I think he just told me we were going.

Suddenly he put his hand on my arm and squeezed his fingers into it. I didn't move.

He's heard something, I thought. I opened my eyes wide, and looked around for anything that would tell me what it was. *This must be the beginning of it,* I thought. *By the time the sun sets tonight we'll either be POWs, or dead. This is the beginning of it all.*

My comrade tilted his head up with his hand still on my arm. He waited, until he was sure. Then he took his hand away again, slumped back against the tree, and laughed nervously as he rolled his eyes. "Ha! Just an owl. Going back to wherever owls go when they've finished hunting for the night."

"*'Just an owl?'*" I found myself sitting bolt upright, staring him square in the face. "He's not hunting. I told you – there's nothing left here for him to *get*. How the hell do you not know that the owl is the harbinger of death? Where do you *come* from, anyway?"

He ignored my question. "You couldn't hear it? You couldn't hear the owl?"

"No. But I know he's come for *one* of us."

"What do you mean, 'No'?"

"Just *'No'*, that's all." I looked away, pretending to adjust my hammock.

"Nyah – *what are you not telling me?*"

I'd hoped we'd be well on our way before he noticed. Out of the war zone at least. I didn't want him to see me as a liability, and ask himself if he should leave me behind. I'd have to prove my worth as soon as we could get moving, but as for now... I just started explaining.

"Well I don't know where *you* were during the air raids of '73, but I was only a few kilometers from where the bombs were coming down. And all we had for a bomb shelter was an L-shaped pit that my grandfather and my uncles had had to dig themselves – all our field hands had taken off, to take care of their own families. When we saw the bombers coming we scurried for our hole in the ground like rabbits when a hawk flies over. My grandparents sandwiched me between them, sitting there in the bottom of the pit – as though *that* would help. Each time a bomb hit the shock waves were so terrible I thought I'd bleed to death, from the inside out. It was like taking a hit in the chest from a kick boxer – and then another, and another. And I was afraid that the shaft of the pit would collapse, burying us alive. I remember sitting there, waiting, watching the faces of my family in the light of the little oil lamp we always kept burning... And you never knew when the bombing was going to stop. Well, I didn't bleed to death, and I didn't get buried alive, but I lost some of my hearing. I lost some more in a UXO explosion after that."

"Really? Then yesterday – when I whispered to you that we should try to escape – how did you hear me?"

"I didn't. I didn't *have* to. I mean, what were you going to say? 'Let's turn around and invite the Vietnamese to tea'? And I can read lips, you know. You said the word, 'home', and that's all I needed to see."

He just shook his head again. "You know, I've been around you for three months now, but I never noticed anything. I guess it was because everyone around us was always... *yelling*. I mean, we were in the *army*. And I really didn't know you before that."

We were from the same village, but then again, we weren't. When the Khmer Rouge had forced his family out of their village, and mine out of ours and then out of Phnom Penh, we'd both ended up in another village – Pong Tuk, in Kampot Province, about a hundred and forty kilometers southwest of Phnom Penh.

Once we'd been "relocated" the Khmer Rouge had "re-educated" us – all work and no play make for a productive and peaceful agrarian society. But because this new peacefulness had been backed up by their semi-automatic machine guns, he and I had never been able to talk to each other. You were watched all the time, and there was always someone just waiting to turn you in for a little extra rice. So you couldn't talk about the Khmer Rouge or the takeover. Your family, or your friends, where you were from or where you'd gone to school. How hungry you were, or how painful it was to watch your family starve. And you *sure* couldn't talk to anyone you had no reason to talk to – we'd learned very quickly that the safest thing to do was to not talk to anyone at all.

We'd been separated shortly after relocation when we'd been sent to different work camps. Then we'd been shuffled from one camp to another – like all the other boys. At one point he'd been transferred into my camp, but into a different work crew. So we *still* couldn't talk to each other.

As the months had gone by it had become harder and harder to recognize anyone you might have known before. The clothes our mothers had so carefully picked out for us had been replaced by government issue. Our neat haircuts had grown out, and we had nothing to wash our hair with. We cleared land, dug irrigation canals or worked the rice fields seven days a week, from dawn until dusk – longer, if the commune was behind schedule. So we'd all acquired a leathery tan from working in the sun. We actually thought the worst of it would wash off, if we could ever get our hands on some soap. Our posture had changed, too – we couldn't straighten up any more. And any distinguishing mannerisms we may once have had had been replaced by a single new one – *scratching*. Head lice, body lice, head lice, body lice... But the biggest change was in our weight. I don't even want to tell you what they gave us to eat. And there was just enough of it to keep us alive – no more.

But when they'd started shuffling me from one camp to another I'd learned to recognize people by the things that never change – their gait, their voice, their dialect, how they move their eyes... When I'd been drafted I'd been terrified, and had looked for *anyone* I might have known before. I'd recognized the other boy from Pong Tuk right away, and had latched on to him before he ever knew what hit him. I would have followed him anywhere. In fact, I was just planning to follow *him* home – I figured *he* knew the way.

"*Damn.* If we just had some landmarks, little brother... You have any idea where we are? They marched us at night on purpose. So we couldn't see anything."

"No landmarks? I crossed the Mekong. And if I did, you did too. They didn't tell us what it was, but when the river's a kilometer across... I'll tell you, I was getting ready to swim. They commandeered a bunch of little fishing boats, and took us over three or four men to a boat. *In the dark.* I was sure my boat was going to go over... But you have no idea where we are? Not even... *sort* of? You were always buzzing around the officers. I thought you were trying to get intelligence."

"Ha! Yeah, well, I soon found out there was no intelligence to *get*. You know what Standard Operating Procedure is? No, I guess you don't. They post locals in each platoon, so the commanding officer can use them to do his navigating for him. So *no one* has a map – except maybe the top brass in Khmer

Rouge headquarters. Wherever *that* is. Even if our commanding officer has a map, I don't think he can read it. Nyah, he wasn't selected because he would make a good officer. He was selected because his family had demonstrated their loyalty to the Party before the takeover. You *know* that, don't you? I mean, I don't know what you know and what you don't, because we were never able to talk freely. And you haven't been in the army as long as I have."

"*Yes* I know that. And I know for sure he can't read a map. He can't read at all. You can tell just by looking at him."

"What do you mean?"

"The way he flaunts his American gear. Makes sure everyone can see it. An educated man wouldn't do that."

He nodded, slowly. "Yeah, none of it's army issue. He went out of his way to get it... But I think our squad leader can read. In '75 we saw them eliminate only the people who were highly educated. We never saw them take anyone away just because he could read. But my father told me to pretend I had no education at all. So that's what I did. And if our squad leader can read, that's what *he* did. You must have done the same thing."

"No, I just didn't say *anything*. I did whatever they told me to do, and didn't say anything. But I listened. Oh yeah, I listened." I started to write my name in the leaves, just to be sure I could still do it – and then scratched it out again. "But in Pong Tuk, they knew we could read. Just because our fathers were important enough to be... put in prison."

"Yeah. We were lucky to have been put into work camps early. Suddenly, no one knew who we were or where we were from. Lucky we were old enough." He looked at me. "You just made it, Nyah."

It was light enough to see now, but my friend did not get up. I didn't know what he was waiting for, but I wouldn't ask him – he was my elder, and if he thought we should wait, we would wait.

"Why," I asked, "do you think we might have crossed the border into Vietnam?"

"Because there were Vietnamese all *over* us yesterday. *Somebody* is invading *somebody*. If we crossed the border we're invading Vietnam, and the Vietnamese are just trying to chase us back into Cambodia. But if we're still in Cambodia, the Vietnamese are invading *us*. I couldn't get enough intelligence to tell me which it is." He rolled his eyes. "So here we are, waiting for enough light to climb a *tree* to try to figure it out."

"What do you mean, 'if we're still in Cambodia, the Vietnamese are invading us'? The Americans are just pushing the Communists over the border, that's all. They're finally winning the war."

"The Americ...? Nyah, are you all right? Did you get hit yesterday? Or fall and hit your head?"

"*No* I didn't get hit. You see any blood? And I didn't fall, either... Why are you looking at me like that?"

"Little brother, the Americans pulled out of Vietnam four years ago. Saigon fell two weeks after Phnom Penh."

"*WHAT?*"

"The Americans pulled out."

"They just… *went home?*"

"Yeah. They just… went home. But Nyah, how could you possibly not *know* that? When they announced it in Pong Tuk they used those awful screechy loudspeakers. Made sure we knew that Communism had triumphed in yet another country."

"Two weeks after we were marched out of Phnom Penh? Is that what you said?"

"Yeah."

"We didn't hear the announcement because we weren't in Pong Tuk. We were still in the first place they put us. They'd dumped us out in the middle of nowhere, with one little hut and nothing else. No one would have taken the trouble to come out to make an announcement, because we were the only ones there."

"So for the last four years, you thought…"

"*Yeah.* How would I know if I never heard the announcement? And who would take the *risk* of telling me, if he thought I didn't know?"

He nodded, slowly. "Well, we'll have to be sure from here on in that you know what I do, and I know what you do. Increases our chances by fifty percent. Do you know *anything* that would help us figure out where we are?"

"No. So you might as well quit asking."

He was quiet for a moment; I was usually more respectful in my reply. And then he got that funny look on his face again. "Nyah, there was *one person* who would have known *exactly* where we are. The *scout*. But I didn't have access to him… Yeah. Local boy. If he was Cambodian, we're in Cambodia. But if he was Vietnamese, working for our army, we're in Vietnam."

"He wasn't Vietnamese."

"How do you know that? You didn't have access to him either."

"Because our commanding officer can't speak Vietnamese. So if the scout was Vietnamese, he couldn't give him a report."

"How do you know our commanding officer can't speak Vietnamese?"

"He's not Khmer Kraum, Puamaak. Can't be. He doesn't speak Khmer with a Vietnamese accent."

"Oh! But that's what the *scout* would have been. A Khmer Kraum would be of much greater value as a scout than a Cambodian or a Vietnamese, because he could speak both languages. He could talk to anyone, no matter where we were. But, more importantly, he could *understand* <u>everyone</u>. So if you were our commanding officer, and you had to choose a scout, which one do you think you'd choose? Even he wasn't that stupid."

"I'll give you that one, my friend. But if he *was* Khmer Kraum, we're in Vietnam."

"Damn." He sighed. "But there's *got* to be a way to figure out where we are… I'll bet you remember a lot from school. What do you remember about Southeastern Cambodia? All I remember is looking at the map, at the area they call 'The Parrot's Beak'. Our teacher pointed it out because it juts southeast into Vietnam like a Hornbill after a piece of fruit. Vietnam surrounds it on every side but the west. Do you remember anything *else?* I sure don't."

"Are you kidding? I was only paying attention to all the places I wanted to go and the things I wanted to see. The great temples of Angkor in the north, the wild elephants of Bokor in the south, the waterfalls of Mondulkiri in the east, the ruby mines of Pailin in the west, the sea at Kampong Saum in the southwest, and the tigers of Ratanakiri in the northeast. The *magical* places. This was before the war, and I thought I'd see them all one day. Yeah, there's a *reason* you don't remember anything about the Southeast. There's just nothing there."

"Well maybe that would explain why we didn't hit many roads when we came through."

"And maybe they kept us *away* from roads for the same reason they marched us at night – so we couldn't figure out where we were... Where's your machete?"

He shot bolt upright. "My knife... Where's my knife! Oh, here it is. *Where's your 'kwaiw'?*"

"Right here." I held it up so he could see it. I'd made sure the night before that I hadn't dropped my farmer's machete.

"Nyah, what's wrong with me? We'd be dead without a knife. I'm the oldest – I should have checked for both of ours when we ditched our uniforms last night."

"Ditched them, and then fell asleep right next to them?"

"Oh, god, you're *right*. If anyone had caught us, and we'd told our story about being just farm kids, and then they'd seen a cuff or a strap sticking out from under the vines... What's wrong with me?"

"Same thing that's always wrong with us."

He sighed. "We'll find some food, as soon as it's safe to look." And he slumped back against the tree again.

"Hey," I said, "do you have a kerosene lighter for our cook fires? I still have mine, but I'm not sure how much kerosene I have left."

"Nope."

"Do you have a flint?"

"Nope. And when your kerosene runs out, there won't be any more. The army will be burning out the villages as they retreat. And all the kerosene will go up with them."

I took my lighter out of my breast pocket; I never carried it anywhere else because it was just as crucial to my survival as my machete. I felt the weight of it in my hand, trying to decide if it felt light. There was no way to measure how much kerosene I had because the wick absorbed it all – shaking it wouldn't tell me anything. "Believe me, if I'd known we were going to escape, I would have filled my lighter. Give me some notice next time."

No reaction from Puamaak. I glanced sideways at him – he still wasn't getting up.

So I just kept asking questions. He was my elder; I could learn from him. And he'd *told* me he was OK. "Why did our commanding officer give the order to retreat *before* the Vietnamese started shelling?"

"I thought you heard it yesterday, when I did. He received information from

Recon – I saw the runner come in. And then *someone* leaked it. I heard the word 'tanks', and the next thing I knew our commanding officer was turning us around. I was thinking they were like the little tanks the Americans brought in during the Lon Nol regime. But then I heard someone say that you can hit them with anything – grenades, M-79s, RPGs – anything in our arsenal – it all just bounces off. *Nothing* can stop them. They're not the little American tanks, Nyah, they're big Russian tanks. And the infantrymen are just like the tanks – they have helmets."

"Helmets? Like the Americans did?"

"Yup. Russian issue, though."

"*Helmets?* You've got to be kidding, Puamaak. Not even our commanding officer has a helmet."

"Ha! Couldn't have found one to fit him anyway. Swollen head. Wait a minute... little brother, I'll bet *he* was the leak. He knew that if he couldn't get us out of there he'd have no more troops to command by sundown. So he dropped the word, 'tanks' to be sure *everyone* turned around. Man, if the Vietnamese had gotten us yesterday... complete massacre." He shook his head. "Nineteen... Hey, you don't know what year it is, do you?"

"No. How would I know?" The Khmer Rouge had abolished the calendar as soon as they'd taken Phnom Penh.

"Ah, doesn't matter. I wouldn't have had a headstone anyway. Wouldn't have been anyone left to bury me. I'd just be lying in the dirt back there, like a dog... Do you know how old you are?"

"No. Twelve, maybe. But I'm just as hungry as if I were eleven, or thirteen. So knowing doesn't make any difference."

He put his hand on his stomach. "So you just looked at me and figured there's not more than a couple of years between us." In Cambodia it's disrespectful to address an elder by his name, so I called him 'Puamaak' (friend). But if I had thought that he was more than two years older than I was, I would have called him 'Bong' (elder brother). "I think I would have been in my first year of high school, if the Khmer Rouge hadn't taken over... Hey, there's the owl again. Did you hear it this time?"

I shook my head. But I could see it clearly, perched on a branch back in the trees. He couldn't – he was looking around for it.

He put his hand on his stomach again, and then the other hand. "We've *got* to find food... Nyah, why the hell is it still so damned *dark?*"

"It isn't."

Day One ~ *All the Degrees of Dead*

How could I have forgotten? I thought. *I guess I've just... gotten used to it, the last three months.* "It's a combination of things, Puamaak. The tree canopy blocks a lot of the light. And... your night vision. You've lost a lot of it."

He shrugged his shoulders. "Like half the other guys in our unit."

"Oh yeah. It'll come back again." But I didn't think it would. And I didn't know what this was going to cost us. We had no idea how often we'd have to move at night. Or how far we had to go.

"You could manage on the plains," I said, "where everything was flat, and all you had to do at night was follow the guy in front of you. Which was always me." I glanced sideways at him again. "You've never been in a jungle before, have you?"

"Not forest like this, no. Forest that's never had *anything* cut out of it..." He sighed. "Tomorrow will be better. We'll be out of here."

I started to get up. "Hand me your cup. I'll get us some water."

My comrade reached into his pack and pulled out a U.S.-GI aluminum cup – old, dented, and dirty. I took it from him and disappeared.

I returned a few minutes later with two cups full of clear, cold rainwater – there are always little pools of it in the jungle, before our summer starts. "This will help with the hunger, too," I said.

He finished his water in one continuous gulp, and handed his cup back to me. "I don't hear a stream, and I don't see a break in the trees. I don't know how you do it, Nyah, but you always do it."

I returned to the puddle and came back with two more cups of water.

He finished his more slowly this time, and then held up his empty cup. "What stories this could tell, little brother. It's seen more years of war than you and I together. You know why it has such a funny shape? It was originally part of a set – the bottom of a plastic canteen fit down into it. Like the canteen our commanding officer has. But the mate to this one went its separate way years ago." He turned the cup over in his hand. "You know, the only reason I have it is because all of its previous owners died."

I looked at my own cup – it was even older than his.

I refilled out cups and returned to my friend.

"Don't listen to me, Nyah. It's just this... *waiting,* for the fighting to start. It's so damned *quiet*..." He looked out at the woods again. "So here we are in the middle of a jungle, with no sign of life at all – except the owl, the harbinger of death. Oh I believe you now, little brother. People call it a 'war zone', but the *owl* was right – it's a *death* zone." He shivered, and a little bit of the water splashed over the edge of his cup.

He started to get up. "Hell, I'd rather hear artillery fire than nothing at all. At least we'd know where the enemy is. OK. I'm Navigation, you're Recon. Find the tallest tree you can find and get up it, so you can see where everyone is. Then we'll know if it's safe to try to move out of here. And if we can look for food."

"OK." I got up, and started to look for a tree.

Now, I hadn't caught on that he was trying to cover for more than night blindness – I was younger than he, and just a village boy. And because I hadn't caught on, I didn't ask myself how much else he might be trying to cover *for*. I looked up to him. If he thought I was the best man to climb the tree, I was the best man to climb the tree. Who wouldn't look up to him? *He* was an infantryman. They'd given *him* a gun. Our squad leader had joked that I was too small. That the recoil of an AK-47 would just knock me over. Because I hadn't been issued a weapon, I'd remained, from one month to the next, just a porter. But the more I thought about it, the more I suspected that our squad leader didn't really care that I might get hurt. I think he cared that I stayed alive. I suspected that, under that Khmer Rouge uniform, he was a nice man with a boy of his own – and had been trying to keep me out of combat.

"A big tamarind's the best choice," I said. "It's the tallest of the big trees thick enough to give me good cover."

"Maybe you'll be able to see the Mekong. That would help us a lot. Eventually we'll have Phnom Treil to guide us. It's the best landmark for finding Pong Tuk. Do you remember it?"

"The rocky one with the funny shape. Always looks blue, until you get close to it. Yeah, I remember it. They used to send me down there to scrape around for bamboo shoots. I'd come back each time with my feet all cut up." Who could forget being made to forage for food because they wouldn't let us eat what we grew?

I started panning the woods for a tamarind from the safety of the tree we'd slept under. My friend, impatient, stepped out from under its shadow.

Our army issue had been a long-sleeved shirt over long pants – it covered you completely. But now, he stood there in his work camp clothes. A short-sleeved shirt over shorts.

He looks so different without his uniform, I thought. *He's so... thin. And I think he's a couple of years older than I am, but he's not much taller. His arms and his legs – they're so... white. My god, he looks like a ghost from hell... Well I've got to be sure he doesn't know it – he might just give up, and tell me to leave him behind. I wonder if he has malaria. No, when I touched his arm when he woke up, he was cold. But that could be malaria, too. There's something wrong with him – he's not alert. Or he would have checked for his machete last night. Both of us have to be able to stay alert, or we're both dead. And how could we have walked all night when he doesn't know where we are, so couldn't know which way to go? He wouldn't have been able to see anyway. No, he's not thinking clearly. If the Vietnamese catch us, they'll probably take me as a POW and just leave him here to die. What would I tell his mother? That he might have made it if I'd just tried a little harder to help him find food? And if our own army finds us they'll send me back to our unit – but kill him by smashing his head in. They're not going to waste a bullet on someone who looks half dead already. But I can't make it without him. I have no idea where we are. He says he doesn't either, but there's a much better chance that he can figure it out than that I can. Am I supposed to go west? What if I do, but miss Phnom Treil completely?*

Maybe if I talk about his family, that will help keep him going. No, that's worse – they're probably all dead. Well, I've just got to keep him alive – somehow. Neither one of us will make it without the other. I woke up before dawn this morning, but just stayed quiet so he could sleep. I think I'll do that every morning. And hope that he always wakes up.

"There are no tamarinds here, Nyah. Come on – we'll have to find one."

I stepped out from underneath the tree, instinctively looking for something I knew should be there. I turned, and spotted some right behind us. Little round fruits, the color of tangerines.

"Look!" I pointed. "That's what we can eat this morning. You can't miss them, even in the thick of the jungle. Wild rambutans. They're like the red ones we used to get in the markets, but instead of growing on a tree, they grow on a vine. You can just close your eyes and pretend you're eating rambutans in the market in your village. They're the best thing you can find to eat in the wild because they have both sugar and water in them. We should be able to find them as long as we're in the mountains; they grow in the lowlands, too, but only in stands of trees."

I walked over to the tree, reached over my head with my machete, and pulled on the vine with the hook on the tip of the blade. My friend had a standard, short-handled machete, but mine was the old Khmer type; the hook was for pulling out roots.

We ate the rambutans as we picked them, peeling them with our fingers and popping them into our mouths whole. Like the little macaques that would have been there before the war.

"This beats even my mother's cooking," said Puamaak. "The last time I had fruit was about six months ago, when the commanding officer let us stop at a commune to pick some. The villagers simply looked away and left us to it – they didn't want us to have their fruit, but they didn't have a choice."

We continued our search for a reconnaissance tree, but I spotted more food first. "Look. Over there." I pointed to a bush about as tall as we were. "It will keep in my pack until we can cook it, and we can eat it raw if we have to." I walked over to the plant, and Puamaak followed me.

"Nyah, *what* will keep in your pack? There's no fruit. Or pods. Or nuts. There's nothing on this thing but *leaves*. Do you eat the leaves?"

I think I must have looked at him as though he were from some other planet. "You eat the root. It's cassava."

He just stood there looking at it.

"You gotta *dig it up*," I said. "Even an elephant knows how to do it. That's their favorite food."

"Nyah, if I've never been in a jungle before, how would I have ever seen an elephant digging up cassava? And where do *you* come from, that you had elephants around? The only elephant I've ever seen is the one people ride around the base of Wat Phnom. The big temple on the hill *in the middle of Phnom Penh.*"

"My grandfather's seen them do it; I haven't. So... you're from Phnom Penh?"

"Of *course* I'm from Phnom Penh. But I just... let people think I'm from somewhere else. *Anywhere* else. Don't want anyone to figure out how many years I spent in school. Figured I could get away with it – not everyone caught up in the march out of Phnom Penh was *from* Phnom Penh. A lot of them were... like you. Not from the city."

"Well I should have guessed you weren't a village boy when the noise of the owl spooked you, but not the owl itself. City people don't believe that the owl brings death. Oh, but it does – I've seen it. But you can trust me with your secret, because I went to school in Phnom Penh. After they had to close our village school because of the shelling between the Lon Nol troops and the Khmer Rouge guerillas. I'm from Prai Anchaan. Just eighteen kilometers northeast of you, on Highway Six. At Bridge Thirteen."

"Bridge Thirteen? The one just before the big market? A few kilometers past where the highway becomes a dirt road after coming out of the city? Oh yeah, I've passed through your village many times. My mother used to buy silk before New Year's each April from weavers just north of you. So you and I actually grew up pretty close to each other. And you went to school in Phnom Penh?" He smiled – he *beamed* – he looked as though someone had just returned his lost *dog*. He shook his head, still smiling. "Only in Cambodia can you find two friends who know absolutely nothing about each other."

"'I guess my village just wasn't that important'? Oh, can you *lie*. Whoever gets control of Phnom Penh gets the whole country!"

Now, if I could lie like that, I'd think it a great accomplishment. But instead of acknowledging my compliment, he deftly turned the subject. "So... your family used to grow rice."

"Yeah, and anything else you can think of. My grandfather was known for his mangoes, especially. He'd developed a method of ripening them by packing them in a special herb so that none of their fragrance would be lost. When you opened the crate and lifted the packing, the smell was like French perfume. His mangoes were in great demand in Phnom Penh. You might have eaten one yourself – when you were a kid."

"Oh, *mangoes*. Don't even talk to me about mangoes. I haven't eaten one since the Khmer Rouge took over. But actually, once we get out of these mountains, fruit should be the easiest thing to find. Even though the mangoes won't be ripe yet."

No, I thought, *there's almost nothing ripe in January. And the fruit trees will have been burned out with the villages.* You had to be able to find the root crops – like peanuts, yams, potatoes, turnips, carrots, radishes, onions, scallions, leeks, taro, garlic, ginger... and cassava. They're what survives when everything above ground has been burned out. But you can only find them by looking for their *leaves*. My grandfather had grown all of them on our farm, and had taught me how to recognize each one. After he'd seen the comet.

And so I came to realize that my friend would have to depend on *me* to find food for the two of us. And I'd thought he knew everything... Well, *almost* everything. I'd spent the entire war learning to survive by watching older boys. You watched them once, and you picked up the skill right then and there –

because, if you didn't, you might not get another chance. And here *I* was, about to teach an older boy how to do something. I felt very old, suddenly.

"OK," I said, "this is how you dig up cassava. You loosen the dirt around the roots with your machete..."

"You'll snap your blade, Nyah. We've *got* to have your knife. We can't afford *one mistake* – all the way back to Pong Tuk. Look," he pointed, "way over there. A much smaller plant. Easier to dig up that one."

"And if we have to run for cover before we get to it? And hole up for a day or more? Yes, we'll find plenty of cassava; it should be all over the place. But why push our luck? OK, watch. I've done this a thousand times. You loosen the dirt around the roots *gently*, so you *don't* snap your blade. Then you loosen them some more with your fingers, until you can pull all the roots out by the stalk. Like this. Do you know why you can always find cassava? Because when you pull it out of the ground the tips of the roots snap off, and don't come out with the rest of it. And those little tips grow back. Since the Khmer Rouge took over, cassava's absolutely the best substitute for rice. Can't eat too much of it raw, though – a little will get you by, but a lot will make you sick. Too sick to walk back to Pong Tuk. OK, you get the smaller one ahead of us." We walked over to it, and he dug up the root.

"Oh," I said, "and never eat anything that's growing near a 'slaing' tree. The tree spreads its poison through the ground somehow, to anything growing near it. There's no 'slaing' around – I checked – so this cassava's OK. I checked the water when I got it, too; if you see that a 'slaing' seed has fallen into it, you know it's poisonous."

"How do you know all this stuff, Nyah? I don't even know what a 'slaing' tree looks like. Never even heard of one."

"Oh, I'm sure you've seen one. You just didn't recognize it for what it was. I'll point out the first one we come to. I don't want you to eat the fruit by mistake – it *looks* edible. It looks *delicious,* as a matter of fact. I know about 'slaing' because my grandfather used to make medicine from it. He was the shaman for our village. Yes, it's poisonous, but the right dose can kill something that's killing *you*. Like you city people would take a tiny dose of arsenic if you had dysentery, to kill the amoeba. You'd be right back on your feet, and the arsenic wouldn't have been enough to do you any harm."

"I never knew my grandfather," he said. "People don't get old in the city, like they do in the country. You're lucky, to have a grandfather. Especially one who knows medicine."

"Ha! He saved my mother's life once – when the Khmer Rouge forced us off the road and into the jungle on the way to Pong Tuk. All of a sudden, she complained of pains shooting up her arm. Then her hand and her arm swelled up – *huge*. My grandfather recognized her symptoms and asked her to describe the last thing she saw before she started feeling sick. She said it was a frog – a frog she'd never seen before. Within half an hour she was slipping in and out of consciousness. No one had any idea what kind of sickness it could be. No one except my grandfather – and when she'd said she'd seen a frog, that had confirmed his diagnosis. He made a medicine that got her back on her feet quickly enough so the Khmer Rouge wouldn't kill her for not being able to work. So he saved her life twice over. He began showing me how to make medicine when I was very young – the simple stuff, I mean. Like how to make a poultice from tamarind to keep a cut from getting infected. He was just beginning to teach me the harder stuff when I was transferred to my first work camp."

He started to pick his way through the underbrush carefully. "So it was a frog like the ones the people in the Amazon use to poison their darts. I thought that was just something you see in the movies."

"Oh, no," I said. "We have plenty of poisonous frogs in Cambodia. And this frog was a particularly rare one. A horned frog. But my grandfather knew of it all the same. He'd learned the formula for the antidote as a young man, and had remembered it all those years. Even though he'd never had to use it. And he was able to recall it instantly, even though he was old. If it had taken him *fifteen minutes* to remember the formula, my mother would have been dead. He wasn't a shaman for nothing – I'll tell you that, my friend."

My comrade paused, remembering the modern pharmacy around the corner from his house in the city. Then he imagined lying on the forest floor just staring up into the trees, sure that you were going to die just because you'd accidentally brushed up against a frog. "So what was in the antidote?"

"If I tell you, you'll start throwing up – and we just don't have time for that... I'll tell you when we get back to Pong Tuk. You wouldn't believe me anyway – remember I told you that."

"Maybe your grandfather would tell me the formula himself. Could I meet him, when we get back?"

"Oh. Sure. Eat your cassava. No, when you eat it raw, you've got to peel it first. Hand me my 'kwaiw'."

"I did recognize the root," he said, "when you pulled it up. My mother used to make little cakes with cassava, for her friends. She used to pour pink icing over them, and I remember watching it as it dripped slowly down the sides. And, of course, she always made an extra cake for me."

"Raw cassava's one of the things that got me through the camps. Ah, but I had a trap – for jungle rats. *That's* what saved my skin. And I learned to use it so well that I never even had to kill the rat myself. I'd balance a chunk of wood over the bait, and when the rat went for the food he'd bonk himself over the head. I used to run for the trap when they let us off for our morning break, so no one would beat me to it and steal my next meal. Then I'd tie the rat around my waist with a piece of string I'd made from vine, and go back to work with the thing swingin' around my waist 'til I got off for lunch. Then I'd skin it, roast it, give some to my closest friends and eat what was left – sure, it was still fresh. You know how I got the trap? I met a man who had no shoes, and I had a pair of Ho Chi Minh sandals I'd found. So we traded. And when I got extra rats I'd trade for other things, too – like a homemade fish hook, or a piece of fishing line. That's how I got my kerosene lighter, so I wouldn't have to start my fires with a flint. So many of us trapped rat that rat meat became just like money. I was even able to make long-term payment arrangements with it. A rat a day for a week gets you a few drops of kerosene for your lighter, and a rat a day for two weeks gets you a lump of salt." Jungle rats had become currency – along with mud crabs, fish, frogs, snakes, and small birds and their eggs – soon after the Khmer Rouge had outlawed the use of money.

"But rat doesn't compare to centipede," I continued. "You know – the ones as long as your foot? If you roast them you can split their shells and pop them inside out to get all the meat. Just like lobster!"

"Once we're back down in the lowlands," he said, "we'll be able to cook. A little more smoke between the smoldering villages won't catch anyone's attention. At least they tell the villagers to get out before they burn their houses. The farmers and their families will be right ahead of the retreating troops."

"Hey," I said, "that's taro over there." I walked over and dug up the root. "We can eat this raw, too. So how did *you* survive the work camps? You must have learned to find food somehow, or you couldn't have stayed alive."

"I wasn't in the camps very long. I'm older than you, remember? The camp you and I were in at the same time – they drafted me out of that one. And you know how it is. Once you're in the army you get a little more food. Ha! Just gives the Vietnamese a bigger target, that's all."

"Man, I'd give anything to see one of their big Russian tanks. Maybe I'll see one when I climb the tree. If I do, you can climb up after me and get a look at it too."

"Oh yeah." And he turned the subject again. "Well it's like I said – *somebody's* invading *somebody*. I heard when I got drafted that whoever's at the top of the Khmer Rouge leadership – the biggest brother of all the Big Brothers – had started sending raiding parties into the Mekong Delta." The top echelon concealed their identities for their own protection; we had never heard the name, "Pol Pot" and didn't know who he was. "He might have kept it up, and the Vietnamese might be invading us in retaliation. Or he might have escalated the raids into a full-scale invasion."

"Brother Number One started sending raiding parties into the Delta? Why?"

"To try to get it back, Nyah."

"Try to get it *back*? The Vietnamese took it from us *three hundred years ago*. There must be just as many Vietnamese living there now as Khmer. You know, if you hadn't gone night blind, you would have been able to find out if he kept the raids up. But you always had to get back to your sleeping area before it got dark. The officers would have been most likely to talk among themselves just before they went to sleep."

"Oh," he said, "I think he did keep the raids up. An extended campaign like that would explain why they're putting kids my age into combat. And think about it, Nyah. My family supported Lon Nol before the takeover. I'm a recognized enemy of the state – and they *still* put a gun in my hand. That tells you how short of troops they are. But surely when he started this, Brother Number One could see the power of the Vietnamese. He couldn't possibly think we could win. But on the other hand, he must be completely mad. He probably did."

Instinctively, I clapped my hand over his mouth. "Do you have a death wish or something? You can't say *anything* against a Big Brother." I lowered my hand. "Don't get *me* killed with *you*."

"Comrade!" Puamaak was still whispering, but I think I jumped a foot. "You misunderstood me. Brother Number One *is* mad – at the audacity of the Vietnamese, taking the Delta from us. Oh, yes, he could see their power – he thought we couldn't *possibly* win. But he forged ahead anyway – for the Cambodian people. Now we have our chance. We can retake the Delta, if we just fight a little harder. You *misunderstood* me, comrade. Don't make that mistake again." And he rolled his eyes.

I stared at him, incredulous. He could lie his way out of anything!

"Puamaak, we'll be twice as safe if I can lie like you can. Give me a lesson."

"Ha! You could *never* do it. Your eyes are too big."

"Oh, no," I said, "I can learn. I can learn anything. Perhaps if I use my eyes to my advantage. I mean, if I open them really wide, and look right into the eyes of the person I'm lying to, and don't flinch... I tell you, I'm going to learn to do it. If nothing else, to help my mother keep the cadres off her back. '"Oh, these eggs? The chicken just... wandered in here and laid them under the bed. I was just about to bring them to the commune cook, so she could make something delicious for you and the other guards.'" And then *I* rolled my eyes.

"Well now you know what's going on – the raids, I mean. Nyah... I think the Vietnamese are invading *us,* not the other way around. They're not going to risk losing the Delta; it's the richest farmland in all of Indo-China. That's why they took it in the first place. And our army won't be able to stop them – if they have tanks, they have a modern army. Like the Americans did."

"So here *we* are, like mosquitoes trying to bring down a big Brahma bull. It's only a matter of time before the bull swats all the mosquitoes dead, using no more than the tip of his tail."

He smiled, and clapped his hand around my shoulder. "You may have gone to school in Phnom Penh, little brother, but they couldn't take the village out of you." And then he took his hand away – but I could see that he was still smiling. I thought he looked a little better.

I stuffed the cassava we couldn't eat into my pack, and we started to look for a big tamarind again. "Try not to brush up against any saplings as we walk," I said, "so that you don't send anything swaying. We're not the only ones who've figured out that there are no monkeys left here."

The jungle was so thick it looked like no one had been there for years. I tried to find a path so we could move more quickly, and quietly. But there were none. And every big tamarind we came upon was smooth all the way up the trunk. We just kept on walking.

"So who do you think," asked Puamaak, "was the leak yesterday, if you were to make a guess?"

"At the top, our commanding officer. I think your suspicion was correct. But I'll bet it was our squad leader who was the leak at the bottom. He didn't want us to die. Well, if he didn't make it up the mountain yesterday, the Vietnamese got him... But our unit was clearly in retreat. Do you really think they would have killed all of them? Or would they have given them the chance to surrender, and taken those who did as POWs?"

"I don't know, little brother. I think it would depend upon whether or not the Vietnamese who got to them first were Khmer Kraum. OK. We know we crossed the Mekong. If the Vietnamese are invading us, we're in Southeastern Cambodia just north of the Delta. And if we're invading Vietnam, we're *in* the Delta. So there's a good chance that some of the Vietnamese soldiers who came up on us yesterday are Khmer Kraum. If they catch us we can talk to them, and they can talk to us. They might even give a couple of lost farm boys some hot Cambodian food. Wouldn't that be the most ironic thing you could possibly imagine? We get caught by 'The Enemy', and they treat us better than our own..." He stopped.

"What's the matter?" I whispered.

"It won't work."

"*What* won't work?"

"Anyone who catches us up here will know who we are, and how we got here. Because of the battle yesterday. And kids looking for their families wouldn't be looking for them up here... No, trying to pass ourselves off as farm kids won't work until we're down in the lowlands again. It's the only story we can use, but," he shook his head, "no one will believe it. And if we're caught by Vietnamese who don't speak Khmer, we can't even *use* the story. You know what? If they see us here in the jungle and think we're Khmer Rouge, they won't even bother to catch us. They'll just shoot us."

"But Puamaak, there are no two people on *earth* who look less like soldiers than we do. We've got our old farm clothes on. We don't have guns. And we're so damned *short*. It's a good thing we're not trying to pass ourselves off as soldiers, because we'd never be able to do it! And we'll lose our cover the minute we step out of the jungle and into the lowlands. Especially if they're burning out the villages. Remember – a tree is always the best place to hide, and when they burn the villages, all the trees go up with them."

We finally found a big tamarind with knobs running up the trunk. "OK," I said, "I know you didn't have anything like this in the city. Watch how I get up it. The villagers will have had to leave their dogs behind, and those dogs'll be hungry. And some will have rabies. With no one left to cull them out, the rabies will spread from dog to dog pretty quickly. If you want to stay alive, you've got to know how to climb the nearest tree you can find – without having to stop to think how to do it." I started for the tree, and then turned back again. "Oh, the Brahma bulls'll chase you down, too, and then snap their heads around to get their horns into you. And the bull water buffaloes are even worse – their horns are sharper and much longer, so they can get at you before they've even caught up to you. They may look fat and awkward, but, believe me, they can outrun you... Just thought I'd let you know, seeing as how you're from the city." I turned around again and started up the tree, leaving him to stare at my shadow.

I climbed down again in less than a minute. "Just not enough for me to get my fingers around. I'll have to make a ladder."

Before he could protest that the noise would give us away I'd cut down a stalk of bamboo, set it against the tamarind tree and tied it in place with a vine.

Then I climbed from branch to branch up the bamboo until I reached the lowest branch of the tamarind. And then I climbed straight to the top of the tree. I was about three stories up.

Now the boy who'd been issued a gun thought that *I* could do anything. Ha! What a joke! He didn't know that I'm no good at the most important thing for any Cambodian – *I can't catch fish!* But I wasn't going to tell *him* that.

I climbed down fifteen minutes later with two pockets full of tamarind fruit. It wasn't quite ripe yet, but it would get us by. And we could pack what we couldn't finish; tamarind keeps indefinitely if you leave it in the pod.

I was very lightheaded now. Getting up that tree and down again took the last of the strength I had. I sat down quickly, as if to eat.

Puamaak sat down next to me. "Who's out there? What did you see? Draw me a map in the dirt if you have to – then I can figure out how to get us out of here. As soon as we're back down in the lowlands we're just farm kids, and can go from village to village to get food from the outlying fields. If there's no cover we'll move at night; the moon is waxing – I'll manage. We still have your lighter to start our fires with, and we can use our water cups for cooking pots. We still have our waterproof hammocks, and can use them as ponchos if it rains. We still have our machetes. And we have enough food now for me to get us out from between the invading and the retreating platoons."

But it was what we *didn't* have that enabled us to think we could get all the way back to Pong Tuk.

I got up again and went back to the grove of bamboo to retrieve my pack. My friend's eyes followed me, as though he were seeing me for the first time.

He looks so different without his uniform, he thought. *He's so... <u>thin</u>. Just a skeleton with skin. But a skeleton doesn't look back at you with those great big eyes. Well it's no wonder he's thinner than I am – I've been getting army rations <u>nine months</u> longer than he has. And as an infantryman I've been getting better food than he has as a porter. But he's not thinking straight. He should have told me about his hearing – that's something I need to know. And when they switched him from carrying food to carrying ammo yesterday, he should have figured out that they were going to put him into combat with me. No, he's not thinking straight at all. And did he just about collapse when he came down from the tree? He tried to cover, but I saw how weak he is. Well, I'm going to pretend that he's in just as good shape as I am. I don't want it to occur to him that he might not make it – he might just give up, and tell me to go on alone. I can't make it without him. How would I find food and water, from here all the way to Pong Tuk? Neither one of us can make it without the other. My <u>god</u> – he's thinner than boys I saw who had starved to death. I've just got to keep him alive – somehow.*

We both knew, with deadly certainty, that one could not make it without the other. But each of us thought that *he* was OK, and could pull the other through. If my friend had been able to see *his own reflection*, and I had been able to see mine, we would have understood that we were *both* half dead.

But we didn't understand – we couldn't. Because neither one of us had a mirror.

Day One – *Recon*

"Nyah. What did you see from the top of the tree?" Puamaak struggled to keep his voice low. *"Anyone coming up on us?"*

"I didn't *see* anyone."

"Maybe we're OK for now. Where're the Vietnamese?"

"I didn't see them."

"Where's *our* army?"

"I didn't see them, either."

"What do you mean? You must have been able to see *forever* from that tree. Nyah – where are the Vietnamese? Where is our platoon? And where are the rest of the Khmer Rouge units?"

"It's like I said the first time, Puamaak – *I didn't see anyone.*"

He looked as though he wanted to shake me. "So *two armies* have completely disappeared off the face of the earth. Impossible. They're out there, Nyah. They're out there *somewhere*."

"Older Brother, I can tie the ladder to the tree again, and you can go up and take a look. But you won't see anything more than I did. I tell you, there's no one out there."

He stopped, passed his hands over his face, then started over again. "I'm sorry, little brother. OK. Tell me what you saw in each of the four directions. *Exactly.* We need to be systematic – like the Americans. My father used to take me to war movies, and he said that that's how they always figure out how to get themselves out of trouble. They analyze every little bit of everything."

"If 'systematic' means 'careful', I was. That's why I was up there so long. OK. First, I used the sun to figure out which way is east. I looked for the Vietnamese who shelled us. Nothing. No infantry, no smoke, no sign of movement. No civilians, either. Next, I looked north, looking for other Khmer Rouge units. Same thing – no military, no smoke, no movement, no civilians. Then I looked south, into the mountain. No sign of anyone. You know, if the unit that started the shelling got ours *before* they got to the mountain, all our guys are dead. The Vietnamese wouldn't have taken POWs in the middle of an all-out assault, even if they were Khmer Kraum. We didn't think of that."

Puamaak shook his head. "I'm glad I didn't know any of them, except our squad leader. They transferred recruits in and out of our unit so fast I didn't even know their names. Except for the officers."

"I didn't know *anyone's* name."

He shook his head again. "That's just how it was... You know, Nyah, you and I were lucky *we* didn't get split up. I'll bet our squad leader had something to do with that..."

He sat down, as if to think. And then his eyes changed, as though he couldn't *think* and *look* at the same time. I sat down next to him and watched him, not knowing what else to do. And suddenly, he snapped his fingers. "*Vultures.* Did you see any *vultures.*"

I shook my head. "But that doesn't mean anything. They were probably all hunted out right after the takeover. Just like everything else.""

His eyes slid out of focus again, but only for an instant. "OK. You didn't *see* anything. But could you *hear* anything? You should have been able to hear much better up there than we can down here, in the middle of this jungle. I mean, your hearing's not *that* bad. *"*

"There was nothing to hear. You don't *hear* anything unless there's something *moving* – and there's *nothing moving*. I'm telling you, there's no one out there."

"Nyah, put your ear to the ground. I'll bet you can pick up vibrations better than I can."

I put my ear to the ground, then I lay *down* on the ground. I sat up again, shaking my head. "Nothing."

"Yeah, I did that when you first went up the tree. I couldn't pick up anything either."

"Nothing makes sense in war, Puamaak. Don't expect it to."

He looked back at the massive trunk of the tamarind. "Nyah... *west*. How about west? What did you see when you looked toward where the Mekong should be?"

"Our army has already burned out the villages for as far as I could see. It looks to me like everyone retreated west. Except our unit. And ours must've been one of the last to retreat, because the villages were burned before yesterday. They're barely smoking now. There are a few plow animals wandering around, but it's as though all the people just... evaporated."

"It must look like a scene from hell," he said. "Well, I'm sure there's *someone* out there – they'll show themselves, when they get hungry enough. Stragglers, deserters, wounded. Surveillance, left behind to report on how quickly the Vietnamese are advancing. Or collaborators, just waiting to help the Vietnamese overthrow the Khmer Rouge. Actually there used to be lots of Vietnamese living in Cambodia before the war. But they weren't welcome here. Some people said they collaborated with the Communist Vietnamese. There were undoubtedly Communist Vietnamese base camps in eastern Cambodia. Phnom Penh people said that's why the Americans bombed us. And there was always that old animosity, because it was the Vietnamese who took the Delta – and then continued to chip away at the rest of our land."

"And with the Thais," I said, "chipping away on the other side..."

"That just increased our determination not to let the Vietnamese get anything more. Lon Nol killed a lot of them. The Khmer Rouge undoubtedly killed some more. And some would have just packed up and gone back to Vietnam. But I can't believe there aren't *any* left. And then there are the families who're mixed – Vietnamese father, Khmer mother, or the other way around. Who's to know which side they chose? And there must be plenty of Cambodians just waiting to help *anyone* trying to get the Khmer Rouge out. If they thought we were Khmer Rouge, they'd kill us. How would they know which side we're on? Yeah, anyone not trying to get to the other side of the Mekong now has got to be surveillance, or a collaborator."

"So now," I said, "we have a fourth scenario. Collaborators, either Vietnamese or Cambodian, mistaking *us* for pro Khmer Rouge. Ha! What a joke! All anyone would have to do to figure out which side *we're* on is to look at how thin we are. Are you sure we ditched all our army issue?"

"Everything except what we ate for lunch yesterday. Well, the Vietnamese army will be here soon enough. If you didn't see anyone out there, that improves our chances for the moment. No one to ask questions of us this morning."

"No one to ask where the hell we are, either," I said.

"Nyah, we won't be able to talk to anyone all the way from here to Pong Tuk. Even if they thought we were just two lost kids, they'd make *up* something so they could turn us in in exchange for food. How many times have we seen that happen?"

"Scenario Five," I said. "Sold out for a sack of rice."

"There's no one out there on our side except our families, Nyah. I knew that. Now we both know it. We'll have to figure out how to stay out of sight the whole way home. We'll have to move at night, like we'd originally planned." He saw my face. "I'll manage."

I shook my head. "Maybe you won't have to. You know how the farmers usually save a stand of trees between one rice paddy and the next? Those stands are what's left of the original forest; they're a lot like the jungle we're standing in. And some would be far enough away from a village so that they might not have been burned. We may be able to move in the daytime, from one stand of trees to another. There'll be plenty of firewood and kindling in there, and if we try to cook in the middle of a stand, I think the trees would cover our smoke. We could have hot food every day! We really need to think twice about moving at night, and not just because you can't see. Look at my feet." We were still sitting on the ground, and I stuck them out in front of me. "That's how I got these two bad toes. When I was marched to my second work camp I got a stick lodged under my toenail." I pointed. "It became infected – and I mean *really bad.* I cried so much from the pain every night that no one else could sleep. So they threw me in the 'infirmary'. A row of cots under a leaky thatched roof, no medicine anywhere. My toe smelled horrible – like a dead body. I thought I had gangrene and was going to die. But I didn't, and the infection eventually healed. Ah, but by that time I'd figured out that if I could convince the attendants that I was still in pain, I could stay there and get out of hard labor. They *fell* for it, and I was there *three months.* The infection should have killed me, but it saved my life instead. I think every bone in my body would have split if I'd had to dig canals again. They had me carrying loads of dirt heavier than I was. Or I would have just starved to death. We didn't get any more food in the infirmary than we did in the camp, but it went a lot further because we weren't working."

"You got lucky, little brother. You were in that infirmary a quarter of a year. And it wasn't just that the food went further. You got a full night's sleep every night, and were able to stay out of the sun and the rain and the mud. I'll bet they even let you boil your clothes to get rid of the lice. Yeah, you got lucky. And because you weren't working, you were much less likely to have another accident."

I nodded. "Sure enough, they sent me back to the camp, and within a few months the whole thing happened *again.* " I pointed to my other foot. "But this time I got even luckier. One of the attendants took a liking to me, and, instead of sending me back to the camp when I got better, she got me to help her with things. I gathered tamarind leaves so she could make the hot-water soaks she used for wounds. I carried water for her. And I did... other things. And then the guy who killed the chickens for the head cadre got transferred! The cook was in a panic, I tell you. She was Communist on the outside, but Buddhist on the inside – she couldn't kill the chickens. I told her that I was an experienced chicken killer, and could do the job. Because I knew I could get more food that way. Yup, she gave me the organs. Sometimes even the liver!"

He smiled. "You'd never killed a chicken in your life. But you just said you could do it, and figured it out later."

I nodded. "It was the protein I was after. My grandfather had explained the difference between carbohydrate and protein to me, and had made sure I understood that I had to have both. So I actually regained some of my strength in the second infirmary. But killing chickens was the hardest thing I ever had to learn to do. I saw the life go out of them because of something *I* had done... Well, that's the end of the story. Just remember, if we mess our feet up, we still have to walk on them. All the way back to Pong Tuk."

"Look at your feet, Nyah. Your toenails are as long as a monkey's. If you cut them just as short as you can get them, you can't get a stick up under them again."

"What would I cut them with?"

"Your 'kwaiw'. I mean, what else have you *got?* And you'd better cut them now, before we start trying to get through any more of this jungle."

And so I set about the task of manicuring my toes with a machete.

"Maybe," he said, "we should move in the daytime around the new moon, and move at night around the full moon. That way we'd always be able to see. The moon will be full again in a week; we can squeeze three nights out of that week. Maybe five, if we have a road to shadow. Oh! I didn't ask you – did you see any roads?"

"Yes," I said. "One. A farm road, but a road all the same. Just to the north of us. Running due west."

"West? *Really?* Then that would be our way out of here *and* our way home! And if it's just a farm road the Vietnamese won't be interested in it. They can't get their big guns down it. And you know what that means – our army won't have mined it."

"And that road," I said, "will surely connect to another road, and that road will connect to another. That's how the farmers used to get their crops to market. Ha! We'll be back in Pong Tuk by the time the moon is full next week – don't you think?"

He didn't answer my question, but asked another instead. "How long will we have the cover of the jungle if we walk parallel to the road?"

"Not sure," I said. "There was another tree blocking my view northwest."

"That's OK. When we run out of jungle you just climb a tree again, and we figure it out from there. Finished your feet? Let's go."

"Don't you want to do yours?" I asked. I looked at his toes only to see that his nails were already cut.

"By the time I'd been drafted," he said, "I'd seen too many accidents like yours."

I got to my feet, extended my hand, and pulled him up next to me. He was my elder, so I did little things like that for him.

"Let's look for a path again," he said, looking around. "How much you want to bet that our platoon made it to the mountain. I don't think the Vietnamese infantry could chase them as fast as they could get away – not with those big guns in tow. And whenever the Vietnamese stopped shelling last night, our commanding officer would've ordered everyone to head for the other side of the Mekong while they could still get away. They'd swim over, if they had to. They can't catch us now, Nyah. They're *gone*."

We couldn't find a path and we were still hungry, so we just went from one rambutan vine to the next – but always moving west. For the first time in my life I was glad there were no birds or monkeys left. They surely would have gotten those rambutans before we did.

"Once we're down in the lowlands," said Puamaak, "we can navigate by the sun. You do the recon, I navigate."

"Do you know how to make a compass?"

"*Make* a compass? With *what?*"

"With your feet," I said. "It's simple. You lay down flat on your back, with your toes pointing due west – lined up with the setting sun. Then you spread your arms out at right angles to your body. Your left hand points south, your right hand points north, and your head points east. If you have to go southwest, you move your left arm halfway to your feet to reduce the 90-degree angle to 45 – now your left hand is pointing right where you want to go. You do the opposite if you have to go northwest – you move your *right* arm 45 degrees. Then you look over your fingers (or your toes, if you have to go due west) and spot a landmark directly in front of them – like a big tree way off in the distance. When you get up in the morning, you just walk toward the landmark. Once you get to it, you do it all again. We just keep going like that, until we see Phnom Treil."

"Where did you learn that, little brother? It's not a bad idea – I think we can use it."

"My first-grade teacher. I think all she was trying to do was make our geography lessons more fun. What would she think, if she knew I'd really have to use that trick she taught us?"

"What would she think if she knew there were more maps in her first-grade classroom than there are in the entire Khmer Rouge army? And that you're *in* the army – instead of in your last year of grammar school."

I knew she must have been killed because she was a teacher. But I didn't want to think about that. I wanted to use what she'd taught me – that's what she would have wanted.

"I'll bet kids in France," I said, "don't have to worry about their first-grade teachers being executed as enemies of the state. And if you ask them what they want to be when they grow up, they say, 'A doctor.' Or, 'A musician.' Or, 'An astronomer.' You ask a Cambodian kid what he wants to be when he grows up? 'Alive.' Yeah, that's the answer you'll get – no matter who you ask."

But we couldn't even have asked the question, or we would have disappeared by morning. The guards would have just told everyone we'd been transferred. If they'd said anything at all.

Puamaak stopped walking and turned to look at me. "What would your answer have been, little brother?"

"A farmer, of course. Like my grandfather. I would have spent my years developing new varieties of mangoes."

"Oh," he said, "but you would have been a *landed* farmer, with all the accomplishment and status that went with it. A horticulturist, and a patron of the village temple – perhaps even an expert in traditional medicine, if your grandfather had been able to continue to teach you. You're smart, Nyah. You could have done it all. You would have had a good life – a good, peaceful, Buddhist life. Had there been no war."

"'Had there been no war.' What would your answer have been?"

"A *pilot*, flying back and forth to Paris." He looked up at the sky through a break in the canopy. "Smart uniform, pretty stewardesses, good food, French wine…"

"You would have made a *good* pilot, Puamaak…"

But my friend had clamped his hand on my arm. *"Don't move."*

He took his hand off, slowly, still looking up. I followed his gaze but couldn't see anything. I couldn't hear anything, either. Perhaps he'd heard a plane? Or a helicopter. *"Dragonfly?"* I whispered.

He shook his head. "There's another scenario, Nyah."

I didn't answer, but watched him instead. I expected him to start looking for a place to hide. But he didn't do anything. Finally he sat down against an old kapok tree, and buried his face in his hands.

I put down my pack and sat down next to him. I figured if there was anything to run from, he'd already be running. So I just did what he'd told me to do – I didn't move.

"How can there be six scenarios," I whispered, "when we've only got five enemies? Our unit, other Khmer Rouge units, Vietnamese, collaborators, and villagers turning us in for rice. Who the hell *else* is out there?"

He raised his head out of his hands and looked me square in the face. "Nyah, where's our platoon."

"Headed across the Mekong with the last of the retreating troops – like you said. They're gone."

He shook his head. "Think about the timing. It was only yesterday afternoon that we escaped. They were running west toward the south side of the mountain as we were running northwest to get to the north side of it. Oh, yeah, they made it all right. But when would they have had time to come down?"

"During the night. As soon as the Vietnamese stopped shelling. They're on their way to the river. But… I didn't see them this morning. I should have seen them, if they're headed for the Mekong. They can't travel very fast on foot. And they're carrying all their gear – food, water, guns, ammo… They can't afford to ditch any of it. Yeah, they couldn't have gotten very far. I should have seen them from the tree."

He nodded. "Look at that mountain, Nyah – it's completely wild. You can't tell me there's a road up it. We had a quarter moon last night, and most of those guys are just as night-blind as I am. They couldn't have gotten down in the dark. So, where are they?"

"Still up there," I said. "And still alive, because if there's no road, the Vietnamese couldn't have followed them. When they got to the foot of the mountain they just... disappeared into the jungle. Like we did."

"Yup. I don't think the Vietnamese got our unit. But we haven't heard anyone trying to get down. And what do you think they're doing up there – *besides* searching desperately for food?"

"They're doing what we are," I said. "Trying to figure out how the hell to get out of here. And because they're not being shelled, they don't know where the enemy is. So they're up there looking for Vietnamese – just like I did, from the tree."

"'They're not being shelled'. That's the key, little brother. For whatever reason, the Vietnamese infantry never advanced from the position from which they shelled us yesterday. Southeast of the mountain. Which you wouldn't have been able to see from the top of the tree because the mountain blocked your view. So what do we look like to our platoon – just two wiry little guys, moving through the jungle obviously trying not to be seen, climbing trees to get a look around?"

"A couple of Vietnamese scouts." We knew nothing of modern surveillance techniques – only what my friend had overheard in *our* army when eavesdropping on the officers. Who didn't know much more than he did. Except for the modern weapons in our arsenal, we might as well have been in the stone age.

"And what will they do if they spot us?" he asked.

"Try to pick us off."

He looked up at the mountain again. "We're just too damned easy to spot down here. As soon as we move out from under the cover of this tree, they'll be looking right down on our *heads*. And when we duck into the brush, they'll see it moving as we make our way through it. Our commanding officer may have a pair of field glasses, you know. An American pair. You don't have to be able to read to use binoculars."

"I don't think he'd be caught dead with binoculars," I said. "I mean, wouldn't they be considered, 'machinery'?" Possession of any kind of machinery was forbidden. "But even if they see us, they can't get us. Not with AK-47s. Firstly, we're out of range; they'd have to be closer to us than half a kilometer away. If they were that close you would have heard them, looking for food and water. Secondly, most of them are guys your age who got no more training than you did. I mean, could *you* pick us off? Thirdly, an AK-47's a *machine gun*. No precision. They'd need a rifle to get us... Do you mean that our commanding officer has a rifle?"

"No, " he said, "he doesn't. I know that for a fact. Even if he did, he'd have to pass it over to someone else to use it – I don't think he can shoot any better than he can read."

"Then who are you worried about?" I asked.

"The *scout*. I think, if anyone spotted us, he could figure out a way to get to us. Local boy – knows every path on this mountain. All *he's* got is an AK-47. But *he* could get close enough to us to get us."

"But he's not *with* our unit," I said. "He never came in yesterday. Our commanding officer turned us around before he got back to us."

"So we don't know where he is. Except that he's above us."

"How do you know that?" I asked.

"Nyah, that's the only way he can see. He's with Recon, so he's been trained. He knows he *always* has to be able to see."

"The runner who came in to tell our commanding officer about the tanks – did he go out again?"

"*I* don't know," he said. "All of a sudden we had a chance to escape, and I had to figure out how to do it. But he's attached to Recon, so he's above us, too. Because that's the only way *he* can see."

"And anyone else attached to Recon is up there, too. These mountains are the only ones around, and the one above us is the highest peak... Puamaak, they'd have rifles – wouldn't they?"

He shrugged his shoulders. "Makes more sense than issuing them AK-47s." He sighed. "Well, we're right back to the two options we had when we woke up this morning. Move out of here quickly, or stay hidden until tonight. Either one is high risk. We move, we could get picked off. We stay, we could get caught in crossfire."

I didn't want to think about this new scenario – I could only keep track of the ones I could count on one hand. So I leaned back into the tree, looked up into the leaves, and just concentrated on our two options.

"I think the second one is more risky," I said. "And if the Vietnamese can't send their infantry up the mountain, they'll start lobbing mortars at it. I don't want to be here when they do. If we move carefully, under the trees, no one will spot us."

"If we could just find a path... Wouldn't you think the villagers who hunted up here would have left some?"

"They wouldn't have hunted here very long," I said. "And after that, well, a footpath in the jungle can disappear in a single season. But I'll bet I can find something. The people who were too poor to own their own land used to work the farms down in the lowlands, but stake out little plots for themselves in places like where we are now. Where no one owned the land. Their paths were well worn; if we're lucky, we'll run into one."

"And when we run out of jungle?" he asked.

"We'll be back to the same two options – move out quickly, or wait and start moving at night. But we'll be away from our platoon, and whoever else might be up there with them. And we might have more information by then, so we could make a better decision."

He leaned back against the tree and closed his eyes, as though he could escape *that* way – if only for a minute.

"What country do you think we're in, Nyah? I mean really. We've just been guessing."

"We're in Cambodia."

"What makes you so sure, little brother? You were just as lost as I was two hours ago."

"It was what I saw from the top of the tamarind. I know that the people who lived in those burned-out villages were good Buddhist people."

"You saw what was left of their temples?"

"No," I said. "I didn't see even one."

"Then how do you know they were good Buddhist people?"

"It was the plow animals I saw wandering around. The villagers were in a hurry – they were running for their lives. But they took the time to untie their animals before they left, so they wouldn't starve at their tethers. Yes, they were good Buddhist people."

"The Vietnamese are Buddhist, too," he said. "I think they would have untied their animals. Their farmers are victims of war just like ours are – none of them would have any interest in Communism now." He paused. "Well, there's one sure way to tell where we are."

"What is it? And why haven't we tried it yet?"

"Because we haven't seen any of the local people yet. The way the Khmer Rouge describe the Vietnamese, they must *surely* have two heads. First farmer we see – if he has two heads, we're in Vietnam."

I burst into laughter – I couldn't help it. I grabbed the bottom of my shirt and clapped it over my mouth; now all you could see was a pair of crinkly cinnamon-colored eyes. His eyes popped open and he started laughing with me, grabbing for his shirt tails. I think it was the first time we'd laughed in four years – I *know* it was. It was the first time we'd had enough to eat! The cassava, the taro, the tamarind, and the little wild rambutans. And we'd found all that food ourselves.

You must understand that we'd survived the work camps only to be drafted for as long as we were still alive. With no pay and no leave, *ever*. With no news, or letters from home, or home to go back to – just a palm-thatched shed on the edge of a relocation village that one good rainstorm would have taken out. We weren't soldiers, we were slaves. No... slaves have a *home*. Is there even a word for what we were? I don't think so – not in any language *I've* ever heard of.

As quickly as it hit us we snapped out of it again. Puamaak got up from the foot of the tree. "OK, let's go! You take us under the trees until we run out of jungle, and I'll follow right behind you." He looked down, toward the farm road. "One thing's for sure – wherever we are, we're in the middle of nowhere."

I looked for a path, found one, and we headed west again.

"But the binoculars," I asked, "and the other American gear our commanding officer has. Like his ammo box, and the canteen he always wears at his waist so everyone can see it. How did he *get* all that stuff?"

"Black market. High-status leftovers from the Americans who were here for Lon Nol, and the GIs who pulled out of Vietnam. He *bought* them. He's an officer. *He* gets paid."

"Paid?" I asked. "With *what?* Not with money – the Khmer Rouge themselves abolished money. So they wouldn't pay their officers with it."

"I don't know with what, but he gets paid with *something*. And he takes bribes, too – I've seen him. A gold ring here, a fancy watch there... rare, expensive leftovers from before the takeover." He shook his head. "Don't think about it, Nyah. Doesn't matter anymore."

We continued walking, but all of a sudden, he stopped. "I just had the weirdest thought, little brother. Maybe it was the extra sleep, or the food you found for us... The Americans put a man on the moon, but the Khmer Rouge didn't want their science. They live in prosperity, but the Khmer Rouge didn't want their education. And they live in freedom, but the Khmer Rouge didn't want their democracy. All the Khmer Rouge wanted from the Americans was their stupid plastic canteens."

Our path suddenly turned down to the farm road, and we found ourselves in thick jungle again. After a while I found another path, but a little way out it turned down to the road, too. We walked through the jungle a little further, but then even it ran out. We could see the road continue west, but the mountain curved southwest. We just stayed inside the curve of jungle and followed the mountain; we couldn't risk leaving our cover. We picked more rambutans as we found them, and ate them as we walked.

We were feeling much stronger now, and started to put some real distance between ourselves and where we'd started out that morning. But we weren't putting any distance between ourselves and our platoon. Or anyone else up there. All we were doing was going around the base of the mountain. If we could just keep up our pace, though, we'd be out of the area by nightfall. Safe from both armies, at least.

"We're doing OK, Nyah. We're doing OK."

And then he heard them.

Day One ~ *Hunted*

Puamaak grabbed my arm, and pointed; then I could hear them, too. Moving through the underbrush on the jungle floor. They were obviously looking for something. And they were trying to avoid detection – they were moving slowly, and they weren't talking.

Instinctively, I looked for a young tamarind. It's the easiest tree to climb, and if you can just get yourself ten meters up, its lower branches will conceal you from anyone on the ground. I spotted one a few meters ahead of us.

"*Follow me,*" I whispered, and we walked toward the tree quietly. I reached it ahead of him, climbed up two meters and turned back.

He was standing at the foot of the tree. He wasn't following me.

He was *trying* – he was just as scared as I was. Could there be one Cambodian in the whole world who couldn't climb a tree? And would that be the Cambodian I'd escaped with? "Put your foot on the first branch!" I whispered. He put his foot on the branch and I leaned down, grabbed his arm and pulled him up into the tree. "When I lift my foot off a branch," I said, "you put your foot right where mine was. Just follow me up the tree like that." We were both about ten meters up in less than a minute. Adrenalin.

This was considerably easier than escaping from our unit the day before – now that we were up the tree, we didn't have to do anything else. Not like yesterday, when we'd had to do three separate maneuvers in tandem in front of all the other guys in our platoon – including the officers – without arousing suspicion. And then *run* for three hours or so.

But as soon as we were settled in the branches we realized that not only could the enemy not see *us*, we could not see *them*. Now all we could do was wait – listening. And if we were discovered, there was nowhere else to go except further up the tree. Which wouldn't have done us any good. This was even more nerve-wracking than yesterday. And of course, there was the other problem...

"Why didn't you tell me you didn't know how to climb a tree?" I whispered into his ear.

"I thought you knew," he whispered into mine. "I thought that's why you showed me how to climb the tamarind this morning."

"I thought you just couldn't climb a *big* tamarind – most people can't. I didn't know you couldn't climb a tree at all. I could have taught you how to climb one of these little tamarinds this morning. If I hadn't had the strength to pull you up onto the first branch, you'd still be down there. And when they found *you*, they'd start looking for *me* – no one would be out here alone. Just let me know when you need me to teach you something. Just let me know."

He nodded, without a sound. He knew I wasn't angry with him – that I was just trying to keep the two of us alive.

We could hear them coming closer now. They were still moving slowly, but at a steady pace.

"Vietnamese?" I whispered.

"I don't think so – they're coming *down* the mountain. Our unit. Or another..."

The worst scenario, of course. "We're going to be up here a long time," I whispered. "Sit on the branch and relax your muscles – this will be the only rest we get today." We sat down right next to each other, but on opposite sides of the trunk; we could still whisper back and forth, but we both had the trunk to hang on to. "I can tie our hammocks up if we have to stay here all night," I continued. "And if you have to pee, do it against the trunk of the tree. It will drip down slowly, and never get to the bottom to give us away." He looked around the trunk of the tree at me. "How," I said, "do you think I used to hide from the village bully in Prai Anchaan?" I'd always been the smallest, so I'd always been the target. "I can hide anywhere. But a tree is always the best place. People look straight ahead, or down; they never look *up* unless they're looking for something. And whoever's coming doesn't know we're here. Unless they saw us earlier..."

Puamaak lowered his head and closed his eyes, concentrating on the sounds coming to him on the wind. "They're getting closer, Nyah. Sounds like there're half a dozen of them. *Damn* it, if they'd just *say* something. Then we'd know who they are."

"And if they speak Khmer with a Vietnamese accent."

He caught my wrist. "Nyah, if they catch us... If they *are* Khmer Kraum, we might be OK. We'd just wait out the war in a POW camp. That would delay us getting back to our mothers, but it would increase our chances of getting back to them eventually. Because *they'd* get us out of here."

They were still moving through the undergrowth on the jungle floor, looking for something. And looking carefully; they still weren't moving very fast.

Now Puamaak was looking down at the ground, clinging to the trunk with everything he had – like a cat at the end of its ninth life. His chest was hollow, his shoulder blades stuck out, and his arms were a couple of sticks. My fears of earlier that morning came rushing back – if anyone found us, they wouldn't bother to capture him. They'd just kill him, or leave him behind. Because they'd figure he'd die before they could get him out of there.

We could hear them coming closer, and closer, until they were right underneath us. But they didn't stop what they were doing – which meant they didn't know we were in the tree. What the *hell* were they looking for?

We couldn't even whisper now. I peered down through the branches and caught a glimpse of hair, but couldn't see the uniform underneath it. *Or* the weapon. I strained my eyes, looking for anything different than what our soldiers would have been issued. But I couldn't see anything.

Now we didn't even dare to <u>breathe</u>. My friend looked around the tree at me and mouthed the words, "*Why can't they just open their mouths?*"

And suddenly, they did. One started barking out orders – and another barked right back at him. Then another started, and another, until they were *all* barking.

"*Dogs!*" whispered Puamaak, and he slumped against the tree. "A pack of *dogs.* Probably scared up here by the combat in the lowlands, and confused by the disappearance of their masters. *Are they rabid?*" He shot bolt upright. "I've never seen a rabid dog. Aren't they supposed to foam at the mouth or something? Can you see *anything?"*

"Shhh! There may be someone with them!"

We waited, listening. And after a few minutes, the dogs began to move on.

"Climb higher," he whispered, "and see if there's anyone with them. Our army, or Vietnamese. You could tell by the uniform."

"Do you *know* what a Vietnamese uniform looks like? And if it *would* be different? The Viet Cong uniform looked just like ours – from the cuffs right down to the Ho Chi Minh sandals. Have you ever *seen* a Vietnamese infantryman?"

"No, I haven't," he said. "My god – and they were about to put me into combat. I wouldn't have known who to shoot at."

"A 'kramaa' – that's how we could tell the difference in the uniform. I didn't get any more training than you did, but we know that the Vietnamese army wouldn't include a scarf with the uniform. The Vietnamese don't use them."

He nodded, slowly. "Good thinking... Now climb higher and look for a 'kramaa'."

"I can't – they'd hear me. Or they'd see the branches moving. We just have to sit here and wait. But the dogs aren't rabid; if they were they'd be snarling, and biting each other. I think they're just looking for food." I shook my head sadly. "Poor dogs. I wish we had something for them... But they'll be hungry enough to be dangerous. We'll have to stay up here until they're at least a kilometer away."

And for the second time that morning all we could do was sit, and wait.

"Well at least they've stopped barking now," said Puamaak.

But I was already picking tamarind. "Just hang on to the tree," I said. "I can get it."

We waited another fifteen minutes. "Can you still hear them?" I asked.

"Yeah, maybe half a kilometer away. Good – let them thrash around and set a few saplings swaying. Our commanding officer will send out a search party for *them."*

I shook my head sadly again. "Puamaak, think about how much those dogs are like us. Free, but hungry and lost. And they've banded together to increase their chances of survival – just like we did."

"No, they're even worse off than we are. They don't have anywhere to go, or anyone to go back to. And if the Vietnamese find them, they'll *eat* them. That's what I've heard, anyway."

I looked down at the ground again. "I got a good look at one of them, after they started barking. He has a cut across his back, his fur is all matted, and he has the beginning of mange. A farmer's dog, but now he just looks... *wild."*

"You think we look any better? I hope I can get cleaned up before I see my mother again."

"Don't even think about it, Puamaak. Because we can't look any different than anyone else – our lives will depend on it."

He didn't say anything. Because he knew I was right.

"But you can look mangy and still look pretty good," I said, trying to rally him. "They do it in the movies all the time. Remember that guy who went down some river in Africa in a little boat, to blow up a German gunboat? Now *that's* mangy. All you need are some fat water buffalo leeches – and I'm sure I can come up with some."

"*The African Queen,*" he said. "That was the name of the movie, because that was the name of the guy's boat. Yeah, the more difficulties he overcame, the mangier they made him look. By the end of the movie he looked just as bad as we do. But he was a big hero, for blowing up the gunboat. You know that actor was short, like us? My father told me that not all Americans are tall. We used to see them in Phnom Penh, pretty often. But I never saw a short one."

"They don't all have yellow hair, either. I mean, look at the guy in *The African Queen*. Oh, but a lot of the actresses have yellow hair. I'll take one of those – you can keep the dark-haired ones."

"I think they were hippo leeches, Nyah. They don't have water buffalo over there."

"How would you know?" I handed him some tamarind.

"Well, if this war is ever over I'm going to store more soap in my house than rice. Nyah… when was the last time you saw a girl?"

"In the infirmary. There were female attendants there – you couldn't call them nurses. But I was always too hungry to notice if any of them were pretty. No women in the camps, no women in the army, and when they marched us here it was at night, so we couldn't even see the village girls. Yeah, I think it's been a year and a half."

"I haven't seen a girl since I left Pong Tuk, three and a half years ago." He shrugged his shoulders. "I never ended up in an infirmary."

I had no reply to that – no reply at all. But maybe *that* was it. Why he couldn't climb. I'd been trying to figure it out ever since we went up the tree. I'd had a three-month break from hard labor each time I'd been in the infirmary, but he'd *never* had one. Yeah, maybe that was it. There were plenty of trees in Phnom Penh, and every kid I ever met in the year I went to school there could climb – although not as well as I could. I couldn't believe he'd never learned.

I leaned around the trunk of the tree again, on the pretense of handing him more tamarind. I looked for any sign of muscle in among the bones . But there was none.

Now, I wasn't kidding when I'd said it was the jungle rats that had saved my skin. But I should have been more precise. It was my *muscle* that they'd saved. Because jungle rat meat is pure protein. He hadn't been eating rats the last four years. Except for a little dried fish, he'd been getting almost no protein at all. With no muscle in his upper body the only thing that had gotten him up that tree an hour ago was me pulling him up into it, and his adrenalin taking over. I had to figure out how to get him up a tree, because we'd surely have to do it again.

So I would simply repeat what had worked. "OK," I said, "next time we have to climb, we'll do just what we did earlier. I'll start up first, lean down and pull you up, and you just put your foot on the next branch when I take my foot off it." I didn't add that I would be sure he was scared enough that his adrenalin would kick in. And that I would pretend, from here on in, that the problem was not that he *couldn't* climb, but that he'd never learned.

"It worked once, it should work again," he said.

"It's a good thing there are two of use. Makes everything twice as easy."

"Or twice as dangerous, if we haven't synchronized our stories. Those dogs that we thought were after *us* – that's the closest we've come to getting caught. Nyah, do you have any idea how different the two of us must look from one another? Our story is that we're trying to find our families. *Plural.* Don't tell anyone we're related, because if they catch us in that lie, they'll assume we're lying about everything else. *God* I wonder what else we haven't thought of."

I was Khmer, quite different in appearance than the people of any of Cambodia's neighbors – Thailand, Vietnam and Laos. And different than Khmer mixed with any of them, or with Chinese. If you want to see classic Khmer features, just look at the statues from the Angkorian era – our Golden Age. A Khmer face is typically oval or round, with high cheekbones, a slightly aquiline nose and almond eyes. There's a distinctive crossbow-like curve to the mouth. A Khmer frame is slight and well-proportioned. Khmer skin is golden or chocolate brown, and Khmer hair and eyes are brown or black. My features were Khmer, but not typical. I had a heart-shaped face and a very aquiline nose – like a little sparrow hawk. And I had the blackest hair you ever saw – blacker than coal still a kilometer down, under a new moon.

My comrade was Khmer and Chinese, which is what you'd expect in someone from the city. He had a rounder face, narrower eyes and much lighter skin than I did. And a squarer frame. His hair was black, but lighter than mine – and wavy.

"Nyah, I think I could get cleaned up a *little* without attracting any attention. Once we find clean water I could scrub my skin with coconut husk. But I'd still have these old clothes – I'd still *look* just as bad as everyone else. And I could brush my teeth with cane fiber, like we did in the camps. I could cut my fingernails just as short as my toenails so no dirt could get up under them. And, if we can find a really big pot, we can boil our clothes to get rid of the lice. But the clothes would still *look* the same. And my hair… I could get some of the knots out of it with my fingers, but it would still look dirty."

"You know," I said, "they cut my hair in the work camps, but they only cut it once in the army. The day I was drafted."

And this time, it was Puamaak who looked around the tree. He ran his hand through his hair and, with a sickening turn of his stomach, realized that his was the same length as mine. *They stopped cutting our hair,* he thought, *because they figured we wouldn't last long enough in the army to make it worth their while. So, sometime shortly after Nyah got drafted, two officers – somewhere – had a conversation, trying to <u>guess</u> at how long the boys in our unit would live...*

"We were always on the move, little brother. How could they cut our hair?" And he quickly turned the subject. "Our mothers would never imagine that we're headed back to Pong Tuk together. I'll never forget the day you turned up in my unit. I was just… standing there, waiting for someone to tell us what to do. And then this walking pair of eyes came up to me."

"And do you remember what you said?"

"*What* the *hell* are *you* doing here?'" He laughed. "Yeah – I remember. But how did you recognize *me?*"

This would be my first chance to see if I could lie. It had been easy to pick him out . His mannerisms were effeminate, and he reminded me of a girl. Except that girls climb trees better. "You just looked like a city boy. Like you were used to nice clothes, and good restaurants." Hell, that wasn't much of a lie. That wasn't a lie at all – I just hadn't told him everything!

"Really? You could tell, even after all those years?" He sat up a little straighter on the branch. "I had three years of French, you know. Before my school was closed."

"I had one. The year I had to live in Phnom Penh. But I would have had it in Prai Anchaan; the village curriculum was the same."

"Oh! That's another thing we didn't think of. Even though we grew up near each other, our speech is just as different as our faces are. So we might be from the same *unit*, but we wouldn't be from the same *village*. And I'm not from a village at all. So if we're using the 'we're trying to get back to our village' story, you need to be the one doing all the talking – I'll just shut up."

And then it hit him; I never would have figured it out. "*That's* it. Your grandfather grew not only rice, but vegetables, root crops, herbs and fruit. And enough of it to sell in Phnom Penh. So he must have owned a *lot* of land. But no one ever figured out that you were from the upper classes, once you'd been put in a work camp. It was your country accent, Nyah. And your grandfather? They looked at his hands, and his weathered face, and knew he was a farmer – but never guessed how much land he owned. *That's* it. That's why they didn't kill him. I've been trying to figure it out."

I looked down at the ground again. "But not all of my grandfather's children followed in his footsteps. Two of my aunts became university professors. I don't know what's happened to them. I heard that, with the highly-educated families, they just kill the whole family at once – they don't take just the father or the mother. So if they found out my two aunts were professors, they would have killed my uncles and my cousins, too." I just hoped that, if they'd killed them, they hadn't tortured them first.

And that's what we were most afraid of – torture. We never talked about it – *never*. But I believe we both had the same plan. Bolt, and take a bullet in the back.

"I guess," I said, "they kill off all the professors and the teachers not only because they're educated, but because they're from the upper classes." Cambodian society mirrored the Indian model; teachers and monks were always at the top.

"No, little brother, there's more to it than that. They want to be sure that, once they've killed off all the educated people, there won't be any teachers left to make *more* educated people. Because they know it's the educated who can organize a resistance movement. I mean, it's perfectly logical."

What we didn't know was that the reason the founders of the Party understood the power of teachers was that most were teachers themselves. They had gone to Paris for university, on government scholarships. And the first Cambodian woman to earn a baccalaureate degree? Pol Pot's wife.

"It's the same with the monks," he continued. "They want to be sure they kill all of them so there won't be any monks left to make more monks... No, don't think about all the killing, Nyah. Just think about how to get back to Pong Tuk. I can't hear the dogs at all now; I think they turned down into the lowlands. Now, how do I get out of this tree?"

"Same way you got up it, my friend, but backwards. When I take my hand off a branch, you put your foot on it. Don't get discouraged; getting down is usually harder than getting up. But at least you can take your time." I handed him more tamarind. "Eat a little more, before you try to get down."

He took the tamarind from me, and we sat quietly looking out over the jungle. The canopy stretched above us in every shade of green. Kapoks, banyans, ebonies, wild jackfruits and mangoes, tamarinds, palms of every description, and wild mountain trees that have no name at all.

"*That* one – over there." I pointed. "Just uphill from the one with the feathery leaves. *That's* a 'slaing'. Remember what it looks like." And I handed him more tamarind.

A pod slipped out of his hand as he tried to split it open – the tamarind was still pretty green. He jumped, and watched it as it fell from one branch to another until it finally hit the ground. I didn't say anything – I knew from his reaction that he understood that a slip like that could cost you your life, if there was anyone at the bottom of the tree.

"It's so beautiful up here," I said instead. "Especially when it's quiet. I can only imagine what Ratanakiri is like."

"Oh I *know* what it's like. The frogs are more lethal than the tigers. Come on – let's go. Before we see mortars raining down through the canopy."

We got him out of the tree, picked up a footpath, followed it, and then continued on where it turned down into the lowlands. We picked up another path, and then another, all with the same outcome.

"We're just getting further and further south," I said. "We need to be going west. At least until we figure out where we are. But I guess we don't have any choice – we can't leave the cover of the jungle until we're further away from our platoon."

"If your instinct is right and we're still in Cambodia, we can probably afford to go quite a ways south without worrying too much about it. Remember, Phnom Penh is in south-central Cambodia, and Pong Tuk is a *long* way south of Phnom Penh. We should know – we walked it. It's probably just about to the Vietnamese border."

But figuring out where the border was was not straightforward at all. When the Vietnamese took the Mekong Delta three centuries before, they took a lot more than just the Delta. The border arched north, then south again. If you didn't have a map and didn't know exactly where you were, you could cross over into Vietnam before you even knew it. Well, we didn't have a map, and we didn't know exactly where we were – we didn't have any *idea* where we were. Our plan had been to navigate by the sun. But the sun is blind to borders.

After an hour or so we found ourselves in foothills. They zigzagged – west, southwest, west, southwest, making a jagged circle around the mountain. We just kept following them, unwilling to leave our cover.

And suddenly, the foothills turned southeast. We found ourselves on a bluff, with our first clear view of the south.

We looked for Vietnamese.

Day One – The Road

"Can you see anything?" whispered Puamaak, his eyes panning the plain that stretched below us. *"Anything moving?"*

"No, nothing. Can you see the Mekong?"

He shaded his eyes with his hand and looked west, toward the horizon. "No. I can't." And then he focused his eyes straight ahead again. We were looking over what was left of little farms – rice paddies abandoned after the harvest because of the army coming through, and then the evacuation.

"Where were we yesterday, when we took off?" I asked. "Can you figure it out?"

"Southeast of here." He pointed off to the left. "Look how these foothills curve around to that little mountain. Then south of the mountain you can just make out more foothills. I think they shelled us from the other side of them... Oh, I was running just as hard as you were, little brother, but I was able to keep track of which way we were going. Lucky, that's all. It was about three o'clock, so the sun was already in the west. Three hours earlier and I wouldn't have been so sure."

He shaded his eyes again. "You see any vultures? The units that retreated before ours did would have come through the area below us, trying to get to the Mekong. But you can't really tell if there was any combat down there because everything's been burned."

"Look for movement on the ground," I said. "That would be vultures." I shook my head. "I don't see anything... Are you *sure* you can't see the Mekong? Your vision's OK in the daytime – it might even be better than mine."

He looked west again, and shook his head. "I can't see it, Nyah."

Now, I should explain why the farms we were looking at hadn't been abandoned four years before, when the Khmer Rouge had seized power and immediately reorganized the country into communes. Farmers known to be supporters of the Khmer Rouge before the takeover were allowed to stay in their villages, in their own homes – they hadn't been relocated, as my friend and I had been. We were what the Khmer Rouge called 'new people' – the educated, the urban, the well off. We'd been relocated for 're-education'; there were more than two million of us from Phnom Penh alone. The farms we were looking over were part of communes now. They were worked by a mix of people – those who hadn't been relocated, and those who had been relocated to communes and kept there (instead of being sent to work camps, prisons or the army). Pong Tuk was administered the same way.

"All we can do is keep our cover," said Puamaak. "Follow the foothills southeast."

"So we'll be heading back toward where they shelled us yesterday. But we'll be on the *other* side of the hills."

"Yeah. We have no choice. Just watch for Vietnamese. Come on – let's go."

But I was still looking out over the landscape. "It's not going to be easy to find food down there. I don't think we should leave the foothills without at least two days' supply. And I mean stuff we don't have to cook – we just don't know where we'll end up. Because we still don't know who's out there, and where."

He fished around in his pack. "We've got four tubers of cassava left."

"Raw, that's four days' ration for the two of us; you can't eat more than half a tuber a day without getting sick. But that's not enough to keep us going. We have lots of tamarind, but you can't really count that as food. Especially when it's not ripe. All it does is fill your stomach for a little while."

"So we keep looking for wild rambutans and taro," he said.

"And 'psat kajo' – wild mushrooms. We can eat *those* raw. Look for 'psat kajo' around the roots of old trees as we walk. And if we're lucky we'll find peanuts just before the last hill meets the lowlands; the farmers plant them on hillsides because peanuts like well-drained soil. When we get over there, look for places where the hillside has been cleared. Even if the plants have been burned out, the nuts should still be down there. But we won't be able to eat the peanuts, either, until they've dried out for a few days; fresh from the ground, they're just like raw cassava – they can make you really sick." I sighed. "What the *hell* are we going to eat? Even for the rest of today? We've each had half a tuber of cassava already, and it's only mid afternoon." I sighed again. "Well it's better to go hungry than to get sick. Just keep looking for rambutans, taro and 'psat kajo', and peanuts as we get closer to the communes. Bananas, papayas and guavas ripen throughout the year, but I don't think we're going to find any. Not in a war zone. Too few farmers, and too many soldiers."

"This bluff is the only place where we've been able to see anything without you having to climb a tree. Maybe once we're out of the war zone you won't have to climb so many. It's dangerous – I know it is."

I nodded. "All of us boys in Prai Anchaan were climbing a big tamarind one day, and one of my friends fell out of it. He shouldn't have – he was a good climber. But a branch broke underneath his foot. When he hit the ground he crushed his shoulder." I looked at Puamaak. "But you know what he did? He learned to climb a tree with one arm. Or, I should say, with an arm and a half; his shoulder was frozen, but he could still use his arm from the elbow down. No matter what happened to him, he just kept right on going."

"Are you kidding?" he said. "Look at you. The Khmer Rouge set Cambodia back to the stone age – I mean, who still uses a flint to start a fire? But you've adapted perfectly. Look how you find food, and hide from 'predators'. I think your ability to survive stems from how your grandfather raised you... It was your grandfather who raised you, wasn't it? You never talk about your father."

I didn't want to talk about that – my grandfather had been more of a father to me than my father ever had. I simply nodded. "But I was the least likely to survive the last four years. Oh I haven't told you that story yet – how I almost died I don't know how many times before the comet went over. I asked my aunt, when I got older, which diseases I'd had – she was the one who nursed me through everything. She said, all of them that she'd ever heard of. Well anyway, my grandparents and my aunt were so afraid I'd die that they never made me get up early, gave me the best of the food, and never made me work hard – except in school of course. Such a coddled child should have been the first to die. But even though I was only seven when we were forced out of Prai Anchaan, I made a pact with myself to survive right then and there. To help my family. But I know I got some immunity from all those diseases – I never got sick after that. Except for the infections in my feet."

We made our way to the little mountain but didn't climb it, for fear of being seen. We saw no movement, and everything was quiet.

Now the little mountain was between us and our platoon. Puamaak saw me look back. "You thinking about our squad leader?"

"Yeah," I said. "He couldn't have been more than twenty-five, by the look of him. I think he had a wife and child, from before the takeover – but of course he could never talk about them. I don't care about anyone else in our unit. That's horrible, isn't it? I wasn't like this before the war. Any time another kid got hurt – got whacked in the head with a paddle when we were playing around on a boat, or walked into a fish trap, or jumped into the water in flood season only to find he'd jumped into the top of a tree – I'd be the first one to go back to the village to get help. But it's like I said before – I never got to know anyone in our unit. Except you and our squad leader. I hope he got away. I think he was trying to keep me out of combat. Did you notice that when he joked about me being too small to handle the recoil of an AK-47, he always did it in front of his lieutenant? And I think he was trying to keep you out of combat, too – it's just that your time was up."

"All that transferring in and out of our unit," he said. "Splitting people up before they could get to know each other well enough to trust each other." He shook his head. "That's the way they planned it, little brother. I *know* it is. They were afraid of sabotage, or escape attempts, or getting their throats slit in the middle of the night. Or all of those things. But think about how well their strategy worked. If you and I had been separated, neither one of us would have tried to escape alone. We'd be on the top of that mountain." He pointed back to the highest peak. "Well, if the Vietnamese get our unit, I just hope they either take them as POWs or kill them quickly. And if they don't get them, anyone with the guts to try to escape still has a chance to get away. But I don't think anyone else would have *tried* to escape, except our squad leader. I think the three of us were the only people who hadn't been completely brainwashed."

"Yeah," I said. "If they're going to brainwash you, they have to do it in your first work camp. The mistake they made with me was that they didn't separate us Pong Tuk boys at night. We all slept in the same shelter, and talked when we thought no one was listening. Like, 'Do you believe all that stuff about turning your parents in if you think they're counter-revolutionaries?' And, 'The more rice you plant, the more rice you'll have to eat.' – when there was only gruel in our bowls, and less of it with every passing month. We stuck together, and talked every night before we went to sleep – that's why they were never able to brainwash us. It must have been the same in your camp. You and I were just lucky."

"Oh, there's more to it than that, little brother."

"Yeah?"

"Yeah. They couldn't brainwash us for the same reason they wouldn't have been able to brainwash our teachers. You don't just memorize facts and figures in school. You learn how to solve problems. And in the process, you learn to reason. What they were telling us wasn't reasonable – so we didn't believe it. Communists know that they can't seize power and hold onto it unless they can brainwash enough people to build a support base. And Communists know who they can brainwash and who they can't. They know they can't brainwash anyone who can reason, and they know that educated people can reason. So what do you do with the people you can't brainwash? You get rid of them – you either kill them quickly, or you work them to death."

"And if you can't work them to death, " I said, "you send them to the front."

He smiled. "And here we are."

"So, the Khmer Rouge made the decision to kill everyone who had an education not only because they might organize a resistance movement, but because they couldn't be brainwashed – which would make it all the more likely that they *would* organize a resistance movement. OK, I get it. But it wasn't our *luck* that they missed us – it was our karma. Our good deeds in our previous lives caused us to be reborn into well-to-do families in this one, so that we could get an education, so that we couldn't be brainwashed – but could make it *look* like we had."

"My family didn't go to temple much, but I think you're right on that one little brother. It all comes down to karma in the end."

"But you're right," I said, "about Communists knowing who they can brainwash and who they can't. I saw the cadres just line everyone up, and sort them all out. But I couldn't figure out how they did it."

"All they had to do was pick out who had to work the fields with his father, and who didn't. I saw them line everyone up my very first day in my very first camp. They went right down the line, looking at each boy's clothes and listening to the way he spoke, looking for calluses and scars on his hands – even observing the way he stood in the line. You could pick out the boys who'd never been in school. But those boys had all had to watch *us* go to school. They'd see us disappear through the gateway every morning, and reappear in the afternoon – but they never knew what went on inside the school compound. They saw us change from year to year, as we learned new things. But *they* never changed very much. They just kept falling further and further behind us – and they felt it. The cadres played on that. They made those boys feel important because they *were* poor and uneducated. Well, those kids played right into their hands; they were brainwashed the very first week. Oh, yeah, I watched them, and I could see them changing. But not from a worm to a butterfly – the *other* way around."

"Those were the other guys in our unit," I said.

"Yup."

"But why were there poor kids in our work camps at all? They weren't 'new people' – their families weren't well off, or educated, and they *certainly* weren't urban."

"They were kids like you, driven into Phnom Penh from the countryside by fighting in their villages. They were labeled 'new people' simply because they were living in Phnom Penh on April 17, 1975. The day of the takeover. On *one day* of their lives, they were in the wrong place. And for many of them, it will have *cost* them their lives."

"Yeah," I said, "I'd forgotten. About twenty percent of my classmates in Phnom Penh were from somewhere else. One in five..."

We just kept walking, and walking, trying to get down to the lowlands. And it seemed we never stopped *talking*. We were hungry, and talking helped take our minds off it. And remember – we hadn't been able to talk freely for *four years*. But, at the bottom of it all, talking helped us to figure out how we'd ended up in a war zone, and how we were going to get out of it. It would take both of our intellects.

"But the brainwashing, "I said. "I think there's another reason they didn't succeed with us. The cadres – we didn't *like* them. And we respected them even less than we liked them. So we didn't listen to them. Well, we listened, but we didn't believe what they said. Now, if it had been our squad leader..."

"No, Nyah. We like him, and we respect him, because we *know* him. If he'd been the one trying to brainwash us that first week, we wouldn't have known him yet."

We finally made it to the last hill before the lowlands, and found a big tamarind for me to climb. I didn't have to make a ladder this time and got up and down pretty quickly. "Still nothing moving out there," I said. "I saw a band of big trees just south of us, and it runs west for several kilometers. There might be farmhouses in there, but we could keep to the northern edge. I saw what looks like a peanut field, too, between us and the band of trees. From the looks of it the sun will be going down in a couple of hours. Maybe I can climb one more tree just before sunset, and then we can find a place to hide for the night. It's like you said – we won't have the light of a full moon until next week."

"No landmarks, Nyah? You still couldn't see anything that would tell us where we are? Or what country we're in?"

"No. Maybe at the next tree."

"And you couldn't see the Mekong?"

I shook my head. "No."

He sighed. "One thing's for sure – we've got to get all the way out of these foothills or we'll be very cold tonight. We can't risk making a fire, and if we can't stay warm, we'll be burning calories we can't replace. How did we even make it through *last* night?"

"I don't know," I said. "Last night was a long time ago."

We walked down into the peanut field and, after scraping around a bit, got enough to fill our pockets. Then we walked down into the lowlands, finally leaving the mountains – and our platoon – behind.

But, as I've said, it wasn't enough to get away from our platoon. We had to get out of the war zone. We knew we couldn't do it by the end of the day – we'd have to get back across the Mekong, and we couldn't even see it yet – but we wanted to get as far as we could before the sun went down. You have twelve hours of daylight in Cambodia, no matter what month it is. Twelve hours, and that's all you've got. We moved west across the band of trees, racing the setting sun.

To our surprise, we suddenly hit a road. Running southwest.

"Looks like the same farm road we shadowed this morning, Nyah. But all these country roads look alike. Let's back up into the woods a little way, just to keep out of sight, and walk parallel to the road until just before the sun goes down. Then we can find a tamarind and have one last look around. As of tomorrow, we'll have you climb just one tree a day."

We walked on until, suddenly, we ran out of trees. I climbed the last big tamarind on the southern edge of the grove. "The road continues southwest," I said. "There's a lake on the other side of it, not far ahead of us. And there's a river further down."

"A river? Does it look like the Mekong?"

"Can't be. It's flowing west to east, not north to south. And it's too small."

"OK little brother, not the Mekong, but certainly a tributary. I wonder how close we are to the Mekong herself? That's going to be some swim when we have to go back across. But you grew up on the Mekong. You must be one hell of a swimmer."

"Oh yeah. Even if the river's a couple of kilometers across, that's nothing to me. And there won't be a killer current this time of year. We can find some wood and just float over, kicking underwater to keep from catching anyone's attention. We'd be the same color as the log and the muddy water – we'd be so camouflaged, we could even cross in the middle of the day. You'll be OK even if you're not a strong swimmer – just hang onto the log." He'd have to. Even if he'd been a strong swimmer before the takeover, he wouldn't be now. For the same reason he couldn't get up a tree.

And then I had an awful thought. What if he couldn't swim at all? Most Chinese kids can't – especially kids from the city. But I thought that, if he couldn't swim, he would have said something...

"Nyah, didn't you say this road keeps going southwest? We can keep going tonight. We'll have more than a quarter of a moon, with no trees to block the light."

"But look at the clouds."

"We'll have just enough light to follow a road. The sun's just going down, which means it's only six o'clock. We could wait another twenty minutes until it's dark, and then walk until nine – or ten. Leave the Vietnamese far behind us. I know how you feel about moving at night, but we wouldn't hurt our feet on an old, dusty farm road. What do you think?"

"If you'll be OK..." I said. "Yeah, you could just follow me, like you always do. The sooner we're out of the war zone, the better our chances. But if we're too tired to go on when we hit the river further down, well, there would have been a bridge over it. We can hide for the night under what's left of it. It should be warm under there, and we'll have some cover. And plenty of fresh water."

"So we have twenty minutes before it gets dark." My friend flopped down under a tree, rolled his hammock into a pillow, and curled up in the grass.

"Hey – not so fast!" I said. "We never did find enough food to get us through the next couple of days. Those mushrooms we were looking for in the foothills – we might find some down here. I remember my grandfather taking me out and showing me how to recognize them, and that was in Prai Anchaan. So 'psat kajō' must be lowland mushrooms. Come on – let's take a look around."

His eyes were already closed, but I knew he was thinking. He was trying to decide which he wanted more – the rest, or the food.

His stomach won. He opened his eyes and stretched out his hand for me to help him up.

"Twenty minutes," he said. "Let's split up just enough so we can cover more ground – keep me in the corner of your eye. OK – 'psat kajō'. Looks like a little sun parasol. The cap's about as big as your palm, and the stem's about the same length."

"Those are the ones you get in the market," I said. "The ones you find in the wild are all different sizes – like the people in the market. 'Psat kajō' are white, so the best way to find them is to look for a patch of snow. Come on – before it gets too dark to find anything."

Ten minutes later he signaled to me excitedly, and I walked over to his patch of snow. There weren't a lot of mushrooms there, but there were enough to get us by.

"I've never had to eat mushrooms raw before," he said. "They're sort of... sweet."

I looked at the mushrooms, and looked at him. I don't know what I'd been thinking. We were in the lowlands now, in the communes – if there were any mushrooms here, there was a reason that no one had picked them. My eyes locked on his. "How many did you eat?"

"Poisonous?"

"*I* don't know. Well I guess we'll find out soon enough. Just tell me if you start feeling sick."

"But Nyah. They look exactly like 'psat kajō'. How can you tell they're not?"

"'Psat kajō' are sweet when they're *cooked,* but not when they're raw – when they're raw they're bitter. Just a little – but enough so that no one would ever call them 'sweet'. *How many did you eat?*"

"Just one. I was waiting for you."

One the size of the tip of his finger, or one the size of his hand? He could be perfectly fine, or he could be dead by morning. I remembered my grandfather's words – "If you're not absolutely sure they're 'psat kajō', don't touch them. And I don't just mean, 'don't eat them'; I mean, 'don't even touch them'."

"Just one?" I said. "Well why didn't you say so. You'll be fine." But I started to look around. If the foothills we'd just come out of were limestone, I might be able to find a cave for us to hole up in if he started to get sick.

But he was already headed back to the road, believing what I'd said. To him, I was the expert on any kind of food we might find out here in the wild. He got to the shoulder, and waited for me.

"Man, you could drive a car on this thing," he said. "It's like a super highway, compared to what we're used to – footpaths and cart tracks, from one camp to another. Three years and six months since I've been on a road. The last one I was on was the one out of Pong Tuk."

"So how big is a super highway?" I asked.

"Maybe twice as wide – two lanes instead of one. The width of Highway Six where it passes through your grandfather's village. Cambodia's a small country, so none of the highways are very big – not like in America, or France. But they would take you to all the places you wanted to go and the things you wanted to see. They start in Phnom Penh and radiate outwards, like the spokes of a wheel on an ox cart. Seven goes east toward the waterfalls of Mondulkiri, and then north toward the tigers of Ratanakiri. Six goes north to Siem Reap, and the great temples of Angkor. Five goes west to Battambang, and then on to the ruby mines of Pailin. Four goes southwest to the port of Kampong Saum, and the sea. Three goes south to Kampot, and the wild elephants of Bokor. Two goes south to Takeo – we'll have to cross it to get back to Pong Tuk. One goes straight through from Phnom Penh to Saigon – cuts through the entire Southeast. Oh, yeah, if the Vietnamese are invading *us*, and not the other way around, their main assault force – not the little one that shelled us – will be sticking to Highway One like a train on a track. That's the only way they can get their big Russian guns into the country. And they'll have packed all their troops and supplies into trucks, so they can keep their men with their guns. If our troops around Highway One retreat as quickly as ours did here, the Vietnamese can invade Cambodia like a blitzkrieg – and they know it. All their guns and all their tanks and all their troops will be *on that road*."

"Trucks?" I asked. "Their soldiers don't even have to walk?" I couldn't imagine such a thing. My friend and I hadn't been able to ride even once since we'd been drafted. Not once since the takeover. And not only had we had to march, we'd had to carry all our own supplies.

"No, Nyah, they don't have to walk, but they're still stuck in the army. Just like the Khmer Rouge they're chasing down. *Stuck in the army,* where the rats taste better than the food. *Stuck in the army,* with commanders who can't find their way off a soccer field. *Stuck in the army,* in a giant game of cat and mouse that no one will ever win. But you and me? We're *out!* We made a clean escape, my friend."

"And once we're out of the war zone," I said, "we can do whatever we want to."

"Yeah… like going after what *we* want to eat, instead of just eating what comes to us. Snake – that's what *I'm* going after. And fish. We could get *fresh* fish. Moist, and tender, and sweet. Not like the dried stuff we've been getting the last four years – you cold break your teeth on it. How are you at catching fish?"

"Oh, a river rat like me?" *So if he decides he wants fish,* I thought, *and we go to a reservoir to catch some, I'll just say that I can tell it's all fished out. How would he know? You can't see the fish – they're under water!*

We made it to the river in less than an hour. "It's not even seven o'clock," he said. "Can't be. We can swim this thing in fifteen minutes and pick up the road again. We'll find some other place to hide tonight. But let's sit down for a few minutes – we haven't rested since the dogs chased us up the tree. We have no cover, but there are no houses here. Nowhere for anyone to hide. Just a *few* minutes... But don't lie down – we'll fall asleep."

"We didn't lie down *last* night," I said, "but we *still* fell asleep."

So we sat down in the middle of the road and leaned in against each other, knowing that if we fell asleep we'd wake up when we fell over. We sat there just looking at the ruins of the bridge, in the moonlight that filtered through the clouds. I wondered how many people that explosion had taken out, and how long ago. The bridge could have been destroyed by the Khmer Rouge when they fought Lon Nol's troops between '70 and '75. Or it could have been hit by the Americans – the carpet bombing, from '65 to '73. Or it might have been blown up by the Vietnamese, or by our army, just yesterday. The last of the blackened, twisted metal hung silently over the water, looking deceptively still. But I knew that it was constantly moving, atom by atom, turning into rust.

And suddenly, my comrade started to laugh. The sound echoed off the end of the bridge, and came back to us like the mocking cry of a ghost. But Puamaak didn't seem to notice.

"Nyah, I've been so *stupid*. There's one sure way to tell if we're in Cambodia." He shook his head. "I wonder how many other clues I've missed."

"What do you mean? The terrain in Vietnam would look the same as here. The crops would be the same. The farmers would raise the same kinds of animals that we do. What do you see that I don't?"

"It's what I *don't* see. Nyah – look at the road."

"A dirt road looks the same anywhere – you said so yourself. When I climbed the tree this morning the houses on either side of it might have told me something, but they were all burned out. You can't tell if they're Cambodian or Vietnamese when there's nothing left of them but *smoke*. What?"

"Look at the bridge, little brother. What do you *not* see that *would* have been there four years ago?"

"I don't know. I'm tired. My brain shut off when I sat down."

He got up, walked to the bridgehead, raised his arms straight up in the air and then spread them to make a V.

I jumped to my feet. "Road signs! The name of the bridge and the tonnage it can take, at the very least. And if we're near the Mekong, there would have been a sign for the ferry."

"Yup." He laughed again. "The Khmer Rouge took down just about every sign in the country. That's why no one ever knows where the hell they're going when they're moved, and where the hell they are once they get there. And the Vietnamese just *weren't that stupid*. Think about it. Not only do we have a Communist government, we have the *stupidest* Communist government in the whole world. Do you think they took down all the road signs in China and Russia? Of course not."

"But," I asked, "don't you think the signs are gone because the blast that took the bridge out took the signs out with it?"

"No. Look – here's the post that one of the signs was mounted on. And here's where they unscrewed it. We're in Cambodia!"

We were excited now – at least we were in the right country. We climbed down into the riverbed, took a good long drink, and got ready to swim the river. I wrapped my kerosene lighter in a strip of banana leaf, then wrapped my 'kramaa' around my head and tucked the lighter up into it – hoping it would stay dry. I could swim the short distance with my head above water.

A 'kramaa' is a rectangle of loosely-woven checked cotton cloth about the size of an extra-long bath towel. As far as I know, we Khmer are the only people who use them. We wind them around our heads like turbans before we go out in the sun. This practice is one way that anthropologists distinguish our Cambodian culture from that of our Vietnamese neighbors. Our culture is Indian-based – the 'turban' we make is an adaptation of the Indian farmer's turban. Vietnamese culture is Chinese-based – the conical hat they use is an adaptation of the Chinese farmer's hat. But we use our 'kramaas' in a hundred other ways. As sarongs, dust masks, scarves, sashes, baby slings, pads for carrying things on our heads, potholders, towels, sacks to carry things in… you get the idea. In the army they were our packs – you just spread them out on the ground, put all your stuff on them, and tie the corners together. If you have a machete you tie the 'kramaa' around the handle and hang onto the handle; it's easier to carry everything that way.

Our 'kramaas' were government issue but not army issue, so we hadn't had to ditch them with our uniforms. The work camps had issued different colors at random; mine was red, and my friend's was blue. Unless we'd gotten them mixed up – they were so dirty now you couldn't even see the color. Remember, we'd had no soap for almost four years now. No clean water, either. I remember the first time I tried to wash my 'kramaa' – it came out dirtier than it went in.

I cut a section of banana stalk, sliced it lengthwise, put the blade of my 'kwaiw' into it and tied it closed with a vine. Now I had a scabbard, so I could swim with my machete without getting cut. I made a second scabbard for my friend, but I cut his much longer than mine. Banana stalks are full of tiny air chambers, and they float very well. I wanted him to have a float because he just had no muscle in his shoulders. How the hell was he going to swim? If he'd ever learned – he still hadn't said that he hadn't, but he hadn't said that he had. And he was my elder – I couldn't ask him. I decided to stay right next to him.

I took the peanuts from my pockets and put them in my water cup, then wrapped the cup in my hammock and stuffed everything under my shirt – in the back, hoping something might stay dry. And then I put the banana stalk scabbard under my arm; I'd paddle with the other arm. My comrade just looked at me and did what I did. It seemed he hadn't caught on.

"What are the chances of me being such a good swimmer?" he said. "Chinese kids are always the ones who don't know how to swim. But because my mother was Khmer, I had Khmer cousins to teach me."

Thank *god.*

We looked out over the water, searching in the moonlight for a place to get in. But there was twisted metal everywhere.

"Let's get in upriver of the bridge," he said. "The longer ago it was hit, the more wreckage there'll be on the downriver side. Especially if they get flash-floods here. And kick right on the surface so you don't kick into metal."

"OK," I said. "But actually, the next time it rains, there could be a flash-flood. There's been no rain since the harvest, and the paddies are sickled flat. Let's choose our hiding place carefully every night."

We walked upriver twenty meters or so, got in and swam across. It was just a small tributary – I wondered how long it would take us to find the Mekong herself. And I wondered how I could find my friend some protein, so he could put some muscle on before he had to swim again.

Now it was well after dark, and as soon as we were out of the water I started getting cold. Especially my feet. Maybe swimming the river hadn't been such a good idea... Well, it was done now. We took another drink, dried our knives with our 'kramaas', climbed up the riverbank away from all the wreckage, made our way back over to the road, and started walking southwest again. I checked my lighter – it was still dry.

About a kilometer later I felt the road beneath my feet tilt upward – as though we were going up a little hill. I ran ahead of my friend, as kids do when they're excited. I was curious to find out what lay on the other side of the hill.

When I got to the top of the slope, the road underneath my feet felt different. *Very* different. It felt wonderful – it was *warm!* I motioned to my friend to hurry up and whispered as loudly as I dared, "We hit another road. And it's a grey road!"

"A grey road? What do you mean, a grey road?"

"A grey road, a black road, I don't know what you call it – it's like the roads we had in Phnom Penh."

"A *paved* road. You call it a paved road, Nyah." He continued walking toward me – and all of a sudden, he stopped.

"It feels great, doesn't it?" I whispered. "My feet are already warm!"

He didn't answer, and he didn't move – I wondered what was wrong with him. But when he told me to stay where I was, I knew. Now it was as though we weren't on a warm road in the tropics at all – it was as though we were in a much colder place. It was as if we'd simply frozen.

"Little brother, there's only one road in the entire Southeast that's paved. And if what we just swam across is a tributary of the Mekong, we're right near the Mekong herself. We're not in the middle of nowhere, we're in the hottest damned spot in the whole damned battle theater. We're on Highway One – right near the Mekong Crossing. Just where our commanding officer would have been ordered to go. Just where he would have been told we'd be most needed."

"So he knew where we were..."

He nodded, slowly. "He knew *exactly* where we were."

He looked southeast, down the highway – toward Vietnam. "With no one left to stop them the Vietnamese will barrel up this road and all pile up on each other at the Mekong – they'll have no way to get across."

Now he stared down the highway as though he could see straight through to Saigon, just one hundred and thirty kilometers away. "Nyah – we've got to get out of here."

"But we can't, can we." It wasn't a question – I knew.

"An intersection at a major highway in the middle of a war zone. We were right in the middle of it before I knew it. I should have listened to you, Nyah – if we hadn't been moving at night, I would have seen it. I should have listened to you."

As we stood there in the moonlight we were thinking the same thing, but I waited for him to say it. "Where do you think they laid the mines..."

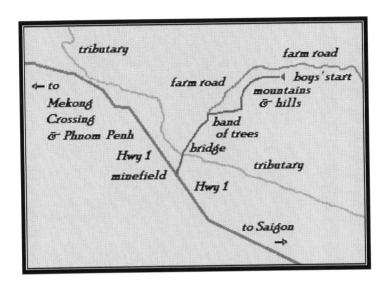

The boys' route, January 6th
(from the north side of the mountains to Highway 1)

10 kilometers (6 miles)

Day One ~ *The Seventh Scenario*

"Just don't move, Nyah. We're safe as long as we're on the asphalt."

"What's asphalt?"

"The stuff a paved road is made of. There may be mines in it, but they're anti-tank mines. We don't weigh enough to trip them. I guess we can sit down. Yeah, let's sit down to figure all this out."

"And hope the Vietnamese don't show up before we *do*. With a good road like this, they'll be moving at night. Just like we are."

"Well, if they show up before we're out of here, we just throw our arms up in the air and surrender. I'm not running through a minefield."

"But they'll *run over* us before they see us. They're not expecting to see two kids sitting in the middle of the road, in the middle of the night – in the middle of a war zone. And if we try to get out of the *way*...",

"...we'll have to run right onto the shoulder of the road, where the anti-personnel mines have been laid. And we'll trip *those* for sure." He shook his head. "The grade, where the road connects to the highway... we were just lucky."

He made his way over to me. "Well if we have to cross the shoulder, Nyah, we don't have to do it here. We can figure out the safest place to cross."

"There's no 'safe' place to cross a minefield. We have to figure out a way around it. Are you listening for convoys?"

"Yeah – I'm listening."

I looked west, toward where I thought the Mekong should be. "What if we just kept walking up the middle of the road until we got to the river, and then just... jumped in?"

"There'd be more mines at the end of the road than anywhere else, little brother. They know that if the Vietnamese can get across the Mekong, they can get all the way through to Phnom Penh. And we have no idea how far the river is."

"Well if the tributary we swam across loops around and goes under the highway, we could jump off the bridge. If it's not too high. Maybe if we walk up the road, we can find the bridge. Or what's left of it."

"Nyah. We wouldn't be able to see where we were jumping. And that river was running parallel to the highway for as far as I could see. If it loops back around, we're nowhere near where it does."

"Well, what's on the other side of the road?"

We looked across to the south side of the highway to see a burned-out stilt house, and the remains of a car underneath it. Perhaps a government official. With the wrong government – it looked like the house had been burned in '75.

We looked behind us, at the road we'd just come off of. There was a burned-out house on each corner. But they hadn't been burned in '75 – they'd been burned in the last few days. Now that I saw the houses, I could smell the ash.

"Nyah – when we came up the grade – we didn't see those houses? We didn't even *smell* them? How long have we been walking?"

"We started shortly after the sun came up, and it went down a couple hours ago. That's fourteen hours. And we've had nothing to eat but what we could find in the trees, or dig up, since mid-day yesterday. *That's* why we didn't see the houses."

"Well I'm glad we didn't see them, or we would have stopped. We're already half way through the minefield. We only have to get through the other half. Increases our chances by fifty percent. So actually, we're lucky."

"I don't feel very lucky. I don't see any way to avoid going over the shoulder." I sighed. "I wish we could measure how much good karma we have left; then we'd know our chances. But we can't measure our karma any better than we can measure the kerosene in my lighter."

"I'm willing to bet that you have more good karma left than I do, little brother – I know you better now than I did this morning. You've been pulling my weight all day. It's my turn."

"*Oh,* no. I know what you're thinking. Look – I only had a few weeks' training before they put me in your unit, but they taught me how to detect mines. I can feel around for the trip wires. Can't see much with what little light there is, but I'll be able to feel the wires."

"If we'd had just *one more day*, we'd have had more moonlight to see the wires. And maybe fewer clouds. And if we'd had just *one more day,* I wouldn't have made this mistake. A little more food, a little more rest, and I would have been thinking clearly…"

"Just one more day and you would have been in combat. You would have been dead by now."

"Yeah. Maybe both of us, little brother… Look. I've been in the army a lot longer than you have. They taught me how to detect mines *and* how to lay them. So I'll be the one to find the mines – you'll be well behind me. Once I've found them, we'll just go around them. If there *are* any. The army may not have wanted to waste anti-personnel mines when they knew the Vietnamese would be moving in on trucks; they may have only laid anti-tank mines. It's like we said – they don't even waste *bullets* if they can kill you with something else. But we can't take the chance."

"Well if we're going to find the mines, we have to think like the guys who laid them. When they taught you how to do it, what did they tell you to do?"

"Get them into the shoulder first, *then* put them in front of the…" He turned slowly, and his eyes locked on mine. "… houses." He sat down on the pavement, and buried his head in his hands. I'd already seen him do that once today. I sat down next to him.

"OK, there'll be mines in front of the houses," I said. "Of course – our army wants to be sure the Vietnamese can't resupply."

"Nyah, there's nothing left here for them to *get.* No rice, no food, no medicine… No, the army wants to be sure no one can get into the houses to *hide.* Collaborators, or surveillance for the Vietnamese."

"But they couldn't have mined in front of *all* the houses – could they?"

"I think they would have just done the ones along the highway. And they would have mined the lanes that lead back into the village."

"So if we can get through the shoulder and over to a house, and then avoid the lanes when we make our way out of the village, we should be OK."

"It won't be quite that easy. You Khmer set your houses well back from the street. If I were to try to come up with an average, I'd say fifteen meters. Add three meters of shoulder... that's *eighteen meters.* By the time I get through all that, the Vietnamese will have come and gone and be sipping their morning coffee in Phnom Penh. Well, we'll think of something, before a convoy shows up. *Damn* – if we didn't have to worry about the Vietnamese we could sleep in the middle of the road tonight, get up tomorrow morning and *see* all the trip wires. Just bad luck that we hit this thing in the dark."

"No, it's like you said before, Puamaak. It's because we hit it in the dark that we're halfway through it. We wouldn't have even gone up the grade if we'd seen the road."

"Too bad I can't use your lighter to see the tripwires. But then the Vietnamese would see *us.*"

"Is there a pattern to the way the mines would have been laid? Something we could use to our advantage? I mean, if the army lays them in rows, we could crawl between the rows. When they taught me how to detect mines they taught me how to find the ones laid by all the *other* armies – the Vietnamese, the Americans, the Thais... They didn't tell me how *our* army does it."

"There's no standardization in anything our army does. The units in one district do things a certain way, and the units in another district do them completely differently. So you can never second-guess them. But training is one thing, and combat is another – anyone laying mines here would have known the Vietnamese were coming. They would have been so scared they would have forgotten everything they'd been taught. And there's so much chaos in our army now that one unit often doesn't know what the other's doing. One might have laid mines around the houses, and another might have come along later and set the houses on fire. With the same purpose. I've been in longer than you have, Nyah. I've seen it all."

"So they might have *skipped* this area, thinking another unit had mined it already. Or skipped it because another unit had burned it."

"No, they wouldn't have skipped it – not an intersection on a major highway near the Crossing. If anything, they would have mined it twice. *Damn* how are we going to get across."

"If we can find an area where there are no houses, all we have to worry about is three meters of shoulder."

We looked up and down the road. We couldn't see very far in the moonlight, and the clouds and the blowing ash made things even worse. But we could make out the shapes of houses for as far as we could see.

"Hey – the dirt road we just came off of," he said, "I don't see it continue on the other side. But it *must...* If that road is paved we can walk down it to get away from Highway One, and then cross the shoulder of that road where there wouldn't be so many mines... Look down the highway for another signpost with no sign on it – *that's* where our road will be. Come on – let's go."

I got up and extended my hand to pull him to his feet. And as soon as I'd done it, he clamped his hand around my wrist in a vice grip. It was clear he wasn't going to let go – and I wasn't going to let him. I wasn't so scared that I couldn't function; that's not it at all. It was that, if he stepped on a mine, I wanted to go out with him. I knew I couldn't find my way back to Pong Tuk by myself. I wondered again who the owl had come for that morning. Maybe for both of us.

But I hadn't realized *why* he'd clamped his hand around my wrist. When I'd extended my hand to help him to his feet I'd been looking down. But he'd been looking up. He'd seen the clouds part suddenly, and by the time he was on his feet again we were spotlighted in the moonlight. Right in the middle of the highway.

"Walk slowly, Nyah. No sudden movements."

"I thought you said we were safe on the asphalt."

"Safe from the *mines* – but *the mines aren't our biggest problem.* Just sneak down the road right in tight behind me."

Oh, I was going to follow him all right – because I wanted to hear what it was that could be worse than a minefield.

"We're totally exposed on this road, little brother. No one who spots us will know who we are or why we're here – and they won't take the time to find out. If you saw someone coming toward you right now, and you had a gun in your hand, what would you do? You'd shoot him – before he had a chance to shoot you. We can't *possibly* be the only ones out here. Collaborators. Deserters. And surveillance, for either side. *Anyone who sees us will shoot us.* "

"I understand," I said. "We were OK until we lost our cloud cover. But the wind's picked up, so we may get it back again."

The wind fanned the cinders on either side of the road, and more ash began to blow up. "Don't cough, Nyah! If you have to hold your breath, do it – just don't cough!"

We inched our way down the highway and hit the continuation of the farm road just a block from where we'd come off it.

"Not a grey road," I whispered.

"And it runs due south – straight to the Delta."

"So this road's probably mined, too."

"Well finding the farm road didn't work. Let's think of something else."

But we *couldn't* think of anything else. We backed up a few houses until we were in the middle of the block again and just stood there, in the middle of the road.

"What do I *smell?*" I asked. "That's not burned houses."

"It's what was inside the houses, when the Khmer Rouge took over. There would have been all kinds of businesses here four years ago, this close to the Crossing. Convenience stores and restaurants, for people headed to the ferry. Repair shops, for all the trucks going back and forth between Saigon and Phnom Penh. When the Khmer Rouge set up the communes they would have left the farmers here, but they would have shut down all the businesses and relocated the tradesmen to the countryside. Like they did with us. The people would have taken with them whatever they could carry, but there would have been all kinds of things left behind. Rubber tires, restaurant supplies, crates and packing boxes, plastic bags... who knows what else. And with all the fuel stops, there would have been plenty of gasoline – no one could carry *that* off."

And then he stopped – and buried his face in his hands.

"Don't sit down!" I whispered. "If this place is full of four-year-old gasoline, we're going over the shoulder *now* – before you think of anything else! *Look again for a place to cross!"*

How the hell had I gotten here? Because I'd survived the work camps long enough to get drafted. And I remembered again how I'd survived the work camps. Now *I* was the rat in the trap, trying to find a way out. I wasn't having any more luck than any of the rats I'd eaten.

The ash swirled all around me, like the ghosts that swirl around a temple at night. The smell of the charred houses conjured up visions of people screaming, running for their lives. And every *pop!* of a cinder beneath my feet sounded like the M-79 shell that had taken some of my hearing five years before. It was all beginning to make me sick.

The rumble of thunder cleared my head. A *rainstorm* – that's what we needed! It would drown the smell of the houses. And put out any hot spots that might be left, so the gasoline wouldn't explode. It might slow the Vietnamese down a little, too, and send whoever else was out there running for cover. Yeah, a rainstorm would buy us some time.

"Nyah, can you hear it? I think that's artillery fire. The wind keeps shifting – I can't tell for sure. Look down the south side of the road. Look for the house closest to the shoulder. Look..." He suddenly let go of my wrist and pointed – and collapsed in a heap on the pavement.

I dropped down next to him. He was sitting up, still pointing. And he was *laughing.*

"I looked, but I didn't *see,*" he said. *"Take a look around."* He opened his arms wide, like a drunken man inviting you into his living room. "It's been so long since I left Phnom Penh... that house, down there. It looks just like my uncle's! A bicycle shop on the ground floor, and a flat for aaaaaaaaaaall my cousins right above it!"

What was he talking about? Did he think he was still in Phnom Penh? And he wasn't getting up – what the *hell* was wrong with him? I was exhausted, I was scared, I was half starved, and there was a kilo of ash in my head.

And then I remembered. *The mushroom.* The one, wild, poisonous mushroom that he had eaten just before the sun went down. Sometimes it just takes one.

"Nyah, look around. Highway One, between *two intersections.* The businesses – that's the key. These aren't Khmer stilt houses, *they're Chinese shop houses!* Chinese houses are right near the street, because they're merchants' houses. And they have a cement floor aaaaaaaaaaall the way across." He sounded drunk again. "The infantry wouldn't have bothered to lay a mine in a cement floor when they could lay one in the dirt. We just need to get from the asphalt over to the floor of one of those houses, and we're safe. *Twenty feet –* that's it!"

He was making perfect sense – and had been, all along. There must be something wrong with *me*.

"OK – OK – I understand," I said. "We need to look for the shop house nearest the road. That one – over there."

"No." He shook his head. "That's on the *north* side."

"Well what the hell's the difference if we walk to the Mekong north of the highway or south of it?"

"We'd have to cross the dirt road we came in on if we walked on the north side. And by the time we got to the Mekong, the Vietnamese would have gotten there, too. The river is very narrow at the Crossing, and the current would carry us south – right in front of them. They could just sit there on the bank and... pick us off. No, we need to cross the shoulder on the south side of the road and get moving southwest again, away from the two intersections and toward the Mekong *below* the Crossing. I want to get us across the river as soon as you can see where it is. First thing tomorrow morning."

"OK," I said. "That house – over there. The one with the door hanging open. We won't have to break in to get through the house and out of the village. And it's closer to the road than the others."

He shook his head. "Nyah, there's a reason the door's hanging open. That house is booby trapped. And there's probably a string of mines all the way from the road to the door. But I know these shop houses – the cement pad is always wider than the house. I'll go across the shoulder on the *other* side of the house, and we can just walk on the cement pad around to the back."

He got up quickly, walked down the road until he was in front of the house, and took a look at the shoulder. "Yeah – six meters. It should take me about half an hour to get through." He untied his pack and handed his machete to me.

"Tell me what we're looking for," I said. "Russian mines, Chinese mines, American mines..."

"... German mines, Vietnamese mines, Cambodian mines. Trip wires, stakes, prongs, and mines sticking out of the ground. But you can't see the mines that are activated by pressure plates. All the parts are buried."

"Look, I'm the one with the better night vision. I *saw* the owl this morning, when you could only hear it. So I'm the one who should go through the minefield first."

He heard me – I know he did. But he knelt down on the side of the road anyway.

He got ready to stretch himself flat on the asphalt, perpendicular to the shoulder, so that he could feel for mines directly in front of him and inch his way across. "Just take both packs and walk a block back down the middle of the road, the way we came. Because I don't know what they put in here, and how far the shrapnel will fly. If you hear an explosion run back here, crawl on your stomach straight toward the house from my starting point, and be sure I'm dead. If I'm not, slit my throat with my machete. Most of these mines are designed to blow your foot off so you'll yell for a medic; the idea is to tie up all the medics. But I'm not walking through – I'm going through on my stomach, so as to put less weight on the pressure-plate mines. So a mine could hit me anywhere."

"If you don't hear an explosion," he continued, "come back in half an hour. You'll be able to see me signaling to you to come across – there's enough moonlight for that. Toss the packs over; just throw them as hard as you can so they land on the cement pad. Then toss the machetes over – away from me, so they don't hit me. Then slide across the shoulder on your stomach, *exactly* where I went through. If the Vietnamese get here before the half hour is up, just surrender. I'll do the same. And don't waste time crying – ask the soldiers for food. No, be sure you cry – they'll be more likely to give you food that way. Got it?"

"Yes."

"Now repeat it."

"I back up the way we came, at least a block, with all our gear. If I hear an explosion I run back, crawl on my stomach over your path to get to you and slit your throat. If I don't hear an explosion I come back in half an hour, toss our gear over and crawl on my stomach over your path. If anything goes wrong I promise to get back to Pong Tuk to tell your mother what happened to you. I just go west until I see Phnom Treil, and then walk straight toward it – that's right, isn't it? Be careful – I don't think I can make it back alone. And then neither of our mothers would ever know what happened to us."

"I think we'll be OK. Our army would have left in a hurry; if they did lay anti-personnel mines, they would have done a sloppy job of it. They might not even have buried them completely. Don't worry – I can do it. Now get going."

I backed up *two* city blocks. And I started looking again for a safe way to get across the shoulder. I couldn't help it – that's just how I was. I just never gave up.

I could see nothing that would help us, on either side of the road. I began to look for trees growing over the roadbed, thinking we could get up onto the first branch, climb over to the other side of the tree, and drop down clear of the shoulder. No luck – no trees. Too many years of war.

But as I looked down the highway I saw something in the middle of it. Something that shouldn't be there. Something black, and flat – maybe a jungle rat that had been trampled. No, we were too near the shop houses – a city rat. So I shouldn't get too close... But maybe it was something else. Something we could *use*, to help us get back to Pong Tuk.

I walked up to this thing to see what it could be. A... shoe. I picked it up. Government issue, but not like the sandals that had been issued to me. It was an infantryman's shoe. Just a little smaller than my foot.

So they *were* putting boys younger than I was into combat. I'd been right – our squad leader had been trying to keep them from getting *me*. But if they'd loaded me up with ammo yesterday morning, that meant he couldn't protect me much longer. They might even have been planning to send me into combat with my friend – <u>tomorrow</u>. *I wonder why he told Puamaak,* I thought, *but didn't tell me. But I wonder if they told <u>him</u>. Oh my god – they didn't want him to know. Because there was a change of plan, and they were going to send <u>him</u> in, too. They were going to send <u>everyone</u> in!*

I sat down on the asphalt and turned the shoe over in my hand. Whoever's shoe it was wouldn't be needing it now. His unit would have been routed, but he would have been too small to keep up. He would have drowned, trying to get across the Mekong alone after running to get away. Dead – and younger than me.

More rumbling in the distance. I couldn't tell which direction it came from – I was too busy throwing up. From finding the little shoe, from the suffocating ash, or from the fear of being left alone, I didn't know.

And then I heard it. *BOOOOOM.*

I had a flashback of the UXO explosion that had taken some of my hearing five years before. I started running back to where I'd left my friend, carrying only his machete, running straight down the middle of the road. The only sound was the slapping of my bare feet on the pavement. I had never felt so alone in my life.

It was the silence that brought me around – the explosion had been *behind* me. And the sound had been exactly like that M-79 shell five years before. I turned around and walked back to where I'd been throwing up, and then continued on toward the explosion.

Oh, I'd figured out what had happened. One of the wandering plow animals had been startled, bolted, and tripped a UXO or a mine. I guess there was still a little bit of Buddhist compassion left in me; I wanted to be sure he was dead.

I walked on until I could smell the ash of an exploded M-79 shell – a smell seared into my memory. I stood there and listened, although I wanted to run – I'd lost two of my friends in that explosion five years before. But I didn't run. I stood there, and listened for the bull. No sound. The bull was dead.

The half hour wasn't up yet but I went back to the shop house anyway, carrying both packs and the 'kwaiw' in one hand and his machete in the other. And there was my friend, standing on the cement floor, waving for me to come over.

I carefully found right where he'd started; there was just enough moonlight to see the path he'd left where he'd inched his way across the shoulder.

I tossed the packs and the machetes over to the house, slid over on my stomach and rejoined Puamaak. I picked up the packs and held up his machete. "Can I slit your throat now?"

He laughed. "Not a single mine, Nyah – not that I could find." He took his machete back. "Now let's get out of the village."

The cement pad of the shop house was still warm beneath our feet. We walked around to the back, and could see what remained of a wooden stilt house. The whole thing had collapsed on itself, and its roof tiles covered the ground.

"There'll be no more shop houses now that we're away from the road," said Puamaak. "The safest place to walk is under the main floor of the Khmer houses; I'm not chancing the lanes. But this house – we'll have to go over it."

We picked our way over the tiles and looked ahead to see how many more houses we had to go. But we just couldn't see that far.

The next house was still standing, except for the stairs. We started to walk underneath the main floor and were almost to the other side, when he heard the whole house start to creak.

"*Run!*" He grabbed my wrist and took off, pulling me behind him. We got out from under the house, and he turned into the lane that led between the rest of the houses – still dragging me behind him. We ran through all the swirling ash, the scorched trees and the fallen timbers, until we were out of the village – and then we kept on running. I tripped – or he did – I'm not really sure; one if us brought the other down. We lay there in a shallow pond, sucking air like a couple of dying fish.

He sat up, coughing. "Are you OK? Did you hurt your feet?" Before I could answer he pulled me up by my shoulders and started shaking me. "Are you OK?"

"*Yes,*" I said, pushing him away so that I could get out of the water. "We've still got to walk tonight, to get further away from the highway. At least three kilometers. Are *you* OK?"

"Yeah. And you're right – we've got to keep going." And we both climbed out of the pond.

We sat down against a tree, if only for a *few* minutes. But as soon as we were off our feet, it was like the night before...

"Don't fall asleep!" he whispered, as loudly as he dared. "We have to rest before we move on, but we *cannot* fall asleep! Stand up – take your shirt off – wring it out and lay it on the bank to dry. Then sit down – *but don't lie down!* No, that's not going to work. Damn it, let's get away from this tree!"

We wrung out our shirts and 'kramaas', laid them out to dry, sat down on the bank and leaned in toward each other. And suddenly, everything was quiet.

It was then that I noticed the breeze. It was sweet. As though it were blowing in from somewhere outside of the war zone. A peaceful breeze – the kind that sets prayer flags fluttering. It cleared our heads a bit, and we leaned back on our hands on the edge of the pond and let it swirl gently around us.

"Sorry, Nyah. I had to make a split-second decision back there. Keep going under the houses, or go through the lane and chance hitting a mine. I thought our army would have been in too much of a hurry to lay mines that far back from the road, so I chanced the lane. Did I break your wrist?" He laughed – if just a little.

"Seems to still work OK," I said, waving it around. "Well I'm sure I'll be hauling you through something or another before we've made it all the way back to Pong Tuk. We're doing OK, for all the scenarios of what could happen to us – getting caught, being mistaken for something we're not, being turned in for rice... and then there was the minefield."

"Yeah, the minefield. That was the seventh scenario. And I'm sure we'll see it again."

Day Two - *Stripped*

We 'new people' had a saying: *'If you wake up in the morning, all it means is that you didn't die during the night. You have another day – or part of one.'*

We'd continued walking the night before, after getting out of the minefield. We'd shadowed the farm road southwest to get away from the highway as quickly as we could. Then Puamaak had remembered that Highway One runs northwest, all the way from Saigon to Phnom Penh. So we'd struck out through the dry rice paddies due west – by taking the shortest route to the Mekong we could actually continue to put fair distance between ourselves and the convoys that would be coming up the highway.

But we hadn't been able to stop after the first three kilometers because we hadn't been able to find a stand of trees. "All the years of carpet bombing," my friend had said. "The Americans figured the Vietnamese Communist base camps were in the stands of trees, so, with their B-52s, they simply took the trees out."

We'd found a place to sleep around midnight – we'd been walking eighteen hours. We'd flopped down on our hammocks, too tired to hang them up. But as soon as we were off our feet we'd agreed that walking eighteen hours *free* was nothing, compared to walking eighteen hours as drones of the Communist Khmer Rouge army. And as soon as those words were out of our mouths, we'd fallen dead asleep.

'If you wake up in the morning, all it means is that you didn't die during the night.' Yes, my friend woke up this morning – but with a hand over his mouth.

Instantly awake, he lay motionless on the ground. But his mind raced – who'd captured him? And who would want him *alive?*

Then he realized that the palm on his face was soft. So it wasn't a farmer, waiting his chance to help the invading Vietnamese. Or anyone from a work camp or a commune. No, it was the army.

But, which one? Vietnamese – had to be. Khmer Rouge would have killed him already. They would have assumed he was pro-Vietnamese just because he was in the war zone. Or could they be Khmer Rouge surveillance, mistaking him for one of their own?

No, not Khmer Rouge. No cuff. The wrist on his face was bare.

They hadn't covered his eyes; it was just dawn, and he strained to see his captors. But he couldn't – the one with a hand over his mouth had something black over his face, and was leaning in so close that Puamaak couldn't see around him. He closed his eyes, and waited – screaming inside that he hadn't tied his hammock up in a tree the night before. That *one mistake...*

It was then that he thought to listen, for any clue that might come to him on the wind. Artillery fire, way off in the distance. And then he realized that he couldn't hear anyone *with* his captor. So he'd been captured by a scout – because the scout thought he had information.

It had been just a few seconds now since my friend had felt that hand over his mouth. But he'd already figured out who'd captured him, and why. That's why we were the very last of the survivors – we could figure it all out, when the other boys couldn't.

"*It's me,*" I whispered. And then Puamaak realized that the hand over his mouth was a little hand – a little hand that smelled of earth.

"Are you awake?" I asked. He nodded, his eyes as big as saucers. "Sorry." I took my hand away and pulled my hair out of my face. "I couldn't take the chance that you'd cry out when I woke you up. We have a problem. Same one as last night. I've already been up a tree and taken a look at the landscape. Nearest stand of trees is *way* far away. We have twenty minutes before the sun comes up – just time to get partway over. Maybe the mist will hide us for the other part. I know you can't see very well – just get up, and I'll lead you. It's over levees all the way, so you don't *have* to see. Be sure you have your machete."

"Nyah – did you hear the artillery fire?" He sat up, and started groping for his gear.

"Yes, I could hear it. But it's far away."

I helped him up, and we made our way over the levees as quickly as we could. We got to the trees and walked in to the middle of the stand. Knowing that I was going to climb another tree, he lay down in the first of the morning sunlight. And then he closed his eyes.

I watched him for a minute. It had been just over twelve hours now since he'd eaten the mushroom, but he seemed to be OK. I thought that, if something were going to happen, it would have happened already. I scrambled up the tree.

He fell asleep the minute I was gone; he needed food, and he needed water. I could go without them longer than he could, but I think that was because I was barely nine when they put me in my first work camp. I noticed in those first critical weeks that I adapted faster than the older boys did.

Fifteen minutes later I dropped down from the tree. That woke him up, and I handed him some tamarind. "This is a *little* more ripe than what we got yesterday. We'll have to swim another tributary before we get to the Mekong. It's bigger than the one we swam last night, but we shouldn't have any trouble. No sign of Vietnamese here, but that doesn't mean they're not up on Highway One – I can't see it any more. We covered a hell of a lot of ground after we got out of the village last night."

"No sign of anyone else?" he asked.

I helped him to his feet. "No, it's just like yesterday – all the *people* seem to have evaporated."

"Any roads between us and the Mekong? I don't want to go through a minefield today – not until I've had something to eat, anyway. But I know there'll be at least one road, running north up the bank of the river to the old ferry crossing. We may be able to find a way around it, though."

"The only roads I saw run east/west," I said. "Probably feeders to the ferry road. And they're just cart tracks. Nothing the Vietnamese will be interested in."

"Good. How about food? Could you see *anything?*"

"Nothing – nothing at all. And we can't stop long enough to catch anything until we're out of the war zone."

"I wouldn't chance cooking it anyway," he said. "Not here. OK, let's figure out what might grow in this area. We're in Prey Veng Province, and we'll be in

Kandal Province once we get across the Mekong. That's where your village is. What did your grandfather grow? Fruit would help us the most – start with that."

"OK… mangoes – but they won't be ripe yet; mangosteens – it's the end of the season; pineapple and jackfruit – too easy to find, and too easy to pick – they'll all be gone; durian – not ripe; longans – not ripe; coconuts and sugar palm – I can't climb the trees without making a target of myself; soursop and cherimoya – not ripe. Rambutans – the red ones don't grow where it's this warm; believe me, my grandfather tried it. That leaves guavas, bananas and papayas – they'd be around the houses. If we can't find anything, well, some of the seeds are edible – rambutan, durian and jackfruit. But you have to cook them, so we wouldn't be able to eat them until we're across the river. And there're no wild rambutans, either; I found vines in among the trees here, but all the fruit is gone."

"OK, Nyah. How about root crops? What did your grandfather grow?"

"Yams, potatoes, turnips, carrots, radishes, onions, scallions, leeks, taro, ginger, garlic… but I didn't see any fields that aren't rice paddies. It's because we're away from the houses; these are the outlying fields. You know, I didn't even see cassava – which is really strange. There's always *some*, growing around the paddies."

"How about vegetables? Bitter melon, eggplant, tomatoes, corn, beans, peas, cabbage, squash, peppers…"

"No – nothing," I said. "The people here never got their winter crops in. Look around, when we get out of the grove."

"*Sugar cane.* Did you look for cane? We could suck the juice out of it – instant energy, kills your hunger, and puts water back in your body."

I shook my head. "This is a war zone, Puamaak. That's the first thing every soldier looks for."

He exhaled very slowly, as if finishing a cigarette. "So that leaves us with the tamarind and the raw cassava we got yesterday, until we can get across the river – I don't want to get anywhere near the houses. It's not enough to get us by, but it will have to."

"And it looks like we're lucky to have even that. I had to climb really high up to get the tamarind; somebody already got everything on the lower branches."

We walked to the western side of the grove, found a levee and set out again.

"We have no cover at *all*," said Puamaak, looking around. "No mist, no smoke, no cane fields, no trees... *Nothing.*" He shook his head.

"Before the harvest we could have walked down in the paddies; we're so short, no one would have seen us."

"Nyah, isn't that where we *should* be walking? Prey Veng must be *full* of UXOs, but the paddies have been plowed up every year since all the fighting began."

"Oh, no, the levees are safer. I know that from Prai Anchaan. The paths along the tops are well worn – by kids, by plow animals, by dogs, by wives taking food out to their husbands in the fields. So most of the UXOs would have been detonated already. And our feet – the levees are nice soft dust, but the paddies are prickly stubble."

"Well we've got to find some cover *somewhere*. Nyah, you said you could hide anywhere. Think."

"Just keep walking, until I can figure something out."

We picked up our pace and walked on, but I *couldn't* figure anything out. And after ten minutes or so, my friend started to fall behind. "OK," I said, "I'll show you a trick I learned from one of the older boys. Follow right behind me, and concentrate on something to take your mind off how tired you are. Watch my hair blowing around. Don't take your eyes off my hair. And then, when you think you just can't go any further, change to something else. Watch the mosquitoes buzzing around my ears. Don't take your eyes off my ears. And then, when you think you just can't go any further, change to something else again. Like my pack swinging back and forth. But always stay right in tight behind me – then you can't fall behind."

So we just continued on. He watched my hair blowing around in the breeze. And then he watched the mosquitoes buzzing around my ears. And then he watched my pack swinging back and forth. And then he watched my feet kicking the dust up as I walked. And then he got an idea.

"Nyah – those dirt roads you saw running west – there must have been houses on them. There should be a line of trees running in front of each house. We could walk just inside the line of trees. Yes, we're trading one problem for another – I didn't want to get near the houses. But that's better than walking *here*. Or maybe everything's been burned?"

We walked on until we could see the outline of a house ahead of us. It looked as though it hadn't been burned, there were trees in front of it, and I knew there must be a garden. We started for the trees, covered the distance quickly, sat down in some tall grass and peered furtively through it at the house.

But it looked as though no one had lived there for years. We made our way to the garden, and, thinking that something might have re-seeded itself, looked around for anything we could eat. Nothing. The empty trellises creaked in the wind, the bean poles had fallen over, and the tomato frames stood in different stages of collapse. We looked for rain barrels. Gone.

And then we looked back out over the landscape. All the paddies should have been green with newly-planted winter crops. The irrigation canals should have been full of water. And there should have been farmers everywhere – with their Brahmas, their water buffalo, their children and their dogs. But everything was quiet, and all we could see was stubble, dust, and ash.

"Take a good look, little brother." My comrade pointed out over the landscape. "This is what a war zone looks like. Bombed, burned, deforested," he tossed his head back toward the house, "stripped, and abandoned. Take a good look."

"You see with the eyes of an infantryman, Puamaak. I see with the eyes of a farmer. The reservoirs haven't been re-opened; there's no one here to do it. There's too much wind because the trees are gone; that stirs up the dust. The dry-season crops should already be in – squash, tomatoes, corn... I don't know when they plant their rice here, but I know it doesn't plant itself. If the paddies aren't replanted, there will be no rice next year. I've never seen anything like this."

"And the Southeast can't be the only place where this is happening, little brother. I wonder if *everyone* will starve. Our staple food the past four years has been rice porridge diluted with water – in the communes, in the camps, and in the army. Next year we won't even have that." He looked out over the landscape again. "And the people here will be the first to starve, because there's been war in the Southeast longer than in any other part of the country. The carpet bombing – it *started* here. Then there was the Khmer Rouge insurgency. And then Brother Number One launched the Delta raids. And now the Vietnamese... Oh yeah – the people will start coming back. Because they have nowhere else to *go*. But there's nothing left for them here."

I started to get up. "Come on. Let's just get over to the Mekong and get out of here."

We walked along the row of trees, crossed a dusty track that served as a driveway, then walked along another row of trees and crossed another driveway. We just kept on walking down the road from one row of trees to another, because that's the only option we had.

"Where are the *dogs*, Puamaak? Every farmer has a dog."

"I think they've all been eaten. Except the ones that ran up into the hills. Where's the tributary? Shouldn't we have hit it by now? How could you have even *seen* it this morning if we haven't hit it yet?"

"I didn't see it – but I knew it was there. I saw two lines of trees winding parallel to one another. You know the city, I know the rivers. It's like the gasoline in the intersection last night. You couldn't see it, but you knew it was there. I wouldn't have."

"Common sense," he said. "How many vehicles have you seen driving around since the Khmer Rouge took over? And if no one's driving, no one's using up any gas. The reservoirs underneath those pumps might not be full, but they *sure* aren't empty." And he put his hand on his stomach.

"Puamaak, if I can get some frogs in the tributary, do you think you can eat them raw?"

He didn't answer, but put his other hand on his stomach at the very thought of it.

"The Japanese eat things raw," I said. "We can learn to do it."

"But they season it with something. And then they smother it in *rice*... Maybe we shouldn't talk about food until we have half a chance of finding some."

"OK," I said. "Just think about how much better off we are today than when we woke up yesterday. Think about what we accomplished in less than twenty-four hours. We got ourselves away from our platoon. We got ourselves away from the Vietnamese. We found food. We found water. And we're not *lost* anymore. I still can't get over how we woke up with absolutely no idea where we were – not even what country we were in – and then were able to figure it out *exactly* by the end of the day. What are the chances of that? If we hadn't hit the tributary of the Mekong, and then Highway One, and if Highway One hadn't been paved, we'd still be trying to figure it out."

"Yeah," he said, "just slogging our way west, navigating by the sun, with no idea which way to go to get out of the way of the Vietnamese except to get away from where they shelled us." He put his hand on his stomach again. "You know, we still have tamarind left. If you can get some frogs, we can cut them into really tiny pieces and wrap them in the tamarind."

"And tamarind's got acid in it. Remember the mint and coriander salad we used to get at weddings? The meat in it was 'cooked' by soaking it in lime juice. Maybe the tamarind would 'cook' the..."

"Nyah – what's the matter?"

"We didn't hear any frogs last night. We're down in the lowlands now – we should have heard some."

"We didn't hear any because the irrigation ditches are dry."

"But the reservoirs are full."

"Maybe the frogs have all been hunted out. Like all the other animals."

"Not the poisonous ones," I said. I saw him look down at our bare feet. "No, the ones in rice country are only poisonous if you eat them. But we didn't even hear *them* last night." I shook my head. "This place is different than where you and I come from. It's like you said – it should be just like Kandal Province, right across the Mekong."

"Yeah. Phnom Penh is only sixty-five kilometers upriver from the Crossing."

"So Prai Anchaan is only eighty. This place should look just like where I grew up. But it doesn't. And no cassava? *Anywhere?* If I didn't know we were in Cambodia, I'd swear we were in Vietnam."

Puamaak started to look around at the landscape again. "What else is different about this place?"

"Well," I said, "look at the way the farmers have cleared their land. It's not just because of the carpet bombing that there are fewer trees – I think they just slash and burn here when they want to clear for a paddy. And there're no mountains, Puamaak. Look around." He turned, and slowly panned all 360 degrees around us. "Last mountains we saw were the ones we came out of yesterday. The only place I know of that has no mountains is the Delta."

Now my comrade looked really worried. "You're right, little brother. Even from Phnom Penh you can see mountains. The peaks of Udong." He stopped walking, and sat down in a patch of tall grass. I sat down beside him.

He closed his eyes and tried to replay every second of his teacher's pointing out the 'Parrot's Beak'. Every word she'd said, and every movement of her finger on the map. "Highway One runs just north of the Delta in the 'Parrot's Beak' – Svay Rieng province, the last one over before our eastern border with Vietnam. And we came south last night... we could have crossed the southern border and gotten into the Delta. Nyah, are you *sure* you couldn't see the Mekong this morning? Another pair of parallel lines of trees? If we're near the Mekong we're either in Prey Veng province, or in the Delta just south of it. *Not* way over toward Saigon."

"Yes, I'm sure. Because I couldn't see very *far*. When we were up in the mountains I had taller trees to climb, and they were high above the lowlands. I could see for a *long* way yesterday. But not this morning."

My friend was quiet.

"And there's another thing," I said. "The irrigation reservoirs here aren't rectangular, or even square – they're round."

"*Round?* The Khmer Rouge always had us dig rectangular reservoirs. Are *all* of them round?"

"All of them that *I* could see," I said.

"OK, let's back up. We know we were in Cambodia last night because there were no road signs at the bridge. *Damn* – if there'd been signs, we'd know if we really are near the Mekong. 'Yes', if there was a sign for the ferry, and 'no', if there wasn't. You couldn't see Highway One this morning, either?"

"No. Are we even sure that *was* Highway One?"

"Yes, because One's the only paved road in the Southeast."

"But," I said, "if the Vietnamese have those great big tanks, and a modern army, One's probably not the only paved road in South Vietnam. We were assuming we were in Cambodia, but *all we were going on* was the fact that there were no road signs at the bridge. Some poor Vietnamese farmer might have unscrewed them just to use the metal for something else. After so many years of war, everyone's desperate. And you said One runs over the border – we could have been on the Vietnamese side last night. Any scenario you look at – whether that road was One, or whether it was some other paved road – we *could* be in Vietnam."

"Or in the 'Parrot's Beak'," he said. "One province further away from Pong Tuk than Prey Veng, and one province deeper into the war zone."

"So I guess we're just as lost now as we were when we woke up yesterday."

Puamaak nodded his head, passed his hands over his face, and rested his chin in his hands.

Suddenly, he jumped up. "No, we're not! That road was a *highway.* It *had* to be One. And that section of it *was* in Cambodia – if it were in Vietnam, the sign for the southern part of the farm road wouldn't have been missing. The government would have made sure of that. But when we shadowed *that* road we could have crossed our southern border. Or we could still be in Cambodia, but in Svay Rieng. So yeah, I guess we *are* just as lost as we were yesterday, because we don't know where the Mekong is." And he slumped back down again, into the tall grass.

"Unless I can see it," I said. "When we come up on a really tall tamarind, I'll climb it and try again. But one thing hasn't changed since we first woke up yesterday – we know we have to go west to get to Pong Tuk."

"*Do* we know? *How* do we know. How did we even come to *that* conclusion?"

"Because when I crossed the Mekong with the army, we kept going perpendicular to it. Wasn't it the same with your unit?"

"Yeah," he said.

"Yeah. They were trying to get us to our next camp as quickly as possible, so they weren't marching us in circles yet. They were marching us due east." I started to get up. "At least we know we have to go west. At least we're going in the right direction. It's *something*."

But my friend was desperately hungry – it would take more than that to rally him.

"You need water more than anything else," I said. "And it will fill your stomach, so you won't be so hungry." I looked out over the landscape again.

He followed my gaze, and then looked up at me from where he sat in the grass. "I don't want to risk going out to one of those reservoirs without cover, but I don't think I'm going to make it to the tributary. Nyah, why am I so thirsty? I should be able to go without water for more than half a day."

"Part of it's the food we're eating. Yesterday we had wild rambutans; there's juice in them, and they're sweet. Today we have raw cassava and tamarind; they're dry, and sour. Don't eat any more cassava – if it makes you sick it will be with diarrhea, and that will take the last of the water in your body. And don't eat the tamarind – just suck on it. But it's not just the food we're eating. It's the heat, too. We're not in the mountains any more. And it's not just the difference in the elevation – the lack of tree cover makes it much hotter down here."

He shook his head. "I wonder how hot it's going to get today. Well one thing's for sure – we can't keep going at this pace. We don't have real food, we walked eighteen hours yesterday but didn't get a full night's sleep last night, and we ran for hours the day before that. If we push ourselves beyond our limits, we'll die. Wouldn't that be the most ironic thing you ever heard of? 'They got away from the Khmer Rouge, they got away from the Vietnamese, but they *still* died – because they didn't know how to pace themselves.' We have to slow down tomorrow, even if we're not across the Mekong. *Damn* I hope we don't run into Vietnamese."

"But you can pass us off as farm kids down here in the lowlands," I said. "Especially as we're going west now. We'd just wait out the war in a camp."

"The dogs, Nyah. The *missing* dogs. Either the farmers ate them, or our army got them. That got me thinking. How many times have we heard that the Vietnamese soldiers eat dogs. That can mean only one thing – that they don't get enough food in their army, either. And do you think they'd share what food they have with their prisoners? I don't think so, little brother. Khmer Kraum or not, if they were hungry enough, they'd kill us – and never tell anyone they'd found us. We'd never make it to a camp."

I shuddered. "Let me look for a rain barrel behind one of these houses. Even a little water will get us to the tributary."

"We're out of houses, Nyah. Didn't you notice? About a kilometer back. But there's a big tree ahead of us – can you take another look around?"

The tree was a mango, and I was able to get up it without much trouble. I spotted a grove of trees ahead of us about half a kilometer across, and felt there should be water in there. But I stayed up in the tree for a few extra minutes so Puamaak would rest in the shade. This was the first time I'd heard him say he didn't think he could make it, and I didn't know him well enough to gauge how serious he was. And he was right, about pushing ourselves beyond our limits. I decided not to take any chances.

I looked around for unripe fruit; we could eat green mangoes if we had to. There was nothing. It was then that I noticed the split branches. Someone heavier than I was had climbed up and stripped the whole damned tree. Everyone was starving, that was all. I decided not to tell my friend, and wondered if things would be this bad all the way to the Mekong.

I climbed down from the mango. "There's a big grove of trees ahead of us. Got to be water in there. Looks like the track we're on runs straight into the north end of it. And there are a few houses before the grove; I can check their rain barrels. You know I always find water – you'll be OK."

"Start with the barrels *furthest* from the houses..."

I helped him up and we started down the cart track again. But how to keep his mind off his stomach, and keep him going? "Look around for flowers," I said.

"Flowers? What for? And where are we going to find flowers in the middle of a war zone?"

"To *eat*. These were farms. Basil flowers. Squash blossoms. Bean flowers. Banana blossoms. Even hibiscus and nasturtiums are edible. And then there's wild water hyacinth... If the villagers left as much as a few days ago there should be some new flowers out. And you can eat all of them raw."

"Hmm. We may even find rose bushes – who knows what they grow over here? I wonder what roses taste like? I know they're edible. I don't remember where I heard it, but I heard it somewhere."

"Oh, yes," I said, "that's right. And you can even make tea out of the seeds."

He began to pick up his pace and look around; my plan had worked. But as for finding flowers that we could *eat*, well, I'd sort of made that up. Most flowers are poisonous, except the few I'd named off. And I didn't really think we'd find any of those.

We got to the first house in less than a quarter of an hour. Farmhouses always have fruit trees around them, and the trees around this house had survived all the years of war. We slipped out of sight quickly.

"Give me your cup," I said. "I'll look for rain barrels while you stay under the trees. Look up into the branches for fruit. If you see any, I'll climb up and get it when I get back."

There was a shed behind the house, and I headed through the trees straight for it. If there was a rain barrel behind it I wouldn't have to get anywhere near the house. I made my way quietly around the back, and peered out from behind a tree.

In our part of the world a rain barrel is a big round earthenware vat, about a meter and a half across. Best drinking water you can get in all of Cambodia, because it's cool – the terracotta wicks the heat away.

Sure enough, there was a rain barrel behind the shed. I stole my way over to it and looked in. Empty – the barrel had cracked. Probably from the repercussion of the bombs.

I saw another barrel at the far corner of the shed, underneath a tree. I made my way over to it.

Ah – *plenty* of water. I dipped in our cups and started to fill them up.

And then I saw it, sitting in the bottom. A 'slaing' seed.

This is one stupid farmer, I thought, *to have put a rain barrel underneath a 'slaing' tree.* I turned back and looked at the tree behind me. It was a longan.

I didn't know how the 'slaing' seed had found its way into the rain barrel, but I knew we couldn't drink the water. I made my way over to the house.

There was only one barrel that hadn't cracked, and I looked inside. But this barrel was much larger than the one behind the shed, and it was in the sun; the water had stagnated. I would have chanced it if I'd been able to see through to the bottom, but I couldn't. I made my way back to my friend, our empty cups in my hand. He didn't ask any questions.

"The water's poisoned," I said. "Any fruit in the trees?"

"Stripped."

"And we still don't know where the Mekong is."

I sat down beside him and put our cups back in our packs. And all of a sudden, it was quiet again.

"Nyah, do you remember when every day wasn't just a struggle to stay alive? Waking up to the sound of the monks chanting at Wat Phnom. Eating warm French bread with your brothers and sisters before you went to school. Watching the sparrows vie for crumbs at the school canteen. Eating ice cream. Playing ball. Hearing music. Seeing a pretty girl. The sound of your mother's voice when she heard you come in from school. Having someone ask you what you wanted for dinner. A warm bath before you went to sleep at night. And all the blankets you wanted. Do you remember, Nyah?"

"Yes. It was a long time ago, but I remember."

My friend lay down quietly, and closed his eyes.

Day Two - *The Sound of Water*

"Come on," I said, as gently as I could. "If you don't get up, you'll fall asleep. You can rest when we get to the tributary." And I wondered again if I'd have to find a place for us to hide, as I'd wondered when he'd eaten the mushroom.

I took him over to the rain barrel and showed him the seed in the bottom of it. "The tree will be nowhere around here because the farmers wouldn't plant one near their fruit trees or their gardens." I pointed down into the water again. "Remember what the seed looks like."

"Nyah... do you think someone deliberately poisoned the water? I mean, if they mined the roads and booby-trapped some of the houses..."

"I don't know. It's more likely a jungle rat dropped the seed into the barrel. But even if someone poisoned every water hole and irrigation reservoir from here to the Mekong, they couldn't have poisoned the tributary. We just have to get to it." And I turned, to start for the road.

But Puamaak didn't follow me.

"Nyah! You didn't *see* this?"

I turned around again. He was still looking down at the barrel. He pointed to the rim of it. "The barrel-maker's mark. *Look at it.*"

I followed the curve of the rim to the signature etched in the clay. 'Van Nida'. A Khmer name. And it was written in Khmer.

Puamaak's eyes met mine over the barrel, and he broke into a smile. "Rain barrels are always made locally, little brother. We're in *Cambodia!* Even if we're not near the Mekong, we're not in Vietnam. We're not that far *east*, and we're not that far *south*. It's *something*."

We made our way back to the road. As I've said, it was only a cart track, and it led us into what looked like a round oasis of jungle. We raised our arms as we walked into the shade of the old, spreading trees, letting the cool air wash over us. I felt sure there would be water here.

There were wild trees around us now; even I didn't know all their names. And then I spotted a mango, and then a durian. Suddenly, Puamaak stopped dead in his tracks. He grabbed my arm to hold me back, and pointed.

A village.

"It will be mined," he said. "They would have started with the pig sties, the chicken coops, the duck ponds, and wherever else the Vietnamese could get food."

"But I don't hear any pigs, or chickens, or ducks. Or dogs."

We looked out over the village, but it appeared to have been abandoned years before. I looked at Puamaak. He motioned that we should go ahead, and we started to look for water.

And then we saw a sign, hung over what looked like the remains of a country store. But we couldn't read it.

"This was a Vietnamese village, Nyah. And from the looks of it, the inhabitants were driven out during the Lon Nol regime. Did you ever hear what happened in Prey Veng in 1970? Everyone in Phnom Penh talked about it."

"No..." I said.

"Lon Nol had eight hundred Vietnamese rounded up and executed in one village alone. He was afraid they would collaborate with the Vietnamese Communists to take more of our Cambodian land. And after he had the people executed, he had their bodies dumped into the Mekong. So they would float south, into the Delta – the land the Vietnamese had taken from us three centuries before."

I shuddered; I had never heard the story. In 1970 I was still in Prai Anchaan, and only four. But I wondered how my family could have supported Lon Nol, knowing what he'd done. Perhaps he was just the lesser of evils.

"The Khmer were such a gentle people," I said, "until we mutated in response to these madmen. The soldiers who killed all those Vietnamese – they were probably just like you and me, until they got their orders. And the cadres who kicked us, and caned us, and starved us, and worked us to death – they were just ordinary people, until the takeover. Farmers, who grew our food. And fathers, who loved their families. I mean, I don't know anything about brainwashing, but weren't they... too old? What happened?"

"'Nothing makes sense in war. Don't expect it to.' Your words, little brother. No one understands what happened; I quit trying to figure it out a long time ago. I just want to get back to my family."

We scanned the little hamlet – quaint wooden houses with footpaths connecting them, all in the cool shade of the old, spreading trees. It was even prettier than Prai Anchaan, before the war. "I wonder," I said, "why Khmer people didn't move into these houses after the Vietnamese were driven out?"

"The Vietnamese were probably killed."

"Oh... of course. Ghosts." Khmer would have been afraid of the ghosts of the dead Vietnamese. Khmer would have been afraid of the ghosts of *anything*. Well, that explained that. "Come on," I said. "Let's check the rain barrels."

We went from house to house, but those barrels that hadn't cracked from the years of bombing had all been looted out.

"There must have been a well in this village," I said. "We just have to find it."

"I wouldn't drink from it, Nyah. There may have been bodies thrown into it. I wouldn't drink from it, and neither should you."

I had to admit he was right. He closed his eyes for a minute, and I watched him, wondering if he would make it to the tributary. And, for the first time, I wondered if *I* would make it.

And that's when I heard it.

I didn't hesitate for as much as a second – I grabbed Puamaak's wrist in a vice grip and pulled him behind me, right through the middle of the village. Then I heard it again. And *again*. I ran both of us straight toward the sound as fast as I could run.

Puamaak started to pull back, exhausted. "But we're almost there!" I said.

"Almost *where*? All I hear are bulls. And you told me we should stay away from bulls."

"That's the sound of water – they're *water buffalo* bulls! And where there're water buffalo, there's water – there's a wallow around here somewhere. Just keep running toward the sound – before they shut up, and we have nothing to follow!"

We ran on until we reached the edge of the grove of trees, and found ourselves looking out over a wide, muddy pond.

And there they were, in all their majestic fatness – all the abandoned bulls and cows had banded together at this waterhole. And they were all wallowing at the northwest corner of the pond, in the shade of the old, spreading trees. The coolest spot. Animals are smart; even domesticated ones find ways to survive in the wild.

"Just follow me," I said. "My first job in Pong Tuk was to keep the bulls from fighting, so I'm used to them. I'll get us around to the south side of the pond, and we'll get our water and be off again before they notice us. I was wondering where all the plow animals were... But farmers use Brahmas, too, so keep an eye out. We'll work on your tree climbing once we're across the Mekong."

I got us around the pond and we stood on the bank, looking into the muddy water. "Don't get in," I said. "There'll be leeches. Told you I could find you some." I filled both our cups from the shoreline, and I started to drink from mine.

"How do you know the water hasn't been poisoned?" he asked.

I tossed my head toward the buffalo. "Ask *them*. If the water had been poisoned, they'd all be keeled over."

He drained his cup and filled it again. "OK, how can you tell there are leeches in the pond?"

"Watch." I knelt on the bank and slapped my hands on the surface of the water half a dozen times, then pulled them back quickly. He watched as leeches swam in from every direction toward where I'd created a disturbance. Big, fat water buffalo leeches – wherever there are buffalo, there are leeches.

I kept my eye on the buffalo as I filled my cup again. "That cow, over there. Something happened to her calf yesterday. Or the day before."

"What calf?" he asked. "There's no calf over there."

"That's my point."

"What are you talking about?"

"The noise she's making is different than the other noises buffalo make. She's calling for her calf. She would have started when she first missed it, and wouldn't give up until a couple of days later. Actually I think it was the cow I heard in the village – not the bulls. Oh, by the way, this is what buffalo piss tastes like. But don't worry, it won't hurt you."

"I don't care," he said. "It's water, isn't it?" And he drained his cup again. "But we could walk around the pond a ways to look for a spring. The water would be better there – cleaner *and* cooler. Water's coming into this pond from *somewhere*. Do you think the bulls would come after us if we looked for the inlet?"

"I think we're OK if we stay on this side." And we started walking around the edge of the pond, looking for a spring.

I spotted something else first. "*Food!* Stay right there – I'll get it." I jumped into the water, picked all of them quickly, got out again and handed him his half.

He was *starved,* but he just stood there and looked at them. "Those mushrooms," he said, "that we thought were 'psat kajō' that weren't 'psat kajō' at all... Are you sure you know what these are?"

"Are you sure you're half Chinese?"

I rolled one of the little brown balls in my fingers until the skin came off, and held it out to him.

"Oh. Oh yeah." He smiled, and popped the water chestnut into his mouth.

"You have to peel them," I said, "just like the rambutans, the cassava and the taro. You have to peel almost anything you find out here."

He ate his share just as fast as he could peel them. "If we walk around a little more," he said, "maybe we can find more food. Are the bulls still looking like they're going to leave us alone?"

"Yeah, I think we're OK. Those lily pads over there – think they're lotus? I could look for seeds."

"But you'd get leeches on you. You'd have to get way out into the pond."

"If I get one on me just scrape it off with your machete. We used to dribble tobacco juice over them in Prai Anchaan. But I don't think we ever got *buffalo* leeches on us – I think they can sense the difference between human skin and buffalo skin." I shook my head. "I hope so."

I ran into the water and over to the lily pads. There was only one plant, and the pods were gone – someone had gotten them as soon as the seeds had ripened. So I just pulled the whole plant up, ran back to my friend, and we peeled the root and ate it.

"Looks like the leeches didn't find you very tasty," Puamaak said with a grin. And he began to pan the shoreline again, looking for a spring. "Hey – there are a few more water chestnuts over there."

I walked over to the chestnuts, picked them and put half of them in my pack – they'd be our reserves, along with the peanuts. I walked back to my friend, and we ate the other half.

"Did you notice anything about this waterhole?" he said, still looking around the pond.

"What do you mean?"

"We never found an inlet. Unless one of those bulls is sitting on it."

"So?" I asked.

"So this is not a natural pond."

"It's an irrigation reservoir."

He shook his head. "We never found an outlet, either. *Look* at it, little brother. Look at how round it is."

"Perfectly round. Whoever dug it did a really great job."

"'Whoever dug it' was an American B-52 pilot. It's a bomb crater, Nyah. A bomb crater that filled with groundwater and rain. And look where it is – right next to the huge stand of trees we ran through. That's what the pilot was aiming for, but he missed his mark."

"So *that's* why all the reservoirs are round," I said.

"Yeah. The Khmer Rouge didn't have to *dig* anything – when they took over in '75, these craters had already been here for years. Well, we just got enough food and water from this one to get us through the rest of the day – that bomb just saved our lives. But I wonder how many others it took."

I didn't want to think about that. "Let's go back into the village – see if we can find more food. And I'll climb another tree and look for the Mekong again. One last drink." And I filled my water cup.

"Well I've got to hand it to you, little brother – you have one hell of a way of finding water. Chasing water buffalo, instead of them chasing *you*." He laughed – he looked a lot better now. "So before we leave, let me give you a little token of my appreciation."

He quickly filled his cup and poured the whole thing over my head. Next thing I knew we were having a water fight, leeches and all. Running around chasing each other back and forth across the bank, each trying to get the other one wetter than he was. If there were any UXOs in there, we never hit one, and the buffalo were too lazy to chase after us that day. As for surveillance and collaborators, well, if there were any there, they just watched us and let us go – so as not to give their own position away.

The sound of distant artillery fire jolted us back to the war zone, and we headed back into the village.

"The gardens may have re-seeded themselves each year," I said. "Look for bright colors. Look around the houses. Yeah... we should be systematic, like the Americans. Start by looking on the ground, for things like squash and melons. Then look a little higher, for things like eggplant and tomatoes. Then look a little higher, for beans, peas, corn and hibiscus flowers. Then look up, for things in the trees."

We looked around and found nothing, until we looked *way* up. And there was a familiar shape, framed against the sky. A *coconut*.

Now, palms are the very hardest trees to climb if you don't have a good, solid ladder. You either have to shinny up, which takes a tremendous amount of strength, or hobble up with a figure-eight of rope stretched between your feet – that takes less strength, but more coordination.

"Nyah, you can't climb that... can you?"

I laughed. "Sure I can, when there's no one around to take a shot at me. OK – I think my next story beats anything you may have overheard in your brilliant career as a spy..."

"Every time I was marched into a new work camp," I started, "I made sure I was at the end of the line. Behind the taller boys, so the cadres waiting for us wouldn't see where my eyes went. *Up*. You see, as I marched in, I'd be taking my inventory. Coconut inventory."

"As soon as I got the chance," I continued, "I'd make two ropes from vines. I'd wait for the new moon so the cadres couldn't see me. Then I'd tie the ropes around my waist, sneak out of our sleeping hut, and climb the nearest palm that had ripe coconuts. When I got to the top of the tree I'd tie the end of one rope around the stem of the first coconut, then twist the stem off the tree. Then I'd do it again, with the second rope and a second coconut. I could never get more than two coconuts at a time because they were so heavy, with the husk still on them and all. And then I'd climb down again. If I'd dropped the coconuts, the guard would have zeroed in on me and fired up into the tree. It was nerve-wracking, I tell you. But I never dropped a coconut. Never."

"And how do you hide a couple of coconuts," asked my friend, "until you can crack them open and eat them? Or do you trade them for other stuff, and say you found them on the ground?"

"Are you kidding? The cadres would never have believed I'd found them. They'd have killed me for stealing. And if they didn't kill me for stealing, they'd kill me for not sharing with my comrades. No, I'd have to eat them all myself. And I'd have to do it before I got caught."

"So how do you hack a coconut open," he asked, "and eat it without anyone noticing? I mean, you have to get through at least three centimeters of husk before you even get to the shell."

"Once you're down from the tree you get as far away from the camp as you can. You find a patch of woods so the trees will muffle the sound. Then you split the husk and crack the shell with your machete, and eat the coconut right there. Then you sneak back to your sleeping hut. I'll bet there were guys in your camp who were doing it, but you just didn't know it."

"I don't think so, Nyah... coconut palms are pretty tall. How tall were the trees you were climbing?"

"About two and a half stories."

"Two and a half stories? You climbed up in pitch darkness, balanced two and a half stories above the ground while you got the coconuts and tied them to your waist, and then climbed back down again? Right under the guard's nose? Nyah, believe me, you're the only person I ever knew who had that much *guts.*"

"It's something you do only when you're starving, not something you do when you're just hungry. You either succeed, and get food, or you fail, and die instantly – either from the fall or the gunshot. But, either way, you're not hungry any more."

He shuddered. "Skip it. We'll find something else to eat."

"No, I'm thinking more along the lines of something to drink that doesn't taste like buffalo piss."

"Coconut *water!"*

We walked over to the base of the tree, looked at each other and burst out laughing – there was one nice coconut just lying on the ground. Which meant not only that I wouldn't have to climb the tree, but that the coconut was ripe. I pulled out my 'kwaiw', and five minutes later we had both coconut water and coconut meat.

"If we'd seen the coconut first," said Puamaak, taking a drink, "we wouldn't have bothered the buffalo."

"But it was a damned good water fight. Even if you did have to lose."

"*Me* lose. Who ended up with a fat leech down his shirt? You're lucky it kept right on going and dropped to the ground."

"You're lucky I didn't make you eat it. But we got *really* lucky here – this coconut hasn't been here more than three days."

"Nyah, how do you know *that?*"

"Because the Khmer farmers would have had every tree in this village staked out, just waiting for the coconuts to ripen and drop. They would have gotten it the first day it fell. They may have been too afraid to move into the houses of the dead Vietnamese, but they wouldn't have been afraid of eating their coconuts."

He nodded. "But we could get stuck without water again. We should always have one coconut with us, just in case."

"We'll find more trees once we're across the Mekong. You rarely find them growing wild, but every farmer has a few he's planted. A lot of the trees will have been burned, but not as high up as the coconuts. Yeah, I think we'll be able to get more."

But Puamaak wasn't taking any chances – he chipped two pieces off the husk and made us each a scrub brush.

I climbed a tamarind and came down with my first *conclusive* reconnaissance report. "I can see the Mekong! And we're almost to the tributary."

"Ha! We'll be out of the war zone by tonight."

"But you should see the craters out there, from all the years of carpet bombing. Looks like a war zone all right. Looks like the *moon.*"

"Except there are probably more people on the moon than there are here," he said. "It was ten years ago that the Americans first got one of their astronauts up there. It was just after the comet went over. They'll have had time to build a whole colony by now. Those Americans – they can do anything."

"Except stop the Vietnamese Communists." I shook my head. "I'll never understand it as long as I live. They could get a man to the moon, but they couldn't stop the Viet Cong – *who were only half their size."*

"But think about why *we're* here," he said. "Because the *Communist* Khmer Rouge are fighting the *Communist* Vietnamese – who were their allies less than ten years ago. Is that any less strange?"

I shook my head again. "The only way this war will ever end is if the Vietnamese win it. Because if the Khmer Rouge win it, they'll just keep on fighting even after they take the Delta back. Almost all of what's now Vietnam originally belonged to Cambodia, so if Brother Number One were to win the Delta war, he's just keep right on going."

"I want all the fighting to stop so I can go *home,"* he said. "And I don't mean Pong Tuk."

"There'll be something left of Phnom Penh because that's where Sihanouk's palace is. So your house may be OK. My mother's, too – we moved in with her when we were forced out of Prai Anchaan."

"Nyah, you're assuming that Sihanouk didn't switch his allegiance. If he did, do you really think they would have told us? But even if our houses are still there, there will be nothing in them. Did they tell you not to lock your doors, when they came with their AK-47s to order your family out of the city? And did they tell you we'd all be able to go back in three days?"

"Yeah. And my parents believed them."

"And did they tell you why we had to leave?" he asked.

"They said the Americans were going to start bombing us again."

"Lies, to get us *moving*. Not a single bomb fell on Phnom Penh; if it had, we would have heard it. Come on – let's get going." We got up, and headed out.

"I want the war to end," I said, "so I don't have to kill to get food. I *hate* killing. Remember when we were kids, when we had the Chinese in the markets to butcher our pigs and ducks for us, and the Muslim Cham to butcher our cattle for us? So all we Khmer had to kill were fish and chickens. And *I* never had to kill anything."

"I didn't either, little brother. Not so much as a half-dead fish."

"That's why I liked my rat trap – I could set it up so that the rat would kill himself. I never had to face a live one. Except once – I got a *huge* one. He was so big the block of wood didn't knock him out. By the time I got to the trap he'd been in there awhile; I tell you, he was mad as hell. When he saw me he started gnashing his teeth, and hissing, just *waiting* to get at me. Well, I couldn't waste the food, but I couldn't face killing him. So I found an older boy who would do it. And he knew just how to do it, too. He took the whole trap and held it under water. So I gave him some of the meat as payment, and shared the rest with my friends – there was *plenty*. That was the biggest rat I ever saw."

"How many years ago was that, Nyah?"

"About three – when there still *were* big rats around."

"Even rats are reincarnated, you know. Not only has he had time to be reborn, he's had time to fatten up again. We can just catch the same one again!"

"Very funny. I don't think it works quite like that…"

More artillery fire.

"We'll hit the next minefield at the road to the ferry crossing?" I asked.

He nodded. "There'll be a village there, but they'll have used a different pattern than they would for a highway. They'll have started with the areas where there's a concentration of food – and right after the harvest, that means the shed where the rice was milled. So from here on in, when you do your recon to get us through a village we can't go around, try to locate the milling shed first so we can stay clear of it. Next they mine around the pig sties, the chicken coops, the duck ponds and the communal mess building. And on their way out they encircle the whole village. But what we're headed for should be just a long string of stilt houses on the bank of the river – we can just walk south until there aren't any more houses, and get into the river there."

"And once we're across it?" I asked.

"We'll just go way out into the country where there aren't many villages. Or roads, either. But once we get through Kandal Province and into Takeo Province, we'll hit Highway Two. Maybe nothing in it, but we can't take the chance."

We finally got to the tributary and took a good long drink. Then I climbed a tree to get another look around. So much for climbing one tree a day; it was just mid afternoon, and I'd already climbed five.

"The end of the village on the Mekong is a kilometer south of us," I said.

We prepared to swim the tributary the same way we had the first one – with our gear in the back of our shirts, our machetes in banana stalks under one arm, and the lighter kept safe and dry in my 'kramaa'.

We both got in and swam across, but I didn't get out on the other side.

"Nyah, what are you doing? Get out of the river."

I just started laughing. "I'm not *walking* that kilometer to the last house on the Mekong – I'm *riding*. And I'm having a very nice time in here, too. I might even be clean by the time I get out." The tributaries of the Mekong were the first clean water we'd been in in three and a half years.

He slid back into the water and swam downstream to catch up to me.

"There are no mines in the middle of a river," I said. "No UXOs either. And no one will see us down here. Even if they do, they'll just think we're dead. A couple more bodies in the water."

"Yeah. This is a *lot* safer than walking the same distance."

"And we'll get a little rest, like we did when we sat in the tree to get away from the dogs." We let our bodies go limp, and were soon carried into the main current.

But my friend was barely floating, because all that was left of him was bones. It looked like the only thing holding him up was a bubble in his shirt. But he didn't seem to notice, so I didn't say anything. The artillery fire had finally stopped, and we were able to relax.

"Ah, it's *cool!*" he said. "It feels so good on my feet. And the water just swirls around you – around and around and around. I've never been in a river where it was safe to float downstream. I've only been in the Mekong. You didn't have a river like this in Prai Anchaan, did you?"

"No, but our house faced a little tributary that fed irrigation canals upstream from us; the Mekong was on the side of our house. There were big trees in front of our balcony, and we could climb up and jump into the water as soon as we got home from school. But in flood season we used to paddle to a temple and jump off the wall into the water. The temple was so small that the Bodhi tree was bigger than the building! And only one monk lived there. I think he was very lonely in dry season, but in monsoon season he was always surrounded by children. He never shooed us away."

The river had widened and the current had slackened; high water had been two months ago. We weren't going anywhere fast.

"Oh!" said Puamaak. "Now I can tell you the story I overheard the day before we escaped. Craziest thing you ever heard." I handed him the banana stalk with my 'kwaiw' in it – it sounded like it was going to be a good story, and I didn't want him to sink before I'd heard the end of it.

"Well apparently," he started, "some of the officers in Phnom Penh got hold of cars and figured out how to drive. Which just confirmed their conviction that *education* isn't necessary. So one of them concluded that if he could figure out how to drive a car, he could figure out how to fly a helicopter. He got hold of a leftover from the Lon Nol regime, got in the thing, started it up, and got it up in the air. He was so proud of himself, he started flying it around. Oh, yeah – he was having himself a good old time, showing off high above all the other officers. But when he went to bring it back down again, he couldn't figure out how to do it. Ran out of gas, and crashed. Now he's dead. End of story."

"Ha! He probably didn't even check the gas gage before he went up."

"Nyah, he wouldn't have known *which* gage was the gas gage, if he couldn't read. He may not even have known the thing *ran* on gas."

"Ha! I never would have thought of *that*. You know, if you hadn't gone night blind, you could have gotten us a lot more stories. But if you were doing all your eavesdropping in the daytime, how is it you never got caught?"

"Because I'm *good* at it, Nyah. I got the cadres and the officers used to seeing me around. And I made sure that I always looked 'insignificant' – no education, no brains, no mind of my own. They became careless, talking among themselves."

"Did you ever find out where the food we grew in the camps went to? The potatoes, and the squash, the corn and everything else. All they gave *us* for vegetables was the water-lily stems we could scrounge in the wild. And the *rice...* I mean, I know the cadres got some of the food, but where did the rest of it go?"

"I heard the commandant talking once about it being sent to China, as payment for munitions. Yeah, all the protein we ever got was a little bit of dried, salted fish. Guess the Chinese didn't want that. Hey... most of us lost our night vision our first year in the camps. But *you* didn't. Why? Was it something your grandfather told you? Is there a medicine for night blindness?"

"Yeah," I said. "What we were just talking about. *Food.* My grandfather told me that sweet potatoes are just about the most nutritious food on the planet, so that's the first thing I started to steal. But in order to steal them, you have to understand how the plant grows. Which of course my grandfather had taught me. Sweet potatoes grow about six to a plant – they're its root system. If you steal more than one from a single plant the leaves will die, and the guards will start watching the potato patch for the thief. But if you steal just one the plant will recover, the leaves won't die, and the guards won't suspect a thing. The best thing about sweet potatoes is that you can eat as many as you can steal raw. And you can stash what you can't eat, so you have something for the next day – I used to make a cache by digging a hole in the ground. Lots of vitamins in sweet potatoes – so you never go night blind. And when everyone *around* you is night blind, but *you're* not, you're the one who's going to survive. But think about it – I didn't lose my night vision because I could steal food at night, and I could steal food at night because I didn't lose my night vision. Full circle. And here I am, still alive."

But there was a twist to this story. When I couldn't get sweet potatoes, I stole cassava. It's high in vitamin C, so I never got scurvy. But like so many things in life, the good and the bad come all mixed up together. Raw cassava contains cyanide. I didn't know that. When I had nothing else to eat, I ate it – and I ate it for *four years*. So it helped to keep me alive, but it could have killed me instead.

We heard a noise on the bank and instantly spread our legs apart, trying to look even deader than we had before. But it was just the creak of bamboo.

"Nyah, think of how many kilometers we walked south yesterday. But we never did hit the border. We weren't 'Border Patrol'. We were *never* 'Border

Patrol'. Because we were never anywhere near the border."

I told him about finding the little infantryman's shoe in the middle of the highway. "So they were going to send me into combat with you – I'm sure of it."

"Yeah, I figured that out yesterday, when you told me they'd switched you from carrying food to carrying ammo. I was going to tell you once we were out of the war zone."

"But did you figure out why our squad leader didn't tell me?" I asked.

"No – that was the strange thing. He told *me* – why wouldn't he tell you?"

"Because nobody told *him* – because they were going to send *him* into combat, too! They were going to send *everyone* in!"

"Oh my god. I think you're right, little brother. Our commanding officer knew he'd need all his men fighting, because he knew we were near the Crossing. I still can't believe we got away, Nyah. I still can't believe it... But I'll tell you, they decided to put us into combat months ago – it was just a matter of when. That's why they stopped cutting our hair. They figured we wouldn't last long enough to make it worth their while."

The river was warm, but I suddenly felt cold to the bone. "Yeah, I thought it was odd that they cut my hair for three years, and then they didn't anymore... When did you figure it out?"

"Yesterday," he said. "When I realized that my hair is just as long as yours."

We drifted for awhile, each of us quiet.

"Puamaak?"

"Yeah?"

"All those movies we saw, in Phnom Penh."

"Yeah?"

"No one's own army was his worst enemy."

"No."

"I don't think any of those movies were real stories," I said, "but they were about things that really happened. The cowboys fought the Red Indians. The sheriffs fought the outlaws. The Americans and their allies fought the Nazis. But everyone had only one enemy."

"Yeah..."

"We have *five*. Our own army, the Vietnamese army, anyone mistaking us for either of *them*, the cadres in the villages, and anyone wanting to turn us in for rice. We have *five.*"

"I know, little brother. But once we're out of the war zone, it will be better. I think we can cross the Mekong tonight, don't you? It's two nights after the quarter moon, and the light will reflect off the water."

"Whether we can cross tonight depends upon how wide the river is. And how much wind there is. And how rough the chop is. Depends on a lot of things. This is the *Mekong,* my friend – not the Seine."

He nodded. "I remember coming across in one of those little boats. I was just as scared as you were. But now I'd give *anything* for one of those little boats. Our army will have taken all of them, though, to get their infantry back across."

We continued to drift with the current, and suddenly, "Nyah! Out of the water! Village ahead – *get out!*"

There was no cover on either bank, so we climbed out of the water on the west side of the river and started walking – slowly – toward the Mekong. But no one gave chase, and no one fired on us. The area was just like the rest of the territory we'd come through – as lifeless as the moon.

"Look at how the landscape has changed," said Puamaak. "More bomb craters, fewer trees. The closer we get to the river, the fewer places there are to hide. This is even worse than where we started out this morning. I think we're going to *have* to cross the river tonight."

The sun set at six, and we hit the Mekong an hour later. There were no lights in any of the houses, and nothing had been burned. The ferry 'road' turned out to be a wide space between the houses on the bank and an irrigation ditch behind them, and we were across it before we realized what it was. We walked under a stilt house, and found ourselves on the top of the bank of the river.

We walked toward the water, mesmerized – like kids do who've never seen the ocean before. There were no clouds to block the moon, and the light transformed the muddy brown river into a sparkling silver sea. It was quiet, the air was clean with the smell of water, and a breeze from upriver swirled softly around us. Such peace, in the middle of a war zone.

But it was not the beauty of the river that transfixed us; no, it was something else. We just couldn't see what we were looking for. We could make out the snags on the bank, the bamboo that hugged the waterline, and a cluster of low palms that had fallen over into the water. We continued to strain our eyes, as though we should be able to see twice as far with two pairs as with one. But we still couldn't see what we were looking for.

We couldn't see the other bank of the river.

Day Two - *Between Hell and High Water*

"Nyah... what do we do now? We can't cross the river here. We can't even see the other side."

I didn't say anything. This was not what I'd thought we'd find.

"Where did we cross when the army brought us over?" he asked. "We could see the other side *there*. It must have been near the ferry crossing." He threw his arms in the air. "But we can't go upriver – we'd run into the Vietnamese. And going downriver is equally pointless; all these big rivers just keep widening out as they flow down to the sea. So we can't cross. But we can't stay *here*. We have no cover. And we're in full moonlight. There's just nowhere to go, and nowhere to hide, and no way to get out of the war zone."

I still didn't say anything.

"*Oh* no Nyah – I'm not backtracking. That's even worse than staying here. And you know what we have left to eat? Raw cassava, which we can't eat until tomorrow, raw peanuts, which we can't eat until I don't *know* when..." he fished around in his pack, "... and one pod of tamarind." He looked up. "Nyah, what are you doing?"

"I'm going to get a drink. And go for a swim. I haven't had a swim in the Mekong in five years."

He followed me as I walked down to the water, still whispering frantically – he sounded like air escaping from a tire. "Nyah – we're *trapped*. Between the war zone and the river. And we have nothing left we can eat."

"Older brother, think about what our biggest problem was today. No water. Without water, you can't do anything. You can't walk, you can't run, you can't swim, and you can't look for food. Here, we have all the water we need. Just watch the current when you go in."

"Oh, so I'm *invited* to your pool party."

"*Pool party?*" I turned around and looked at my comrade, wondering what had happened to the cool, level-headed infantryman that had gotten us through the minefield the night before. "What's the matter?"

"*What's the matter?* What do you mean, 'what's the matter'? This is like standing in the middle of Highway One, just waiting for the bullet that's going to take you out. But last night, *I knew what to do.* I knew how to get us through the minefield, and once we were through, I knew where to go to get away. From both armies."

So *that* was the problem – he was completely out of his element here. Yes, we were in a lot of trouble; we had to get across the river. But we hadn't even started to talk about it yet. I wondered how he could panic so quickly.

And then I remembered throwing up in the middle of the highway last night. From the suffocating ash, from what the shoe had told me, from the fear of being left alone, and from the realization that I had no control over *anything*. Not the mines, or the moonlight, or the gasoline, or the Vietnamese – or anyone else who might have been out there.

"Nyah, did you hear me? *We have nowhere to go.* The currents out there in that river? They could drown a fish."

"Just give me a few minutes to think. Go get a drink, and go for a swim. By the time you're done, I'll have figured something out."

I continued to walk down to the river, staring straight ahead of me at the unbroken expanse of water. I walked toward the shoreline as I'd done every day as a child. And suddenly, an old memory began to seep into my brain. I walked a few steps further, and stopped.

I turned back to my friend. "We do have a place to go. You'd be able to see it yourself, if we weren't standing here in the middle of the night."

"OK, I know I'm night blind. Are you telling me *you* can see the other bank of the river?"

"No," I said, "I'm telling you that I don't have to see our escape route to know it's there."

"Would you just tell me what we're going to do?"

"There are islands in the Mekong, Puamaak. Every few kilometers. Like Koh Dach, just north of Phnom Penh – you would have passed it going up Highway Six every time you went with your mother to buy silk. And the islands are always just south of where the river widens out."

"How do you know *that?*"

"Think of how the islands were formed," I said. "The river split, then rejoined itself – leaving an island in the middle. Or the currents pushed sand ahead of them and created a sandbar, which eventually became an island. Then, over the years, the current ate the north end of the island away, leaving a wide spot in the river. It's just the pattern of the Mekong, and it repeats over and over again. We'll start across, the current will carry us south, and I'll see an island pretty soon. Then we can get in to shore, make camp, and, if there's no one on the island to bother us – which there probably won't be – we can rest for a day or two before crossing the other half of the river."

"And just how are we going to *get* to this island?" he asked. "Hanging onto a *log?* Oh no – I'm not leaving the shoreline unless I can see land in front of me. *Especially* in the middle of the night."

"We'll find a boat. Once the boat's ready, we can push off into the river." I looked out over the water again. "It's actually pretty calm out there."

He just stared at me, as though trying to determine the degree of my delirium. "You're going to find a *boat?* Nyah, you've never been here in your life – how would you even know where to look for one? Even if you did, our army will have taken every boat they found."

"Ah – every boat they *found*. That's the key. Most people don't know how to find them. But *I* do – because I know how the fishermen hide them. And the fishermen here can't be that different than the fishermen in Prai Anchaan. It's only eighty kilometers upriver, remember?"

"Well, tell me how you're going to find a boat then. I can't think of a better way to pass the time."

"You look for a stick in the shallows," I said, "stuck into the mud. Once you find one, you feel around under water to see if there's a rope tied to it. If there is, you feel along the rope to see if it's attached to the bow of a boat. If it is, you feel around for a big rock – that's what's holding the boat under water. You get in the boat, lift the rock, and push it out over the gunwale."

"What's a 'gunwale'?" he asked.

"The side edge of a boat."

"Oh. OK. Now I know what a gunwale is, and you know what asphalt is. Keep talking – what do you do next?"

"You start bailing the silt and the water out," I said. "If we don't get all of it out, that's OK; I mean, we're not trying to win a race. We just need to get the boat to float well enough to get us across the river."

"So every fisherman hides his boat the same way?"

"Pretty much," I said. "Because the method works so well."

"So you're like the guy who found Tutankhamen's tomb. He didn't know where it was, but he knew where to search for it. He knew it had to be in the Valley of the Kings. And although he'd never seen it before he knew what it would look like, and what would be in there. He knew there would be a staircase leading down to a sealed door, then a narrow passageway, then a burial chamber with paintings on the wall and gold treasure inside. Because the Egyptians buried all their kings the same way."

"Exactly," I said.

"But another fisherman would know exactly how to find the first fisherman's boat."

"But a fisherman would never *steal* another fisherman's boat. It's the Law of the Mekong. Except in wartime. That's why we're going to 'borrow' one. When the war is over I'll return it, and take the ferry back across."

He shook his head. "The villagers who evacuated would have taken all the boats – they wouldn't swim if they had a boat. And if they had extra boats, they certainly wouldn't have had the time to bury them. And then the army would have gotten them. You're delirious, Nyah. Those mosquitoes I watched buzzing around your ears this morning – now you have malaria, or dengue. Or mad cow disease. Or *something*."

"We're not completely out of food, you know." I reached into my pocket, pulled out a water chestnut and handed it to him. I figured if he had something in his mouth, maybe he'd stop *talking*.

He peeled the chestnut and popped it into his mouth – and then started talking anyway.

"*I* know what's the matter with you. Seeing the Mekong again. It reminds you of home, doesn't it. Well I'm sorry, but this is no time to be getting homesick – we've *got* to get across the river."

"Puamaak, there's *nothing* the *matter* with me. OK, look at all the houses on the shoreline, and calculate it out. They were all fishermen, which meant that they all had a boat. And some of them had two. Each family that had a spare would have taken only one boat because they'd want to be sure they'd have one when they came *back* – I mean, how else would they be able to catch their food? And as for having the time to bury the spare, *three minutes*. All you have to do is rock it enough to get one gunwale under water. The hull will fill, the boat will sink, and the Mekong will do the rest. Believe me, she'll drop enough silt in the boat to bury it; you don't even need a rock, if you don't have time to look for one. And remember – some of these people would have been drafted. Just like we were. And some would have been relocated. Just like we were. Or sent off to work camps. Just like we were. So what do you suppose they did just before they left? *They buried their boats.* So there should be plenty of boats down there – even *you* could find one."

"Well supposing I do," he said. "How do we know the fisherman didn't just *junk* it because it wasn't seaworthy anymore? We could sink out there, Nyah."

"Once you find a boat, you can figure out if it's seaworthy. If it holds water, it is; if it doesn't, it isn't. If it isn't, we go find another boat. It's just *not that difficult.*"

"Really? Do you really think we can get across?"

"Hell," I said, "I'd rather face the Mekong than a minefield any day – even *without* a boat. Not much that can go wrong between us and an island when it's calm like this. OK, I told you how to find a boat, so go find one. Just look for a stake. You're more likely to find one south of here than back toward the Mekong Crossing, so once I've finished I'll walk south along the bank to look for you."

"'Finished?'" he asked. "Finished what?"

"Getting us more food."

"Food? Where? Where are we going to get food? I'm not going in any of those houses."

I pointed to a tree not far up the bank. "I took my inventory the minute we hit the beach. Look at the silhouette of that palm."

"It's a… sugar palm," he said.

"Yeah. And because we're in a village, there should be a good solid ladder already tied to it. I wouldn't risk climbing a palm here in the daytime, but I'd risk climbing one at night."

"And why do you think," he asked, "that someone else hasn't gotten to the fruit ahead of you? Especially if there's a ladder tied to the tree?"

Boy, he just wouldn't quit. I pulled out the rest of the chestnuts and handed them to him. "Because only an experienced climber can get all the way up to the crown, where the fruit is – even with a ladder. The tree starts to sway when you're halfway up. Hey, if they put a gun in *your* hand, anyone who could climb that tree was drafted months ago. So the chances that no one's been up there to get our fruit are actually pretty good."

"OK, you climb the tree, I'll go look for a boat. But I'm going to get a drink first." He started for the water.

"Hey! Remember to watch for the current!" I went after him and caught his arm. "Let's get in south of that big snag jutting out into the river – the water will be slower there." He started to pull away from me. "OK Puamaak. Next time I want to go swimming in one of those blue pools with lines on the bottom like you have in Phnom Penh, *you* can show *me* how to do it."

"Ha! There *is* a trick to it. They put a chemical in the water to keep it clean. If you open your eyes under water, the chemical will sting them. So you can't swim under water at all. But the chemical's invisible – so if no one tells you about it, you don't know it's there."

"*Really?* There's not even a sign?"

"Nope."

We got to the shoreline, walked around the pile of logs to the downriver side, and I started to wade in.

And this time, he caught *my* arm, "Nyah, this is not the Mekong you knew as a kid. There are bodies in all of these rivers. Remember – we're just south of the Crossing. Who knows what went on up there. Be sure you look carefully before you fill your cup – that way you won't be filling it next to a body that got snagged. Be careful, little brother."

We scanned the shoreline and the snag, waded out and took a good long drink. Then we just stood there, letting the cool water swirl around our tired legs as we watched the moonlight dance on the tips of the waves. "I don't know much about the Mekong," said Puamaak, "but I've heard of kids in Phnom Penh who drowned just because they ran into the river after their soccer ball. It happens, once in awhile. You hear a couple of stories like that, and you learn to watch for the current."

He handed half the chestnuts back to me, turned around and started out of the water. I whispered after him, "Do you think you can see well enough to look for a boat?"

"Apparently all I have to see is a stake sticking out of the water. A straight line shouldn't be that hard to spot. The rest is just feeling around in the muck. I've been night blind so long that I'm used to feeling around for things I can't see. So I'm probably better at that than you are – for a change."

He took off down the shoreline and I headed for the palm. The bamboo ladder was still intact, and I found fruit up in the crown of the tree. I figured I'd end up with some nasty scratches, trying to climb that tree at night. But I couldn't resist the chance to get us some sugar palm. It's sweet, and it's soft – it melts in your mouth. And it always reminded me of home.

I climbed down, split open the pods, picked out the fruit and ate my half.

Then I started to think about where to look for a couple of paddles – the boat would be useless without them. But Puamaak hadn't figured that out yet.

Well, if I'd been a fisherman and had been ordered to evacuate, I would have stowed all my paddles inside my house. But I wasn't about to go into any of those houses – much safer to stay out here and make my own paddles. I found a large bamboo and cut it down, cut a meter and a half from the bottom of it, then split the piece in half lengthwise. Two minutes – two paddles.

I was glad we hadn't had electricity in our village; I wouldn't have learned all the things I'd learned from my grandfather if I'd been watching TV. My comrade and I wouldn't have made it to the Mekong, that's for sure. We wouldn't even have made it out of the mountains. I wondered how many generations his family had lived in the city – how many generations it takes to lose your knowledge of the natural world. As I've said, our families hadn't been allowed to get to know each other in Pong Tuk. I wondered if his mother had survived.

I caught up to my friend and gave him his half of the fruit. Then we split our last pod of tamarind.

"What are we going to do about paddles?" he asked.

"You remembered. I was wondering how long it would take. I made us a couple."

"You *made* us a couple? That's just about as fantastic as me finding a boat."

"Where is it?"

"Over here."

"Buried just like I said it would be?"

"Exactly."

"Did you see any fish traps?" I asked. "We could get whatever's in them, and cook it once we get to the island."

"Nope."

"Yeah, they're probably in the houses. With the *real* paddles. *Damn.*"

We stepped into the boat. "Man, this thing's been down here awhile," I said. "Loosen the silt with your fingers and scoop it out with your cup."

We worked on the boat for half an hour and finally got the gunwales to surface. "Keep loosening the silt," I said, "and stir the water up, so we'll be bailing the last of the silt and the water at the same time. I'll be back."

I scouted around until I found a low-growing palm with fronds that were wide at the base. I cut off a couple, sliced off the bottom meter and shaved off the thorns – I'd made us a couple of big scoops. I brought them back to the boat.

"Hold the frond by the narrow end," I said, "and flip the water and the silt over the gunwale with the wide end. We should have this thing out of the mud pretty quick."

Within half an hour we had the boat afloat. "Rock it," I said. "Rock it side to side. If we can get the last of the water in the hull moving back and forth, it will begin to slosh over the gunwale."

He smiled. "Inertia."

We rocked the boat until we got enough water out for it to be seaworthy; there were about fifteen centimeters left in the bottom. But that was as it should be – Khmer fishing boats are made with a long, shallow open compartment that runs the length of the keel. The water serves as ballast, and the fisherman drops his catch into it to keep everything alive.

We put our gear in the boat and began to turn the bow toward the open water. "Did your feet blister today?" I asked him. "I can drain the blisters with a sugar palm thorn and wrap them with tamarind paste. I should do that now, before we take off. We can't afford an infection in your feet, especially when you have to walk on them."

"No, I'm OK. You?"

"Are you kidding?' I said. "The bottoms of my feet were like shoe leather before we were even marched out of Phnom Penh. The only time I ever wore shoes was to go to school, and to the temple. I don't like shoes."

"Then why did you give me that look, when I said we had to ditch ours?"

"I wanted to keep them to *trade*. Remember how I got my rat trap?"

"Oh," he laughed. "Yeah. But why didn't our feet get swollen, for all the hours we walked yesterday and today?"

"It was the tamarind we ate. Tamarind's good for a lot of things; you can even preserve food with it. And it kept us from starving this morning. If we'd had nothing but the raw cassava, I don't think we would have made it to the buffalo wallow – not after yesterday. Yeah, we wouldn't be sitting here on the bank of the river now."

"We wouldn't have *found* the river, Nyah – almost all of your recon trees have been tamarinds. And we wouldn't have escaped from the pack of dogs, either."

"And you can only sleep where you can hide. Once we're across the Mekong, it will be a tamarind that we sleep in each night."

"Oh, don't talk to me about sleep..." He closed his eyes for a moment. "There should be lots of trees on the island. We can just tie our hammocks up and..."

And that's when we heard them. They were so loud I think I actually heard them first.

"Quick!" I said. "The big snag on the bank above us. We'll pull the boat to the downriver side of it, tip it over and crawl underneath. Anyone coming in from the Mekong Crossing will just look right over the logs and never see us."

I think he finally knew me well enough not to ask me any questions. We turned the bow back around and started to pull the boat out of the water, but it was just too heavy. "Stay here!" I said. I ran back to where I'd made the paddles, found the bamboo I'd cut down earlier, and cut another piece. I ran back to the boat and slid the bamboo underneath the bow. "Let's push the stern to get the bow up onto the roller. Then we can push the hull up onto the bank and flip it to get the rest of the water out. Come on – we'll have to get back into the water to push."

We got the bow up onto the roller and got the boat onto the bank. "OK ," I said, "on three we flip it. One... two... *three*."

It would have helped if we'd been taller – we had an awful time. We finally got the boat flipped, and I rescued the roller before it slid into the river.

"Now let's flip the boat back over, " I said, "get the roller back under the bow, and push the boat up the bank and up against the snag. Hurry – once you hear the first one, you never know how much time you have!"

"Who did you hear, Nyah? I didn't hear anyone."

"What do you mean? How can you *not* hear them? They're all around us!"

"All I hear are frogs."

"And you don't know what that means???"

"No."

"Just help me get the roller back under the bow!" I whispered frantically.

"Are they poisonous frogs?"

"No, they're not poisonous frogs. *Just help me with the boat!"*

Suddenly, we felt a gentle breeze stir the evening air around us – like someone had turned on a ceiling fan. We looked up at the moon, a gleaming white opal in the clear sapphire sky. And then the breeze started to pick up, as though someone had turned the fan up a notch. Just as my friend began to relax, it hit us – a *wall* of rain. The temperature dropped about ten degrees, and rainclouds smothered the moon. The whole thing happened in less than thirty seconds. *That's* a Cambodian rainstorm.

"That's what the frogs meant!" I yelled to him over the hammering of the rain. "We're not going anywhere tonight. You never get into the Mekong in a storm. The river turns into a monster – she'll swallow you alive."

The rain stung our backs and our necks, but it got our adrenalin going. We got the bow back onto the roller and started trying to push the boat up the bank to the snag.

This was even harder than getting the silt out of the boat. The bank was uneven, the boat was heavy and awkward, and the snag was six meters above us.

"Just keep pushing!" I yelled. "If we can't get the boat well above the waterline, we'll be stuck out here all night!" I knew that if the storm was of any duration the river would rise quickly; the rice had been harvested after the last big rainstorm and the winter crops had never been put in, so the runoff tonight would be the worst in twelve months. And the deforestation from all the years of carpet bombing would make it even worse. If we couldn't get the boat far enough up the bank, we could be awakened by rising water in the middle of the night – only to realize that we were going to drown underneath the overturned boat.

We pushed another ten minutes and finally got the boat up to the snag. We turned it parallel to the river, flipped it, pushed the uphill gunwale tight into the bank, and crawled in under the downhill side.

"Now I believe you, Nyah. You can hide anywhere."

"Hand me your hammock and your 'kramaa'." I pushed his hammock into the crack between the bow and the uphill side of the bank, and I pushed our 'kramaas' into the crack at the stern. Then I spread my hammock out underneath us. "We need to stay in the middle of the uphill side – that's where it will be the driest. It's about fifteen degrees, we're soaking wet, and we're going to be here all night. Get whatever sleep you can, because tomorrow we're pushing off at first light. No one will be out in this rain tonight, but I want to be on the river before anyone can see us tomorrow."

The rain was so loud we could hardly talk, and the frogs were still singing their hearts out. My mind kept going over how we'd ended up underneath a stolen boat in a storm on a flooding riverbank, still in the war zone, with nothing left that we could eat.

"Do you know what day it is?" I asked my friend, over all the noise.

"It's the day they were going to put us into combat."

"We're still in the war zone…"

"… but we're still alive. And that's all that really matters."

Day Three ~ *The Mekong*

We awoke cold and wet from a night spent in the mud. All the boat had really done for us was keep the wind off – it hadn't rained very long, but the runoff had seeped in around the bow and the stern relentlessly throughout the night. I crawled under the gunwale, out of the boat and into the cold morning air.

Puamaak crawled out behind me. "See anyone?"

"No, but let's be out of here before the mist burns off." We'd slept until after sunrise because we hadn't seen its light; we'd been under the boat.

He began to rub his arms. "How's the lighter?"

I took it out of my shirt pocket and checked it. "The wick's wet. Water got up underneath the cap. How wet are the peanuts?"

"Don't even ask. Come on, let's get a drink."

I followed him to the shoreline, but my eyes were turned downriver. There was an island out there, all right. I could barely see it through the mist – but I could see it.

We checked for bodies, waded into the river and ducked under water to scrub off last night's mud. The water turned out to be warmer than the air, and we really didn't want to get out.

"Do you think if we just sat here awhile our lice would drown?" asked Puamaak.

"I already tried it, my friend. Before I even got drafted. No, it doesn't work."

I looked out over the river. He followed my gaze, not sure how much he should worry. "Do you really think it's safe to cross?"

"A lot safer than staying here. It's not raining, there's no chop, and there's not much wind. That's the thing you have to watch out for on the Mekong this time of year – the wind. Actually, if it were September or October, I wouldn't get into the river at all; that's when she's a killer. But she's had a couple of months to calm down now, and we can't make a fire until we get out to the island." I pointed out the spit of land that split the river in two. "If we can't get warm, we're going to be in trouble. Let's just eat and shove off."

And so, that's what we did. We ate a quarter of a tuber of cassava each; we'd eat another quarter in the afternoon. We checked the hull of the boat for holes and splits, found none, flipped it back over and slid it down the muddy riverbank into the water. Then we rinsed the mud out of our gear, threw it in the boat, pushed off and climbed in over the stern.

He moved right up into the bow.

"Move back toward me a little," I said.

"Why? When we get to the island I can jump out and pull the boat in."

"We'll have a lot harder time *getting* to the island if you don't move back. The bow is too low in the water because you weigh more than I do. You should actually be in the stern."

"Switch places then."

"The person in the stern has to *steer*."

"OK. Never mind." He moved back, and the bow came up a little.

"Paddle on the downriver side of the boat," I said, "and I'll switch back and forth from one side to the other to keep us on course. You can move forward just before we hit the island. I'll tell you when."

Now, I'd never known anyone who hadn't learned how to handle a boat before he'd learned to ride a bike – if my classmates in Phnom Penh didn't know how to do it, well, they'd never let on. My friend put his paddle into the water, and the current immediately ripped it out of his hands.

I didn't think twice. I dove over the side and retrieved it, then turned around and swam back to the boat. I hauled myself in over the stern and handed it up to him.

Why didn't I make an extra pair of paddles last night? I asked, talking to the wind. *It would have taken me two minutes. And we're both too cold and hungry to paddle as hard as we need to. I've never seen a stretch of river this wide – I wonder what the currents are like...* I called up to Puamaak. "Do you know what to do if the boat capsi... turns over?"

"Find you, and then we'll swim for the island together."

"No. Swim back to the boat and climb on top of it." *And hope we can get it turned over,* I thought. "Can you see anything on the island yet? Any smoke?"

He shook his head. "But it would just blend in with the mist."

"Can you see how long the island *is?* We can't afford to overshoot it."

He shook his head again.

"Then just paddle like hell."

I kicked myself for not trying to get into one of the houses to steal a decent pair of paddles. And why hadn't I looked just a little harder for a fish trap? If there had been anything in it, we *could* have eaten it raw – it was better than starving. And all those *frogs* – why hadn't I taken five minutes to look for some?

I looked behind me to see how far we'd come, only to see how fast the current was carrying us south.

"This is almost worse than being in the war zone," I called up to Puamaak. "We can't control where we're going, there's no place to hide, and we have no way to get more food."

And as soon as I'd said it, I could feel us change direction. "Stop paddling!"

But I quickly realized that it was nothing Puamaak had done. The boat had been pulled into the main current, and now, instead of heading toward the island, we were shooting straight down the middle of the river.

The boat moved faster and faster, and suddenly, the bow came around. Before Puamaak could ask me what to do, we were spinning in the current.

He dropped his paddle onto the keel, grabbed the gunwales and just held on. And all of a sudden, it was as though I wasn't there. The mist swirled around him as he continued to spin, like the toy boat he'd played with as a child. It was as though the river had made plans for him, but had decided to play with him first. Before she opened her ragged mouth, to swallow him alive.

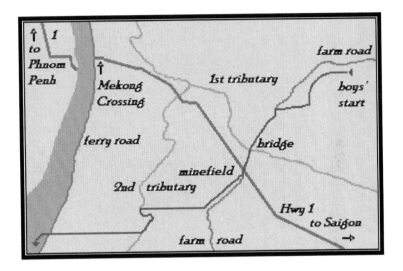

The boys' route from the morning of January 6th
(from the north side of the mountains)

to the morning of January 8th,
(into the Mekong)

22 kilometers (14 miles)

Book Two ~ *The Water Glass*

Day Three ~ *The Turning Point*

There's a festival called Bun Ōm Touk that's been celebrated in Cambodia for a thousand years. It commemorates the victory of our mightiest king, Jayavarman VII, over the Kingdom of Champā. In 1177 the Cham came by land from the east to invade Angkor, the capital of the Khmer Empire during our Golden Age. The following year they came back to finish us off, but this time, they came by water – up the Mekong from the South China Sea, then up the Tonle Sap River, then up the Great Tonle Sap Lake to take Angkor. A pretty slick piece of work, but later that year Jayavarman VII defeated them in an epic naval battle to save the Khmer Empire. Ever since that time we've commemorated his victory with Bun Ōm Touk.

Every schoolboy knows the story, and, although my friend and I hadn't known each other before the war, both our families had always celebrated Bun Ōm Touk in Phnom Penh – on the boardwalk along the Tonle Sap River.

It's undisputedly the most wonderful festival that could possibly exist anywhere in the world – any Cambodian will tell you that. It always falls in November, and the exact date is determined by the phase of the moon. But we must all wait for something to happen first. A phenomenon of nature, oblivious to both peace and war, that happens in only one place on earth – at the south end of the boardwalk, right in front of the Royal Palace. Let me tell you all about it.

Where the snows of Tibet melt into the streams of the Himalayas, the Mekong begins her twisting journey down to the South China Sea. She flows southeast through China, then southwest to snake between Myanmar and Laos, then southeast again to wind between Laos and Thailand. She spills into Cambodia over a great waterfall on our northern border, and reaches Phnom Penh after a journey of forty-thousand kilometers. There she meets the Tonle Sap River, which connects the Great Tonle Sap Lake in the north to the Mekong at Phnom Penh.

At the end of our dry season, the water level in the lake is higher than the level of the Mekong – so the Tonle Sap River flows southeast, carrying water out of the lake and into the Mekong.

With the beginning of the monsoon rains in June, the water level in the Mekong rises quickly. Once it's higher than the lake, the current in the Tonle Sap River *reverses* – to carry water out of the Mekong and into the lake.

With the end of the monsoon rains in November, the water level in the Mekong begins to fall. Once it's lower than the lake, the current in the Tonle Sap River *reverses again* to carry water southeast – out of the lake and into the Mekong – until the monsoon rains begin again.

The Tonle Sap is the only river in the world whose current reverses in this way, and the reversal begins where the Tonle Sap and the Mekong collide – at the south end of the boardwalk. Bun Ōm Touk, in addition to commemorating Jayavarman VII's victory, celebrates this Reversal of the Current. It marks the end of the flood season, and the replenishment of the land with topsoil from upriver.

And so, because of a freak of nature caused by something as simple as the pull of gravity on water, we get a week off from school, our moms make us all our favorite foods, and we get to go to the boardwalk in Phnom Penh.

But wait – I haven't told you *why* we go to the boardwalk. My family sure didn't go all the way into the city to watch the water in the river slosh back and forth. Here's a clue – "Bun Ōm Touk" means, "The Holiday of the Rowing of the Boats". People row boats. *Lots* of boats. For *three days.*

What, that doesn't sound exciting? Well, let me try to explain this again. *Ten thousand rowers* race *a hundred and fifty dragon boats* through the stretch of river where the Tonle Sap and the Mekong collide – straight through to the Royal Palace! There are sixty men to a boat, I tell you, and each boat is sponsored by a *very* prestigious temple. The starting line is under the bridge that spans the Tonle Sap just north of the Mekong, and the finish line is at the south end of the boardwalk – so everyone can see the winners. Elimination heats are run the first two days, and the cries of the coxswains urging their rowers on can be heard from one riverbank to the other. On the third day the finalists race the three kilometer course, to finish in front of the king himself! And now you see why we have to wait for the Reversal of the Current. If we didn't, the finish line would be under the bridge, the king wouldn't get to see a thing, and we wouldn't get to see the king!

OK, does *that* sound a little more exciting? But that's just what's happening on the water!

Yes, the boardwalk is the place to be. Fortune tellers vie with one another to look the most exotic, and therefore the most clairvoyant. Boys squeeze enough room in the crowd for a circle of their friends to kick a shuttlecock back and forth. Sometimes you'll see a pretty girl who's slipped away from her family to meet a special boy, if only for a few stolen moments. Clusters of Buddhist monks stand on the low stone wall that overlooks the river, cheering on the boat sponsored by their temple – peaceful, restrained cheering, as their saffron robes drift in the breeze that comes up from the water. Vendors sell balloons, small toys for the city folk who can afford them, and *firecrackers.*

Oh, but I haven't told you about the *food.* Hawkers wheel their carts up and down selling everything imaginable, from roasted squid with pickled green papaya to peppered steak on bamboo skewers to local escargot. Across the street are the restaurants – Indian, Chinese, Vietnamese, French – and Khmer, of course. At the north end of the row there's my mother's favorite café, where she and her cousins share little French pastries while their husbands watch the heats. You can see Wat Phnom from there, serenely watching over the city from the top of the hill she stands on. And Saambō the Elephant, carrying families around the base of the hill, two people at a time.

Our moms give us enough change to meet up with our friends, get our firecrackers, ride Saambō, and scout out the street vendors for the best hot snacks for watching the heats. As long as we show up to meet her at the prearranged place and time, we're free to do whatever we want. This is the first taste of freedom in the life of every Cambodian boy.

If Puamaak and I had known each other then we would have hung out at the dragon boat races together every year. But now, we were sitting in a ditch, peering out over the edge at a house. Trying to figure out if it was empty. And we were *still* in the war zone – we weren't on the west bank of the Mekong, we were on an island in the middle of it. But not the island we'd been shooting for. The next one, a couple of kilometers to the south.

"I'm starving, Nyah. And we've *got* to get warm… Remember the first tree you climbed? The *very* first one – the morning after we escaped. What did you say was the only sign of life you saw? Plow animals wandering around. Instead of watching this house, climb a tree and look out over the island. If the plow animals are loose, you'll know it's been evacuated. And climb a tamarind, so you can get us something to eat."

We made our way over to a stand of trees, but we flushed a couple of birds. They took off into the air, squawking noisily.

I sighed. "That was an alarm call. Most kinds of birds have one. And a farmer would recognize that call for what it was; he'd know *something's* out here. Back to the boat – quickly."

We retraced our steps to the shoreline and put our gear in the boat. Puamaak started to get into the bow.

"I don't want to get caught in the main current again," I said. "We're so near the north end of the island that we can walk the boat up the shoreline and around the tip, then paddle across the *other* half of the river. If we get caught in a current there it will take us one of three ways – over to the west bank, which is what we want, or back to the island, where we'd just have to start over again, or straight downriver – in which case we just paddle like hell."

"What are we going to do about the fishing village that will be across the river?" he asked.

"Let's figure that out when we get around the point of the island, and can get a look at it."

We took turns pulling the boat behind us up the shoreline. And we talked about food all the way. *Hot* food. We were going to find a stand of trees and cook ourselves something – *anything* – even if it was only a tadpole.

We got around the point and surveyed the village on the opposite bank. Unlike the one we'd left this morning, this one stretched north and south for as far as we could see. So we couldn't go around it.

I climbed a tree, climbed down again and handed my friend some tamarind. "The plow animals here are tied," I said, "but I don't want to walk through that village in the middle of the day. It's not in the war zone, so *it* hasn't been evacuated, either."

"Nyah, what are our choices? Think about it, and tell me."

"Stay here and get caught, or go over there and get caught."

He shook his head. "Stay here and get caught in the war zone, or go over there and get out of the war zone.”

"And get caught by the cadres," I said.

He shook his head again. "Look at that village, Nyah. It's *huge.* Anyone who sees us will just figure we're from some other part of it."

"Puamaak. You're half Chinese. They'll figure you're not from *any* part of it. How many Chinese families do you think there are out here in these fishing villages?"

"So we'll keep our heads down," he said. "If anyone challenges us, well, you know me – I can lie my way out of anything. 'We got separated from our families when our village in Prey Veng was evacuated, and we're trying to catch up to them. Perhaps you've seen them? Did any Prey Veng families come through here?'" We'd pose as kids whose families had supported the Khmer Rouge in the Lon Nol years.

"But they'll know we're 'new people'," I said. "We're just too thin. We look like we just walked out of a death camp. And you may be short, but your voice has changed – they'll know you're old enough to be in the army. And that I am, too, because I'm with you. They'll figure out we're deserters the minute you open your mouth."

"So I'll keep mine shut and you open yours," he said.

"I'm no *good* at lying, Puamaak. Not like you are. Let's sneak through the village at night, so no one can get a look at us. If no one sees us, no one will question us."

"But I can't *see* at night. We'd get caught, and I'd have to lie. But I can't *lie* at night any better than I can *see.*"

"*What?*"

"Nyah – think about it. People are trusting when the sun's shining, and they can see everything around them. But at night, when it's dark, they're afraid. Far less trusting. It's human nature – think about it."

"So what the hell are we going to do?"

"Walk right through the village in the middle of the day with our heads down," he said. "If anyone challenges us I'll use the 'we got separated from our unit' story. And you're an *infantryman.* Just like me."

"How's that going to help?"

"Nyah – you're *kidding.* You really don't *know?* OK. It's not the army we have to worry about here, or the villagers. It's the *cadres.* The village guards.*"

"I know that. That's why I'm afraid."

"But an infantryman *outranks* a village guard," he said. "A porter doesn't."

"Really? Oh. So… how do we convince them we're infantrymen? Without our uniforms or your gun?"

"We don't have to convince them," he said, "unless they give us trouble. Then we order them to clean their guns – and tell them exactly how to take an AK-47 apart to do it. Yeah, that'll shut them up. They'll leave us alone after that."

"We really outrank them?" I asked.

"By a longshot."

"Even though we're only fourteen and twelve…"

"Yup."

"And only four and a half feet tall…"

"Yup."

"And they've had more food than we've had for the past four years, so they still *weigh* something…"

"Yup."

"And *they* have the AK-47s…"

"They'll be out of bullets by now," he said.

"Who said anything about bullets? They have bayonets. We don't outrank a bayonet."

"Nyah, trust me. I can bluff well enough to get us through… They *did* teach you how to clean an AK-47, didn't they?"

"Yeah."

"Then we're fine."

"OK," I said. "We'll walk through the village and vanish into the first stand of trees we come to. But let's watch the shoreline for an hour or so; I'd at least like to know what we're up against."

And so, from the cover of the trees, we watched the village for signs of movement. Nothing.

"Nyah, there's no one over there. I don't know what's going on, but it looks like that village has been evacuated too."

"Dogs? Brahmas? Water buffalo bulls?"

"Nothing," he said. "It's just like the east bank of the river. As lifeless as the moon."

"Well if the plow animals are tied over here, why isn't there anyone over there?"

"Maybe the people here never got the evacuation order," he said. "No one in the village would have paddled across the river to warn them. They would have just taken off to save themselves and their own families. And then the village would have been mined."

"No, there should still be cadres around because this village isn't in the war zone… What if we try to avoid the villages entirely? We could go further down the river until we find a break between villages, and try to get through there."

"The chances," he said, "of us finding a break between villages is not as good on this side of the river, Nyah. This is the *Phnom Penh* side. The fish caught here used to end up in the markets our mothers shopped in. Remember the blue lobsters?" He pointed down into the water. "Right here. And the further we are from the military action around Highway One, the less likely it will be that the villages have been evacuated. In the one across from us, we'd be facing cadres. In the ones down the river, we'd be facing cadres and their 'old people' accomplices. And we couldn't pass ourselves off as infantryman – we'd be too far from Highway One."

I looked at the village, exhaled very slowly, and tossed my gear in the boat. "OK," I said. "Two infantrymen separated from their unit. Let's go." We got into the boat and shoved off.

My friend moved into the bow and pulled the rope back into the boat, then moved back toward the stern a little. He put his paddle in the water and started paddling left. Everything, exactly right. Oh, he wasn't stupid – I'll tell you that, my friend. It's just that, in the city, he'd never had anyone to teach him things. And I wasn't trying to make a village boy of him – I was just trying to keep him alive.

The current ran straight down the middle of the river, as I'd expected it to. But we had no real trouble with it. We got to the opposite shore, pulled the boat up, walked through the village confidently, and then started out over the levees.

But there were no stands of trees for us to duck into. And the village we'd just walked through *was* empty – not as much as a chicken running around.

"I don't believe this," said Puamaak. "We're still in the war zone we've been trying to get out of. If there were cadres here they would have challenged us already. I mean, a Chinese kid pulling up in a boat?"

"So this village has been mined," I said.

"Yeah. Including the perimeter, right ahead of us." He looked at me as though he wanted to ask me what to do, but knew that I'd have no answer.

"Turn around," I said. "What we need most is food, and the fastest way to get it is to go back to the river. Pull up a fish trap, get anything still alive out of it, and put it in our packs so we have something to cook when we can finally make a fire. I saw at least one trap; I took my inventory as we pulled into shore. We can walk back in our own footprints so we don't hit any mines."

We turned around and walked right back through the village.

There were a couple of good-sized fish in the trap, still alive. I looked up at my friend and smiled. "They could hunt out the plains and the mountains, but they couldn't fish out the Mekong." I took the fish out of the trap and handed them to Puamaak to kill and clean. "I left the back of the trap open," I said, "so that no more fish will get caught. When the fisherman comes back, he can close it up again… You *can* clean fish, can't you?"

"Nyah. I'm half Khmer. What do you think." He pulled out his machete and proceeded to clean the fish. I watched him for a moment, and saw that he was actually doing a pretty good job of it.

"You know," he said, "one of my teachers told me that the word, 'Mekong' is feminine because the river gives life. I didn't think much about it at the time, but now I get it."

I started laughing. "Oh, *now* you *like* the river – when she tosses you a bit of fish. Wish you could have seen yourself this morning, hanging onto the gunwales for dear life. Were you screaming, too? I couldn't hear you, from the stern."

"Very funny."

"And was she a pretty teacher?" I asked. "Oh, no, I'm sure you paid just as much attention in *all* your classes as you did in hers. What else do you remember?"

"She said our society used to be a 'matriarchy' – ruled by women, not by men."

I started laughing even harder. "'*Used* to be'? Who held the money in your family – your mother or your father?"

"My mother."

"And how about in your uncle's house?" I asked. "Your uncle or your aunt?"

"My aunt."

"And when you went to the market to buy fish, who did you hand the money to – the fishmonger or his wife?"

"His wife," he said.

"Mmm hmm. And if our families are still in Pong Tuk, and have a choice whether to stay or go, who will make the decision? Regardless of whether or not any of our male relatives have made it back."

"Our mothers." He smiled. "Yeah, my mother will be waiting for me."

It was midday now. Our clothes were dry and we were warm again, we were finally across the biggest river we'd have to cross, there was no one around, and we were looking forward to the first fresh fish we'd had in four years.

"Hand me your lighter, Nyah – I'll carry it in my hand so the wick dries out. We won't be able to cook until we can light a fire."

"Oh you figured that out did you? Well if the wick doesn't dry out, I'll show you how to start a fire without a lighter." I took it out of my pocket and handed it to him. He took off the cap, blew on the wick, fanned it, waved the lighter back and forth through the air, and finally raised it over his head – as though an arm's length closer to the sun would surely make the wick dry faster.

"I never asked you," he said. "Do you have another striker when this one gives out? Or another wick?"

"I sewed them into the hem of my army shirt. And you know where *that* is."

"That's the way my mother hides her gold," he said. "You can sew a chain into a seam and no one will ever know it's there. When she had to get something to keep us alive, or when she had to bribe someone, she'd cut off a couple of links. That's how she used to get us extra rice – when there was still rice to *get*."

We headed out of the village and passed the point where we'd turned back to raid the fish trap. And suddenly, we saw what we'd been looking for – for *three days*. Fields that had been plowed for replanting. *The end of the war zone.* All there was to mark the boundary was dirt – but dirt that had been turned over. We looked at each other and laughed, then hurried on, due west.

"*Temporary* evacuation," I said. "The people are probably on their way back right now. We'll find a place to hide, cook our fish, and then get out of here."

"Yeah. And the army won't have mined here because they know the people will be returning. And that the Vietnamese wouldn't come this way – they'd stick to Highway One."

"OK," I said, "If you want some good fish, start looking around for lemon grass and ginger."

"Can you make our fish taste like what we used to get on the boardwalk at Bun Ōm Touk? The guy who used to park his cart at the north end, a few blocks before you turn off Sisowath to go over to Wat Phnom to ride Saambō – can you make it taste like *that?*"

"I told you," I said. "Look for lemon grass and ginger. You know, if this war is ever over – if they ever start the dragon boat races again – you should try out for a spot on a boat. Now that you know how to paddle. You just need practice, with a team. Which temple would you row for?"

"Wat Phnom. Of *course.*"

I rolled my eyes. "The most *prestigious* one. Why did I even ask... But you can get your nose out of the air. You'd be competing with *me,* on the boat sponsored by our Prai Anchaan temple."

"You're too small," he said. "They wouldn't take you."

"Oh yeah? I'd be the *first* one they'd take. For the coxswain – they'd need a flyweight. And I wouldn't even have to row!"

He laughed, and slung his arm over my shoulder. "Now you can tell me – *how* did you get us over to the island this morning? I thought we were going to drown. You weren't even scared, when the boat started spinning like that?"

"Oh, if this were September or October, I would have been terrified. But it isn't, and the wind wasn't bad – like I said, it's the wind you have to worry about this time of year. I knew you can't fight the Mekong, or she'll fight back. So when I realized we were caught in the current I knew we'd just have to ride it out. The minute it slackened I got us over to the island."

I paused. "But we weren't alone in the river, Older Brother."

"What do you mean? Oh! That *something* set us spinning like that."

I looked him square in the eye. "Maybe a Giant Mekong Catfish. They're *monsters* – three and a half meters long and two hundred and seventy-five kilos. One could easily have capsized our boat and swallowed the two of us alive. They're an endangered species, so there aren't more than a few of them left. But they're out there all right – oh, yeah – they're out there."

He just stared at me.

"Or it might have been just a little Irrawaddy Dolphin. Or a hungry *pack* of them, circling us like sharks. Or a Siamese Crocodile. I heard they find Chinese-Khmer especially delicious. You know – a little contrast in the taste. Like sweet and sour."

"Nyah, would you cut it out. But there *was* something out there. I felt it hit the boat."

"And then it started *hissing.* You heard it, didn't you?"

"Oh come on," he said. "It wasn't a 'neak'. This is the *Mekong,* not Loch Ness. If there were any water dragons left in the Mekong someone would have spotted one. Or *run into* one – for god's sake, the things are so big they'd be a navigational hazard. You *know* what hit us. Stop teasing me and tell me."

"Well," I said, "when the river rises quickly like that, stuff that's hung up on the shoreline gets dislodged and sucked into the main current – just like we did. Yeah, I think we were attacked by a giant *log.*"

"So we didn't hit a whirlpool?"

"A *whirlpool?* You've got to be kidding. Those are around the rocky places. You see any rocks around here? All I see is mud. Oh... I get it. If you try to tell your mother that you got sucked into a giant whirlpool, I'm *not* backing you up."

"Well how about a Siamese Giant Carp," he asked, "trying to get at us by tipping over our boat? They can grow to over ninety kilos, you know. And I'll bet they're very hungry this time of year."

"Would you stop... fishing?" I said. "We hit a *log*. Maybe when we cross the Bassac I can find you something a little more exciting..."

Now there are things I need to explain to you, before I continue our story. My friend and I were only fourteen and twelve, but we had escaped from the Khmer Rouge army, figured out where we were, found enough food and water to keep ourselves alive, and gotten out of the war zone – by ourselves. The Khmer Rouge had taken our families, our homes, our religion. But there was one thing they couldn't get away from us, no matter what they tried. Our *intelligence*. And that's what we'd used to take our freedom back.

But how do I explain what we were *really* trying to do? And that's why I described to you the Holiday of the Rowing of the Boats. We remembered our childhoods. And we thought, rightly or not, that by taking back our freedom, we could get our childhoods back.

But we weren't children any more. We'd been taken from our families as children, then beaten, starved and worked nearly to death. As though that would make us into adults faster – so they could send us to the front sooner. Now we were neither children nor adults, but some kind of mutant hybrid instead. A hybrid created by perpetual war.

But as soon as we were out of the war zone it was as though we were on holiday again. On the boardwalk in Phnom Penh, watching the dragon boat races. Just kids, honing their storytelling skills so they could tell their mothers all that they'd seen and done on their first foray into the world – as soon as they got home.

"OK, OK," I said. "If you want to tell your mother we were sucked into a giant whirlpool, I'll back you up. *If* you don't tell *my* mother I was so *stupid* as to not have snagged us some frogs last night."

"Don't worry, Nyah. I won't tell your mother. And I don't want anything – *just the address of the prettiest girl in Prai Anchaan!*"

"Oh, yeah, like I can remember it after all these years... But I can tell you how to find her *house...*"

"Oh, that will do!" he said.

"Ha! You haven't seen a girl in three and a half years. They'll *all* be pretty, your first day back. Even the ones with big teeth."

"And I'll impress every one of them," he said, "by telling them how I plotted our escape."

"In all of a second and a half?"

"Well it worked, didn't it?" he asked. "And when I tell them it went off without a hitch even though it was completely unrehearsed, oh, they'll be impressed all right."

"And I'll tell them that *I* was the one carrying the grenades. Nerves of steel – that's me... Don't you dare tell anyone I was just a porter. You tell them I was an *infantryman*. Especially my mother."

"OK Nyah, you take the log out of the whirlpool story and throw in a giant catfish, and you've got yourself a deal."

We raced along the levees to find a grove of trees. Now we were climbing out of the river basin; the paddies were terraced here, each one higher than the last. We continued stepping up from one paddy to the next, until we hit the highest one. We weren't paying much attention – we were looking for lemon grass and ginger, and comparing recipes for fish.

In every life there's a single second in which childhood ends forever. This was ours. We stopped, dead in our tracks. We were looking at another highway. And on the other side, farmland, for as far as we could see. Unplowed, and abandoned.

"Where did this *god damn* road come from, Nyah? It's not one of the seven national highways – I don't know *what* it is. And it runs due north, straight up from Vietnam. We're not out of the war zone, we're in another minefield. And none of it is paved. Well, I'm not crawling on my belly through this one. The east shoulder, then the roadbed, then the west shoulder? That's *twelve meters*."

He continued to stare in disbelief, then suddenly punch the air and screamed in a whisper, "What did I expect? This is *Cambodia*."

And then he stopped, and picked up his pack – I thought he was OK. "Oh, screw it," he said. "I'm just going to walk right across the road."

And I think, if I hadn't been there, he would have done it. By this time we'd seen all the ugly faces of war. When we'd been forced out of Phnom Penh we'd been made to walk for days in temperatures nearing thirty-four degrees, finding our own food and water as we could. My family had been split in half because we were living in two different boroughs of Phnom Penh. My mother's half had been forced to go southwest, to Pong Tuk. But the other half? I didn't know. I didn't even know if they were still alive. Our fathers had been taken away with a single knock on the door, never to be seen again. Other family members had just disappeared – you never knew if the Khmer Rouge had relocated them, or executed them, or whether or not they'd tortured them. We'd seen children report their parents in exchange for food, not understanding that both their father and their mother would be killed. We'd seen children killed by UXOs. We'd heard of people blinded or crippled by land mines, of families where one person had stepped on a mine and another had rushed in to help him, only to step on a mine himself. We'd been relocated more times than we could keep track of, first from village to village, then from work camp to work camp, and then from one army camp to another. We'd seen people try to escape, only to be caught and have their legs sliced open so they couldn't get away. We'd found people who'd committed suicide, unable to bear the hard labor, the hunger, and the loss of their families any longer. We'd seen boys as young as eight forced to work forty-eight hours straight, and then sit down on a levee only to fall asleep instantly, roll into the paddy, and drown in ten centimeters of water. And then *we'd* had to bury them. Boys we'd worked right next to the day before. And as we dug their graves we asked ourselves, would we be next? There were dead bodies everywhere – on the roads, in the rivers, in the camps and in the communes. In shallow mass graves with their fingers sticking out. If you could find gold jewelry you could trade it for rice, so we'd learned to pick over bodies before we even left Pong Tuk. We did it so our mothers wouldn't have to.

And after all of this, we didn't *care* if we died – even after our escape. But we desperately tried to stay alive. I don't quite know how to explain this, but I'll try.

Firstly, we were Buddhist. We believed that, during your lifetime, you earn good karma for good deeds and bad karma for bad ones. There is no god to absolve you of your bad karma, as Jesus Christ absolves Christians of theirs. You must live your life so as to tip the scale in your favor – more good karma than bad means you'll be reborn to a good life, instead of to a miserable one. We were both good kids, which meant that when we died, we'd be reborn to a good life. We knew this.

And *anywhere* would be better than here. Which brings me to my second point. Even if we went into some metaphysical black hole when we died – even if we weren't reborn – we'd be out of all *this*. The hunger was endless, and the sorrow of watching your family either die or disappear ended only when you had no one left for them to take.

Which brings me to my third point. Whenever we had a *good* day – and believe me, you can count escaping from the Khmer Rouge army as a good day – we thought we were invincible. Hadn't our experience proven it? If nothing had killed us in the last four years, nothing could kill us now. Oh, we *talked* as though we understood that we were in danger every minute. But we were *kids* – kids who'd grown up with war. We didn't *really* understand. And had we understood, we wouldn't have cared anyway.

But on the other hand, we desperately tried to stay alive. We had to assume that our mothers hadn't been killed – we couldn't leave them on their own. And we didn't want them to never know whether or not we were still alive. For Puamaak, there was always that *one percent chance* that his father would return. Or maybe it was just our instinct to survive. Or our memories of the good times – our friends, the holidays, and the adventures of childhood. If the good times ever came back, we didn't want to miss a thing.

So here's how it was. We didn't care if we died, but we desperately tried to stay alive. And if all of this makes no sense to you, well, don't worry about it – you'd understand it if you'd grown up with war.

But if we were going to die, I didn't want to go this way – I wanted to go *quick*. I reached out my hand to stop my friend. What could I say that would stop him from crossing that road?

"You know, Puamaak, if you hit a mine, it's probably not going to kill you. It'll just take your foot off. Maybe both of them. You'll bleed to death in the dust, screaming in pain. And I'll be here all alone... You know you're an idiot? You get like that, when you're hungry. But because I can go without food a lot longer than you can, one of us is still thinking. We don't have to *cross* the minefield – we can go *under* it. We have to walk north, but not far. Follow me." And I backed away from the shoulder and took off north, quickly, shadowing the road.

At first he didn't follow me. I kept walking, like a mother does who knows her recalcitrant toddler has no choice but to try to catch up to her. I wanted to look back, but knew that would only betray my fear that he wasn't right behind me. So instead I called casually over my shoulder, "When we were coming across the river this morning, I saw a canal emptying into the Mekong. There must have been a bridge over it before the war, but it's gone now. We'll just keep walking north until we get to the canal, and then climb down into the canal bed and walk west." And then I slowed my pace a bit, so he could catch up to me.

"Can't we swim it?" he asked. "There might be mines down in there, too..."

"Can't swim it – we'd be swimming against the current. Can't paddle the boat up it, either. But we can walk in the water."

We got to the canal after just a kilometer, climbed down into the canal bed, and picked our way through the wreckage of the bridge until we were clear of it. Let me tell you, it was rough going – but it was better than hitting a mine. And then we walked back up above the waterline, and walked up the canal.

"You know what that was, Nyah?" Puamaak pointed back to the road. "That *god damn* highway. It's the road that runs north up the shoreline to the ferry pier across the river from the one on the east bank. Of course there'd be a road there – I should have been looking for it."

"I should have been looking for it too... But this is easy walking now. And no one will see us down here in the canal bed."

"Let's get at least two kilometers away from the road before we stop – you never know what's going to come up it. This one'll be good enough for the Vietnamese to use, after they de-mine it."

We walked on for half an hour, came upon a grove of trees, climbed out of the canal bed, and *finally* made our fire.

"How do you want me to cook the fish?" I asked. "Over the fire, clamped between two pairs of sticks? Or underneath the coals, wrapped in banana leaves?" We Khmer don't like smoked food, so I always roasted mine in the coals. But I would give my elder the choice.

"If we use the clamp method we won't have to wait for the coals to burn down. And I can butterfly the fish so they cook in half the time."

I looked up from the fire. "You can *cook?*"

"Yeah. Don't look so surprised – I'm half Chinese, for god's sake."

"OK. Get started on the fish. I'll find some cassava and we can roast it in the coals. We can eat as much of it as we want, when it's cooked."

I returned with cassava just as he was taking the fish off, and I pushed a couple of tubers down into the coals. I hadn't thought to take the time to wash the dirt off, and he hadn't thought to ask me to – that's what years of hunger do to you.

I wrapped the peanuts in a piece of banana leaf and pushed them into the coals next to the cassava. Now it was time to eat, and we split one of the fresh, hot fish. I remember to this day how wonderful it tasted – better than anything in the finest French restaurant in Phnom Penh, before the war.

"We'd better roast the banana leaves while we're waiting for the cassava to cook," I said. "The malaria mosquitoes will be out in squadrons because of last night's rain. Without a double layer of banana leaves inside our hammocks they'll bite us right through them. They'll start coming out before the sun even goes down, so we actually don't have much time. You start on the leaves while I tie the hammocks up. I'll tie our gear to a branch after we're done with everything – we can't leave anything on the ground."

I found a young tamarind that had a wide fork about eight meters up, and I tied the hammocks above the first layer of leaves. Anyone prowling beneath the tree would never know we were there. Puamaak passed the warm banana leaves up to me.

"Don't forget," I said, "to put your 'kramaa' over you before you wrap yourself up for the night. It will be colder than you think – we're not sleeping on the ground."

"If we can eat like this every day we'll put on a little weight. And then we won't feel the cold so much."

After we finished the hammocks we checked the cassava. Now, cassava with no herbs or spices isn't anything to write home about, but the fact that it was *hot* – oh, it was delicious.

"This is a better way to eat," said Puamaak, "than wolfing everything down at once." We couldn't eat much without getting sick because we'd been on near-starvation rations for so long. "Maybe by the time we get back to our mothers we'll be able to eat a full meal again."

"There won't be a full meal there to *eat*," I said. "We're going back to Pong Tuk, remember? To the cadres in charge of the village. They give most of the food to the 'old people', and whatever's left goes to the 'new people' – but never more than what it takes to simply keep them alive. I'm sure nothing's changed – have more cassava."

"Yeah. Even if we can convince them that we outrank them, we still won't get much. And the area around Pong Tuk will have been hunted out."

We finished our food and started to pack what we had left over in my 'kramaa', to tie it up in the tree.

"You *know,*" I said, "there must be dogs back there in that village. And they'll eventually smell our food." I shook my head. "Somehow we've got to get you to the point where you can climb a tree. It's only a matter of time before we meet up with a dog that's rabid. Or something else that's rabid – whatever the dog bites gets it. What if you have a rabid water buffalo after you? Oh, don't laugh – it could happen."

"So five meters or so, do you think?"

I shook my head. "I've seen dogs climb trees before, trying to get at something. You need to be able to get up eight meters." I pointed to the fork in the tree. "And that's how high your hammock is. But don't worry – once the mosquitoes come out, you'll get the hang of it."

I climbed up and tied our food to a branch near my hammock, and tied our gear up next to it. Then I climbed down again and we sat in front of our fire.

"Did you notice there were no road signs at the bridge?" asked Puamaak.

"Yeah. And did you see the highway number imprinted in the bridgehead? '101'. So now you know what to call it. Other than, 'that god damn highway'. But I knew we didn't get into Vietnam without having to look to see if the road signs were missing."

"How?" he asked.

"Listen."

"I don't hear anything, Nyah."

"Exactly – no birds."

"Oh ... of course. Except on the island. I wonder if there really was anyone there?"

"The plow animals might have just looked like they were tied," I said. "Maybe the farmers untied them but didn't take their ropes off. Or maybe the people never got the evacuation order, like you said. We'll never know."

"So if we didn't get down into Vietnam, we've missed our opportunity to find out if the Vietnamese have two heads."

"I know for a fact they don't," I said. "They have three. One for outsmarting the South Vietnamese, one for outsmarting the Americans, and one for outsmarting the Khmer. From the sound of the artillery fire yesterday, now they're in Phnom Penh."

We were quiet for a moment, remembering the shaded boulevards that had smelled of frangipani. The neighborhoods of French-Khmer bungalows, with their gardens of jasmine and roses. And the boardwalk, with the smell of French coffee and baguettes floating on the breeze from the river. They'd called Phnom Penh 'the Pearl of Indo-China', before the war. We wondered what was left of it now.

"Well how the hell would they have gotten across the Mekong?" asked Puamaak. "With all their tanks, and their trucks, and their big guns?"

"Maybe they did what the Cham did when they attacked Angkor in the twelfth century – brought a boat up the Mekong from the South China Sea. And then used it like a ferry, to get their men, their guns and their tanks across the river at Neak Luong and back onto Highway One. Instead of continuing on up the river, like the Cham did."

"Or maybe," he said, "they hot-wired the old car ferries."

It never occurred to either one of us that the Vietnamese might have bridging equipment; as I've said, we knew nothing of modern warfare.

I poked the coals and passed his 'kramaa' over them to make him a warm blanket. As I've said, he was my elder, so I did little things like that for him.

"You know," he said, "if we hadn't escaped, we would have been ordered to follow the Vietnamese as they made their way up to Phnom Penh. And snipe at them from the rear. We would have been dead by now."

"Ha! I would have been dead before anyone else. I mean, I wasn't about to shoot anyone. Our first commandment is, 'Take no life.'"

"It's mutated somewhat, little brother. 'Take no life, *unless* someone is shooting at you. Then, fire in their general direction and fire as fast as you can, to make them think that there are more of you than there really are so they'll go bother someone else. Don't aim real well because you might just hit someone.'"

"You can't aim real well when you're running the other way – that's what I would have been doing."

"Ha!" he said. "You would have turned around to see my back in front of you."

He managed to climb up to his hammock, and we wrapped ourselves up before the mosquitoes came out – about 5:30. We'd get plenty of sleep tonight.

As we rocked back and forth we talked about the old days – the Holiday of the Rowing of the Boats and the boardwalk on the river. We took turns recounting our exploits when we'd been out of the sight of our mothers. We talked of the dragon boats and the firecrackers, of Saambō the Elephant and the temple of Wat Phnom, of the uniquely-Khmer music and that first glimpse of our king. But we agreed that the best thing of all was the hawker with the painted cart – the one who'd sold us our roasted squid with pickled green papaya. We laughed, and told stories, and laughed some more, until we fell asleep. If we could never again be children in life, at least we could be children in our dreams.

Day Four - *Swamped*

I was warming myself by our fire underneath the tree we'd slept in. I'd gotten up at dawn, as I always did. I'd collected firewood and kindling, lit our fire, found more cassava, stuck it in the coals to roast and refilled both our water cups from the canal. Puamaak was still trying to get out of the tree.

I just couldn't understand it. How had he stayed alive the last four years if he couldn't get up and down a tree? Well, all I could do was try to help him acquire the skill. Because if anyone found him, they'd start looking for *me*. And even if they didn't, they'd probably kill *him*. So I might as well be dead.

"Drop the fish down," I said, "so I can put it in the coals. It's tied to a branch near my hammock." I figured that, once he smelled the fish, he'd figure out a way to get down – and it wouldn't be so hard for him the next time.

He made his way over to my 'kramaa' and dropped the fish down. OK, at least he could go sideways. It was *something*.

"So you're Recon this morning," I said, as though I weren't concerned. "That's good. If you can do what I can do, and I can do what you can do, that improves our chances by fifty percent. Can you see the Bassac? I know it's much smaller than the Mekong, but I've never seen it before – it starts more than two kilometers south of the Royal Palace, way past the end of the boardwalk, and I've never been down there. Was your house in Phnom Penh near the Bassac?"

"You've seen it before, little brother. We both had to cross it to get to the war zone. It runs pretty much parallel to the Mekong, and it's the only other river you would have had to cross. The only time *I've* ever seen it is when I crossed it with the army." He sighed. "But I don't see it now. It's all swamp out there."

"Swamp?" I pushed our fish down into the coals. "So how do we get around it? By going north, or going south?"

"Nyah, it's everywhere. Except where we came from."

I jerked my head up; this was not what I'd expected. I hadn't crossed swampland to get to the war zone, and I knew my friend hadn't, either.

"We can't cross it, Puamaak."

"How do you know that? You've never been here before."

"Because the swamp down here can't be that much different than what we had behind our paddies in Prai Anchaan. We'll cut our feet to ribbons on broken clam shells on the bottom. And we'll slice up our arms and legs on the saw grass before we even slice up our feet."

Now my comrade was quiet. And for much too long a time. "Puamaak – what else do you see?"

"Come up here and take a look for yourself."

I left our food in the coals in case there were dogs around, and climbed up into the tree next to him.

"Look." He pointed out over the landscape. "There's still no one out there. There are houses out on that last hammock, before you get into the main swamp, but everyone's gone. What the *hell* could have happened? And if the Vietnamese *did* get across the Mekong, and *did* take Phnom Penh, why don't we see helicopters, or troop transport planes bringing in reinforcements? Or *something?*"

"And why didn't we hear more artillery fire?" I asked. "The only day we heard it was the day before yesterday. How could the Vietnamese have taken Phnom Penh in *one day?*"

"Maybe what we heard was one of our units firing at another. *Everyone's* fighting now."

He looked out over the landscape again. "Nyah, if there are no people this far west, what's waiting for us in Pong Tuk?"

"But the villages that far over can't have been evacuated."

"Pong Tuk is far from our eastern border with Vietnam, but it's probably not all that far from our southern border... But maybe the Vietnamese will pass it by, because it's not near a highway."

"Are you kidding?" I said. "It's out in the middle of nowhere. Prai Anchaan may have been just a farming and fishing village, but we were much more educated and worldly than anyone in Pong Tuk. They'd never even seen people like us."

He raised his eyebrows, and nodded. "Oh, I remember our first day. How the women looked at my mother's clothes, and her jewelry... Well if the Vietnamese didn't take Phnom Penh in one day it's just a matter of a few more. I mean, we don't see any sign of them retreating, do we? I don't think they would go back the same way they came. They would take 101. They'd figure they could get away faster on 101 than they could trying to go back across the Mekong at the Crossing – they'd figure they could just slip into the Delta quickly, and not have to cross the Mekong until they were back in Vietnam. No, if they were retreating, we would have heard them as they hit the mines on 101. We could have heard them even from the island."

"So once they do get Phnom Penh..." I said.

"They'll fan out and take the rest of the country as quickly as they can. They'll de-mine Highway Four first so they can use the seaport at Kampong Saum. And they can start de-mining 101 when they start Four, because they can start from the Delta end. Then they'll de-mine Highway Three so they can use the river port at Kampot. Then they'll start on Two – which we have to cross, to get to Pong Tuk. But if they have enough manpower, they'll start de-mining all four highways at once. Yes, we'll run into Vietnamese sooner or later. Probably in Takeo Province first, at Highway Two."

"Do you remember any Vietnamese?" I asked him. "From the market?"

"*Remember* any? I never *knew* any. If my mother didn't buy from Khmer, she bought from Chinese. Do you know any?"

"Oh yeah, I know a lot. We used to buy from Vietnamese all the time. I can ask where their fish is from – 'Tonle Sap? Mekong?'. I can ask if they have cuttlefish today." I wiggled my fingers like tentacles. "Or lobster." I pointed to the blue in his 'kramaa' and pinched my fingers together. "And I can bargain down the price of anything." I held out five fingers, and then folded one under to make four.

He laughed, if just a little. "Well I had three years of French – I could try that. But I don't think any Vietnamese young enough to be a soldier would understand me. We got our independence in 1953, and they got theirs *years* before we did. How about English? Do you know any English?"

"No. Where would I have learned English?"

"*I* don't know. Just checking..." He shifted his weight on the branch. Both of us were keenly aware that Vietnamese and Khmer are in the same language family, but we can't understand them, and they can't understand us. Even though our two countries are right next to each other. So here we were, up in a tree, talking about trying to communicate with them in some European language. It was beyond ridiculous.

"Puamaak, I was trying to make a point. Sign language will work. Think about it – that's how people have traded in Southeast Asia for thousands of years. If it worked with the Vietnamese in the market, it will work with the Vietnamese in the infantry." And I threw my hands straight up in the air, then brought my right one down slowly, brought all the fingertips together, and raised them to my mouth.

He nodded. "Perfectly clear."

We looked out over the landscape again. "I can't even see plow animals wandering around down there," he said. "Can you?"

"No. I can't even see anywhere where they could graze. No Brahmas, no water buffalo. And no pigs, or chickens... no *ducks*. If it's too wet here for pastureland, there should be ducks and geese. If only to feed the greedy cadres."

We looked toward the horizon, for *any* sign of life. We saw a curl of smoke – but it was only the mist coming up. We saw a goose fattened for slaughter – but it was only a rice sack blowing in the wind. And then we saw a boat, moving across the water – but it was empty. "I wonder how long ago all the people left this place..." I said. We looked out over the marshes in silence.

Puamaak was the first to speak. "I think this is the only place in Cambodia where you'd find so many kilometers of marshland – between the two big rivers. It looks like... an endless sea."

Those words, 'endless sea'. They triggered a memory. "Puamaak, I *recognize* these marshes. I was in a work camp on the edge of them. A really long time ago. I remember climbing onto the highest levee I could find to see if I could see the other side." I shook my head, slowly. "I couldn't."

"Do you have any idea where you were?" he asked.

"No. No idea at all."

"Then you were west of where we are now. You were on the Bassac side of the marshes, looking back this way – or you would have seen the Mekong. And you would have recognized that."

"That's true," I said. "That's why you're our navigator – I wouldn't have figured that out."

"You would have, eventually. It's just common sense. But think about this, little brother... as we got older they marched us further and further away from our families, so we couldn't get back to them. Long before they put you in the army, you were across the Bassac and a full province away from Pong Tuk. Oh! *That's* why you don't remember crossing it – because it was such a long time ago. But do you remember anything at all about these marshes from when you were in the camp? Anything that would help us figure out how to get across them?"

"No," I said. "I used to go to the edge, to catch whatever I could from the bank. But I never went in."

"The clam shells?"

"Yeah."

"But did you ever see anyone *else* go in," he asked. "With a boat, or a raft..."

I shook my head, still looking out over the marshes. "Never."

"Well we have to figure out *something*. Because there's nowhere else to *go*. Wait a minute... Nyah, how did our army get us to the combat zone without us crossing this swamp? We crossed the Bassac, and we crossed the Mekong, but we didn't cross *any marshland* in between."

"Well, I crossed the Mekong before the harvest – before the end of monsoon season. The marsh would have been a lake then. But I didn't cross a lake... I walked across dry land to get to the Mekong. But I don't know where it was."

"So did I – but I don't know where it was, either. Because there were no landmarks. And I don't know how we'd *ever* figure out where it was."

"So we're stuck with trying to cross here..." I said.

"But look. This canal goes all the way over to a lake," he pointed, "and continues on the other side. We can walk along the edge of the canal just above the waterline, swim the lake, and then pick up the canal again."

"If we're not swimming against a strong current in the lake," I said. "The current in the canal will tell me what the current in the lake is like." I started down the tree. "Stay here."

"I'm not going anywhere, Nyah. I can't get down, remember?"

I checked the current in the canal and went back up the tree. "The current is slower than yesterday – the rainwater's drained out into the river. But I wonder how far over the canal goes. Let me climb a little higher."

I climbed up another eight meters or so, and quickly climbed down again. "Dead end," I said. "The canal doesn't go much beyond the lake.*"*

I shook my head, remembering. "'Don't go in the marshes'. That's one of the first things they told me, when I was a kid. So, of course, I went in. They just patched me up when I got home – figured there was no need to yell at me."

"This is like when we got to the Mekong," he said, "and couldn't see the other side..." He turned and looked at me, as though he thought I could figure out what to do.

"What if we went back to the village," I said, "and tried to find some shoes?"

"They'll all be gone, Nyah. That's the first thing you'd take, if the cadres told you to evacuate and you had to go on foot. You'd take every pair of shoes you could get your hands on. There won't be any long-sleeved shirts or long pants back there, either. And the village *must* be mined – we can't look for anything."

He leaned back against the trunk of the tree. "Nyah... It's not just the clams and the saw grass. First our feet in the mud of the canal, then in the lake, then in the canal again, then in the marshes... even with shoes..." He turned to me with that same knowing look I remembered from the moment he'd told me we were going to escape.

In the work camps we'd dug irrigation canals in the dry season, but in monsoon season, we'd worked the paddies. Sixteen-hour days shin-deep in water, in the rain. Then, overnight, our waterlogged skin would dry out, leaving cracks between our toes. They'd start to bleed, but we'd have to climb back into the paddies the next morning anyway. When our feet hit the water the pain was excruciating – like someone rubbing salt into our open sores. We'd get wet again. And dry out again. And get wet again. And dry out again. And then an infection would set in, and our feet would just never heal up. Trench foot. And *everyone* got it – no possibility of being rotated out and sent to the infirmary. And if you wonder how we could have worked sixteen-hour days when there are only twelve hours of daylight in Cambodia – they just put torches out.

"What if we could *oil* our feet before we start out tomorrow?" asked Puamaak.

"With what?"

"Coconut oil. Peanut oil. Palm oil. *Motor* oil. *Anything.*"

"No way to get any," I said. "Especially if the village is mined."

He exhaled, very slowly. "This just keeps getting worse... Do you realize we'll have to cross all those marshes in a single day? Because there'll be no place we can sleep, or make a fire to cook – there'll be no place high enough to make camp at night."

"Cook *what?*" I asked. "If we have to cross all the marshes in one day, we won't have time to catch food."

"The clams! We wouldn't *have* to catch food – we could eat the clams. We'd have to eat them raw, but we could do it."

"Nope," I said. "You can't get the shells open unless you cook them. Not even with a kni... *The fish!* I forgot about the fish!"

I climbed down, took the fish and cassava out of the coals, and called back up to my friend. "Don't think about how to get out of the tree, just think about how to get down to the next branch."

He got down pretty quickly after that. Whether it was my instructions or the smell of the fish, I don't know.

I served him his food using a square of banana leaf as a plate.

"Nyah," he said between bites of fish, "remember that movie, *The Great Escape?* I think I saw it three times. It was a true story – how Allied prisoners of war escaped from a German POW camp in World War II. They were in just as much trouble as we are – more, if you count the guns the German guards had trained on them twenty-four hours a day. But seventy-six POWs got out of that camp. You know how they did it?"

"I don't know," I said. "I was too young to watch war movies."

"They knew how to *plan,* Nyah. It's a little bit different than just thinking systematically. When you plan, you think *ahead*. Those POWs – they *planned everything* before they *did anything*. That's just the way they do it in the Western countries. And the higher the stakes, the more they plan. To get across those marshes we're going to have to plan just like those POWs did. What if we go back to the village and get the boat, then pole our way up the canal to get back here. Catch food all day today – enough for several days. Smoke it tonight so it won't spoil, and get an early start tomorrow. Pole up the canal to the lake, paddle across the lake, pick up the canal on the other side and then, where the canal ends, pole our way through the marshes. We can sleep on the boat, and if we can find a big wok to put our fire in, we can even reheat our food."

"*And* cook the clams," I said. "And if we bring the fish trap with us, we can put it in the water every night and get fresh fish for the next day. We'd have to bring all our firewood and kindling, but it's possible. When we run out we just eat the smoked food cold."

But then my comrade thought of what had gotten him up the tree so quickly the night before. "The mosquitoes – dengue mosquitoes in the daytime and malaria mosquitoes at night. Oh yeah – if we got sick, we'd die before we got back to Pong Tuk. Both of us. And then neither of our mothers would ever know what happened to us." He sighed. "Every time we figure out how to get across, we think of something else that will prevent us. This damned swamp makes crossing the minefield on One look like a walk in the park."

"And the Mekong look like the Seine," I said.

We finished our food in silence.

"But we've been asking ourselves the wrong question," I said. "'How to get across the marshes.' We've never asked ourselves the most *obvious* question."

"What question is that, little brother?"

"'*Why are we going back to Pong Tuk?*' After three and a half years, you really think our families are still alive? And if they are, they've probably been relocated again – Pong Tuk was the *third place* my family was sent to after they marched us out of Phnom Penh. First they dumped us out in the middle of nowhere, with one little hut and nothing else. After a few weeks they moved us into a village – the conditions for 'new people' were little better there. Then a couple of weeks later they moved us to Pong Tuk. Then they split us up, and sent everyone to a different place. Except those too old or too young to work. The only reason they kept our mothers was because they needed them to work the fields. But the chances that they're still there are just about as good as our chances of getting across that swamp. *Why* are we going back to Pong Tuk?"

"Because there's nowhere else we can *go*, Nyah. OK, we're agreed we can't go to Phnom Penh, but even Prai Anchaan eighteen kilometers upriver from *there* will be crawling with Vietnamese. They'll be demining Highway Six so they can get up into Northern Cambodia. So we can't go to your home, or to mine. *Where* would we go, Nyah – *tell* me."

I thought of the only other places I knew – all the places I'd dreamed of as a child. Angkor in the north, Bokor in the south, Mondulkiri in the east, Pailin in the west, Kampong Saum in the southwest, and Ratanakiri in the northeast. I couldn't think how to get to any of them – not on foot, anyway. They were all even further away than Pong Tuk was. "OK," I said, "let's do what we did the first time I climbed a recon tree . Let's run through the four directions."

"North, more marshes. And north of that, Vietnamese, and whatever's left of our own army. South, more marshes. And south of that, Vietnam. East, the war zone we just came out of – no food. And who knows what the hell's going on over there now; if we haven't seen any transport planes or heard any mines go off on 101, then the rest of their army is coming up Highway One. That leaves us with... going west. Across the damned marshes."

He exhaled very slowly, as though finishing a cigarette. I'd seen him do that twice before in the last three days, but only when he couldn't see any way out of the trouble we were in. I felt that, because he was older, he would try to shield me from the worst if he could. Like not telling me he'd figured out that they'd planned to send me into combat. So I learned to look for that behavior, and to worry when I saw it. I could use it as a gauge of just how much trouble we were in.

"Puamaak... is there anything you're not telling me?"

"No. Because I can't figure out how to get across the swamp. I need your brain, Nyah. *Think.* I haven't found anything yet that you can't do – you're like a damned *ninja.*"

"I can't find my way back to Pong Tuk, I'll tell you that right now. I don't know how you're going to do it."

"I have a way," he said. "As soon as we're across the Bassac, I'll show you. *Damn,* it's *so close* – if we had levees to walk on we'd probably be over there by tonight." And he exhaled slowly again.

"Assuming we get through," I said, "how much further is it to Pong Tuk?"

"Well, let's try to figure it out. Pong Tuk is in the eastern part of Kampot Province. Takeo Province is between Kampot and Kandal provinces. We're in the eastern part of Kandal – Phnom Penh is northwest of us."

"Northwest of us?" I said. "I thought it was straight up the river."

"It is. But rivers aren't straight – especially the Mekong. It curves northwest at Neak Luong. So we aren't as far west as Phnom Penh yet."

I just stared at him in disbelief. "We started out in Prey Veng Province, on the western side. So we've gone across... not even a quarter of one province. We have four quarters of Kandal, four quarters of Takeo, and one quarter of Kampot to go. That's *nine quarters* – and we haven't even crossed *one.* We're less than *one tenth* of the way back."

"It's not as bad as that, little brother. Kandal Province is very narrow down here in the south, and Pong Tuk is not a quarter of the way across Kampot Province – it's only a few kilometers from the Takeo border. I think, as the crow flies, we're almost two-tenths of the way back to Pong Tuk."

"Poor choice of words – there *are* no more crows. They've all been eaten."

"Sorry. Look, Nyah. We can knock off for a day, if we feel like it. What difference is a day going to make when we've been gone three and a half years? We no longer have to get out of the way of the Vietnamese invasion force, and we're away from *our* army, so we can go at whatever pace we want to. I just wish I knew how far *south* we have to go from *here.* Pong Tuk must be pretty near the Vietnamese border, but I think the border's much further south in Kampot. If we were across the Bassac I'd have some landmarks. But we're *not* across the Bassac."

"If we had a map," I said, "we could figure out how many kilometers we have to go. We could find the north end of the second island down from Neak Luong and measure the distance to Pong Tuk. We'd be able to see *exactly* how far away we are – and how far south Pong Tuk is."

"But we don't have a map, and we won't be able to find one. Don't think about it, little brother."

"Well we've walked for three days – more, if you count the running we did the day we escaped. If we're not even two-tenths of the way, it will take us twelve more days to get back to Pong Tuk."

"No it won't," he said. "We were half dead until this morning. Not enough rest, not enough food, not enough water... But now we have *fish,* and we can cook, and we'll be able to eat a little more each day. We'll be much stronger from here on in. We may even put on some weight before our mothers see us again. And once we see Phnom Treil we can make a beeline for Pong Tuk."

"OK, let's say ten days. Takeo will be crawling with Vietnamese by then. Kampot too."

"Well there's nothing we can do about it, Nyah. We'll just have to take it one day at a time."

"I thought we were supposed to be planning ahead, like they did in *The Great Escape.*"

"Oh my god, you're *right.* We can't even do *that.*"

"And where the hell have all the people gone?" I asked. "This is our fifth day since we split off from our unit, and we haven't seen even one person. Why is there no sign of the retreating Khmer Rouge army? Were there no deserters, aside from you and me? And no wounded, or stragglers? Impossible – our army is on foot. How about escapees from the work camps and the prisons? Where are they? And the villagers? Most of them would have been women, children, and the very old – there was not one person who couldn't keep up? And the people who could keep up – they're all on foot, too. How did they get out so fast?" I just looked at my friend, hoping that he could make some sense of it all simply because he was older. But he just shook his head.

"Do you remember what happened," I said, "when they dropped the atomic bomb on Japan in World War II? I saw pictures of it on TV. Look at what the blast and the radiation did to the people and their city – some of the people were even vaporized. That was about thirty-five years ago. What if the Americans developed a *new* kind of bomb in those thirty-five years? A bomb that would vaporize people without burning everything around them. They got a man to the moon – they could make a bomb like that. Maybe the Vietnamese dropped one on everyone in the lowlands during those twelve hours that we were asleep on the mountain. A bomb the Americans left behind."

"What would make you think of a thing like that, Nyah?"

"Because it's not just that we haven't seen any people. *We haven't seen any bodies, either.* This is our fifth day and we haven't seen even one. *No bodies in a combat zone?* And none in the rivers, either? Even in peacetime you see bodies in the rivers once in awhile – the dead of the families too poor to cremate their relatives. We've crossed three rivers now. No bodies in the water, no bodies on the banks, no bodies on the island. Where are all the bodies – *tell* me."

"I don't know, little brother. I wish we *would* find some bodies – we could get the damned shoes off them so we could walk through the damned swamp! Then we'd be able to get across in a day. But we saw live animals, Nyah; first plow animals, then dogs. Then birds, on the island. So there was no bomb that vaporized people – it would have gotten the animals, too. But we should have seen bodies. And we should have seen stragglers. Maybe they just drowned themselves in the Mekong, in terror of the two-headed Vietnamese. Or because they couldn't cope with being relocated a hundredth time. Or because they had no family left. And then their bodies washed clean downriver, because of the rainstorm. There have been plenty of people who've committed suicide in the last four years."

I nodded. "When I was in the infirmary I got up one morning and went outside to take a leak. The mist was so thick I could hardly see. Suddenly, something brushed against my elbow. I looked up to see one of the boys from the infirmary hanging from the tree above me. It was his foot that had brushed against my elbow. Finding a body is one thing, but if it's someone you know – someone you talked to just yesterday..."

"Don't think about it, Nyah."

I shook my head and looked west again. "I wonder if there will be anyone left in Pong Tuk, by the time we get there. I really wonder."

He put his hand on my shoulder. "Let's at least get the boat and bring it back up here. Float down the canal back to the Mekong, then float down the river to where we landed. Pole back up here, or pull the boat – whichever's easier – catch food all day, cook it up tonight and get an early start in the morning. The only problem we haven't solved is the mosquitoes. Let's sleep on that one – we may think of something before tomorrow morning."

We prepared to float down the canal just as we had to cross the tributaries; none of our gear was expendable, so we couldn't leave it at our campsite. Now we had all our earthly possessions with us – there would be nothing left in Pong Tuk, in Prai Anchaan, or in Phnom Penh.

"Just remember," I said, "as soon as we pass the wreckage of the bridge, swim to the right side of the canal and stay tight into shore when you turn the corner. If you don't, the current in the canal will shoot you into the current in the river. And I might not be able to get out to you..."

We slid into the canal and let the cool water carry us down the shoreline. The corner was far ahead of us.

"Did you lose anyone," I asked, "in the march out of Phnom Penh?"

"No. It was just my mother, my father, my two sisters and me. I don't know what happened to my cousins, and my aunt and uncle – the ones with the bicycle shop. A different group of soldiers ordered them out of the city. What about you?"

"I almost got split off from my whole family. I got ahead of them somehow, with one of my sisters and a cousin. Suddenly the road split ahead of us. My sister and my cousin just went straight. I told them we should wait for my mother – that if we didn't, she would have no way of knowing which road we took. But they wouldn't stop. I was only eight, and they were younger than I was – not old enough to understand what I was trying to tell them.

There was a roadside shed at the fork – you know, the kind that travelers use to get out of the sun for awhile. When the soldiers weren't looking I ducked into it and hid, and began to watch the road for my family.

But they didn't come – hour after hour after hour. My younger brother was just a toddler and my other sister was a baby, so I guess my parents couldn't go very fast. I just kept waiting, looking at every face that passed me on the road. And then the sun began to go down.

I knew I wouldn't be able to see them in the dark. The next twenty minutes were the worst in my entire *life* – worse than anything that happened to me in the camps. And then, I saw my grandfather's face... Or recognized the way he walked. Or *something*. I stole out of the shed and over to him, and took his hand. I'll never forget the look on his face – he'd thought he'd lost me, too.

My mother asked where my sister was. I told her what had happened, and that we'd catch up to her and my cousin eventually. But then a soldier shouted to us to go *left* at the fork, and waved his AK-47 at us. My mother stopped, and asked her two brothers to go ahead on the other road to look for her daughter. We sat on the side of the road, and waited. This was about six thirty.

Finally, at about ten o'clock, my uncles returned. Just the two of them. We never found my sister."

"I'm sorry, Nyah. Were you close to her?"

"No, because I didn't grow up with her. She lived in Phnom Penh with my mother the years I was in Prai Anchaan."

Puamaak shook his head. "If people had been able to talk freely after we'd all been relocated, I'm sure we would have heard many stories like that. It was mass confusion, and the soldiers waving their AK-47s and yelling at everyone made it even worse. I'm sorry, Nyah. But I'm glad you weren't close to her."

We rounded the corner into the Mekong safely and floated back to where we'd left the boat. I stole a pair of paddles from a house – one whose door was not hanging invitingly open. Then we pulled up lemon grass. The root was for the fish, and the leaves would keep the mosquitoes off – they don't like the smell. You just mash it up and rub it on your skin.

We pulled up the fish trap and put it in the boat, then made our way back to where we'd started out that morning. I sat down on the bank, and he set the trap in the canal. "We might get something by dinnertime," he said, "especially as there's still a current."

"How?"

"With the trap, of course."

"What kind of trap is it?"

"What do you mean, 'what kind of trap is it'? It's a fish trap."

"You mean your cousins didn't teach you about traps when they taught you how to swim?"

"What is there to teach, Nyah? You close the back of the trap and throw it in the water."

"What is this trap meant to catch?"

"*I* don't know. Do I *look* like I know? I have no idea."

I just rolled my eyes and then rolled backwards onto the bank, flinging my arms out dramatically. *"What did you cook last night?"*

"River flounder."

"So I guess it's a flounder *trap*, isn't it? And what do you have to do to catch flounder?"

"*I* don't know."

"You have to *bait the trap*."

"Bait it? With what?"

"With dead fish. Flounder are bottom feeders."

"You mean, you have to *have* fish to *catch* fish?"

"Yeeeeeees... And once the circle is broken – when you have no more fish to bait the trap with – you won't catch any more. Come on, pull it up. We can fool the fish by using slugs as bait."

He pulled up the trap and started to hunt for slugs. And I got up, to show him how to do it. I started rolling logs.

"Dead ones work the best," I said. "And the deader they are, the better they work. The fish can smell them."

Puamaak looked down at where the log had been. "Plenty of slugs, but no dead ones."

I was standing behind him and just rolled my eyes again. "Pick them up and hand them to me."

I spread the slugs out on a rock, in the sun. "Give them an hour. Believe me, they'll smell bad enough to catch us lots of fish. Don't look at me like that – *I'm* not killing them. The sun is."

He brought more slugs over and spread them out on the rock. "We need to catch as much food as we can today, Nyah. We have no idea how long we'll be out there on those marshes."

"Once we get the trap back in the water, I'll watch it. As soon as we catch something I'll take it out and clean it. We can re-bait the trap with the guts."

"So we don't have to waste any of the meat," he said.

"*Ah* – you're catching on. Tonight I can make jerky out of whatever we get, and roast our cassava with tamarind so it won't spoil as quickly. But, yeah, we're going to need a lot of food to get all the way across those mashes. More than we're likely to catch in the trap. And not little tiny stuff that we have to peel or pick off the bone, like crayfish and frogs. We're going hunting, my friend. We need to get the biggest thing we can get. And I know just what that would be."

"A *bull*? Nyah, I know you're not going after a bull."

"Think top of the food chain, my friend. A ferocious predator. And your very favorite food."

"*Snake!* But snakes aren't very big. We'd get a meal out of one, if we were lucky."

"Not just any snake, Puamaak. I'm taking about a King Cobra. If we can get one it'll get us through a whole week – they're about four meters long! And fat, too. I saw some boys in Pong Tuk get one; I think it was after you left. One of the boys in my first work camp got one, too. Yeah, just one King Cobra and we'd have enough food to get us all the way across the marshes. And probably all the way back to Pong Tuk. Think of the time we could make if we never had to stop to look for food. Think about it."

Now, I knew that one bite from a King Cobra would kill me in less than thirty minutes; there would be no chance of survival. But I was confident that I could get one simply because I'd seen other boys do it. And I could still picture the meat they got; it was as though I had a photograph in front of me. You cut a big cobra into steaks – they're lean, all protein, and easy to cook and eat. I knew how much faster that meat would get us back to Pong Tuk – and how much the protein would increase my friend's chances of making it at all.

But I had never asked myself why the only boys I'd ever seen get these big snakes were very young. The answer is quite simple. Had we all been older, we would have more carefully weighed the risk.

Day Four ~ *The Snake*

We were sitting on the bank of the canal in the breeze coming off of the marshes. We were making a couple of spears to hunt for our snake. It's very easy, if you have any kind of a knife. You just cut a two-meter length of bamboo – the thin kind – and sharpen one end to a point.

"The boys in Pong Tuk who got the cobra," I said. "They showed me just how you do it. As the snake runs away from you, you follow it and spear it through the back of the neck. Then you cut its head off with a 'kwaiw' – if you try to do it with a short knife you'll have to get too close, and it'll bite you for sure. Then you hang it up and let all the poison run out with the blood. Yeah, they showed me how to do everything. They said it was delicious, and it fed their whole family for a week. Cobras are out in the daytime, not at night, so this is just the right time to look for one. And remember – the trick is to follow it so you can get it in the back of the neck. They don't eat humans unless they can't get anything else, so it'd be going *away* from us."

"So where do we look for one?" he asked.

"Well, they live in stands of trees. That's another reason I hung our hammocks high up last night."

"That's not the cobra that spits poison, is it?"

"*No* that's the Indo-Chinese Spitting Cobra."

"But aren't we in… Indo-China?"

"Yeah, the spitting cobras are around, but that's not what we're after. Too small."

"Oh. OK."

"Tell me how you usually prepare your snake," I asked, now that I knew he could cook. "After you skin it and take the guts out, what do you do?"

"I just split a piece of bamboo almost all the way to the end, coil the snake up, insert it between the two halves of the bamboo, tie up the split end, balance the whole thing over the coals and roast it 'til it's done."

"You don't use any herbs, or seasonings, or anything like that?"

"Wait – let me send the maid down to the market… Nyah, we're in the middle of *nowhere.*"

"Exactly – we're in the *country*. *That's* where you get the best food. My family was always very particular. We grew the best varieties of vegetables and herbs on our farm, and didn't pick them until just before they went into the pot. We got the freshest fish from the Mekong. We got our pepper from Kampot – the same pepper that's shipped to Paris, to the finest restaurants. All our salt came from the sea. And everyone in my family could cook very well – even the men. I've spent a third of my life now under the Khmer Rouge, eating what we wouldn't even give to pigs before the war. Now you and I can get *fresh* food again, and we have the time to make it taste *good*. Yeah, that's *my* idea of freedom… Now you know I have to make jerky out of most of the snake, but for tonight I can take a big piece…"

"Yeah…"

"… slice it down to the bone"

"yeah…"

"… rub the inside with tamarind"

"yeah…"

"… stuff it with our roasted peanuts, a little coconut and some lemon grass root"

"yeah…"

"… then tie it closed with lemon grass leaves, wrap the whole thing up in a banana leaf and steam it in the coals. Six additional ingredients that we can get right here. And each will add a different flavor. But most importantly, if the snake is wrapped and steamed like that the meat won't dry out."

Puamaak closed his eyes. "I can almost taste it."

"Well we've got to get the snake first. Come on." I got up, and helped him to his feet.

"So do we look on the ground, or up in the trees? And what does a King Cobra look like? I've never even seen one."

"The one the boys in Pong Tuk got was black," I said, "with yellow bands around the length of the body. But the one the kid in the work camp got was olive green."

"You mean, they're not always the same color? Then how are you supposed to recognize one?"

"Flared hood, big fangs…"

"Oh. Yeah."

"You look for them on the ground," I said. "Look where they'd have a place to hide. There aren't any rock piles here, but there're logs. A pile of logs would be the best place to start. And look for holes in the ground."

We found a log here and a log there, but not a pile of logs. So we just looked around the biggest log. No snake, no hole in the ground.

"Let's roll it and look for giant centipedes, Nyah. You said there's a lot of meat on them."

"OK, you roll the log and I'll whack the centipedes. Just jump back after you get the log turned over – centipedes sting, and they're poisonous. But they don't move very fast, so you should be OK. *Damn* I wish we had shoes."

We rolled the log and saw a couple of baby centipedes burrow quickly into the earth. "Too small to bother with," I said.

We rolled a couple more logs, but all the centipedes were small. "This just isn't worth it," I said. "Let's keep moving back into the trees, to try to find a cobra."

We kept walking through the grove until we came… out the other side. We found ourselves in paddies.

By this time Puamaak had had some time to think about my commentary, 'They don't eat humans unless they can't get anything else'. Well, *we* certainly hadn't been able to get anything else. And we were, presumably, smarter than a snake. "Why don't we look for bullfrogs?" he suggested casually.

"OK. They have enough meat on them for me to make jerky. Let's go to one of the smaller ditches. We may have to reach into their holes to get them, but we'll get them if we work at it long enough." And figuring he couldn't tell a frog from a toad I added, "Just go for the green ones and the grey ones – leave the brown ones alone."

"What's wrong with the brown ones?" he asked.

"Cane toads. They're poisonous."

"Poisonous enough to kill you? Like the frog that almost killed your mother?" He started to watch his step again.

"Yeah, but cane toads only kill *greedy* people. So you and I would be OK."

"Nyah, that's ridiculous. Is that some kind of village superstition? You sound like the headman of Pong Tuk."

"Oh, no – it's absolutely true. They're poisonous, but only if you eat them. The farmer who shares with the rest of his family? He doesn't die – he just gets sick. But the farmer who *won't* share, and eats the whole toad himself? He's dead by morning. Because it takes one whole toad to kill a man. I saw it in the newspaper the year I had to live in Phnom Penh. Cane toads aren't very common, and in peacetime most farmers don't eat frogs because they have plenty of other things to eat. So you only hear about a case every once in a while. But you and I aren't greedy – we split everything we get 50/50. So we wouldn't die. But we *would* get really sick."

"But why not hunt in the main irrigation ditch?" he asked. "More frogs there – it's like shopping at the big Central Market in Phnom Penh instead of at the local open-air market in Prai Anchaan."

"Because that's where the people in the village," I tossed my head back toward the Mekong, "would have gotten rid of their UXOs from all the years of carpet bombing. I mean, they have to put them somewhere. So they dump them where people are least likely to walk. The main ditch always has some water in the bottom of it, so people don't walk there. But let me tell you what happened to me...

When I was seven, after the first of the skirmishes between the Khmer Rouge insurgents and the Lon Nol troops, my friends and I found an unexploded M-79 shell in one of the paddies on my grandfather's land. We were just kids – and *boys* – and we wanted to see it explode. So we took turns throwing it against a tree. There were four of us.

After a little while the people working the paddy realized what we were playing with, and told us to stop. To go bury it where other kids wouldn't find it. So I went to the main irrigation ditch, and then I went to the section furthest from the village – I did just as I was told. My friends followed me with the shell and waited on the bank while I climbed down into the ditch and started to dig a hole.

Suddenly, I heard a metallic *squeak, squeak, squeak.* I tell you, they did *something* to that shell. Then one of them threw it against a tree again. But this time... *BOOOOOOM.*

I looked up to see a fireball. And then... dead silence. Black ash started to float slowly to the ground – I remember it fluttered as it fell. It came down on my face, and I remember that it was very soft... Then my ears started ringing. I climbed out of the ditch and saw all three of my friends flat on the ground, unconscious. Blood everywhere.

Some of the villagers heard the explosion and came running. No one ever *ran* in Cambodia back in those days, unless we were being bombed – no one was ever in a hurry. But when they heard that explosion, let me tell you, they *ran*. It was my aunt who got there first because we were still on my grandfather's land. She grabbed me and was trying to say something to me, but I couldn't hear her. She hauled me back to a shed on one of the levies between the paddies – you know, the kind the workers use to get out of the sun at lunch. I tell you, she walloped me like I'd never been walloped before. She was so afraid that I'd do it again – and be killed the next time – that she didn't even know what she was doing. To her, I was her son. She and my grandparents raised me together.

Then she stopped whacking me and just squeezed the life out of me, sobbing. My hearing came back – or most of it. Yeah, that walloping was just what I needed. Because when I came out of that ditch and saw my friends, I went into shock.

We found out later that day that two of them had died, and the third had had part of his face blown off. I didn't even have a scratch. My grandfather said it was my good karma – I'd been doing exactly what the adults had told me to do."

"Your grandfather was right, Nyah. It was your good karma that saved you."

"Well, I was below the explosion and the fireball – I was about two meters down in the ditch. And because I was digging, my face was down. But I often wonder if it was my *bad* karma that saved me. My two friends – they died before the Khmer Rouge took over. They never had to go through all of what you and I have had to go through, in the camps and in the army. And they never saw their fathers taken away. They never knew that edginess that eats away at you every passing minute of every day after that – the nagging fear that the Khmer Rouge will come back, and take your mother. Or your grandfather. Or your aunt. Or *you*. You're never the same, after they've taken that first person away. Those boys who died – *they* were the lucky ones. Yes, I often wonder if it was my bad karma that saved my life."

"And you were just about to bury the shell," he said. "Another five minutes, and *no one* would have died. What kind of karma is that?"

"But I have to tell you why the M-79 shell was there in the first place. Why there was fighting in Prai Anchaan. When the Khmer Rouge guerillas were trying to overthrow the Lon Nol regime, the army decided to shell them from our village. And guess where they decided to shell them from? *Our school yard.* So when the guerillas returned fire, guess what they fired at? The shells that missed the schoolyard landed in my grandfather's fields. One of them was the one that killed my friends."

"So *that's* why your school was closed before the Khmer Rouge even took over. And that's why your grandfather moved the family into Phnom Penh – not just to get away from the fighting, but to get you back in school. But it was the Lon Nol army that got your friends killed, Nyah. Not the Khmer Rouge guerillas. That's the stupidest place I've ever heard of to put a gun emplacement – in a grammar school."

"Hey," I said. "I just saw something go into that hole. Over there. You take that one, I'll take this one."

I reached in, felt around, and came up with nothing. He reached in, yelled, and yanked his hand out – with a snake still attached to it.

"Stand still!" I shouted. "I'll get it off you! Stop jumping!" I grabbed his elbow and pinched the snake on either side of the back of its neck until it let go of him. He put his bitten finger in his mouth, and I cut the snake's head off.

"You would've been fine," I said, "if you hadn't just sucked out all the poison and swallowed it."

He yanked his finger out of his mouth, and I began laughing like hell. "Does that look like a cobra to you? *No hood.* It's a Water-lily Snake, and they're not poisonous. I've been bitten by one three times and I never even got an infection – it's not like getting bitten by a rat. But I'll make a poultice from tamarind for you, just in case. The acid will kill the bacteria."

He looked at the snake, and then back at me. "Good to eat?"

"*Yeah* they're good to eat. Why do you think I didn't just let it go?" I handed him his prize. "Go on – get the fire started." And I gave him my lighter.

I followed him back to our campsite and watched him as he skinned the snake. He knew just how to do it – you turn it inside out at the neck, and pull the skin off all in one piece.

Fortunately King Cobras are not common, and the few that there were at the beginning of the war had probably been hunted out. We never did come upon one, and ended up using the spears we'd made to catch bullfrogs instead. Good karma, that's all. Just good karma.

Day Four - *The Map*

"Nyah. You still awake?"

"Yeah."

"How come?"

"Same reason you are."

He paused. "We can't get through those marshes, little brother."

"I know."

It was about eight o'clock. We'd talked until seven, mostly comparing recipes for things our mothers had made. And I'd told him about all the different kinds of fish traps, and how you use each one. I just thought he should know.

"OK," he said, "let's run down the list. One – we just don't know how far we can take the boat. If the marshes get really shallow, we won't even be able to pole our way through. If we have to abandon the boat, we can't make it to the Bassac without shoes, long sleeves and long pants because of the saw grass and the clam shells. So we'd have to sleep out there. But there might not be any place high enough to sleep. Even if there were, we'd have trench foot before we finally made it out. And the mosquitoes – even with the lemon grass... Man, I didn't get past 'One' and we're already dead."

"There's something you haven't thought of," I said.

"Water snakes."

"They wouldn't bother us if we didn't bother them. *Think.* What would I be worried about, as Recon?*"

"No trees."

"*That's* our biggest problem, Puamaak. If there were trees we'd have a place to sleep – all we'd have to do is tie our hammocks up. We could even take a break in the middle of the day and get our feet out of the water. But what I'm most worried about is not being able to see where we are. We could be just fifty meters from a stream that would take us right into the Bassac, but never know it and slog through kilometer after kilometer of marsh instead. That's what happened in *The African Queen,* you know. They couldn't see where *they* were in relation to the lake they were trying to get to. But they got lucky – a rainstorm washed them right into it. Well, my friend, this is not Hollywood. There will be no rainstorm for us – we just had one. But even if we don't have to ditch the boat, once we lose sight of the Mekong, all we'll have to navigate by is the sun. So what happens if we have a really cloudy day? We could get totally lost out there. And then run out of food. Hey – you don't know how to navigate by the North Star, do you?"

"Are you kidding? We always had so much light in Phnom Penh that we could barely *see* the stars. People used to stay up late because it was so much cooler at night. My parents never ate dinner before eight o'clock – ever. 'Do you know how to navigate by the North Star'. Who do I look like – Galileo?"

We were both quiet again, the only sound the creaking of our hammocks.

"Nyah..."

"Yeah."

"We never asked ourselves what the retreating army would have done."

"They had no place to go, either," I said. "They would have had to cut straight through those marshes. But they had shoes, and long sleeves and long pants, and their AK-47s. And they had some food with them."

"They wouldn't have gone through the swamp, little brother. They would have crossed the Mekong at Neak Luong and then gone up Highway One to defend Phnom Penh. *If* they'd followed orders. If not, well, as soon as they were north of the marshes, they would have turned and run west. They would have ended up well south of the city. And don't even think about us trying that – if we didn't run into our own army, we'd run into Vietnamese."

And then he snapped his fingers. "*That's* where they got us from the Bassac to the Mekong over dry land. And by running west, the retreating troops who didn't go up to Phnom Penh simply retraced the route they'd taken to get to the combat zone. But we ended up further south, because we shadowed the lower part of the farm road."

"How do you know," I asked, "that the marshes end well south of the city? When we looked north from the top of the tree this morning we couldn't see the end of them."

Puamaak lowered his voice. "Nyah. I have a *map*."

I didn't say a word. He didn't have a map. Why did he think he had a map? I braced myself for whatever it was he was going to say next.

"Nyah – you still awake?"

"Yeah."

"I have a map in the same way that you have a schedule of when the moon will rise each night. In my *head*. My fifth-grade teacher put it there. The map is of the Water Glass. And the border is just south of it."

I still didn't say anything.

"I'm not crazy, Nyah. OK. The Bassac flows southeast from Phnom Penh – just a little. And the Mekong flows southwest from Neak Luong – just a little. The two rivers get closer and closer together as they flow south. And then, at the border, the Bassac takes a sharp turn east and runs halfway over to the Mekong. You can see it very clearly on a map, and it sticks in your head because the two rivers make such a distinctive pattern. 'The Water Glass', she called it. Actually, I thought it looked more like one of those Coca-Cola glasses we used to get in restaurants. Maybe that's why I remember it."

"Puamaak, Kandal is your home province, so your teacher would have spent a lot of time on it. She would have shown you the map over and over again, and pointed out the pattern each time."

He nodded in the dark. "She was a good teacher… Like the one who taught you how to make a compass. You've remembered that for six years now – *half your lifetime.*" He raised his brows and nodded again. "Good teacher."

"OK," I said. "So now you have a *map* of the swamp. But it's still a swamp."

"But it's a swamp in the shape of a Coca-Cola glass, little brother. OK. The top is just below Highway One at the western ferry crossing – just north of us. The bottom is where the Bassac runs west to east, instead of north to south. And that's where the marshes are the narrowest. We can't get *around* them, Nyah, but there's a much better place to cross them than up here. The bottom of the Water Glass. The swamp should be only a few kilometers across down there."

"So we just turn the boat around and shoot down the west bank of the Mekong?"

"Yeah," he said. "What do you think?"

"Now that we have real paddles, I think it's safe to try it."

"But think about this, too," he said. "The Bassac is the 'unknown' – you and I have only seen it once. When we had to cross it – me, to get to the war zone, and you, to get to the work camp you were telling me about. What if we cross the marshes up here, and then cross the Bassac only to find more marshes on the other side of it?"

"Wouldn't we have the same problem west of the bottom of the Water Glass?" I asked.

"I don't think so. The next province over is Takeo. Remember how many mountains there are in Takeo? I can't think of their names, but I remember that almost all of them are in the south. Like Phnom Da, the ancient temple site. So the landscape down there must be higher than it is up here. I think if we cross the marshes down by the border, the chances that we'll hit more marshes on the other side of the Bassac will be *much* less. So now we have two reasons to try to cross further south."

"It's a good plan," I said.

"Are you sure? You don't think it's good just because we're going back to the Mekong? That's like home to you, so you feel safe there."

"Hey – it's the only plan we've been able to come up with, so it's a *really good plan*. We're just lucky that you remember the map, and I know the Mekong. Because I sure as hell don't remember the map."

"You would if they hadn't closed your school before you got to the fifth grade. And I was in private school. Chinese school. Our curriculum was pretty much the same as yours, but I think we were a year ahead."

"My teachers concentrated on world geography," I said. "I can probably find my way to Tonga faster than I can to Takeo. But… why didn't it hit you this morning that we're in the Water Glass?"

"Nyah, do you realize that today was the first day since we were driven out of Phnom Penh that we got enough to eat? Your brain needs food to function, just as any other part of your body does. I think my brain switched back on sometime after dinner."

"And the longer you're free, the more will come back to you from all your years in school. I'll make a bet with you on that. Well, I don't have anything to bet you with, but as soon as I do, I'll bet you."

"Maybe it wasn't the food," he said. "Maybe, way in the back of my mind, I was trying to figure out how I got to the combat zone without crossing over swamp. Maybe *that's* why I finally remembered the map."

"Maybe it was both," I said.

"Well, we're not out of the woods yet. We'll have to get a lot closer to the border than I wanted to."

We continued to rock in our hammocks, neither one of us able to sleep.

"Nyah..."

"Yeah?"

"Doesn't it seem to you that every day is more dangerous than the last?"

"What do you mean?" I asked.

"It's just that we keep moving further away from the combat zone in Prey Veng, but things don't seem to be getting any safer."

"Yeah... Go on."

"Day One," he said, "we were in the mountains, and we thought that was the worst place we could possibly be because we were sandwiched between the Vietnamese and our platoon. Then we thought Highway One was the worst place we could be because of the minefield, and because we were spotlighted in the moonlight. Day Two we thought the west side of the combat zone was the worst place because we couldn't find food and water. Then we thought the east bank of the Mekong was the worst because we couldn't see the other bank, and we had no cover again. Then, on Day Three, we had to put in to the Mekong *twice,* then walk through a huge village at high noon. Only to find ourselves staring at 101 on the other side of it."

"And this morning," I said, "we saw the marshes. Which place do you think is really the most dangerous, of all of them?"

"The marshes, little brother. Think about it. In all the other places we were able to gain control. Maybe not of everything, but of enough things that we could get through. In the mountains we were able to use the tree cover, and we found food and water as soon as it was light. At Highway One I was able to feel my way through the minefield. After we left the lower part of the farm road, you were able to find food and water by following the sound of the buffalo. And then we were able to find a boat at the Mekong, and the village on the other side turned out to be evacuated. Then when we hit 101, you were able to get us under it. But in the marshes, I can't see that we can get control of *anything.* Anything at all. Even if we take food with us, it's like you said – if we get lost, we'll run out. We could *die* out there, Nyah."

"And we'd die slowly. Ha! *The African Queen* seems like a luxury cruise compared to what it would be like for us out there in that endless swamp. They had real food, and barrels of good water, they had a map so they knew where the hell they were, and they were able to get the boat all the way through. And it was a much bigger boat than ours, too. So they had a bunk to sleep in, with *blankets.* And a place to cook, a place to get warm, a place to dry their feet out, and a place to get out of the sun. They even had shoes, and more than one set of clothes... and *cognac.* Sign me up for *that* trip."

"Their boat had a motor on it, too," he said. "Even though it broke at some point. And there were no god-damn *cadres.*"

"Yeah. Good actor, good actress – made you think they were really in trouble, didn't they?" I rolled my eyes. "Hollywood."

"But how," I continued, "do we figure out where to get out of the river? I don't think the border's marked. We'll have to put in to shore north of it, but close enough to it to cross the marshes at the narrowest point."

"I have an idea," he said. "OK – why can't we cross the marshes up here? Because there's *too much* water to camp at night, but, because it's not monsoon season, there's *not enough* water to take the boat all the way through. So we need *less* water, or *more* water. As we go down the river we just keep looking at the bank on this side – more trees, less water; more canals, more water. When we find either one, that's where we get out."

"Yeah," I said. "Makes sense... Hey! I know how to find the highest ground around. It's my grandfather's method. And it's more reliable than using an American altimeter."

"What is it?"

"Where do farmers take their plow animals when the Mekong rises above all the grazing land?"

"Nyah, I'm not from the country, I'm from the *city*. That's my whole problem out here."

"OK, what was the highest ground in all of Phnom Penh?"

"Wat Phnom... Of *course* – we look for a *temple!*"

I nodded in the dark. "Always built on the highest ground around."

A Cambodian temple is not only built on the highest ground, it's built on a multi-level platform to make it even higher. Railings are built around each level of the platform, to make terraces.

"Never saw anything so funny in my life ," I said, "than the terraces of our temple in Prai Anchaan full of Brahmas and buffalo the last time we had a really big flood. And the monks trying to get around them to get into the temple for their six o'clock prayers. The things you miss in the city..."

Puamaak pictured a monk turning around to free his saffron robe from the long, sharp horns of a buffalo, only to be met with the glassy stare of the beast. He laughed, but the sound died far too quickly.

"Your grandfather's method would have worked four years ago, little brother, but it won't work now. All the temples were destroyed in '75. Whatever remains of the temples south of us won't be visible from the river."

"I'd forgotten that..." I sighed. "I wish the Americans had won their war with the Vietnamese. Then we wouldn't have to worry about the border, and could start moving west again *south* of all the marshes. Down in the Delta. And if the Americans had won, the Vietnamese wouldn't be *here*. And they wouldn't be *Communist*. One Communist regime is about to replace another – so we'll always have war. If we get back to Pong Tuk and our mothers aren't there, let's just go to Thailand."

"But Nyah, if the Americans had won, we wouldn't have been drafted and sent to the front to fight the Vietnamese. We'd still be *in a work camp*. With no way to escape."

"Oh... no, it'd be worse than that. It was the army that threw us together again. We'd be in *separate* work camps. Alone."

He shook his head. "I don't even want to think about that... But we've got to get to Kampot Province even to get to Thailand, little brother. To get to the ocean, so we could walk west along the beach. Well one thing's for sure – we'll get an early start tomorrow. We'll certainly be awake long before sunrise. Maybe we can get to the border while it's still dark. *I* might not be able to see, but *you* will."

"But we can't get out of our hammocks," I said, "until the sun's up, for the same reason we had to get into them so early. Held hostage not by an enemy soldier, but by a tiny little insect with a bayonet for a nose."

"Man, if it's not one thing it's another. Well, all we can do is take one day at a time. At least we know what we have to do tomorrow."

"We just have to be *sure* we don't go over the border, Puamaak. We'd be sitting ducks, in our little boat. We'd be captured for sure."

"No, they'd just shoot us... Don't think about it, Nyah. Don't think about anything. Go to sleep."

The map in Puamaak's head

Day Five – *The Messenger*

It was three in the morning, and we were wide awake. We were rocking back and forth in our hammocks telling stories, waiting for the night mosquitoes to go wherever they go for the day. We had about three hours to kill.

"There were bodies *all over* the beach," I said to Puamaak.

"No... *Really?*"

"Yeah. All lined up in rows. Like someone had dragged them out of the water and lined them up for quick removal. I couldn't understand why no one had come with trucks to pick them up."

"They were just *lying* there?" asked Puamaak.

"Yeah. And then one of them *moved*."

"Oh! I guess they weren't all dead then. But if you were only three, you weren't there by yourself..."

"I was with my grandmother," I said. "I was so scared I grabbed her hand and started to pull her away. And then you know what she did?"

"What?"

"She *laughed*," I said.

"Huh?"

"She told me they were French – and that *none* of them were dead. She'd been to Paris, you see, so she knew their customs. She said they just like to lie in the sun like that."

"All in rows... like how we dry our fish," he said.

"Exactly! And then every once in awhile they turn over."

"Like I said – just like how we dry our fish. You line 'em up on the beach, all the heads pointing the same way, and after a couple of hours or so, you flip 'em. They really lie in the sun like that? That's bizarre. Did she say why they do it?"

"She didn't know," I said, "but she said they were 'on vacation'. That they don't have to work all year long."

"They weren't farmers, then," he said.

"Well of course not – every farmer knows to get out of the sun when he doesn't have to work."

"Oh," he said, "I'll bet I know what they were doing. We dry fish to preserve them. I'll bet they were lying in the sun to preserve themselves. So they'd stay young longer."

"That's what I thought. But when I asked my grandmother, she said that's not it. She said the French are just... *strange*."

"Well, she'd been to Paris, so she would know. They must be very strange indeed."

"So how will we know," I asked, "if we've gotten too far south today?"

"Other than bullets whizzing over our heads? Look for *anything* that doesn't look Cambodian. People walking around in cone hats instead of 'kramaas', houses that don't look like ours, cars, trucks, or anything else that looks modern. Like a boat with an engine. Or buoys, or navigational signals – you know, like we used to see at the port in Phnom Penh. *Anything* that doesn't look Cambodian, we walk back up the bank until we're sure we're in Cambodia again."

"Signs!" I said. "If we see signs…"

He laughed. "But we'll put in to shore before we hit the border. Remember Nyah, all we need to do is find more water – more canals coming into the river – or less water – more trees."

"Well, we have enough food to last us two days. And that's not counting the peanuts. But I'm not leaving the fish trap behind until we have to ditch the boat."

"Yeah – the peanuts," he said. "Why didn't you stuff my snake last night? Like you were talking about – with tamarind, and lemon grass, and peanuts."

"Stuff your snake? It wasn't any bigger around than my thumb. I could have stuffed the peanuts with the snake."

"Well maybe we'll get a bigger one in the marshes," he said. "One of those huge Burmese pythons."

"Your spear wouldn't go into the neck, it would just push the snake under water. And you'd keep right on going, into the water – with the snake."

"Inertia. I'm glad we discuss these things… You know why you remembered how to spear a King Cobra and how to get the poison out? Because you so admired the boys who got the cobra in Pong Tuk. They were *heroes* to their families, to bring home that much food. We all wanted to be like that."

"But I got a beehive the next week," I said. "Full of honey. I'd already figured out how to provide for my family by the time they took my father away. I got a lot of stings, though, getting that hive for them. And after we finished the honey, we ate the bee larvae. Even more nutritious than snake! Oh, I forgot – we have another kind of cobra in Cambodia. The Monocled Cobra."

"You mean we have three different kinds?"

I nodded. "The King, the Indo-Chinese Spitting, and the Monocled."

"Well if I meet up with any of them, I'd rather it be the spitting one – at least it doesn't bite."

"Oh yes it does."

"You're kidding, Nyah. It spits *and* bites?"

"Yup."

"Is there anything out here that doesn't kick, gore, scratch, pinch, sting, bite or spit poison?"

"Nope."

He sighed. "You know, once the Vietnamese have solidified their control and things settle down a bit, maybe I can live in the city again."

"I can't imagine anything more boring. You guys have to go to the zoo to see a *cow*. In the matter of city life versus country life, of the two of us, I'm the expert. I'm the one who's experienced both. Let me impart to you my wisdom on the subject of city life, my friend.

Lesson One: Soot is not a spice. Yes, you get very good Vietnamese noodle soup in the sidewalk cafes around the Central Market, but the black sprinkles on top are supposed to be our world-famous Kampot pepper. They are in my soup in Prai Anchaan. But in your soup in Phnom Penh? Plenty of black sprinkles. Definitely not Kampot pepper.

Lesson Two: Why do you city people swerve your motorbikes through oncoming traffic like fish swimming upstream? We country people know where to drive, when we have to go into the city. Behind a Mercedes. Everyone makes way for a Mercedes. So you just cruise on through behind it.

Lesson Three: In the country, a person approaching you with his hand outstretched is trying to give you something. In the city, a person approaching you with his hand outstretched is trying to get *you* to give *him* something.

Lesson Four: In the country, mud has a purpose. We make bricks out of it – that's what your commercial buildings are made of. Water buffalo use it to keep themselves from overheating – without them, you would have no rice. Some of your most delicious food comes from it – like those succulent little mud crabs. But your city mud? It's just… *mud*.

Lesson Five: People in the country don't have to flip a switch to get a cool breeze. We just move out onto the balcony.

Lesson Six: The prettiest girls are not girls at all. Don't ask me to explain that one to you – I think you can figure it out. Every big city has them, and my grandmother told me she even saw them in Paris. They don't hurt anyone. On the contrary – she told me they were the most fashionable ladies she saw in all of France.

Lesson Seven: Women are not born with striped hair. I remember crossing the bridge over the Tonle Sap to go into Phnom Penh with my grandfather. On our side? Black hair. On your side? Striped hair. The bridge is less than a kilometer long, my friend – *you* tell me what's going on. No, don't tell me; I don't think I want to know.

Lesson Eight: In the country, we have prettier girls. Actually our village girls are just like the ones you have in the city, but ours take the time to smile at you."

"*Oh,* no, Nyah – I'm not giving you that one. You just don't understand. Our girls don't smile at you on the street, but they smile at you inside. Like when they take your order at a nice restaurant. Or show you where your classroom is the first day of school. Or give you a tour of the National Museum – some of them look just like the statues from our Golden Age. Oh, no, they smile at you, Nyah. They just don't smile at you on the street."

"Tell me about the striped hair…"

"It's called 'highlighting'. My sisters used to do it. They go to the pharmacy, you see, and they get this chemical…"

"Shhh! What was that!"

"An *owl,* little brother. Don't worry. Not every owl brings death. I mean, nothing happened after we heard the last one."

"No, but this owl is after something that's smelled our fish. And that something is either heading for our tree, waiting at the bottom of it, or already climbing it. Probably a snake. There are plenty of poisonous snakes in Cambodia besides cobras, and most of them can climb trees. I'll jettison the food."

I untied the 'kramaa' with the fish in it from the branch I'd hung it on. When it hit the ground I heard something scamper away through the underbrush. Whatever it was, the owl would get a nice meal out of it.

"Not a snake," I said. "I'll go down and get the fish."

"Hell, let's just get up and get going. Neither one of us will be able to get back to sleep. If we get out into the middle of the canal there should be enough of a breeze to keep the mosquitoes off. If not, well, we've got the lemon grass."

I helped him get out of the tree and we threw everything in the boat. We shoved off, toward the Mekong.

There was still a current running toward the river, and the breeze was at our backs – we made good speed down the canal. It was beautiful, in the moonlight. Little bats swooping back and forth for bugs, the stars the clearest I'd ever seen them, and the moon reflected in the water. You could forget it was a war zone, in the dark. But in less than a quarter of an hour we hit the twisted wreckage of the bridge. We continued on, to the Mekong.

I don't know what it was, but when we turned the corner it was as though someone turned a key in my head. Now I was looking straight down the river – and I knew just what we had to do. But we had to do it before the sun came up.

"Keep paddling," I said. "I want to keep us moving quickly." I didn't tell him what I knew.

"Look," he said, "that's the southern tip of the island we landed on the day before yesterday – I can just see the silhouette of it."

Islands in the Mekong are eye-shaped, with a point at the north and south ends. The river narrows where the islands widen in the middle, and then widens out again where the islands narrow at the points.

"Now," he said, "we must be almost in the main river again. Yeah, the current is picking up."

He turned around and looked at me – I could tell that he was afraid. I knew that all he could see was the shadows of the shorelines. I think, for him, this was worse than the minefield at Highway One. But he knew he just had to trust me – that's the only choice he had. I remembered that feeling of helplessness from the night on Highway One. And the day he'd told me they were going to put him into combat? That had been a thousand times worse.

So I just pretended that nothing could go wrong, and, knowing he couldn't see, told him what *I* saw. "We're past the island now. OK, just remember, if we come up on another one we want to stay to the right of it. But don't worry – I'll steer. And what's the plan if the boat capsizes?"

"We both swim back to it," he said.

"And just climb right back on. Easy." Yeah, if he could see it. Maybe this hadn't been such a good idea after all. I suddenly remembered my uncle and his friends talking about how dangerous the Mekong could be at night – even commercial captains moored their boats at sundown. But no, this was the only way we could do what we had to do. I knew I just had to trust in our karma – that's the only choice *I* had.

We were shooting straight down the river now. The banks squeezed the water between them, and we continued to pick up speed. I knew what he was thinking.

"No waterfalls south of the Lao border," I said. "And the river will widen out again, so the current will slacken. Always does." And by the time I'd finished my sentence, the river had widened again.

"Look," he called back to me, "another island. Much bigger than the one we landed on. So if we stay to the right the river should narrow, because we'll be out of the main river again."

"Not necessarily. The main river might be on this side this time. But it does look like it's narrowing – we should start going faster in a minute."

"I learned to swim in my cousins' village," he said, "but I never went down the river in a boat. Once you get used to it, it's sort of fun. After the war, I'm buying a boat."

Oh great, I thought, *I've done too good a job – now he's not afraid* enough. I wondered how much further we had to go.

We were parallel to the island now. We passed the southern tip of it, and I looked nervously to my left – due east. I just didn't want that sun to pop up yet. It looked as though I still had a little time.

"Can you see much on the western shoreline, Nyah? Either more trees, or more canals coming in? I think there are a lot more trees, don't you? The only trees on the shoreline where we came from this morning were right around where the canal emptied into the Mekong."

"Yeah, there are a lot more trees here, but they're not solid – there're trees, then a paddy, then trees, then a couple of paddies, then trees again... But you were right – we're definitely better off down here. Some of those trees might have fruit on them. We'll look when we get out."

"Do you see anything moving on the shoreline?" he asked. "The fisherman will be getting up just about now, don't you think? In my cousins' village they used to get up around 5:30 – about half an hour before sunrise."

"It's pretty much the same everywhere," I said. "I'll start looking for fishing boats pulling out into the river. As soon as I can see people, I can see if they're wearing 'kramaas'."

"But they could be Khmer Kraum – *in Vietnam.*"

"OK," I said, "if I see anything moving – anything at all – we'll pull into shore right away. Ditch the boat and walk north until we're sure we're in Cambodia."

"And if we find another canal, one that looks like it goes all the way over to the Bassac, and we've already ditched the boat?"

"We steal another boat," I said. "Have you been paying attention?"

He laughed. "OK. Hopefully the next one will be easier to get out of the muck than this one was. It's so waterlogged we could've cooked in it without a wok to hold the fire. Nothing could ignite this thing."

The river widened out, then narrowed again, then widened out again. But it was different down here – we couldn't see any more islands. The river narrowed again, and suddenly, we saw a solid wall of trees running down the bank.

"Look, Nyah – high ground! Let's pull in to shore."

"Not yet, comrade – not yet."

"Why?" He stopped paddling and turned around. "Nyah, you're *crazy* if you think we can go any further south. We've found what we were looking for, so let's get out of the river. Yes, this was my idea, but I don't know where the border is."

"You mean, *that* border?" I pointed straight ahead of him with my paddle. He turned around to look downriver, and I heard him suck in his breath.

"You can only see it at night," I said. "That's *electric* light. Look – it doesn't flicker. But as soon as the sun comes up, the border will disappear. Then, at sundown, it will appear again. I was trying to do what you said – get us as close to the border as I could so that the strip of marshes between the Mekong and the Bassac would be at their narrowest. It occurred to me when we pulled into the river this morning that if I looked for electric light, I could find the border. Come on, paddle left and we'll get in to shore."

I'll tell you, our timing was perfect, because dawn was just beginning to break. As the electric light that gave the border away began to fade, the first sunlight of the morning lit the western bank. And suddenly, I could make out a familiar pattern. A row of old trees on either side of a wide, dusty footpath, running inland from the river.

"Paddle hard!" I cried. "It's a good omen, I tell you. It's a sign from my grandfather that this is where we should cross the marshes. He knows that we're in trouble. *You* can believe that or not, but *I* believe it. Paddle hard!"

The current had already carried us past where the footpath met the river. We pulled in to shore, beached the boat, hid the paddles and started to walk back up the shoreline. As the rays of the sun began to warm the earth, the mist began to rise. It swirled around us in the breeze from the river.

We found the path and looked up it, through a tunnel of old, spreading trees. And suddenly, something flashed above the mist. *Gold.* And then we could see orange and green, too – the roof tiles of a temple.

But the Khmer Rouge had destroyed all the temples. How could there be one here?

We started up the path as though walking into the past. And as we got nearer and nearer to the flashes of gold and green, my friend started walking faster, and faster – afraid that it was all a mirage, and would burn off with the mist. Then he stopped, and looked back – waiting for me.

I remembered what it was that had set us on our way before dawn that morning. The only way we would have ever found the border. It was the owl. I wondered how many other signs my grandfather had sent me since we'd escaped six days ago. That I'd missed, because I hadn't thought to look for them. I wouldn't make that mistake again.

Day Five ~ *The Ruined Temple*

"Nyah! Pay attention! *Watch for mines!* We're right near the border – and they *always* mine the border. We traded one problem for another when we came south. I stopped as soon as I remembered; I won't go any further until you've caught up to me. Look – I'm on a concrete walkway now. You have only a few meters to go. *Look down* as you walk."

I'd been walking up the path just looking into the air. An abandoned temple is always eerie, even in the middle of the day. But in the mist, just before sunrise... the ghosts haven't even gone in yet. I thought they'd be floating about two meters above the ground, so that's where I'd been looking. I don't know why I thought they'd be *there*, but I did. I guess it's because my grandfather had told me that ghosts try to warn you of danger. Two meters would be just above my head – yeah, just the right height for a ghost to come talk to me. *If* he had anything to say.

The walkway led into the temple compound between two 'chaidey' – miniature pagodas, one for each of the temple's patron families, used to keep the ashes of all the generations of their dead together. My family's 'chaidey' had been in our temple in Prai Anchaan – the temple my grandfather and his forefathers had chosen to patronize.

I caught up to Puamaak. "Did you see any ghosts," I asked, "and did they come talk to you?"

I expected him to say, "What? Another village superstition?" But I guess he remembered my story about the cane toads; he just said, "No. I didn't."

As we came up the walkway we could see the orange and green roof floating on the mist, with a single golden water dragon slithering down the tiles. This temple had fared better than most; it was partly burned out, partly blasted out, but there was one corner wall left standing. The Khmer Rouge had obviously been interrupted in their work.

Temples are always the first casualty when Communists seize power, but in Cambodia, the Khmer Rouge had been particularly intent on knocking them out quickly. You see, they're seats of learning. Many a poor farmer has sent his son away to become a monk, not because either of them had any interest in religion, but because the father wanted his son to have an education. After secondary school, the temple would have been the only opportunity.

The temples had been destroyed just after our families had been marched out of Phnom Penh, but we hadn't been allowed anywhere near the one in Pong Tuk. So we'd never seen what the Khmer Rouge had actually done. Now, we found ourselves looking out over the ruins of what must have been a thriving monastic community. A school, with the monks' quarters next to it; the nuns' quarters, off in the distance; the kitchens, in a building by themselves; and a little shrine in the middle of a large, open plaza. All quiet, just when the monks should have been coming out of morning prayers.

And then we saw something from a dream – or, should I say, from a nightmare. The burned-out shell of the dragon boat the temple had entered into the races at Phnom Penh every year. The roof meant to protect it had collapsed on it instead. We turned to look at each other, but didn't say a word.

We were standing between the two 'chaidey' now. 'Chaidey' are constructed as commissioned, around the perimeter of the temple compound. The older the temple, the more 'chaidey'. If they complete a square all the way around the compound, the temple is very old indeed.

As we stepped out from between the 'chaidey' we could see that the square had been completed, but that the Khmer Rouge had blasted several 'chaidey' away.

"Do you know what it means," I asked him, "to have the 'chaidey' destroyed like this?"

"No. We just went to the temple for festivals. So I never knew much about it, except what my mother told me. We buried our dead in the Chinese cemetery. We didn't use a 'chaidey'."

"That's because it was your father's family that was Chinese, not your mother's; otherwise, it would have been the other way around. Your family would have gone to the Chinese pagoda, but had a 'chaidey' at your father's temple. It's always the mother who decides the religion of the children. So if the mother is Khmer, the family goes to the Cambodian temple – even if just for holidays."

"I guess after a few more generations we would have stopped using the Chinese cemetery and commissioned a 'chaidey' for our family. But actually that would depend upon whether I married a Chinese girl or a Khmer girl – I'm the only boy. I never thought about it before. Whoever arranged my marriage would be the one to determine which way my family would lean, in the generations ahead; toward the Chinese culture, or toward the Khmer culture. Oh, but I'll have to choose my own wife, if neither of my parents has survived. How would I do it? There's no way to meet girls in Cambodia. Maybe you could introduce me to one of your cousins... Nyah, I want to be sure I *always* have a family."

I nodded. I thought he was only fourteen, but I could understand why he was looking so far ahead. "Let's see who's left in the end. Your parents? My cousins? Let's see."

"So what *does* it mean, to have the 'chaidey' blasted away like this? That the ghosts have nowhere to go?"

"No, I think they just go back to where their 'chaidey' was and go into the ground or something. By destroying the temple the Khmer Rouge were trying to destroy religion, and education. But by destroying the 'chaidey', they were trying to destroy the family unit itself."

"Of course... but they weren't successful. I mean, look at us. We could have tried crossing the border at night, then taking the boat all the way down the Mekong – through the Delta, to the South China Sea – and then walked or paddled west along the beach to Thailand. And made a new life for ourselves there, in a *free* country. But instead, we're trying to get back to our families."

"The kids who've been brainwashed," I said, "they're the real victims – more than you and me. Because at the end of all this, we'll still have *some* relatives left. Maybe even our mothers. But those kids? They turned their backs on their families when the cadres and the officers told them to. They'll have no one at all."

"Like those dogs on the mountain who treed us our first day... How much do you want to bet the high-ranking officers don't do what they tell their underlings to do? They don't turn their backs on their families – they send them out of the country. And when all of this is over they'll just send for them."

"My parents were going to send me to France, when the carpet bombing got so bad. My mother came out to Prai Anchaan to talk to my grandfather. She was going to send all her children out. But I told them I wouldn't go – I wouldn't leave my grandfather. So she dropped the idea."

He nodded. "My parents had the same discussion."

"If we had only known... The Khmer Rouge tried to *annihilate* us 'new people'. All that talk of 're-education' – that was just a lie."

"Nyah, I think they wanted to leave just enough of us alive to grow their rice for them. Didn't want to get their own hands dirty. What kind of Communist equality is that? But they never calculated how many people they would *need* to grow their rice for them. With so many of us dead, who will feed them now?"

"The 'old people' working the communes can't do it by themselves, that's for sure. Yeah, the people who set up the system four years ago should have been trying to keep us *alive*. But they did just the opposite. I mean, look at the food distribution. They usually starved us, in the camps. But just after harvest season they brought in tons of food, and told us we could eat as much as we wanted to. They knew that people who've been starved will eat so much when they finally get food that they'll either get sick, or die. The first year I didn't know any better, and kept on eating even when I was full. I finally stopped when I started to have trouble breathing. But one of the other boys – he never stopped. All of a sudden he said he couldn't breathe, and the next minute, he fell over. The cadres told us later that he was dead. You remember, up on the mountain, you said we couldn't have escaped if it hadn't been right after harvest season – that the extra rations were what gave us the strength to run like that. If we'd still been in the work camps when the Vietnamese invaded, instead of in the army with a little more to eat, we might have eaten ourselves to death yesterday. The first day that we finally had enough food."

"Are you kidding? If we'd escaped from the camps, we would have been too weak to escape at all. We'd be lying in the dirt somewhere." He shivered. "Well, if we don't make it back to our families, we'll probably die. That's just the truth of it. So until we get back to Pong Tuk, let's just think about the problem at hand. There might be a road from this temple over to the Bassac. We won't know until we've had a look around."

The compound had been cemented over at some point, probably to keep the dust down during dry season. So there would be no mines – we could move around freely.

We walked out onto the plaza from the perimeter marked out by the 'chaidey', climbed the terraces to where the main temple had stood, then slid into the shadow of the one remaining corner wall. We looked over to where the statue of the Buddha should have been – now just a pile of rubble. I saw one eye, lying on the floor. I walked over to it and just looked at it, mesmerized by the staring pupil against the swirling pattern of the mosaic floor beneath it.

Suddenly, I could feel a presence behind me. And then I heard someone whispering – the sound was as soft as the mist around me. "Pick it up, Nyah. It isn't right to leave it on the floor."

I reached down and picked up the eye, without really knowing what to do with it. I looked for a proper place to put it. A high place, as a show of respect for the Buddha. I finally set it on the highest spot I could find – a shelf that had once held an oil lamp. I turned around, but the presence I'd felt behind me was gone. *A ghost,* I thought. *I wouldn't have been able to hear a living person whispering that low. But... he knew my name. Oh, of course...*

I suddenly remembered where I was. And who might be watching me. "I could be shot for that, you know."

But just as I'd remembered where we were, Puamaak had remembered, too. "Oh my *god!* We're right in the middle of a village! We need to be sure it's been evacuated. Why didn't I think of that before?"

We both walked slowly back to the corner wall and slid behind it. We looked out over the landscape, toward where we thought the village should be.

We found ourselves on the highest terrace on the south side of the temple. We looked over the southern row of 'chaidey' only to see jungle on the other side. Except that it wasn't quite jungle – there was a pattern to it. It was what was left of the monks' garden.

"So the village is on the north side," whispered Puamaak. "I'll go over there, and hide, and just listen for a few minutes. This is the time of day when people are making all kinds of noise, getting ready for the day ahead. And you go back to the east side of the compound and look down the footpath out to the river. Look for fishing boats. Between the two of us, we should be able to tell if this area has been evacuated. Meet back here in twenty minutes."

We met back at the corner wall half an hour later, each with an armload of firewood and kindling. Neither had to ask the other if he'd seen or heard anyone – if either one of us thought the area hadn't been evacuated he wouldn't have bothered to collect the firewood. And we'd gotten all of it from what had fallen onto the cement in the last four years. The villagers would never have risked coming here.

"There's no road running west, Nyah. Only 101, going up to the ferry. No, there's nothing coming up it. But since we're so much higher here than where we were this morning, I'll bet we'll be able to find dry levees to walk on." He started to pass me firewood and kindling, and I began to build our fire.

"Show me how you do that," he said. "I've never seen anyone make a fire the way you do."

"I used to go with my grandfather to our outlying fields – too far away from the house for us to come back for lunch. So he'd have to reheat our food out there. First, you dig a hole about thirty centimeters across. Then you dig a forty-five-degree trench on each side of it. Then you put the kindling in the hole at about a 30-degree angle, and light it up. Then you feed sticks in through the trenches. You know how a candle burns faster if you tip it until it's almost upside down? Same principle with the kindling and the sticks – they burn faster because they're at an angle. And a crossdraft starts up through the two trenches. You just sit back and wait until you have coals, after that. But think about it – the faster you can get your coals, the sooner you can put your fire out – less chance that someone will see it. But the biggest advantage of doing it my grandfather's way is that, if there's a big gust of wind, your fire doesn't spread and get out of control – because it's down in the hole. That alone can save your life. Well, I can't dig a hole in the concrete here, but if you can pass me some big chunks of rubble, I can make a circle out of them instead. Oh, and we have *fresh* fish this morning. There were fish in the trap when I pulled it up. We can save the smoked food."

"*Fresh* fish?" He smiled. "You were right, little brother – your grandfather's looking out for us. I can't wait to meet him – he must be a very *powerful* shaman. We're going to have a good day today. Ha! We'll be over to the Bassac and across it by sunset."

While we waited for our fire to burn down we looked over what was left of the monks' garden. The trees looked liked they'd been scorched in '75, but not burned – as though a rainstorm had swept though after the fire had been set. Perhaps that's why there was a corner of the temple left standing. Perhaps a storm had sent the Khmer Rouge scurrying for cover, and the rain had put out the fire.

"Look for bananas, guavas and papayas,' I said, "Yellow, green and orange." We had plenty of fish, frog and cassava, but nothing that would help Puamaak regain more of his night vision. I tried to imagine what it must have been like for him, feeling his way through the minefield on Highway One. He might not have the survival skills that I did, but I'll tell you, he had guts. I think that's why he was able to lie so well. I think lying takes the most guts of all.

"Looks to me like all the fruit's gone," said Puamaak. "No vegetables, either. There's a banana blossom over there, but it's not worth risking hitting a mine. How are you going to get to a tree to do your recon? The thing about mines is, they're not always in any kind of a logical place. When you have your commanding officer yelling at you to lay them faster you just put them... anywhere."

"The roots of the trees along the path we walked in on are so old they're popping out of the ground. We can walk on top of them to get to a recon tree, and then back out to the river. Then we can find a levee to walk west on."

We ate our fish and quietly retraced our steps out of the compound and over to one of the old, spreading trees. I climbed a couple of stories up, and came down with my report. "You'll never believe this. We thought, with the trees and the temple here, that this area would be drier. It's the opposite – it's *wetter*. Because we're in the bottom of the Water Glass. It looks to me like we can get all the way to the Bassac in the boat! There's a canal just south of us, running through the marshes. And then beyond that, there are lakes."

"So the land this temple was built on is probably a man-made hill. Like the hill that Wat Phnom stands on, in Phnom Penh. Hey, if you don't have a high point to build a temple on, you just make one. Khmer engineering at its finest."

"By taking the canal we won't have to worry about mines, we can keep the boat and the fish trap, and we won't have to walk today." I just shook my head and laughed.

"Nyah, that canal's not in Vietnam is it?"

"Nope – no boats on it. It's in Cambodia. But barely, judging from where we saw the lights this morning."

Puamaak started for the river, but I hung back a moment. I turned and looked behind me – I wanted to pay respect to the Buddha. Because it was he to whom we owed the good karma that had caused my grandfather to lead us to the canal. Because it was he who had taught us about the law of karma, and to make good karma instead of bad.

The Buddha is not a god, but a perfect human being – one who has reached enlightenment. He learned how to become enlightened by studying Hindu meditation and ancient scripture, taking from it what he could, and then boldly experimenting on his own. When he reached enlightenment he decided to remain on earth to teach others how to do it, instead of escaping the cycle of death and rebirth right there and then. That was a great personal sacrifice; that's why we pay respect to him. But we don't ask him to do things for us, because he taught us that we have to make our own good karma to get what we need in life. We don't thank him for his sacrifice, either – I don't know why, but we don't. Instead, we chant a prayer three times, aloud: "Namo tassa bhagavato, arahato, samma sambuddhasa". This chant is in Pali, an ancient Indian language similar to the Buddha's mother tongue, and the one he usually spoke when teaching – it's a cousin to Sanskrit. The chant means, "Honor to you, the illustrious one, the venerable one, the fully-enlightened one". I didn't say the chant aloud that morning, standing on the old path to the river. But I said it.

I caught up to Puamaak. "There are double the ghosts here now," I told him, "than there would have been before the war. The ghosts of the ancestors of the patron families who commissioned the 'chaidey' are here, of course. But there would have been scores of monks and nuns and students living in that compound. And the Khmer Rouge would have killed all of them. Yes, there are many spirits here. Did any of them talk to you, after I asked you the first time? Did any of them try to warn you of danger?"

"No. Did any of them come to you?"

"None of them tried to warn me, so I think we'll get to the Bassac OK."

He nodded. "If the ghosts had anything to say to us, they would have said it."

We walked in the water back to the boat, put our gear in and recovered the paddles. We turned back for one last look at the temple – I think I said one last prayer. And then we pushed off, to cross the marshes.

Day Five - *The Omen*

Now, I've told you about the Festival of the Rowing of the Boats that's been celebrated in Cambodia for a thousand years. But what's a thousand years, in such an ancient land? Let's go back *another* thousand, to what was there before – the bustling commercial enterprise known as Funan. Where goods were traded between Europe and Asia through a strategic port in the Mekong Delta, Oc-Eo.

The people of Funan built a web of canals to bring export goods into the port from the north – rhinoceros horn, exotic woods, cardamom and other spices, kingfisher feathers, ivory, *gold...* even elephants. I can tell you that Roman coins have been found at the port, and Indian commercial seals, too. But as to who was buying the elephants and how they were transporting them, that I can't tell you, my friend.

So, unbeknownst to us, we were now in the oldest part of Cambodia. But actually, we'd been there all along. The mountain on which our platoon had been holed up? That was Ba Phnom, believed by some to be the ritualistic center of Funan two thousand years ago. And the canal that we were headed for? A thread in that ancient web of mercantile canals.

The traders built a trunk canal to connect Oc-Eo with Angkor Borei, a town just west of the Bassac. Angkor Borei eventually became the capital of one of the principalities that succeeded Funan and preceded Angkor – Water Chenla. Jayavarman VII made Buddhism the state religion in the middle of the Angkorian era, but, before his time, this area was Hindu. The people built a beautiful little temple on a small mountain near Angkor Borei – Phnom Da. And in the early years of the Angkorian era they built another one, right on the top of the mountain.

Now, it should have occurred to me that we were in what used to be Funan and Water Chenla when I'd climbed the tree at the temple and seen a land of... water. But it hadn't, and here we were, drifting down the Mekong watching for the spot where the canal connected to the river.

"We need to make rollers," I said, "in case we have to port over a low spot or a dike. There won't be any more bamboo until we get over to the Bassac. And we should reinforce the bow rope – we may have to pull the boat at some point."

We spotted a grove of bamboo ahead of us and paddled over to it. I cut down two trunks, trimmed them and cut them into rollers while Puamaak cut a length of vine to repair the bow rope. We didn't even have to get out of the boat.

We switched places, and I began to reinforce the bow rope.

"Little brother, is there anything we've needed out here that you haven't been able to make?"

"What'd I make?"

"The bamboo ladder to get up your first reconnaissance tree, the banana-stalk scabbards (which were really life preservers – I knew what you were doing), the scoops we bailed the boat with, the roller we used to get the boat up the east bank of the Mekong, our first pair of paddles, the clamps we used to cook our fish and make our jerky, the banana-leaf linings for our hammocks, the spears to get a cobra, and now more rollers, and rope." He peered over my shoulder. "Where'd you learn how to do that?"

"I used to make the neck ropes for our Brahmas' cowbells. The rest of the stuff was easy – you just have to know what kind of bamboo to use. Some kinds are thick, and virtually unbreakable; the ladder I made was just like the ones we used to put on our coconut and sugar palms. Other kinds are easy to split, or flexible and easy to bend. And then there's the kind I used to make our spears – very thin, and rigid. Banana trees, well, they're all about the same."

"I remember my mother," he said, "complaining to my father about his Chinese friends calling the Khmer 'primitive'. 'We are not *primitive*,' she would say. 'If you have the materials and skill to make what you need, it makes a lot more sense to make it than to buy it.' But he was from a long line of merchants – he couldn't see it her way. Oh, you wouldn't have wanted to be there the day they had *that* discussion..."

I smiled as I continued to plait the rope. "When we lived in Prai Anchaan, my grandfather made just about everything we needed. He was an exceptional basketmaker – he could make any kind of basket my grandmother could ever want. He made her cooking pots, too, and fired them in a kiln he'd dug in the ground. He even made our Brahma carts, and our wooden plows – he'd buy the metal blade from the blacksmith, but he'd make all the other parts himself. And although he wasn't a fisherman he could make any kind of fish trap, or mend any type of net. He even made our bomb shelter without any concrete."

"I wish he were here now," he said, "to make us one of those little melon-sized fish traps you were telling me about . We could take it with us after we ditch the boat." He peered over my shoulder again. "You're left handed?"

"Of course not," I said, without looking up. And, of course, I was. But I had quickly switched to my right when my teacher had whacked my left the first time I picked up a pen.

So now it was *I* who deftly turned the subject. "But you know, if we were in Germany like the guys in The Great Escape, I wouldn't have been able to make any of those things. No bamboo, no banana trees, no heavy vines..."

"Yeah," he said, "if they'd needed a ladder they would've had to 'borrow' one. And as for 'borrowing' a boat – all the boats would have been padlocked. But actually, if this were Germany, we wouldn't need anything at all."

"What do you mean?" I asked.

"We would have frozen to death our first night, on the mountain!"

"Puamaak – we just about did."

"OK," he said, looking over the contents of our boat. "We have two days' supply of smoked fish, smoked frog and roasted cassava."

"But we have nothing for your night vision. Once we get into the lakes, look for white morning glories floating on the water. I can cook the vines up tonight. Lots of vitamins for you in those dark green leaves. And we can get some snails. Easy to catch – you don't have to chase them around. Even *you* could get some."

"Very funny," he said. "But why don't we drop the trap every time we stop?"

"OK. We won't get river flounder in the marshes, but we might get other bottom feeders. Maybe even *crabs*... Get some more vine and I'll tie the trap to the stern. Actually, that's what I should have done in the first place – if we'd capsized this morning, we would have lost it."

"Who taught you about the river," he asked, "and how to handle a boat? It wasn't your grandfather; he was a farmer."

"My oldest uncle. But he didn't teach me the way our teachers taught us in school. That's the French way. He let me watch how he did everything, and then let me ask questions. That's the Cambodian way. That's how I learned to cook, too – my aunt let me watch her. So did my mother. How did you learn to cook?"

"From my mother, the Cambodian way. And from my father, the Chinese way."

"What's the Chinese way?"

"'Pay attention, and don't ask questions!'"

I laughed. "Yeah, I had another uncle who didn't have the patience of his older brother. But he didn't know as much, either, so I didn't mind not learning from him."

"He didn't know as much," he said, "because he didn't have his brother's patience."

"Guess so. Never thought about it. But he'd had a head injury – I think that had something to do with it. Hey – tie your 'kramaa' around your head to keep the mosquitoes off." I emptied my pack into the boat and wrapped my 'kramaa' into a turban.

He looked at me and shook his head. "Khmer – dead giveaway. Even from a distance. If we get into Vietnam by accident, or if you see anyone at all, take your 'kramaa' off and hide it. Don't even bother to unwind it – just *rip it off*. No 'kramaa', no way to tell if we're Cambodian or Vietnamese."

We drifted the rest of the way down to the canal and I turned us into it. "You know what we should be carrying with us?" I said. "Marijuana. It grows wild – start looking for some. Most of the medicines my grandfather made were teas; if one of us gets hurt the other can make a tea from the marijuana leaves, to ease the pain. I'm not sure if it will work, but we can try it. Look for tamarind, too."

"OK," he said. "Oh – brace yourself for finding bodies. The people in the village we just came from had to go *somewhere,* and they probably did just what we're doing. If a child or an elder died from the trauma of the evacuation, they would have had to roll him over the gunwale and just keep right on going."

We found ourselves paddling through an orchard, but these were all tall trees – no banana, papaya or guava. In a few minutes, though, we came up on a tamarind. Puamaak pulled on some reeds to get us over to the bank, and I climbed the tree and got all we'd need.

In a few minutes he turned back to me and pointed to a low bridge in front of us. He held up his index finger and mouthed the word, 'one'. Then he made a circle with his thumb and index finger and mouthed the letter, 'o'. Then he held up his index finger again and mouthed the word, 'one'. We slipped under the bridge without a sound, circumventing the minefield exactly as we'd done two days before – except much further south.

We paddled on and finally hit the dreaded marshes, but the canal took us right on through them. Now we were in a lake, with a light wind blowing across it – enough to keep the mosquitoes off.

"You think the canal we just came out of continues," asked Puamaak, "on the other side of this lake?"

"I don't know. Not a tree to climb anywhere. We might as well be in the Sahara. I'd guess we just go straight west to pick it up again. The wind's not enough to blow us off course."

We paddled on across the lake and picked up the canal again. Someone had stuck a stick in the bank and had tied a piece of an old rice sack to it; it was the flapping that had caught our eye. "So *this* is how they mark the canals," said Puamaak. "We'll see more of these flags."

We paddled on for another couple of kilometers or so and hit a river that ran north / south. But it wasn't the Bassac – it was too small. We crossed it and beached the boat on the bank.

"You look for morning glories," said Puamaak, "while I take a look around." And he headed north, up the bank.

I baited the fish trap and dropped it, then walked to the top of the bank and looked out over... another lake. We could probably port the boat if we had to, but the bank was steep, the boat was heavy, and all we had were my homemade rollers. So I headed north to look for a better portage – and my friend.

Well, it seemed he'd disappeared. I looked over the bank again, to see if he was swimming in the lake. Nope. Swimming in the river? Nope. This was not a good idea, splitting up. Not a good idea at all.

I walked a little further north and saw a tree ahead of me. There was quite a racket going on in it. A couple of birds flew out, and then I heard... *swearing.*

"Can you get down?" I asked.

"Yes, although head first or feet first I have yet to tell you." He climbed down, feet first. "There's a split in the bank south of where you beached the boat. We won't have to port over."

"You're Recon now?" I asked. "Make me Navigation and we'll end up back at the mountain."

"I knew I didn't have to get up very high. I thought I could do it, and I did. Tired of feeling helpless, that's all."

We returned to the boat, pulled up the trap, put back into the river and paddled south to find the split. I tell you, it couldn't have been easier to spot if someone had sent up a flare; there was a sea of lavender flowers on either side of it. "You didn't see these from the tree?" I asked.

"See what?"

"The morning glories."

"You told me to look for white flowers, Nyah."

"That's the Cambodian kind. This is the Vietnamese kind. We never got them in the markets in Phnom Penh because they taste just like the Cambodian kind, and that was always available."

He leaned over the gunwale and started picking vines. "So how did you *know* that?"

"Know what?"

"That the Vietnamese kind has purple flowers. You've never been to Vietnam in your life."

"My uncle told me," I said. "The one who taught me how to handle a boat. And took me on the fishing trips. Oh, but I never told you about those…" I took over picking the vines, and Puamaak settled back into the bow seat to hear my story.

"I was always my uncle's favorite, and he took me on fishing trips with him. Just the two of us. We'd paddle all day, to the prettiest spot we could find – just as many fish there as at the ugly spots. We'd anchor, and then we'd cook dinner on the boat. Then we'd reel his net out for the night. We'd go to sleep on the deck, counting shooting stars. Then I'd wake up early, as I always do, and get breakfast started. He'd wake up to the smell of jasmine rice and Chinese tea. Then we'd reel in the net, and it was always full of fish! He'd pick out the little ones for our breakfast, and while he was cleaning them, I'd lean over the gunwale and pick morning glory vines. And then we'd cook everything up. We'd start for home when we just couldn't eat any more. The Vietnamese and the Chinese call Cambodians lazy, but life was easy back then. If your net fills up with fish all by itself, what else do you have to do?"

"Sometimes we had Vietnamese houseboats pass by our house," I continued. "They used to come up the Mekong from the Delta and pass by the boardwalk in Phnom Penh. Most would go up the Tonle Sap River to the Great Tonle Sap Lake, to fish in there. But some would pass the Tonle Sap River and come up the Mekong as far as Prai Anchaan. Some even had a gigantic fish cage underneath the boat, with a hatch in the deck to get into it – so if they didn't catch any fish that day, they could take some from under their boat. They used to pick morning glory vines from the deck, just like we did. So you see they never ran out of food, and they never had to come in to shore for it. I don't think they liked going into the city, either. I think if you're not born there, you never learn to like it."

Puamaak leaned forward to take the vines from me. "I wonder what the Vietnamese army will find left of Phnom Penh? Must look like a ghost town. I remember the market that my mother liked the best. All kinds of fresh seafood just waiting for you when you walked in the door. Her driver would take her every morning, in her white Mercedes. But if she was too busy to go herself, she'd send her maid. Yeah, my mother could cook all of the meal herself, or part of it, or none of it – because she also had a cook. So how do you cook morning glory vines?"

"Tonight I'll make a soup," I said, "with the leaves and the stems from the tip of the plant, and some clams and snails. We can eat it with roasted cassava. You know, I'm sure you've had morning glory vines before. It's just that they take the flowers off before they cook them, so you might not have known what they were. They usually dip them in boiling water for a couple of minutes – not longer, or you lose the color – then braise them with garlic."

"Oh! We used to eat those all the time. But I'll look around for something we can substitute for the snails and the clams – we won't be able to get any without cutting our feet up."

But I was already tying some of the morning glory vine to the bow rope, to make it longer. We paddled through the split, I steered us back into shallow water, and I tied the end of the bow rope around my waist. Then I carefully slid into the water.

"Nyah, what are you doing?"

"Watch."

I floated on my stomach and felt around on the bottom with my fingers. After a few minutes, I pulled up a snail the size of my fist. I held it up so my friend could see it, then put it in my pocket. After a few minutes, I got another. "A snail each!" I called back to him. Then I got us some clams the same way I'd gotten the snails. "A dozen apiece! That's all we'll be able to eat today." I swam back to the stern, untied the bow rope from around my waist, and hauled myself back into the boat.

"So that's how you get clams without cutting your feet to shreds," he said. "And snails, when the water's so murky you can't see them. And you could pull the boat wherever you wanted it to go just by swimming. But... your fingers." I held them out in front of his face, and smiled. "Nyah, why didn't your fingers get cut up on the broken clam shells?"

"There was no *weight* on my fingers."

"Oh. Of course."

"Country people learn to improvise when they're very young."

"Are all your cousins as clever as you are?" he asked.

"Well, my oldest uncle's son..."

"No, I mean the *girls.* And are any of them pretty?"

"*Yes,* if there's no one to arrange a marriage for you when you get older, I'll see what I can do... You're not planning to get married at fourteen are you?"

"No, Nyah. I'm just thinking ahead."

"Well be sure to wait until you're taller than four-foot-eight. I mean, we want the wedding pictures to come out nice..."

"Very funny. But you didn't answer my question. Are any of them *pretty?*"

"The prettier they are," I said, "the less likely they're going to want to marry *you.* Ha! It's going to be up to me which one you get, isn't it?"

I wrapped my 'kramaa' into a big, round turban – like the fortune tellers on the boardwalk do. Then I stuck a morning glory behind my ear and pretended to read the cards.

"I see... a boy with a Khmer smile and Chinese eyes, talking to another boy, about four-foot-six... I see a chubby girl with brassy hair... no... now I see a new Mercedes, with the shorter boy at the wheel... and a very *pretty* girl!" I burst out laughing.

He ripped off my 'kramaa' and stuffed it into my mouth. "That's what your cooking tastes like."

"Well I don't see you turning any of it down. And I want a *green* Mercedes."

"A *pretty* girl, or all you'll get is a tractor."

I pretended to read the cards again. "Now I see a pretty girl – who can't even boil an egg!"

He rolled his eyes and handed me my paddle. "But how are we going to keep our food alive until we can cook it?"

"The compartment that runs along the keel," I said. "That's for keeping fish alive."

"In this heat? They'll be dead in an hour." He picked up the fish trap, lined the cage with the morning glory vines, and poured the snails and the clams into it. Then he lowered the trap over the gunwale and tied it right in tight to the stern. "City people can improvise, too – especially Chinese."

We continued on, and I made sure to steer us straight west. After an hour or so we could see land ahead of us. And another canal flag.

The 'land' turned out to be a long, narrow island, and the canal went right on through it. Now we were in... another lake. We paddled across it and came to another island, and then *another* lake.

Puamaak turned around from his place in the bow. "The bottom of the Water Glass."

"If it hadn't been for your geography class, we'd still be staring at the swamp up north."

He shook his head. "It wasn't geography class, little brother. It was *history* class. Have you ever seen so many kilometers of canals as you have down here? Anywhere?"

I shrugged my shoulders. "They grow a lot of rice around here – somewhere."

"You farmers just assume that every canal you see is an irrigation canal. But I see things with a merchant's eye. The dry season is just beginning; these lakes must dry up to marshes at the height of it. And that's when they would have dug the canal we came in on. But they would have continued it right on through the marshes so that they could always get a boat through to the Bassac. So every time we've been in a lake, we've been paddling over the top of the canal. And it's perfectly straight – I could see it from the tree I climbed when I was looking for the split. A direct route for getting from one river to the other. *With cargo.* And this canal will meet up with another – one that connects this area with the Delta. And the Delta connects to the sea. Am I getting through to you?"

"Oh... we're in what used to be called, 'Water Chenla', I said. "Not too hard to figure out how they came up with that one, eh?"

"You know, your ancestors were probably some of those ancient traders. They probably came from the Delta."

"Really?"

"Yeah," he said. "Their children's children would have slowly made their way north up the rivers, each generation a little further than the last. Until they reached Prai Anchaan."

He was right. They would have had two routes they could have taken – the Mekong or the Bassac. The Bassac would have been shorter. If they'd gone up the Bassac to where the Royal Palace is now, and then gone up the Mekong instead of the Tonle Sap, Prai Anchaan would have been only two hundred and ten kilometers from Oc-Eo.

"My grandmother's father was a trader," I said. "I'd forgotten that... Well if my ancestors were from the Delta, they traded with the people who traded with *your* ancestors. The Indians who came east to the Delta were on their way to China."

"If they didn't go on to China – if they wanted to just take the goods they got here and go back home – they had to be sure the conditions in the ocean were right for their journey. Sometimes they had to wait for *months*."

And in those months ideas went back and forth between the Indians and the Khmer, and came right up these canals. That's why we Cambodians do so many things the Indian way. Like eating only with our right hands, making turbans with our 'kramaas', and elevating our monks and our teachers to the highest positions in society. We adopted one of the South Indian alphabets to write our language down (but then we changed the letters a bit). We even use fresh cow dung like they do in India, to line our threshing floors and kilns. But that only makes sense – it must have been from the Brahmins that we got our Brahmas, don't you think? The Indians brought us Hinduism, too, and Hindu architecture. We continued to build our temples in a Khmer style, but we adopted an Indian form – just look at Angkor Wat.

"And what do you think the Indians did," asked Puamaak, "while they were waiting to go back home? Besides chit-chatting with the locals."

"I don't know."

"When was the last time you looked in a mirror? Your *nose,* Nyah. It's not Khmer – it's Indian. *That's* what made me think that your ancestors were from here."

I had to admit he was right. Most Khmer who met me didn't realize that I was Khmer until I opened my mouth.

"And I wonder," he continued, "if the reason your grandfather knows so much about medicine is that he's descended from those ancient people in the Delta. I wonder if some of what he knows originally came from India. You know, growing up in Phnom Penh, we used to hear about the village shamans. We called them, "witch doctors". But it was your grandfather who brought you through when you were a baby, when the doctors in the French hospital said they couldn't save you. And he saved your mother's life when she brushed up against the horned frog – I don't think those French doctors could have done that. So at least *some* of his medicine works. And it came from *somewhere,* little brother. Maybe all of it's Khmer, or some is Khmer and some is Indian, but I'll bet you a lot of it came over on the trading ships from India."

I didn't know even the smallest fraction of what my grandfather knew of Khmer medicine, and I knew nothing of Ayurvedic medicine, but I wondered if my friend might be right.

"There are canals in eastern Takeo, too," he said. "There's one that goes to Phnom Da."

We started across the new lake. We paddled on, and on, expecting to see land at any moment. But we didn't. I thought we should stop and rest, but there was no shade anywhere. We put our 'kramaas' in the water, wrung them out and made turbans out of them, trying to stay cool. But the glare of the sun on the water was blinding. I pulled the end of my turban loose and let it fall over my face – the fabric was so thin I could see right through it. Now the still water ahead of me looked like an endless sheet of ice.

Puamaak suddenly stopped paddling and turned around, slowly. "Nyah – straight ahead – there's something moving! Something *big."*

"What is it? A Vietnamese patrol boat, do you think?"

"I can't see what it *is* – I can only see that it's *moving.* Look – it's the color of aluminum. But it's not a boat. There's nothing sticking up out of the water."

"Can you see which way it's going?" I asked. "North? South? Or... toward *us?"*

"It's not moving in any direction. It's just... *moving."*

"How big is it?" I asked.

"Maybe... twelve meters?"

"Twelve meters!" My mind raced. *I'll bet no one's been out here for years. And twelve meters would be just about the right length...* "Is it slithering in and out of the water? Are you sure it's not *green*?"

"No, Nyah. It's not a water dragon. But you should be able to see it just as clearly as I can. Get your 'kramaa' out of your face!"

I flipped the end of my 'kramaa' back over my head.

Now, when Puamaak had turned around, they'd started watching us. And now this sudden movement... They started to move, slowly at first, and then faster, and faster – right toward us, across the water. And then they began to climb.

"See their webbed feet?" I pointed up into the air. "They're pelicans!"

We watched the birds as they circled overhead, over our tiny boat.

"It's an omen, Puamaak. If the Vietnamese can kick the Khmer Rouge out we won't be as free as those birds, but we won't be locked up in communes any more. We can go *home.* And I don't mean Pong Tuk. You can go back to Phnom Penh."

"And *you...* you can go back to wherever the hell you came from." And he pushed me into the water.

We splashed around and chased each other for a long while. It was like the old days, swimming with our cousins. We were out in the middle of the lake – this was the first time in *four years* that we were *sure* we weren't being watched. We played around as though we wanted to collect on our omen before its bearers were even out of sight. And then we hauled ourselves back into the boat.

"Do you want me to take the stern for awhile," asked Puamaak. "The boat would ride better that way. And there's no steering to do – we just go straight ahead."

"OK. Pull the end of your 'kramaa' over your face, like I did. It'll keep a little of the sun out." And I moved forward, into the bow.

Oh, this was *much* better. I could see everything without having to look around my friend. I strained my eyes, looking for another flock of birds.

But within an hour I was bored. No birds, no land, just endless water.

It was then that I started to pay more attention to the boat. How it was riding, I mean. It should have been riding better, with me in the bow and

Puamaak in the stern. But it was riding the same as it had before.

Which meant that he wasn't any heavier than I was.

I turned back to look at him. Instead of pulling the end of his 'kramaa' out of his turban and letting it fall over his eyes, he'd taken his shirt off and wrapped it around his head to make a bigger turban.

I'd never seen him with his shirt off. Not in Pong Tuk, not in the work camps, not after we'd been drafted. Never.

It was a grizzly sight, I tell you. A skeleton with a paddle in its hands. I knew that all that was left of him was bones – I should have been prepared. But I wasn't. I looked away quickly and tossed him my 'kramaa'.

"Use mine with yours to make a bigger turban," I said. "And then pull the end of it out, and pull it down over your eyes." *Like I told you to do an hour ago.*

"The end will just blow around in the wind. It's not going to do me any good."

"*Then put it in your mouth.* I'll buy you a pair of shades just as soon as we hit Hollywood!"

He put his shirt back on, but the sight of him without it haunted me. Despite all the food we'd gotten in the last five days, he was losing weight.

I took a big piece of jerky and passed it back to him. "I just finished a piece," I lied. "Take a break – I can paddle."

He laid his paddle on the keel and took the jerky from me.

I continued to paddle on, across the endless lake.

Day Five – *The Trap*

"Land! *Look,* Puamaak. I can see trees."

My friend slid his turban off, and we put our paddles in the boat. We drifted slowly toward the shoreline, watching nervously as it came into focus. There was no way to conceal our arrival.

"Which story are we using?" I whispered back to him.

"'Old people' kids separated from their parents in the confusion of the evacuation. Say we're from the village next to the ruined temple – those people would have come through here."

I turned around and looked at him. "But you're half Chinese."

"It shouldn't matter, this far south. There are a lot of Chinese in Vietnam, and some would have come up here and mixed with the locals."

"You're guessing," I said.

"Yes, I'm guessing, but this close to the wrong side of the border I sure don't want to be an infantryman."

I turned around again and strained my eyes, trying to see the paddy ahead of us. But this could not be right… I jumped out of the bow before we even hit the shore and landed in the mud. I waded over to the paddy, picked up a fistful of earth, turned back to my comrade and let it sift through my fingers. The wind blew it away before it even hit the ground. "How could we still be in the war zone?" I asked.

"'Nothing makes sense in war – don't expect it to.' Better to concentrate on how to get across the Bassac than to try to figure out what happened here. But we have to find it – the canal doesn't go all the way through." He shook his head. "And I was so sure it did."

We beached the boat and I climbed a tree. I came down with more unsettling news. "We're almost to the Bassac, and the river's very narrow here – easy swim to the other side. But the other side is Vietnam."

"Vietnam? But we started out north of the border. And we came due west – I know we did. I've been watching the sun all day. I have to be sure we stay on course; it's my responsibility as our navigator, and the older of the two of us."

It was then that I noticed his eyes. Bloodshot, both of them. If he hadn't put his shirt back on he could've been taken for a ghost from hell – even in the middle of the day.

"Vietnam…" he said again. "I don't believe it. Wait – which way is the Bassac running?"

"Straight north / south."

He leaned back against the boat, put his palms on the gunwale and exhaled, very slowly – as if finishing a cigarette. I held my breath and braced myself for whatever it was he would say next. "Oh – OK. I know where we are. I know *exactly* where we are." He pushed himself off the gunwale and handed my 'kramaa' back to me. "We're just below where the Bassac runs due east, toward the Mekong. We have to go north, but we shouldn't have to go far."

I exhaled all at once. "So we just put back into the water, paddle up the shoreline as far as we can, and I'll climb a tree again. Then we can rest for a few minutes, and eat."

"But Nyah, how do you know it's Cambodia on this side of the river and Vietnam on the other? It's broad daylight – you can't tell me there are any lights on over there."

"I saw houseboats on the far shore. They're the same kind we would have seen from the boardwalk in Phnom Penh, on their way up to the Great Tonle Sap Lake. The kind with the big eyes painted on the bow – you can't mistake them for Khmer houseboats. And look at the scarecrow in the paddy over there. He's wearing a 'kramaa'."

"Come on," he said. "Back in the boat."

We paddled north another kilometer or so and hit rice paddies again. I could see trees in the distance, but there was nothing to climb here. It looked as though we'd finally have to ditch the boat.

We pulled it onto shore and set the fish trap on the bank to drain. We made our 'kramaas' into packs again, then put our gear and the smoked food in his and the food from the trap in mine. We headed north on foot, toward the trees.

The trees turned out to be fruit trees, which meant there was a village ahead. So I climbed the first tree we came to. Puamaak stayed hidden in the underbrush, in case there were cadres around.

I came down again pretty quickly. "There's a small river north of us, through a line of houses along the bank. It empties into the Bassac. Looks like everyone's left."

"OK. We'll sneak between the houses, get into the river, float down to the Bassac, walk north to where it turns west, then walk along the north shore straight toward Takeo. Swim the Bassac there. But we'll have to walk in the water all the way – mines will be our biggest problem here."

I shook my head. "No. And we can't get into the river here, either."

"What's worse than mines? Did you see cadres? Or Vietnamese? I thought you said everyone's gone."

"It's what the villagers left behind that's the problem. There's a *monster* in the river."

"*What?* Nyah, what the *hell* are you talking about."

I simply pointed up. "Climb the tree yourself, and have a look."

He headed for the tree, muttering. "A water dragon, undoubtedly. Like the one in the middle of the lake…"

I helped him get about ten meters up, and he looked out over the river. "So now you see," I said, "why I told you to climb the tree. How could I describe *that?*"

We were looking out over a whole network of interconnected bamboo frames, ropes and poles – and who knew what else underneath the water. All old, and abandoned. Each section was pulling apart from the next where the ropes had rotted out. Poles that had once served a purpose jutted into the air at random and swayed back and forth in the current, as though they were alive. The nets had all torn at the seams, and we watched them, mesmerized, as they flapped endlessly in the current.

"Fish traps," he said. "I can't even see the end of them."

"You're not up as high as I was. They go all the way down to the Bassac. About a kilometer."

He stared down into the water. "Those *nets*... if we were to get caught in them... we'd drown."

"Yeah. You'd just cut your way out of the first one and get swept into the next one."

He pointed to the center of the river. "The current. You can *see* it. Even from up here. This river must be draining all those marshes we were trying to get around by coming south on the Mekong."

"That's why they put the traps here – to get all the fish coming out of the marshes. We had a network of traps like this one in Prai Anchaan. Much smaller, but the same kind of system. It's designed to get the fish coming straight down the main current – the big ones. Not the little ones that feed in the shallows."

"So if we were to get into the river here, we'd be..."

"... a couple of *really* big fish."

We looked out over the river in silence. The scene looked like a huge Picasso painting, with the poles jutting out of the water and the ropes and the nets all tangled up in each other – 'Civilization Collapsed'.

"But with so many people starving," asked Puamaak, "why wouldn't the fishermen have maintained the trap?"

"Let me explain how it came to be in the first place. The fishermen get together, and each agrees to attach his trap to the next one over – so none of the fish can get through, and everyone catches something. The conglomeration of traps is a collective system, but each trap is a private trap – it's maintained by one family, and it feeds only that family. That's not the Communist way. So the cadres must have made everyone stop maintaining the system."

"In their usual manner," he said. "With a gun at everyone's head. But think of how many people these traps could have fed. Think how many people would not have starved to death. You know, Nyah, the only trap we saw at the village on the west bank of the Mekong was the one we picked up. There should have been more. Think about this... In Pong Tuk, the cadres allowed the 'old people' to continue to work their own fields. But the 'new people' – they forced them to work communal fields. So I'm guessing it was sort of like that on the rivers; the 'old people' were allowed to fish, and the 'new people' weren't. To keep them dependent on the 'old people'."

"But in this conglomerate trap," I said, "the 'old people's' traps were connected to the 'new people's' traps. So as the 'new people's' traps came apart in the current, the 'old people's' traps came apart with them. And the whole *system* collapsed. The cadres here weren't just uneducated – they were *stupid*."

"Which made them twice as deadly." He looked downriver. "What if we walked along the south bank and swam the river where it meets the Bassac, below the nets? No, that wouldn't work – we'd be swept down the Bassac. And we'd be in the open, right across from the border."

"Let's walk up this river," I said, "for a couple of kilometers or so. Maybe we can find a place to cross up there. Come on – let's go."

Puamaak looked down to get out of the tree, grabbed onto the trunk and held on with everything he had. And suddenly, there was the cat again. The cat at the end of its ninth life. His shoulder blades stuck out, his chest was hollow, and his arms were a couple of sticks. But now he looked even worse than he had four days ago, when we'd been treed by the pack of dogs.

"You need to eat," I said. "We'll stay here awhile, and I'll cook the clams and the snails."

"No, I want to get away from the border. I'll be fine."

I helped him get out of the tree and we started walking east. And less than two kilometers along, the river dead-ended into a canal that ran perpendicular to it.

We swam the canal just south of where the river started – where the water had lost all its power. Then we walked up the east bank of the canal about half a kilometer, and swam the canal back the other way – north of where the river started. And it worked. We managed to get to the north side of the river without ever getting into it.

"Pretty slick," I said, smiling. "And we're away from the border now. I can make our soup."

We went back in the trees, and I lit a fire and put our water cups on. As soon as the water boiled I dropped the snails in. "They take the longest to cook," I explained to Puamaak. But it seemed he'd fallen asleep.

When the snails were done I fished them out of the broth, took them out of their shells, cut them up and put them back in the broth. I dropped the clams in, and then the morning glory vines.

I took our soup off a couple of minutes later. I hated to wake him up, but all he'd eaten since we'd left the temple that morning was a single piece of jerky.

I ate my soup quickly. As soon as his was cool enough I fished out all the clams and took them out of their shells for him. Then I woke him up.

He finished his soup slowly, as though he weren't feeling well. And he didn't say anything. But he was my elder, so I didn't ask him any questions. I knew if he needed something, he'd tell me.

The sun would be down in half an hour, so I decided to refill our water cups before hanging our hammocks up. I came back to our campsite to find Puamaak already asleep under a tree, his hammock rolled up to make his pillow.

I climbed the tree, tied my hammock up, climbed down again and slipped my friend's hammock out from underneath his head. He didn't wake up. Well, that was no surprise – we'd been up since three that morning.

I returned to the tamarind and tied his hammock up. I climbed down again, to help him get up into the tree.

"Hey – wake up," I whispered. "Your hammock's not too far off the ground." I nudged him. "You can't sleep down here. Get up."

But my friend did not get up. He rolled over, slowly, and groaned. He open his eyes, but then closed them again – as though I wasn't there.

I didn't know *what* to do. I climbed back up the tree and retrieved the hammocks, then rolled his into a pillow again and put it back under his head. Then I put mine over him, like a blanket.

That woke him up. "Hot," he said. "Get it off. Too *hot.*" And then he asked me for water. I raised his head to help him drink; it was then that I realized just how hot he *was.*

He wasn't dead, but he might as well be. And I might as well be, too. Because we'd never make it home now. My friend had malaria.

I sat there in the dark, alone.

Day Six – *The Power of Water*

"Nyah. Are you awake?"

I jumped. It was dawn, and I should have been up already. But I'd been awake until midnight.

"Yes – yes, I'm right here. Do you want some water?"

He'd managed to raise himself on one elbow – I could see his silhouette against the trees. "I have some. You must have put it here for me last night. Thanks."

He began to sip the water – slowly, but as though determined to finish all of it. Well, I was going to have to tell him. I was going to have to tell him this morning. But how do you tell someone he's going to die?

The first rays of sunlight were making their way through the leaves, and we should have been surrounded by the sounds of life. Birds. Cicadas. Crickets. Macaques. Bees. Frogs. Fish, jumping in the canal.

But there was nothing. Except the sound of my friend sipping the water from his cup, determinedly, just a few drops at a time. Slow motion in a bad movie.

"Good spot we found to make camp in," I said. "Away from the border and the village, but near the canal and where the river starts. And completely hidden back here in the trees. This is the same strip of forest we were looking at from across the river yesterday – I'll bet it goes all the way over to the Bassac. We could stay here for days, if we wanted to. If we felt like taking a break."

No sound. No sound at all. And then he started sipping again.

He could have survived malaria before the war, in Phnom Penh – with a French-trained doctor in a clean, white hospital. But not out here – not without medicine. I'd decided last night where I'd bury him – I'd seen a pretty grove of wild cassia on the bank of the river yesterday.

"There'll be plenty of food in the canal," I continued. "Snails, crayfish, mudskippers... I'll bet I could even get us a Water-lily Snake, if I looked around."

He finished the last of his water and collapsed back onto his hammock. "Can I have some more?"

I handed him my cup. "I'll get you some *cold* water from the canal, when you finish this." And he started sipping again.

I tried to think what a doctor would say who knew he was going to lose his patient. "How're you doing?"

He put down my cup, raised himself on one elbow again and shook his head, as though trying to clear it. "Hot. Hot as *hell*."

Now I could see that his face was flushed – the fever must be terrible. Well, I couldn't keep pretending there was nothing wrong. I had to tell him. Better to just get it over with.

"You have malaria. All those damned mosquitoes the night before last, when we slept next to the swamp."

He shook his head. "Too hot. Dengue."

I'd turned my head to watch the woods, as I always did. But when I heard that word… I whipped my head around and looked into his face. But he wasn't looking at me – he hadn't seen me do it. I looked away again, quickly.

Dengue – I hadn't thought of that. The fever gets so high it's like a demon cracking your bones. I wondered how much he knew about dengue. Well, I wasn't going to tell him. I would find him some marijuana.

I began to look around and spotted a vine of wild rambutans, back in the trees. I got up, to pick them.

"Nyah – where are you going?"

"I saw food." And then I realized that the question he'd asked was not the one he wanted an answer to. "Don't worry. I won't leave you alone."

I picked the rambutans, sat down next to him, peeled one and put it in his mouth. Sugar and water, in one tiny little package – if he couldn't chew it, he could get everything from it just by sucking it dry.

He chewed it, and swallowed it, and I handed him another. One by one, slowly, determinedly, he finished all of them.

"You know," I said, "if you had dengue, you'd be in pain by now." I spoke to him gently, as one speaks to the very old. "And remember when the mosquitoes came out? Just before sunset – not at dawn. Dengue mosquitoes come out at dawn. You have malaria."

He looked up at me. "So how come you don't have it? You were just one hammock over."

"Because I had it when I was two. My aunt told me."

"Malaria, or dengue?"

"Both. But not at the same time."

He was quiet for a moment. "But you survived? You survived both of them? Oh, of course you did – you're sitting here next to me."

Yeah, I'd survived – because they'd put me in a hospital in Phnom Penh.

"Nyah – last night – you didn't… *hear* anything, did you?"

"No. No owl."

"What about this morning?"

"No." I shook my head.

He paused. "I wasn't delirious last night, or anything like that – was I?"

"No, I just had trouble waking you up."

"Hmm… Well I'm awake now."

He was on his feet before I could stop him. And then, he started to *walk off*.

"Where are you going?" I jumped up and went after him.

"I'm going to lie down in the canal."

Well, I didn't know what that would do, but I didn't think it would do him any harm. I mean, he was going to die anyway.

I'd tried to remember last night if my grandfather had ever talked about a cure for malaria – that's why I'd lain awake. Just staring up at the stars… as though they could help me think.

When that didn't work I imagined myself walking through my brain, peering into every cell for a memory of my grandfather healing someone. My friend who'd crushed his shoulder falling out of the tamarind – my grandfather had made him a tea for the pain. The smallest monk at the temple – my grandfather had treated him for ulcers, and recommended he leave monastic life so he could eat more than twice a day. The woman next door – my grandfather had burned herbs underneath her cot to help with the pain of childbirth. Everyone had come to my grandfather in the old days, when they needed help. But I couldn't remember anyone ever coming to him for malaria.

When walking through my brain didn't work I tried something else – I just never gave up. Going through the alphabet might jog a memory. A – anise – for a bad stomach. B – bitter melon – for chills. C – coconuts. I knew they were good for something, but I couldn't remember what. I came to the end of the alphabet, with nothing for malaria.

So I'd just tried to remember my grandfather sitting on his balcony, talking with his friends about medicines. I'd remembered the breeze that came up from the Mekong every afternoon – my great grandfather, when he'd built our house, had positioned the balcony to take full advantage of it. I could see the faces of my grandfather's friends as they sipped their coconut water, and talked of him curing many things. But malaria was not one of them. Neither was dengue. I think that's why he'd taken me to the hospital.

I helped my friend get to the canal and we got his shirt off. He walked into the shallows, lay down and curled up – as though to go to sleep. And then he closed his eyes.

He was *so thin.* Suddenly, he looked like a thousand other boys who'd been put in the rivers because there was no one left to bury them. I wondered how much time he had.

He opened his mouth to speak, too weak to open his eyes. "Nyah, if I could get to where you saw the houseboats – do you think those fishermen would help me? The worst thing they could do is kill me. But they must have hospitals in Vietnam. Like we did, before... Maybe someone would help me."

But I knew they wouldn't. Fishermen are poor, and can't afford to take their own children to the hospital. And those who live on houseboats? They're the poorest of all – they don't even own land. Not even a square centimeter, to drive a mooring stake into. I had no way to get him back there, anyway – he certainly couldn't walk. I could make a bamboo raft pretty quickly, but I knew that once we hit the Bassac we'd just be swept into the current and down the river. That is, if we made it past the fish traps.

I wondered again how much time he had.

I'd thought about that last night, too. Just a few kilometers after swimming the Bassac I'd be in Takeo province. But Takeo is *vastly* wide – much wider than Kandal. I knew I wouldn't be able to see Phnom Treil once I was across the river. Phnom Treil wasn't even in Takeo. It was in Kampot – the *next* province over. I wasn't even half way back to Pong Tuk.

And Takeo was different. That first day after our escape, Puamaak had figured out where we were by hitting a tributary of the Mekong and then hitting a paved road. I remembered when I'd had to walk from Phnom Penh to Pong Tuk in April of '75 – I'd walked the entire length of the northern half of Takeo. At eight, it had seemed to me to be an endless sea of rice paddies. There were no great rivers to tell you where you were. And as for figuring it out by whether the roads were paved? I couldn't remember which ones were, and which ones weren't – if I'd ever known at all.

So I would have to find out from my friend, before he died, how he had planned to navigate once we were across the Bassac. He'd said he had a way.

I filled my cup from the canal. "I have to go back to start our fire," I said. "I can't wait any longer." I always timed our morning fire very carefully. I lit it when the morning mist came up and had it out by the time the mist burned off, so no one would see the smoke. "But I'll sit with you while I'm waiting for the fire to burn down to coals. I'll be back in a few minutes."

I hung back a moment. *I should ask him how he was going to navigate,* I thought. *I should ask him now.*

But I couldn't do it. He was my elder – and he'd know why I was asking.

I headed back to our campsite, looking for marijuana plants as I walked. *How very ironic,* I thought, *that he survived four years of the Khmer Rouge, only to die now – when he was finally free. And how very strange – if he was going to get malaria, he should have gotten it years ago. Especially as we've had no mosquito nets since the Khmer Rouge took over.*

But the more I thought about it, the more it did make sense. The damage from the last four years would have been cumulative. I remembered him when I'd first met him – in Pong Tuk, after the march from Phnom Penh. Then I remembered him in the work camp – he'd been much thinner, because of the forced labor and the starvation rations. Then I remembered him when I'd first been drafted. He should have put on a little weight on an infantryman's rations – but he'd *lost* some. And then I remembered him the day after we'd escaped, when I'd first seen him without his uniform. And yesterday, when he'd had his shirt off. There was nothing left of him. First trying to get us out of the mountains and away from our platoon, then trying to get us through our army's stinking minefields... The Khmer Rouge had finally gotten everything he had.

And then I wondered why I was trying to figure anything out at all. The owls knew everything. The first one – the morning after our escape. Why had I even asked myself who it was he'd come for? My friend had been in much worse shape than I. And the second one – the owl my grandfather had sent to get us up and headed down the Mekong. He must have come just after that *one mosquito* had delivered its single drop of death. I'd thought that second owl had delivered one message, but in fact, he'd delivered two.

I collected wood and started a fire, but with no intention of cooking breakfast. I was glad my friend couldn't see himself; he'd turned a strange color that I'd never seen before. I put the water on to boil and started to look again for wild marijuana. I would make him a tea from it – I thought that's what my grandfather would do. It would make my friend feel better, at least. Yes, that's exactly what my grandfather would do. He always made people feel better – especially when he couldn't help them.

But, hard as I searched, I found no marijuana. I headed back to the canal, forcing one foot in front of the other, dreading what I'd find when I got there.

I thought of all the other boys I'd seen die in the last four years. And in the work camps, *we'd* had to bury them – the cadres certainly weren't going to do it. So I knew how much work it was. And I wondered how strong *I* was now – I'd been through the same four years my friend had. I didn't even have a shovel – what the hell would I dig with? Oh, it would be so much easier, to just push him into the current.

But I wouldn't do it. He was my friend, and I would bury him under the cassia trees. I'd dig his grave with my hands if I had to. Had it not been for him, *I* wouldn't be alive. Had he not included me in his plans, when he'd decided to escape.

I reached the shoreline and looked for my friend in the mist – in the shallows, where I'd left him.

I found him sitting up. "Nyah. What's for breakfast?"

What's for breakfast? He has malaria, he's going to die, and he's asking me what's for breakfast? "We still have some fish jerky, and cassava."

"It's not malaria, little brother. Or dengue. It's..." And he said a Chinese word. "I should be OK by tomorrow."

"No, you have a raging fever. That's why your skin's that funny color."

"Oh, *that*. That's just..." and he said another Chinese word. "You've never seen it before, have you?"

"No, I haven't. And no, I don't speak Chinese. You *know* I don't."

"Well there isn't a Khmer word for it, because Khmer don't get it. 'Chan tngai' is the closest."

"*Chan tngai...* 'Defeated by the sun'."

"Quaint," he said, "but yeah, that's it. Sunstroke. The sun burns your brain. And your skin – that's why my skin is red. It's just like cooking a pig."

"Oh! *Really?*"

"Really. Khmer are too dark – they don't get cooked. Those French people you saw on the beach when you were three? *They* got cooked."

"So you're not going to die?"

"No, I'm not going to die. Not today, anyway. Hey, you didn't eat my share of breakfast, did you?"

"*No!*" I sat down next to him. "Could *you* eat breakfast, if you thought *I* was going to die?"

He laughed. "Don't ask." He slipped under water and started blowing bubbles.

Now he wasn't acting sick – he was acting *drunk*. Well I guess I would too, if I'd just figured out that I wasn't going to die. But I was *confused*. I knew he'd never had this thing before, or he would have been more careful yesterday.

"OK," I said, "so now I understand why *I* don't know what you have. How do *you* know what you have?"

"*Lawrence of Arabia*. Oh, a whole *lot* of characters got 'chan tngai'd' in that movie. Probably the whole cast and crew, too – except Omar Sharif of course."

I just shook my head. "Puamaak. Really. How do you know what it is? You didn't figure it out from a movie you saw four years ago."

"OK. OK. When we were marched out of Phnom Penh in '75 I got it. I'd just... forgotten. That was a lifetime ago."

"Well you'd better put your shirt back on, or you're going to get cooked some more. And move into the shallows under that tree, will you?" I pointed to a big banyan. "Before the mist burns off."

He slid over, under the branches.

"But how could your skin get cooked so fast?" I asked. "You didn't have your shirt off that long. It couldn't have been more than a couple of hours."

"Nyah, I haven't had my shirt off in *three years.* Do you remember, in the work camp, when someone stole my hammock? After that I was so afraid that someone would steal my shirt, I never took it off. I worked with it on, I slept with it on, I even swam with it on – hoping it'd get clean in the bargain. And when they gave me my army issue I just did the same thing. I was lucky I got another hammock; the army gave me one."

I tell you, I'd never been so glad to be Khmer in my life. We could have our shirts on *forever*, and then take them off for an afternoon – and have *nothing happen.* Let alone just about *die.*

"But your arms and your legs," I said. "They're all burned up, too."

"I was drafted a year ago, Nyah. Not *three months* ago, like you. I've lost all my work camp tan, and my old camp clothes don't cover me head to foot like my uniform did."

"Oh. I see." I didn't, really. But he was my elder, so I just said I did.

"Well, I guess I'm going to be sitting in this canal all day, trying to get cooled back down to normal. I guess you're Recon, Navigation, Nurse, Housekeeping *and* Cook today."

"No, I'm beginning to feel more like your mother. And the next time you're on the water, put something over your eyes. You're lucky you can still *see.*"

I went back to the fire, pushed our food into the coals and returned to the canal.

"Oh little brother... I heard crickets while you were gone. Do you remember how we all ate deep-fried crickets after the harvest every year? Even us city people. You'd get yours from the paddies, we'd get ours from the markets. Hmm... 'Nyah' – doesn't that mean, 'gecko'? Geckos are supposed to be very good at catching crickets."

"*Crickets?* Risk my life catching your lunch? That's why I was going to get all our food from the canal. *No mines.*"

"Wait... listen... I think I hear... *bees.* There's a hive around here somewhere." He put his hand to his ear. "Yeah – over there! Can't be more than a hundred meters up." He put his hand to his forehead and groaned. "Oh, I think it *is* malaria. Or dengue. Or maybe even the *plague.* I've heard honey has excellent curative powers."

"Do you want me to show you where I was going to bury you? Nice little spot... yellow flowers..."

"Ha! You were just going to throw me into the canal."

I dropped the piece of grass I'd been twisting and looked up. "Why do you think I helped you over here."

He closed his mouth, his eyes got big, and he slid quietly back into the water. He just lay there, looking up into the banyan, not wanting to look at me.

"Hey – I was kidding! *Really* – I had a nice little spot all picked out for you. *By* the river – not *in* it."

He raised himself on one elbow. "Well, when did you pick *out* this little spot?"

"Last night – when I had trouble waking you up. I couldn't sleep after that. I was trying to remember if my grandfather had a cure for malaria. And then I remembered seeing a little grove of wild cassia trees as we were walking up the river yesterday. It just looked so pretty, across the water. With the flowers, and the river flowing by..."

He shuddered, as though he were not overheated, but chilled to the bone instead. "Nyah, either one of us could go out like a light at the flick of a switch."

And he was right, you know.

"Well if *you'd* died last night," I said, "*I* wouldn't have made it. I don't know how the hell to find my way back to Pong Tuk from here."

"Then why didn't you ask me this morning how to do it? If you thought I was going to die."

I didn't say anything.

"Nyah. Once you're across the Bassac, you'll see Phnom Da. Straight ahead of you. It's like Phnom Treil – you can't mistake it for any other mountain. Because there's a little bump on the top of it. So when you see the bump, you know *exactly* where you are."

I still didn't say anything.

"Well why the hell don't you ask me what the bump is?"

I just shrugged my shoulders. "I don't know."

"The bump is a *temple*. That's why it's so easy to spot – it's man made. Straight lines. Dead giveaway."

"Could you just stop using the word, *'dead'*?"

He slid back into the water.

"Well that does me a lot of good," I said, "knowing exactly where I am, but not in relation to anything else. What do you *do* when you see the temple? How do you figure out which way to go?"

He sat up, excitedly. "The temple is *very* old, little brother, and *very* powerful. You climb Phnom Da, you get up to the temple, and you go inside. Then you wait. There used to be an oracle there; he could tell you which way to go. You wait, and if he doesn't show up, you know he's dead."

"Could you just stop using that word?"

He started to laugh and rolled over in the water – he was acting drunk again. "Nyah. There's no oracle. And you don't have to climb anything. You just go forty-five degrees southwest after you see the temple. First you'll hit a road running southwest. Shadow it – it will take you to Highway Two. Then just continue to shadow that first road, and eventually you'll see Phnom Treil."

"How do you know all that? You didn't learn it in school. Because we'd never even *heard* of Pong Tuk. Did your mother tell you?"

He shook his head. "She saw them start taking the children away, and knew it was just a matter of time... But all she could tell me to do was to find Highway Three, and then look for the Phnom Sanhaan range. She drew me a map in the dirt and showed me where we were in relation to Three. And then she rubbed it out before the cadres saw it. She drew me that map several times, to be sure I understood."

"I would have gotten lost," I said. "I never could have found Highway Three. You had the advantage of being two years older than I was. And having a mother who knew the highway system. She must have traveled a lot."

"She did – looking for silk. Always looking for silk. She loved it, you know. We went north of your village for 'pamuuong' – brocade. We went to Kampong Cham Province and Takeo Province for 'hōl' – ikat. We went to Kampot Province for silk kramaa. And we went to that island just south of you for 'anloung' – those fine, colored pin stripes. 'Very slimming,' she would say..." And he ducked underwater quickly.

He came up again, composed. "She figured I would recognize the Phnom Sanhaan range because it always looks blue – like Phnom Treil. And you can always see Sanhaan sticking up above the mountains that surround it."

"Man," I said, "we're *lucky.* If the place we were trying to get back to had no landmark that you could see from a long way away..."

"Good-old rock-solid Phnom Sanhaan. *Dead* giveaway." He laughed, and I jumped into the water to choke him.

"How about my breakfast, Nyah?"

"Keep your shirt on – it's not hot yet. Well *I* knew there was something wrong with you before you did. Yesterday afternoon, when we were looking out over the fish traps. When you looked down to get out of the tree, you froze."

He rolled over in the water and propped his face in his hands. "Nyah, have you really never figured out why I can't climb a tree? *Really?"*

I started to say, "Because you have no muscle in your upper body," but said instead, "*I* don't know. How would I know?"

"*I'm afraid of heights*, Nyah. Terribly afraid. I can't look down." He tried French this time instead of Chinese. "'*Vertige*'. Yeah, I don't think you Khmer have a word for that, either. Who could imagine a Khmer who's afraid of climbing a tree."

I just couldn't grasp this '*vertige*' thing – I'd been climbing trees so long, 'up' and 'down' were the same to me. "So if you're afraid of heights," I asked, "what was all that about wanting to be a pilot?"

"Oh, that was absolutely true. If I were a pilot, I wouldn't *be* afraid of heights."

This must be some kind of Chinese logic – because *I* certainly wasn't getting it.

"Well, little brother, you don't tell anyone I have 'vertige' and I'll tell everyone you were an infantryman. And a good one, too – I'll tell them you shot a dozen Vietnamese. No I won't – everyone will be siding with the Vietnamese now because they'll get the Khmer Rouge out. But I'll tell them you're a good shot. I just won't tell them you never shot anything. And don't tell anyone I was so *stupid* as to get myself 'defeated by the sun'."

But I was not convinced that all that was wrong with my friend was sunstroke. The fear I'd had since the day of our escape had never really left me –

that he was just not going to make it. He was *half* dead then – now he looked even worse.

"Even if you're OK by tomorrow," I said, "we have to slow down. And eat more, now that we have jerky that we can carry with us. We can eat a piece every hour or so."

"I wish we could get something with fat in it, though. We'd put a little weight on, before we see our mothers again. Pork would be the best thing. But I haven't seen a pig since I left Pong Tuk. Maybe there're none left in the whole country."

"Oh," I said, "there's *one* – the roasted one sitting in the canal here in front of me."

"Very funny."

"Some kinds of fish have fat in them," I said. "But I don't know which kinds they are. I'll look for butter fruit – it has vegetable fat in it. And the trees are easy to climb."

"Avocado. Yeah. How do the French eat it?"

"I don't know. Never been French. However it comes off the tree, that's how we're going to eat it." And I went to get our breakfast out of the coals.

I returned to the canal and gave him more than half the food – which is something we *never* did.

"Nyah, take your full half. You need it. I didn't want to tell you, but… I think I should. You're getting thinner."

"Me? *ME?* I was kidding when I said I was going to throw you in the canal, but I wasn't kidding when I said I'd picked out a spot to bury you. You're *much* thinner than I am."

He shook his head. "That's not possible. If I just had a mirror, I could prove it to you."

"Shall I prove it to *you?* There's nothing left of you but bone – and most of that's in your *head*. You're not going to die on me – I won't let you." I stopped, not knowing what else I could say to him. "OK, that's it. Get out of the canal."

He didn't move.

"Comrade – *OUT!*"

Now he looked at me as though I'd gone completely mad. He got to his feet, slowly, not taking his eyes off mine.

"Look at me," I said, "standing here in my camp shirt." I thrust my arms straight out to the side. "Look how big it is on me." I pulled my shirt to one side and pinched it in at the waist. "Now I'm going to *measure* how much too big it is. Look – you see? From my wrist to the tip of my fingers. One hand-length. You see that clearly, don't you? Now – *YOU* put my shirt on. And we'll measure *again*."

I unbuttoned my shirt one button at a time, never taking my eyes off his. And then I held it out to him – and waited.

He walked toward me slowly and took the shirt from me, still watching me. He took off his shirt and put mine on, and buttoned it up. I pulled the shirt to one side and pinched it in at the waist. And I measured with my hand, the same way I'd done on myself.

He looked at my hand, and looked at my face, and looked at my hand again.

"Tell me how many hand-lengths, comrade," I said. "You're not going to die on me."

He didn't say anything.

"TELL ME."

He glared at me like an infantryman glares at the soldier who's just captured him. *"ONE AND A HALF."*

He turned, walked to the bank, and sat down with my shirt still on. He just sat there, staring into the water. And then he picked up a piece of jerky, and started to chew on it.

"We can get as much food as we need from this canal," I said. "It's *full* of stuff coming out of the marshes. No one could fish or hunt up there because no one could get in there. Did you really hear a hive? After we've finished the honey we could eat the bee larvae. *That* would put some weight on you."

"I was just teasing, Nyah. No hive. No honey. No bees."

I sighed. "And no crickets, either. I thought as much. Well as long as you'll be chilling down in the canal all day, I'm going back to the boat for the fish trap. We can put it in the canal and have fresh fish tonight. It can't be more than four kilometers, back to the trap – eight, round trip. So I'll be back in an hour and a half. I don't think you're going to die while I'm gone. Not if you finish your breakfast."

He was still sulking. "Not me – *you*."

"What do you mean?" I asked.

"The mines. We were lucky we got through the first time."

I just rolled my eyes. "I'll do what I've been doing all morning – retrace our steps *exactly*. Like we did at the big village. I should be able to see our path clearly. Don't worry – I'll be back."

"It is a good plan, Nyah. Getting the trap. And after you take the fish out of it tonight, you can put it back in the canal. There'll be something in it by breakfast-time tomorrow."

"But it's not going to be easy, getting that big trap back here. You were right – I wish we had a 'turoo'. One of those melon-sized traps."

"Don't look for one in the village," he said. "Too risky."

"Are you kidding? I'm going to be through that village, retrieve the trap, and back through the village as fast as I possibly can. What's the first thing I warned you about, the day after we escaped? *Rabid dogs.* If the Vietnamese catch us, maybe we're dead and maybe we're not. If our army catches us, maybe we're dead and maybe we're not. If the cadres catch us, maybe we're dead and maybe we're not. But if we get bitten by a rabid dog? We're dead. End of story. If I *trip* over a 'turoo', I'll pick it up. Now get back in the water."

I went back to our campsite and retrieved all our gear, then returned to my friend. I tied his hammock out of sight up in the banyan tree and put all his gear in it. All my gear would go with me – that's the way we always did it, in case something happened.

"Hey," I said. "I can make it back here in *less* than an hour and a half. I'll ride the current down to the village, instead of walking."

"You'll get sucked right into the traps. That's how we ended up here in the first place – trying to get around them."

"No," I said, "I'm not going to get into the main current. I'm going to ride down right next to the south bank. And grab onto one of those big snags sticking out into the river as soon as I see the village. I should be back in an hour – if I'm not, send out a search party, will you?"

"Not funny, Nyah."

"I'm leaving you all the jerky, cassava and morning glory vines. I'll tie them up next to your hammock."

"But that's all we have," he said. "If something happens to you, you'll have no food."

"If something happens to me, I won't *need* food. But nothing will happen to me. Lie very still in the water in case there's someone around. And keep your machete in your hand. Man, you'd *better* be here when I get back." And I took off, after the trap.

An hour went by, and my friend began to watch for me. Another hour passed – he began to worry, but there was nothing he could do. And then another hour passed. And another. But I did not return.

Day Six - *Four Hours*

I left my friend sitting in the water underneath the banyan tree. I swam back across the canal to float down the east side, so I could get into the slower current on the south side of the fish trap river.

I wanted to wave to him, once I was across the canal. But I couldn't take the chance. Cadres, stragglers, deserters, surveillance or collaborators for either side… by now you know the list. I looked back, then started floating south. I was soon out of the sight of my friend.

I began to look anxiously for the mouth of the river. I might have to do some strategic swimming to stay on the right trajectory. I may have lost a little weight since we'd escaped, but now I was in much better shape. We'd never been allowed to sleep a full night since we'd been marched out of Phnom Penh, but now we were averaging ten hours a night. We'd been able to get enough to eat since the end of our third day, once we'd finally gotten across the Mekong and had 'borrowed' the fish trap. Remember, too, that I was only twelve – you can recover very quickly at that age, if your body gets what it needs.

And then there were the other factors. After three years and nine months – one third of my life – I was *free!* And my friend wasn't going to die after all. Not today, anyway. And now I knew how to get back to Pong Tuk from where we were. Oh yeah – I was beginning to feel like my old self again.

I strained my eyes as I floated down the canal, watching for the turn into the river. But the current was slow, the clouds were pretty, and I had no one to talk to but myself. I started to think.

I'd never been to the temple of Angkor Wat, one of the six wondrous things I'd wanted to see as a child. I'd never been there – but I'd seen pictures. *Five stories* of massive stone blocks, carved with dancing spirits all the way to the top. It was an incredible feat of engineering, a thousand years ago. But the canal builders of Funan – they went back *another* thousand. That's *twice* as golden as our Golden Age. I wondered how many kilometers of canals they'd built, and what wonderful places they could take you to.

And then I began to think about the river. It didn't start at any natural place – there were no headwaters. No headwaters at all. It just… rushed headlong out of the canal. And at almost a right angle. I began to wonder if it was a river at all.

The canal builders would have known they could create a rush of water by digging a canal deeper than the one that flowed into it. And I think that's what they were after – a surge that would make it easy to catch fish. That rush of water had had two thousand years now to create a river – there was probably a canal at the bottom of it.

And the maze of fish traps at the end, just before the river collided with the Bassac? I wondered if it had been built right after the canal had been finished, and maintained steadily ever since. Every time a rope had rotted out, it had been replaced. Every time a net had torn, it had been mended. Every time a bamboo pole had snapped in the current, a new one had been put in in its place.

For two thousand years. Until the Khmer Rouge came, and destroyed two millennia of civilization in less time than it takes a child to learn to read.

I reasoned that there must be a huge drop-off where the river rushed out of the canal – maybe even a whirlpool. I didn't remember seeing one yesterday, but then again, I hadn't looked. I decided to get out and walk.

I got to where the current picked up, a harmless sheet of ethereal rippling on the surface of the water. A few paces further along and the rippling gave way to churning. A few paces further still and the churning turned to rolling. I kept on walking, mesmerized, until I reached the mouth of the river. The water was suddenly *sucked* out of the canal in one continuous gulp, as though by an enormous water dragon. I climbed a tree just to watch it.

But it was not the sight of the water that betrayed its strength – it was the *sound*. All that power, created not by a water dragon, but by men two thousand years ago who were probably not much bigger than I was. And Puamaak was right – I was descended from their line, most certainly. I wondered how far from Oc-Eo I was, as I sat there in the tree. Eighty kilometers as the crow flies, and one hundred and ten, if I were to use the Bassac and the canals. I didn't know the distance because I didn't have a map, but I knew that I must be close.

But as I sat in the tree watching the river, I remembered my friend. And then I remembered what he'd said about the Mekong – that the Khmer call it by a feminine name because the river gives life. And that's when I finally made the connection. The real power of water is its power to heal. It was bringing my friend's body temperature back down to normal, and it had given him all the clean drinking water he'd needed to rehydrate. It had provided him with the fish he'd needed to rebuild the muscle he'd lost, and the morning glory vines to restore his night vision. When I'd gone through the alphabet the night before trying to remember medicines, I'd gone right by 'w' without ever thinking of 'water'. I'd thought of 'worms' instead; my grandfather had given me coconut water with earthworms in it when I'd had smallpox. How ineffectual the human mind can be – I wondered what else I was missing.

But then I thought of how lucky I was. I thought of all the boys I'd met who hadn't made it, and the differences between them, and me. I had *one advantage* that no one else had – that I could always find water. And that was the *critical* advantage. Because wherever there's water, there's food. But as I said, I was lucky. Because the way that I found water could not be learned, or taught.

It had all started the day we were driven out of Phnom Penh at gunpoint. People packed rice because that's our staple food – but they didn't pack the water to cook it in. Most families were on foot, and water was just too heavy. It was April, our very hottest month – so everyone drank what little water they *had* brought much too quickly. Along the hundred and thirty kilometer journey I was always able to find a pond, or an irrigation ditch, or a reservoir, or a stream, when other people couldn't. So I got myself, and my family, all the way to Pong Tuk. When I'd been marched from one work camp to another I'd had to find my own water again. And, once again, I'd been able to get myself to the next destination. Then when I'd been drafted – oh, they gave us water, but it was never enough. And they marched us all the time. If I hadn't been able to find my own water, I wouldn't have made it this far. I wondered again how my friend had.

And, as I've said, wherever there's water, there's food. Even if you couldn't catch the frogs and the crabs and the fish, you could get the snails and the clams and the mudskippers. If you couldn't get out to the lotus, you could get to the morning glory vines and the water chestnuts. And think of all the animals that go to a waterhole to drink. That's where you get the most snakes – even Puamaak could tell you that. Yes, if you could find water, you could find enough food to keep yourself alive.

I sat in the tree, still mesmerized by that single spot where the water in the canal was sucked into the river. And I thought again of the water dragon.

Khmer are raised on stories of the 'neak'. Some people say they're real, some people say they're not. Like the Loch Ness monster (who's probably not a monster at all – I mean, has he eaten anybody?).

I believed that water dragons had once existed, and wondered if they really were extinct. They must have ranged over half the earth – even the Vikings depicted water dragons in their art. I knew that the Stegosaurus had not gone extinct in Cambodia until historic times – one was carved into a temple doorframe during the Angkorian era. Then there was the monitor lizard who'd just... *shown up* in Prai Anchaan after the firefights between the Lon Nol troops and the Khmer Rouge insurgents, and started eating the dead soldiers. The thing was the size of a Komodo Dragon. If you want to know the truth, I thought there must be one or two water dragons still out there. And this must be just the kind of place they liked – lots of clean, fresh water, plenty of fish, no one to bother them... I climbed higher in the tree, to look for one.

But then I remembered Puamaak. The longer I was gone, the greater the chance that something would happen to him. And I had to make sure he *kept eating*. I would have to keep on going – perhaps I could look for a 'neak' tomorrow.

As I looked down to get out of the tree I saw the canal below me. The *south* side of it – the little bit of water that hadn't been sucked into the river. The merchants of Funan and Water Chenla had built the canals for trade, so each canal *went* somewhere. But where did this one go?

I was still about fifteen meters up, and I looked due south from the tree. Why hadn't I realized it yesterday? There was only one place for this canal to go – into the lake. *The lake where we'd left the boat.*

And suddenly, a plan unfolded in my head; I tell you, I didn't even have to think. I'd float down the canal to the lake, make a right at the shoreline, go to where we'd left the boat, and *get the boat.* And the trap. Then I'd pull the boat up the canal and back to where I'd left Puamaak. As soon as he could travel we'd shoot down the fish trap river into the Bassac (staying right of the traps *somehow),* and pull the boat along the north bank until the river flowed north / south again. Then we'd pull the boat up the east bank just far enough to compensate for the current, and paddle across the Bassac straight into a canal. If what Puamaak had said was true, we'd be able to get all the way over to Phnom Da in the boat! What a plan – he'd love it. Because he wouldn't have to walk much, and we could keep the trap.

I climbed out of the tree, slid into the canal, floated down to the lake, made a right at the shoreline and walked in the water back to the boat.

As I stepped onto the bank I remembered where I was – in rice paddies. *That's* where you find crickets; that's why we hadn't heard them on the canal. They're one of the most nutritious foods you can find anywhere. And you know how we Khmer eat them? Fried, and stuffed with peanuts. Yes, that's right – I still had our peanuts. I couldn't fry the crickets because I had no oil – but I could roast them. If I could get those down my friend he'd be *fat* by tomorrow.

You find crickets by finding their nests; you look for a hole of a certain size and shape in the sides of the levees. I began to look around, watching for trip wires of course.

After a few minutes of searching and straining my ears I picked up a chirping sound. I followed it, found the entrance to the nest, and dug along the tunnel with my 'kwaiw' until I found a cricket. I picked it up, apologized for having to kill it, apologized to the Buddha for having to kill it – and snapped its head off.

I returned to the shoreline and filled my cup, went back to the nest and poured the water into it. Three more crickets came out.

Three nests and an hour later I had a dozen big crickets for my friend. I would have gotten them a lot faster, had it not been for the twenty-four apologies. I put them in my cup, put the cup under the bow seat and began to push the boat into the water.

And then I *finally* remembered. A – anise. B – bitter melon. C – coconuts. Coconut *water. For sunstroke.* Why had it taken me so long to remember? It's not that Khmer don't *get* sunstroke – it's that we know how to *prevent* it. I remembered my grandfather and his friends, when they'd come in from the fields – they'd reach for a coconut before they even sat down. I'd seen them do it in my mind last night because I'd seen them do it a thousand times in life. And I figured, what prevents sunstroke will probably cure it.

Well it was *my* lucky day. I knew where to find coconuts without even having to climb a tree. I found our tracks from the day before and walked back to the village. And you know where I was headed.

I got to the bank of the river and cut down a banana tree. I cut two thirty-centimeter pieces from the stalk and put them up the front of my shirt, so I couldn't possibly get sucked underwater. Then I swam to the side of the trap nearest the shore – not the front of it, where I'd get sucked in. I grabbed onto what was left of the frame and cut a coconut out of the net. But it could have been trapped there for years... so I shook it. *Plenty* of water. I pulled a banana stalk out from under my shirt and replaced it with the coconut, and then repeated the process. Two coconuts should be enough.

I swam back to the shoreline, hacked the husk off the coconuts, picked up my tracks and walked back to the boat. Now I'd have to get back to Puamaak just as quickly as I could to give him the coconut water. The crickets would be a surprise.

I started to push the boat into the water and saw... an earthworm. A little one, trying to get out of my way.

An earthworm. An *earthworm!* Why had it taken me so long to *remember?* My grandfather had given me worms in coconut water not for smallpox, but for the *fever* of smallpox. And Puamaak's biggest problem was that he was *hot.* I picked up the worm, put it in my pocket, and started to hunt for more. The secret ingredient – I'd have my friend back on his feet by nightfall.

I pushed the boat back into the water with six worms in my pocket, and started to paddle up the shoreline. As I made my way back to the canal I imagined how excited Puamaak would be when I told him we could get all the way to Phnom Da in the boat.

I started to pull the boat up the canal, and in less than a kilometer came to the mouth of the river. I glanced over to see if I could see a water dragon, but decided that that was ridiculous – a 'neak' would be too smart to be out in this afternoon heat. But I determined to look for one when Puamaak and I came back through in the boat.

I continued on another half kilometer or so until I was right across the canal from the banyan where I'd left him. I walked up another thirty meters to compensate for the current, got into the stern, shoved off and started to paddle across the canal.

I landed just above the banyan. I jumped out of the bow and pulled the boat underneath the branches that overhung the water, expecting to see my friend on the other side of them.

He wasn't there.

I looked up into the tree, expecting to find him asleep in his hammock. But his hammock was *gone.*

My head reeled. The day had started with my navigator – my friend – about to *die.* Then, miraculously, he *wasn't* going to die. Then he'd told me how to navigate back to Pong Tuk. Then I'd figured out how to get us all the way over to Phnom Da in the boat. And now my friend was... *gone?* What kind of karma was this???

But my head never reeled for long. If someone had found Puamaak, I reasoned, they might still be around. And if they'd figured out that he wasn't alone, they'd be looking for me. I hid the boat as best I could under the branches of the banyan and climbed up into the tree. I kept climbing until I was a couple of stories up – no one would see me there.

I wondered if Puamaak had gone back to where I'd made breakfast. I looked toward our campsite, but couldn't see it through the trees. *Well,* I thought, *I'll look along the path I took back and forth this morning – he might have collapsed in the heat.* That's the only thing I could think of to do.

But I couldn't find the path.

Because this was the *wrong tree!* This was not where we'd been this morning.

So where *had* we been? North of here? South? *Where?*

I looked south, for another banyan. I didn't remember seeing one walking back up the canal, and I didn't see one now. I turned around, and looked north.

There was another banyan about sixty meters up the canal, and I started to

look for movement on the shoreline. Nothing. I looked for *any* sign of my friend
– a flash of skin, a curl of smoke, branches swaying when there was no wind –
any sign at all.

But there was nothing.

It was then that I saw the body, floating in the canal.

Day Six – *The Body in the Water*

I climbed down from the tree and hid behind the branches that overhung the water. I watched, and waited, for what seemed like longer than I'd been *alive* for the body to float by.

I knew it was not Puamaak. It couldn't be. A person who's died *today* – his body doesn't float. But whoever it was might give me a clue to what had happened to my friend, because his body might tell me something about what was going on in this area. If it wore a uniform, there had been combat here recently. If it was a civilian, this place hadn't been evacuated very long. And if it was a child... the Khmer Rouge were in control here, not the Vietnamese.

The branches blocked my view upstream, so I couldn't see the body until it was right in front of me. As it floated past in the current I looked at the clothes it wore. A faded black work camp shirt, a pair of shredded shorts, and a 'kramaa' that had once been blue.

There was no time to think about what might have happened to him – or what might happen to *me* if I went in after him. I'd promised him that I'd bury him – that he wouldn't end up in a river. But I had to catch him before he got sucked around the bend; once he was in the river I'd never be able to get to him. So I ran through the shallows as fast as I could, and dove into the water.

I swam harder and faster than I ever had before, caught up to the body and clawed at its shirt. I got hold of it and *pulled*, as hard as I could, to get it out of the current.

I pulled so hard that the head came up. And then I saw the eyes... Like so many of the bodies I'd seen in the last four years, the eyes were still open. And then... the mouth began to move.

"Nyah – it *is* you! I couldn't tell. When you didn't come back I climbed up into the banyan to watch for you. Then, *finally,* I saw you on the other side of the canal. I was never so relieved in my life. But then you didn't come back to the banyan. But, I thought, it *must* be you. Short, skinny, with the same color clothes, and the 'kramaa' tied the way you always tie it. So I took a chance, and floated down the canal exactly the way we floated down the tributary after we left the buffalo wallow. Trying to look dead. I figured, if it wasn't you, whoever it was would leave me alone. And if it *was* you, you'd come in after me – because you'd promised me you'd bury me."

We made it back to the bank and hauled ourselves out of the water. "Nyah, I'm *sorry*. It was the only thing I could do. Did you really think I was dead?"

I lied with the shake of my head. "Someone who's died this morning doesn't float. You know it – I know it – any Cambodian knows it. But you did a very good job – of looking dead, I mean. You could have fooled anyone who didn't know you were alive this morning... You know, four years ago you could have signaled me with a bird call from up in the branches of the other banyan. But there are so few birds left that if you tried it now, you'd have someone start shooting at you. That's why I never taught you how to do it."

We started walking back to where I'd hidden the boat, and I explained how

I'd retrieved it. How the canal connected to the lake. Then I told him how I planned to use the boat to get us all the way over to Phnom Da.

We got back to the banyan and he lay down on the bank. "All the food and my gear are up at the other tree," he said. "If we're going south tomorrow it makes more sense to bring them back here than to take the boat up there. I'll go back for them in a minute."

I asked the next question not to hear his answer – I knew what that would be. I wanted him to acknowledge that he needed my remedy. "Have you gotten your strength back?"

"Ha! Just enough of it to act *dead*."

I took a coconut from under the bow seat and hacked off just enough of the end to slip in the secret ingredient. Then I brought the coconut over to him. "Drink it, my friend. Drink it all the way down to the bottom. And I've got a second one for you, because it's the cure for being 'chan tngai'd'."

He looked up at me. "How would you know? You'd never even heard of sunstroke until this morning. And now you have the cure for it?"

"Khmer don't *get* sunstroke because we know how to *prevent* it. And I figure the prevention is also the cure." I told him how I'd remembered that my grandfather and his friends had always reached for a coconut as soon as they came in from the fields. "Be sure you drink all of it. I need my navigator back."

He drank the coconut water down to the bottom – and started spitting like a cobra.

"Nyah! *What did you put in here?*" He turned the coconut over and whacked the bottom of it. The secret ingredient fell out onto the bank. "*Worms?* Oh my *god* – did you save me just so you could kill me?"

"You don't have to eat them," I said. "The medicine is on their skin, and it mixes with the coconut water. You've already swallowed it." And I started to hack the end off the second coconut.

"Man," he said, "if I didn't need you to climb trees, I'd kill you. Is this what was in the antidote your grandfather mixed up for your mother when she brushed up against the horned frog?"

"Oh no – that was *much* worse... You've never heard of worms in coconut water? It's the most common Khmer remedy there is. It's for fever, and you're hot. You feel better now, don't you?"

"You know, as a matter of fact I do. Can anything really work that *fast?*"

"The old Khmer medicine can. You're used to French aspirin – twenty minutes." I dropped the rest of the worms into the second coconut and held it out to him.

He looked at me, horrified. "You can't even wash them *off?*"

"Of course not. That would wash away the medicine that's on their skin. Just wait for a minute and the dirt will settle to the bottom... Just be glad they were still alive when I dropped them in there. If they're dead, the remedy doesn't work."

He had to admit that live worms were better than dead ones, and took the coconut from me. "You... don't have a cure for 'vertige', do you"?

"If I did, would you take it?" I asked.

"*Hell* yeah. If I could see what you see as Recon, you know how much faster we'd get home?"

He finished the coconut water, split the nut in half and started to pry the meat out with the tip of his blade.

"You mean, I said, "a dead body just floated down the canal clutching a machete in its hand?"

He laughed as he looked up. "Oh *yeah* it did."

I got the crickets from under the bow seat while his back was turned, then walked up the shoreline and retrieved our food and his gear. I carved a couple of skewers out of bamboo, stuffed the crickets with the peanuts, skewered them, and hid them in my pocket.

I returned to find Puamaak watching the fish trap intently. "We'll get something by tonight," I said. "OK. Tell me about this 'vertige' thing. What happens to you?"

"Well, I spend all that time getting myself up into a tree, only to get dizzy once I'm up there."

"Hmm… And it's gotten worse as you've gotten older, hasn't it? You didn't have it when you were in grammar school."

"Nyah, if you don't even know what it *is*, how did you know *that?*"

"How did you know to get these beetles?" I held out his cup. "Excellent cure for 'vertige'. I'll roast them up for you tonight."

"All I knew," he said, "was that you can eat them. I dammed up a puddle on the shoreline so they couldn't get back into the canal. Then I just cornered them one by one. You can catch a lot of diving beetles in *four hours*. Trying not to think about whether or not your Recon is still alive. But you didn't answer my question. How did you know that I didn't have vertige when I was younger?" He paused for a moment. "Nyah, do you think you *inherited* some of your grandfather's gift for healing? Through some kind of… strange biological process or something?"

"I don't know. Never thought about it."

"But you should. Ask your grandfather how *he* knows what he knows. Did he learn it all from his father, or from another shaman? Or did he experiment, and develop some of his cures on his own? Or did they just… come to him in dreams or something. Ask him. See what he says. You'll see him soon enough – once we're across the Bassac, we should be more than half way back to Pong Tuk. And Takeo is easy walking. Should be long, straight levees most of the way."

"But there'll be people," I said. "And very little cover."

He was quiet for a moment. "I know that's why you went back and got the fish trap. So that we could make more jerky. Once we're across the Bassac we may not be able to forage for *anything* without being seen."

"Or make a fire," I said. "And there'll be double the night guards in the villages, to watch for Vietnamese. They'll shoot at anything that moves."

He nodded, without a sound.

"How about Highway Two?" I asked. "Is it paved?"

"It wasn't when I used to go down with my mother to buy silk. But it shouldn't take me more than a couple of hours to get us through it."

Now, I had a plan for getting us across Highway Two. And it wouldn't take me any two hours. Because I wouldn't have to look for mines. But I'd explain that to him when we got there. And I had a plan to get him to eat more, too. Simply make what his mother had made.

"What was your very favorite dish," I asked, "when you were a kid?"

"Fish 'amok'. Isn't that everyone's favorite? I mean, it's like our national dish. Well, it was..."

I tied our hammocks up and ordered him into his. I wanted to sleep, too, but we'd need cassava as much as we'd need fish if we were going to get ourselves across Takeo without stopping to look for food. So I did what I had to do – I got us more cassava.

Puamaak awoke after sundown to the smell of hot food.

"Nyah, what are you cooking down there? It smells like... *home*."

"Come down and find out."

He climbed out of the tree and I handed him a skewer of the roasted crickets.

"Where did you *get* these?" he asked. He pulled a cricket off the end of the skewer with his teeth.

"We beached the boat in paddies, remember? The crickets were right there. Another excellent cure for 'vertige'."

I handed him the beetles he'd caught, roasted and cracked open. And then I pulled the steamed fish out of the coals and opened the banana leaf wrapper.

"It smells like... *'amok'!* Nyah, how did you *do* it?"

"Well, I didn't have coconut milk, so I butterflied the fish, slit it at intervals, and put coconut strips in the slits. There was a kaffir lime tree right near where I got the coconuts this morning, so I got some lime leaves to put in. I added a layer of weaver ants, put in the last of the peanuts, and wrapped everything up in banana leaf. Then I just steamed it in the coals. I got lucky, finding the ants. There was a tree with a nest in it right near the canal. I just wrapped my 'kramaa' around the nest and plunged the whole thing into the water before the ants had a chance to bite me. Excellent cure for 'vertige'."

"Nyah, how is it that all of your cures just *happen* to be things we found out here. Crickets, beetles, ants... Oh, I get it. Any kind of insect. The medicine must be in the exoskeleton – like the whatever-it-is on the worms' skin."

"Slime. It's the slime."

He rolled his eyes, and we started in on the fish.

"Nyah, you still haven't told me how you know I didn't have 'vertige' when I was a kid."

"Because I've never heard you complain about it from watching the dragon boats line up at the start, looking down from the bridge. Or from looking down from the terrace of Wat Phnom. And if you'd had 'vertige' back then, you'd never have ridden Saambō – I mean, she's *huge*. No, you didn't have 'vertige' in grammar school because the Khmer Rouge hadn't taken over yet."

"What's that got to do with it?" he asked.

"You remember our first day, after our escape? You said, 'Here we are surrounded, and all I can do is talk about my mother's cooking. What's wrong with me?' And then, when you realized you hadn't checked for your machete before you'd fallen asleep the night before, you said, 'I'm the oldest – it was my responsibility. What's wrong with me?' What was my answer?"

"'No food – same thing that's always wrong with us.'"

"Exactly," I said. "You didn't have 'vertige' before the takeover because you were getting enough to *eat*. The dizziness after the exertion of climbing a tree? You're just out of gas by the time you get up there."

"Then why don't *you* get it? You're not getting any more food than I am."

"Because I only use half the energy you do – because I know how to climb. But I wonder you never learned. There were plenty of trees in the city, and every kid I ever met there could climb pretty well."

"They weren't Chinese kids. You know how we are – we're always inside doing... *homework*. Especially the kids in Chinese school. And when I wasn't doing homework my father had me helping him so that I could learn the business. I'm lucky I learned to swim on my vacations. But as for the cure for 'vertige' being food, well, you just might be right."

I pulled the last course off the fire. The coconut meat – roasted to perfection. I blew the ash off a piece and handed it to him. "But there *is* another thing. If you really are afraid of heights, don't look down. If you don't look down, you won't be afraid. It's simple logic – not anything I inherited from my grandfather. You can feel for the branch below you with your foot, without having to look for it. Get the jerky started, will you? I still have to finish up for tomorrow."

"What else do you have to do?" he asked.

"Make a wrist strap for each of our machetes in case the boat goes over." I held out my hand for him to pass his machete over to me. "But actually, you're not Navigation tomorrow morning. You're *ballast*. You're going to lie down flat along the keel to give the boat more stability." I passed him more of the roasted coconut. "Have another piece."

I put the corner of the end of his blade in the coals and, when it was red hot, burned a hole through one side of the handle of my 'kwaiw' – near the end. Then I heated the blade again and did the other side. I passed a vine through the hole and tied it tight, to make a wrist strap. Then I did his machete, using the hook on my 'kwaiw'.

I handed him back his knife. "Go cut us a couple of lengths of banana stalk to put under our shirts tomorrow. I'm going to steer us around the north side of the traps. We'll start right after breakfast so that we hit the north shore of the Bassac at about seven thirty – the sun will be up, so no one will mistake us for something they should be shooting at. We'll just walk due west, pulling the boat behind us, until the river takes that sharp turn north."

"Bare-headed, " he said, "with our 'kramaas' hidden, so no one across the river can tell if we're Cambodian or Vietnamese. Just a couple of fishermen's kids, too far away for anyone to realize that they wouldn't recognize us if we were closer."

"I got a good view of the area from the tree overlooking the traps the first time I went up. I think the furthest we'll have to haul the boat west will be four kilometers or so. And if we don't have trouble getting across the Bassac, I'll be climbing my next tree around lunchtime tomorrow. Then we'll just keep going until dark."

"*If* we don't run into people," he said.

"How many of our scenarios have we eliminated?"

"One – our unit. We got away – One down. Two – other Khmer Rouge units – probably all up around Phnom Penh. Three – the Vietnamese – yeah, they'll be out there, especially around the highways. Four – collaborators who might mistake us for pro-Khmer Rouge – still out there. Five – people who might turn us in for food – still out there. Six – people who might mistake us for Vietnamese – still out there. Seven – mines – still out there. Did we have an eighth scenario?"

"Yeah, we did," I said. "Pushing ourselves beyond our limits. Your sunstroke..."

"And we'll have a ninth one, as soon as we're across the Bassac. The village cadres – especially the night guards."

"That's Six – 'people who might mistake us for Vietnamese.'"

He laughed. "But... what would you do if something were to happen to me tomorrow?"

"Follow the directions you gave me. Look for Phnom Da, and then head forty-five degrees southwest to pick up the road I'm supposed to shadow over to Phnom Treil."

"You have another option," he said.

"Are you kidding? I'd have enough trouble just finding Phnom Da. You have a map in your head – I don't. If there's another way, I wouldn't be able to figure it out."

"Nyah, you're so damned *smart*. You'd have it all figured out in five minutes."

"And what *is* it that I would have figured out?"

"What have you always told me you knew the best? The Mekong. If something happens to me while you're still near the Bassac, get yourself to the Bassac and walk up the bank until you hit the Mekong. You'd be a few kilometers south of the boardwalk, at that point. Swim east across the Mekong right there – before you get into Phnom Penh. Then walk up the east bank of the Mekong and swim it back west twenty kilometers or so upriver – to Prai Anchaan. Yes, there'll be Vietnamese going back and forth on Highway Six, but you can hide way back from the road on your grandfather's land. Because you know the place. You'd just hide the same way you did from the village bully – and he *never found you,* did he? Even though he was from Prai Anchaan himself. You'd know just where to hunt, and fish, and you'd have all the clean water you need. From the size of the area that's been evacuated I'll tell you, little brother – the Vietnamese have taken Phnom Penh. So pretty soon things will calm down, and the Vietnamese will tell everyone to leave the communes and go home. Whoever in your family made it through the last four years will eventually show up in Prai Anchaan. Your grandfather, your grandmother, the aunt who nursed you through all the tropical diseases, your cousins, your *mother*… If anything happens to me, go up the Bassac to the Mekong. And then on to Prai Anchaan."

His words were meant to reassure me, but they had the opposite effect. Was *he* afraid that he wasn't going to make it? Was he keeping something from me?

"Is everything ready for tomorrow?" he asked.

"Yeah. I just have to tie all the food up."

We climbed the banyan, I tied up our packs, and we wrapped ourselves up for the night. As we rocked back and forth I told him why I thought there really could be a water dragon in the deep hole at the head of the river – why they might not be extinct. I told him about the Stegosaurus on the doorframe of the Angkorian temple, carved less than a thousand years ago. And about the Water Monitor that had just… *shown up* one day in Prai Anchaan – a lizard the size of a Komodo Dragon. I told him about the Viking water dragons. And that the 'monster' in Loch Ness *must* be real – it had been spotted by too many people who simply weren't drunk. But he just laughed at me.

"Nyah, you're going to *look* for a dragon tomorrow, but you're not going to find one. Wait – if I can just find you some marijuana… Then you'll see dragons flying all over the place!"

"Oh! *That's* why you don't believe me. Because you're Chinese."

"What? I'm half Khmer too, you know. I'm not one of those Chinese who calls the Khmer stupid and lazy. This has nothing to do with me being Chinese."

"Yes, it does, but for a different reason. You're thinking of the *Chinese* dragon, and you think that all dragons are the same. The dragons you would have seen at the Chinese cemetery, in your father's temple, in paintings in Chinese restaurants and in the Chinese zodiac – oh yeah, you Chinese have dragons flying all over the place. But they're dragons of the *air* – they're not *water* dragons."

"Well… yeah," he said, "I guess I never did think much about it. I just assumed that all dragons are the same, and that they're not real."

"Because of the way they're depicted in Chinese art. Flying around on wings that are too small to bear their weight, and that aren't even aerodynamic. Or flying around with no wings at all!"

"Well how do you know," he asked, "that the 'neak' isn't a dragon of the air? You find them on the rooves of Khmer temples – *up in the air.* Explain that to me."

"Most Khmer temples don't have ponds, like Chinese temples do. So the 'neaks' end up on the roof instead. *Where you can get a good look at them.* A dorsal fin that runs all the way down the back, *another* fin at the tip of the tail, huge eyes for seeing in low light, and a crest on the top of the head to make it streamlined for diving. And the eyes always have a startled look, as though someone has just caught the animal and yanked it out of the water. Hmm…"

"Caudal fin, Nyah. The fin at the tip of the tail – caudal fin."

"OK. You had two more years of school than I did. Which should have made you more observant. Which way is a 'neak' always going as he slithers along the roof? *Always.*"

"Down," he said.

"Not a dragon of the air, or he'd be going *up*."

Puamaak stopped rocking. "You're twisting my head around, Nyah. Like you always do. It's the fins that have got me thinking… So a 'neak's not some kind of giant water snake – a reptile. Or something like the Water Monitor – that's a reptile, too. Or a dinosaur-like creature, like the Loch Ness Monster – they say he swims with flippers. And a separate caudal fin? I used to go with my mother to buy eels in the market; I remember very well what an eel looks like. Their dorsal fins are joined to their caudal fins. So the 'neak' isn't some kind of giant eel. That leaves… *fish*. Yeah, they can get as big as a dragon. You said a Giant Mekong Catfish can get up to two hundred and seventy-five kilos, didn't you?"

"They found one even bigger than that, Puamaak."

"*Really*… Well there must have been a lot of 'neaks', centuries ago, or there wouldn't be so many cultures that have water dragon stories. What makes a species go extinct? What would have made the Stegosaurus disappear?"

"Ha!" I said. "Just look at what the Khmer Rouge had us doing. Clearing jungle for paddies. And I did it for *three years*. You know how many animals' homes we destroyed? And that's been going on all over the country."

"They must have cleared a lot in Angkorian times, too," he said, "because the amount of rice they were able to produce is legendary. The cadres used to throw that in our faces all the time. Perhaps the sculptor who carved the Stegosaurus into the temple doorframe a thousand years ago saw one that was killed when his territory was cleared for paddies – like the King Cobra you saw in your first work camp."

"Perhaps that sculptor saw the very last one," I said.

"And the Khmer Rouge must have made many animals extinct during the last four years simply because people were forced into hunting when they no longer had enough to eat."

"It's been more than four years," I said. "The Water Monitor that showed up in Prai Anchaan and started eating the dead infantrymen – that was before the Khmer Rouge even took over. And you know what happened to him? They *ate* him. My neighbors *ate* him. Because they couldn't farm any more – not with the shelling back and forth. And they ate him knowing that *he* had been eating human flesh – that's how desperate they were for food. I never saw another one after that."

"The Khmer Rouge hunt too, Nyah. But they hunt *people*. They followed our fathers to Pong Tuk – mine because he had a lot of money, and yours because he had money or power. They stalked them, and then they killed them."

I was quiet for a moment. My father had been an officer in the Lon Nol army, but of course I had never told anyone that. I didn't think the Khmer Rouge had followed him to Pong Tuk; I don't think they ever figured out exactly who he was. But he was a career soldier – you could tell by the way he walked, and the way he talked. I believe they took him away simply because they suspected he was in the army. But I had no way of knowing what had happened at my school, now a prison called 'S-21'. As we were later to find out, Puamaak was right. Once the Khmer Rouge had targeted a suspect, they hunted him down.

Then tortured him, until he was dead.

"And with each passing month, more people starve," said Puamaak. "If the Vietnamese can't stop the Khmer Rouge, the *Khmer people* will become extinct. And that's the truth of it. Especially if there's no rice next year."

I didn't say anything, but nodded my head in the dark.

"I'm sorry, little brother. I just don't know when to keep my mouth shut. Go to sleep – forget about what I said. Just go to sleep, and dream of your dragon."

Day Seven ~ *The Bassac*

Puamaak awoke to the sound of leaves rustling in the wind. But there was no wind.

I shook his hammock again. "*Wake up.*"

"Nyah – what's the matter?"

"I climbed to the top of the tree so I could be sure of where the border is, before they turn their lights out. But there *are* no lights. Puamaak, everyone is *gone.* But I should have realized that the day before yesterday – I saw houseboats, but none in the *water.*"

"Either something's already happened, or something's about to happen. And I don't want to stick around to try to figure out which it is. Come on – we're heading north. The hell with taking the boat."

"But the fish trap," I said. "*Damn* I hate to leave it behind."

We got out of the tree quickly, packed up and started walking up the canal.

"To tell you the truth," I said, "I never did figure out how we were going to deal with the current in the fish trap river. I was just going to take the chance that it wouldn't shoot us straight into the current in the Bassac and down into Vietnam."

A few minutes later we struck out northwest, thinking we could still make our way over to the Bassac while putting distance between ourselves and the border. We'd try to hit the river exactly where we wanted to swim it – half a kilometer north of where it turns east.

We reached the shoreline a couple of hours later. I found a stand of trees, and roasted the fish I'd taken out of the trap just before we'd left the canal. I wanted my friend to rest as much as I wanted him to eat; now that we were on foot again, it was going to be much harder for him. Especially when we'd have to start circumnavigating inhabited villages on the other side of the water.

"We got lucky," he said. "The river's pretty narrow here, and it looks like there's a canal on the other side. There should be a road running up the west bank, all the way up to the boardwalk in Phnom Penh. We can use the canal to go under it."

"*If* we don't see people. I'll climb a tree and take a look. We can go further north to get to a less populated area if we have to. Then find a buffalo crossing and cross the road there. Buffalo are creatures of habit – they go back and forth in the same spot, morning and evening. Even if there's no one to shoo them along. So they would have already tripped anything in the roadbed or the shoulder." I smiled. "So now you know my plan for crossing Highway Two."

I climbed a tree and came down again. "No one on the canal." I pointed across the water. "See that rocky bluff next to it, jutting out into the river? We'll aim for that. But let's rest an hour or so before we swim across."

"We won't have to swim, little brother." He got up, and returned a few minutes later with four banana stalks. He laid two of them side by side, and joined them by inserting a stick just below the top and another above the bottom. Now he had a float, like a short surfboard. He handed it to me and then made one for himself. "We can climb the outcrop, and you can climb a tree on the top of it. You should be able to see *forever* from up there." And he picked up his float and started for the water.

Now, I'd been worrying all morning about him getting across the Bassac. Ever since we'd realized that we couldn't take the boat. So I had all kinds of good stories lined up, to distract him and keep him going.

He looked out over the river. "Looks like it's almost a kilometer across."

"Oh, much less Puamaak. Always looks further than it is." It's actually the opposite; I thought we were in for a much longer swim.

"Well, you know the rivers. I'll take your estimate over mine any day."

And we pushed off, to cross the Bassac.

I immediately launched into my calculated conversation. By the time he noticed he was tiring, we'd be on the other side of the river. "We'll be in Pong Tuk in a couple of days. Who will be waiting for you?"

"My mother and my two sisters. But I don't think their hair will still be striped." He laughed. "Who will be waiting for you? Besides your grandfather, and your mother."

I knew his sisters wouldn't be waiting for him – they'd be in work camps, if they were still alive. But I didn't say anything.

"My younger brother and sister," I replied. Two of my mother's brothers had come with us to Pong Tuk, but they'd be in work camps, too. Time to launch into a story – I didn't want him asking any more questions.

"Didn't you wonder," I started, "how my grandfather made us a bomb shelter without concrete?"

"Yeah… I was lucky I lived in Phnom Penh." The Americans hadn't bombed it because it was the seat of Lon Nol's government.

"Well, he started by digging a shaft straight down. Oh, no, he didn't do it by himself. He had two of my uncles to help him. Then they lined the shaft by setting bamboo poles vertically into it. Big ones – the trees must have been thirty centimeters across at the bottom. Then my grandfather braced the poles with crossbeams – more bamboo poles. Then the three of them dug a room at the bottom of the shaft. When it was finished they lined the floor with big papyrus mats my aunts had made. Then they lowered a wooden cot down the shaft, set it in the room, and put food underneath it. Things that wouldn't spoil – dried fish, tamarind in the pod, pickled vegetables, dried mangoes, coconuts in the husk, pickled eggs, rice…"

"How were they going to cook rice down there?" he asked.

"They put pans and a 'kwaiw' under the cot, too – and firewood. And we always had bottles of water filled and ready to go; when we saw the planes and ran for the hole, we'd each grab one. If we didn't have time to grab water, we'd cook the rice with coconut water from the coconuts under the cot."

"But Nyah, why didn't you suffocate from the smoke of the cook fire?"

"My grandfather had built a ventilation system in."

"So he doesn't just know medicine, and farming, and the wisdom of the Buddha. He has some knowledge of engineering, too. Where'd he get it?"

"I don't know," I said. "Khmer people just seem to… *have* it. I mean, look at Angkor Wat. A thousand years ago they just stacked a bunch of rocks one on top of the other and made the biggest religious complex in the world. Bigger than Notre Dame in Paris. Just as famous, too. If your father were Khmer, you wouldn't be so incredulous. My grandfather made some kind of drainage system in the shelter, too. And he kept rainwater out by roofing over the shaft. We got in through a crawl space on the side that had a rain flap over it. Yeah, we'd lift the flap, step onto a ladder and scurry down the shaft into the underground room."

"I would have been claustrophobic," he said. "What was the longest your family ever had to stay down there?"

"You know, I don't remember. But I know we were down there a *long time*... The air strikes went by quickly, but during the worst of the fighting between the Lon Nol troops and the insurgents, it wasn't safe to stay in our house. So we had to go back down into the pit. And it wasn't just waiting out the fighting, it was waiting to find out who'd *won*. The last time we came up we didn't even bother to find out – we just packed up quickly, went to Phnom Penh, and never went back to Prai Anchaan again. But the waiting, underground... that's one of my worst memories from childhood." And I looked up into the sunlight, thankful to be swimming in clean water in the middle of a beautiful cool-season morning with a stomach full of fresh fish.

"Which uncle is the impatient one?" he asked. "The one with the head injury?"

"The youngest. And I'll warn you right now, he has a temper – if you ever meet him, stay out of his way. But I wonder if he survived... he probably crossed a cadre a long time ago. Sometimes he doesn't realize what he's saying."

"How'd he hit his head?" he asked.

"He and his friends were rolling logs in the Mekong, and he slipped. Smashed his head on a log. They hauled him out of the water before he drowned."

"Or washed downriver..." Puamaak looked at the shoreline ahead of us to try to gauge how fast we were being carried south.

"Slow current in the Bassac this time of year," I said, as though I were an authority on this river I knew nothing about. "See that coconut in front of us? Look how slowly it's moving." But the coconut was on the *other* side of the main current – we weren't even halfway across. "So... how old are your sisters?"

He laughed. "Nyah, if I don't know how old *I* am, how would I know how old *they* are? But I do know they're too old for you. Too bad – they're pretty. But you know... if the Khmer Rouge married them off after you and I were put in camps, that would increase my family's chances of survival. That would bring two more men into it. Men the cadres and the army didn't plan to kill."

"What do you mean, 'if the Khmer Rouge married them off'?"

"Oh, I guess you never heard... The cadres just *tell* you one day that you're going to get married. And that they've already got the girl for you. And you haven't even met her. And then they marry you off in a mass ceremony."

"*Really?*"

"Oh yeah. In the story I heard, there were fifty-two couples. They started the ceremony just before dark because they wanted to show the newlyweds a movie afterwards. To make the occasion more memorable. As if getting married to a complete stranger at gunpoint wouldn't be memorable enough. Well, this guy was married to the girl they'd picked out for him in less than a minute – when there are fifty-two couples, you have to move things right along you know. Then they separated all the brides and grooms for the movie, brides on one side and grooms on the other. When the movie was over the grooms were instructed to retrieve their brides and go to their assigned huts for the wedding night.

Well, this guy couldn't remember what his bride looked like. He couldn't see, anyway – there were a few palm-leaf torches lit, but that was all. So he thought, I'll just wait until all the other grooms have retrieved their brides, and the only girl left will be mine. So he waited, and waited, as the other fifty-one grooms went round and round looking for their brides.

When all of the other couples had left for their huts, there was one girl left. He went up to her and apologized for not claiming her earlier. When she told him that that was all right, he saw that she was missing some of her teeth. He thought it very odd that he hadn't noticed that when he'd been married to her.

And then he realized what had happened. *Her* groom had taken another bride, knowing he could get away with it in the confusion. So *she* wasn't his wife – someone else had taken his!

But you know what he did? A rumor got started that the camp was going to be attacked by the Vietnamese that night, and everyone decided to sneak out under cover of darkness. But he wouldn't leave this girl to fend for herself. He told her that if she wanted to come with him, he'd do his best to look out for her. She said politely, no, thank you, she could fend for herself, and that she had family nearby. So he snuck out of the camp, and never saw the girl again."

"Well," I said, "I'd just tell them I'm 'ktui'." (homosexual)

"Wouldn't make any difference, Nyah. They'd marry you off anyway."

And by the time he'd finished telling me his story, we'd hit the eastern shore of the Bassac. We hid our floats and started up the rocky bluff we'd seen from across the river. We climbed to the very top of it, and then I climbed the tallest tree.

I found myself looking out over farmland, from the foot of the bluff below me out to the horizon. I could see the Vietnamese villages to the south, over the border. And the long, straight canal coming up from the Delta, from what had been Oc-Eo. There was a mountain off to the west that I knew must be Phnom Da, although I couldn't make out the temple on the top of it. I could see the terrain we'd have to cross if we simply headed forty-five degrees southwest from Phnom Da – all paddies, with long, straight levies in between them.

But no matter where I looked, I couldn't find what I was looking for. Any sign of *life*. A curl of smoke from a cookfire, a fishing boat on the water, the green of the winter crops in the fields. But there was nothing. We were still in the war zone we'd been trying to get out of. And I couldn't see the end of it.

I climbed down from the tree, to tell my friend.

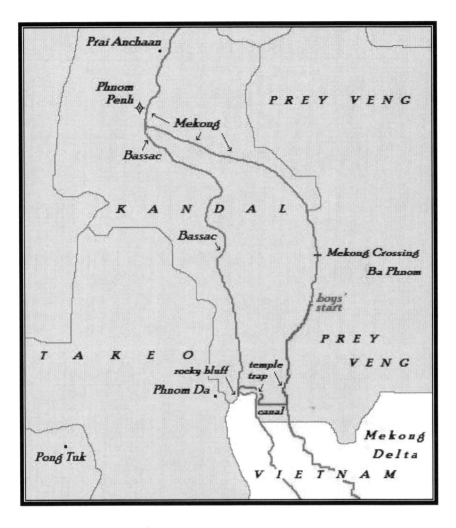

The boys' route from the morning of January 8th
(from the east bank of the Mekong, south of the Crossing)

to midday January 12th
(to the rocky bluff on the west bank of the Bassac,
where the river turns east)

60 kilometers (37 miles)

Book Three - *Takeo*

Day Seven - *The Temple on the Mountain*

I dropped down onto the crest of the rocky bluff on the west bank of the Bassac.

"Nyah, could you see Phnom Da?"

"I think so. There's a mountain due west of us, and there's *something* on the top of it."

"Man! We finally got a break. We'll just walk west until we can see the straight lines of the temple. Then… forty-five degrees southwest. Straight shot to Pong Tuk. But, what else did you see? Who's out there?"

I shook my head. "No one."

I guess it was the tone of my voice – he remembered it, from six long days ago. "No one at *all?"*

"I can't lie to you, Puamaak. We're still in the war zone, and I can't even see the end of it. There's been a 'gkeeah'."

"A gk… *what?"*

Chinese, I thought. *No wonder he doesn't know the word.* I turned away from the barren landscape and looked out over the Bassac, slowly making its way to the Delta as it had for a thousand years. *The only thing as constant as the flow of the river,* I thought, *is the recurrence of war.* And then I sat down on the rock so that my friend would sit down next to me. A 'gkeeah' is not something that can be explained easily.

"It's a purely Khmer word," I said, "not a loan word from any other language. It's a very old word, left over from Angkorian times. From when the Cham came up the rivers and sacked Angkor in the twelfth century. You've never heard it because it never happened to you Phnom Penh people until April of '75, and, after that, we weren't allowed to talk about it."

Puamaak hugged his knees and waited for me to continue. Like I'd waited that very first night, on the mountain, to hear the rest of his escape plan.

"It has only one meaning," I explained. "'Scrape'. But it's not a verb – it's a noun."

"It's the reason all the people have disappeared."

"Yes," I said. "It means everyone's been *scraped* off the land. It only happens in a cataclysmic war – that's why you only hear the word every thousand years or so."

"So there will be no one left in Pong Tuk."

I could see the tears well up in his eyes; he wasn't as used to war as I was. Phnom Penh people had had only four years of it. I'd had six – half my lifetime.

"But that doesn't mean that everyone's dead," I said. "It just means they got pushed somewhere else. I don't know how we're going to find our families. Do you want to float down the Bassac to the coast, and walk west along the beach to Thailand? Wait until the Vietnamese have solidified their control, and then go back to your house in Phnom Penh? If your mother and your sisters are still alive, that's where they'll go – eventually. I can't think of any *other* way to find them."

"We wouldn't even get out of the Delta, Nyah. Someone would catch us. It would be easy, because neither of us knows anything about Vietnam. We wouldn't remember the map, because we never *knew* the map. We wouldn't be able to understand what the people around us were saying. We wouldn't be able to look for food because there will be villages down both sides of the river. All the way to the sea. How could we even get out of the water without getting caught? And once they'd caught us, they'd take all our gear. Your lighter, our water cups, our hammocks... They've been at war much longer than we have – they'll be all the poorer for it, and all the more desperate. Someone might kill us just to get our machetes."

"Well, what do you want to do?" I asked.

He looked out over the river. "*I* don't know... Why do you never cry? I never see you cry, Nyah."

I sat as still as the stone beneath me. "Because my grandfather is already dead."

He whipped his head around and looked into my face. And then just stared at me, in disbelief.

"He died of starvation," I said, "just before they took me away, to put me in my first work camp."

Puamaak put his head on his knees, trying to keep his shoulders from shaking. His tears dripped onto the rock.

"That's how I survived that camp," I said, "if you want to know the truth. I was in shock, so I was very quiet, and did everything the cadres told me to do. I think they thought I'd been brainwashed before they even got me. I saw kids *die* in their first camp – they never made it to a second. So my grandfather's death probably saved my life."

My friend raised his head. "But I thought you said he would *be* there when we got back."

"He will be. He's buried there. In the stand of big trees south of the village."

He was quiet for a moment. "I'm sorry, Nyah. I'm so *sorry*. Is... is that how you know about the owl?"

I nodded.

"But the uncle who took you on the fishing trips," he said. "You were close to him. Perhaps he's grown to be like his father, since you saw him last."

"If he survived," I said. "He has a heart condition. And I don't know where he is. He didn't end up in Pong Tuk – he's with the *other* half of the family."

Puamaak scraped his hands over his face to try to dry his tears. "I'm sorry about that too... Well, what do you think we should do?"

"We have to get closer to the mountain," I said, "to be sure it's Phnom Da – *if* we decide to go on to Pong Tuk... Hey, do you think you can climb? There should be an easy way up to the temple for the people who used to go there to pray, centuries ago. And for the people who used to come down from Phnom Penh for the day, when we were kids. We'd be able to see much more from the top of the mountain than I can see from here. So we could make a better decision where to go. Because we'd be able to better guess the extent of the 'gkeeah' – how far west the people have been scraped off the land."

"Yeah, I can climb," he said. "So when we get to the top of the mountain, we'll have three choices – Pong Tuk, Phnom Penh, or Prai Anchaan. I don't want to go to Thailand, Nyah – I want to find my mother."

"OK then. These are our options. One – Continue on to Pong Tuk, and hope our mothers are still there. If it looks like the 'gkeeah' didn't go over that far. Two – Go to Phnom Penh and hide out somewhere until the Vietnamese can solidified their control, and wait for your mother to come back. Three – Go to Prai Anchaan and hide out on my grandfather's land until the Vietnamese can solidify their control, and then go back into Phnom Penh to look for your mother."

"What about *your* mother? Why do you never talk about her, Nyah?"

"Because I don't know her very well. We lived in Prai Anchaan, she lived in Phnom Penh. I didn't even know she was my mother until I was five. She used to come out to Prai Anchaan once a year, and the year they put me in school, they told me who she was. Then when I had to move into Phnom Penh, she was always at work. And by then she had three other children. My father didn't pay me much attention, so I just stuck with my grandfather."

"And you were only with her for a few months in Pong Tuk – and then she was out in the fields all day. One hell of a life *you've* had, Nyah. I'm sorry."

"Oh, no, you don't understand. My grandfather was as good to me as any mother could have been. My aunts were, too. And my grandmother. I know my mother loves me, in her own way – all mothers love their children. But it's less likely that our mothers will still be in Pong Tuk than it is that they've headed back to Phnom Penh... We have to get to the top of Phnom Da to see the extent of the 'gkeeah'."

"All the Phnom Penh people," he said, "will be going back together. Safety in numbers."

I shook my head. "They'll all still need to hide from the cadres. Because the cadres will be more ruthless now than ever. They know the Vietnamese are coming – they'll be like rats backed into a corner, watching the cobra flare its hood just before it strikes. They'll be *robbing* the evacuees, trying to survive themselves. Stealing their food, and leaving them on the side of the road to die. No, I think it's much more likely that each family will go back separately. And you know there will still be cadres in Pong Tuk, even if our mothers are gone. The cadres are always the last to leave. They're the 'clean-up' detail."

"'Clean-up'?" he asked.

"Shoot anyone who doesn't get out. Or bayonet them, if they don't want to waste their bullets."

He shuddered. "Nyah – how do you *know* all this?"

"I got 'gkeeah'd' out of Prai Anchaan, remember? My grandfather had to explain to me why we had to leave, and what would happen if we didn't. And then we all got 'gkeeah'd out of Phnom Penh. So I've been 'gkeeah'd *twice*. Now, let's talk about Option Two."

"Go to Phnom Penh," he said, "and hide out until the Vietnamese can solidify their control. Wait for my mother and my sisters to come back."

"Not a good choice. Even if we could manage to hide, there's nowhere to get food. When was the last time cassava and rambutans and mushrooms grew wild in Phnom Penh? Before it *was* Phnom Penh – before the capital was moved south from Angkor half a millennium ago. And how about the other stuff we've been living on the past four years – snakes and frogs and jungle rats? Same answer. And, no, I'm not eating city rats."

"But we'd have the Tonle Sap," he said, "and the Mekong, and the Bassac…"

"… but no fish trap. And the rivers flow swiftly in that few kilometers where they converge; there are no shallows. Nowhere to catch crabs and snails and clams and mudskippers, or to gather morning glory vines and water chestnuts and lotus."

"Nyah, I just had a *terrible* thought. What if our mothers go back to Phnom Penh, and they starve there? At least they had *something* in Pong Tuk."

"They might have thought of that, too. Pong Tuk 's not all that far from the ocean – they may have headed for the beach, to try to get to Thailand."

"What do you think *your* mother would do?" he asked.

"Just what we're doing – look for *her* mother. I think she would try to get to Phnom Penh, and then wait there until she could get through to Prai Anchaan."

"That makes sense," he said. "Yeah, that makes more sense than anything else. OK – that's our third option – go to Prai Anchaan. What do you think?"

"Well, it's like you said Puamaak. We'd be able to find food there, and hide there. Straight shot up the Bassac, cross the Mekong just south of the city, then cross back again opposite Prai Anchaan. Once everything calms down and the Vietnamese de-mine Highway Six, we can walk back to Phnom Penh to find your mother."

"Or float down the shoreline of the Mekong," he said.

"You know, you don't sound so much like a city kid anymore." And I patted him on the back.

"OK," he said, getting to his feet. "Let's start for Phnom Da so we can get a better look at the landscape. See if we can make it to the foot of the mountain by the time the sun goes down. Pick up a path to the temple as soon as we can see in the morning."

We climbed down off the rocky outcrop and retrieved our banana-stalk floats. We kicked our way under the bridge on the road that ran up to Phnom Penh, then got out of the water and walked due west.

As the sun began its final descent, Phnom Da lay straight ahead of us across the plain. We made camp for the night, started our fire and tied our hammocks up.

There wasn't that deadly silence here – there were cicadas in the trees above us. We counted them as they knocked off for the night, one by one. When the coals were ready I pushed our food down into them, and we moved to the northern edge of the grove to watch the last of the western light play on the walls of the ancient temple.

"Nyah, if we do head for Pong Tuk tomorrow, we have to take a landmark forty-five degrees southwest from here before the sun is gone."

I lay down and pointed my feet straight at the rapidly-sinking sun. Puamaak made sure that the top of my head pointed straight back to the Bassac. I extended my left arm out at a right angle from my body, and he moved it halfway down to my feet. "Look over your fingers, Nyah, and take our first mark."

"That huge kapok tree. It must be more than thirty meters tall."

"That's a good mark, but there's probably a village under it. Someone would have planted that tree in our grandfathers' time, to use the cotton wool for pillows and mattresses. But it's the only thing out there that's tall enough. We'll deal with the village when we get to it."

"*If* we go that way," I said. "Prai Anchaan's our best option. We can make a fish trap as soon as we get settled on my grandfather's land. Then we can go into Phnom Penh to find your mother and your sisters, and bring them back to Prai Anchaan with us. My village is our best option – believe me."

I retrieved our food from the coals and returned to the edge of the grove. We watched as the moon rose over the mountain, turning the little temple on the top of it into a glistening jewel. The moon would be full tomorrow.

The roof must have collapsed, because the moonlight disappeared into the walls. I wondered if there *had* been an oracle there, a thousand years ago – what kings had consulted him, what predictions he'd made, and what stories he'd had to tell. Certainly there would have been a healer associated with Phnom Da. I wondered if he'd been anything like my grandfather.

"Nyah! *There's someone up there!* I just saw him move. Look – there goes someone else!"

It seemed we weren't the only ones anticipating the full moon. The sound carried over the open plains, and echoed in the walls of the temple. One at first – their leader. Then another, and another, until they all started in. A pack of wild dogs, howling at the moon.

"What was I thinking," I said, "when I suggested we climb Phnom Da? There would have been plenty of people living there before the war, to sell food and water and trinkets to the day-trippers. And they would *all* have had to leave their dogs behind, because they would *all* have been relocated – because there's a temple on the top of the mountain. What the hell was I thinking?"

My friend shook his head. "We won't be able to climb that mountain even in the daytime."

We walked back into the grove and sat down at the last of our fire. I tossed some kindling onto it and poked the coals, trying to keep it going.

"Where did you live, anyway?" I asked. "Would your mother try to go back to Phnom Penh by shadowing Highway Two, or Highway Three?"

"Three – we lived in Pochentong."

"*Pochentong?* I thought you lived on the east side – by the boardwalk. Twenty kilometers from me. But if you were on the west side it was more like forty. And the Khmer Rouge probably mined the city when they realized that they couldn't stop the Vietnamese. How would we cross *that*, to find your mother? And whatever's not mined is full of Vietnamese."

"Nyah, logistically, it would make more sense for us to split up. For me to go to Pochentong by going northwest from here, and for you to go to Prai Anchaan by going north. But splitting up is not an option – neither one of us will make it without the other. So we have to agree on *one* of our three possible destinations, and stay together."

We sat in silence, staring into the last of the glowing coals.

"Which way would *your* mother go back?" he asked. "Highway Two, or Highway Three?"

"Three, because that's how we got to Pong Tuk. So that's the only way she knows. She'd go to Pochentong, and then find a place to wait until she could get through the city to Highway Six."

"Pochentong..." He suddenly sat bolt upright. *"Pochentong! Why have I been so stupid?* The international airport, from before the war – it's all set up for them. They'll start flying their troops into Pochentong. And as they bring their troops in, they'll commandeer all the abandoned houses around the airport to convert them into barracks." He nodded his head, slowly. "Including ours. My mother's smart – she will have thought of that... So she'll have gone somewhere else." And he buried his face in his hands.

I remembered the day I'd realized that the Khmer Rouge would have burned my grandfather's house, and all the trees around it. And I remembered how I'd felt. That's how my friend was feeling now. No, this was worse, because he no longer knew where his mother would go. I started to think, grasping at anything I could to rally him.

"Hey," I said, "all we've heard of the Vietnamese since we escaped a week ago was artillery fire the day after we started for Pong Tuk. We didn't hear *anything* after that. And the artillery fire might have been our army, one unit firing at another. Maybe all the people have disappeared because they *thought* the Vietnamese were coming. Maybe they never came."

But my friend just shook his head. "I think they got across the Mekong at Neak Luong sometime after we got across Highway One."

"You're just guessing."

"No, I'm not," he said. "Think about it. Think about how fast our army retreated. And think about how short of troops they must have been even before *that*. It's like I said before – I'm 'new people'. A recognized enemy of the state. And they *still* put a gun in my hand. I think we didn't hear much shooting because there was no one left to shoot at."

I was quite for a moment. "So the Vietnamese are here... and almost certainly using the airport."

I poked the coals again, and, this time, a lick of flame came up.

"Your mother's mother," I said, "Is she still alive? I mean, was she, the last you knew?"

"Yes."

"Where did she live?"

"With my mother's older sister."

"Where?"

"Pochentong." He put his face in his hands again.

"Yes! Don't you see? My mother will try to get to Prai Anchaan to find her mother, through Pochentong and then through Phnom Penh. And your mother *will* try to get to Pochentong – to try to find *her* mother. But because the Vietnamese will have commandeered the airport, they'll have closed *off* Pochentong. So, *if* our mothers left Pong Tuk, they're on the same highway and will get stuck at the same place – on the western edge of Pochentong."

He lifted his face out of his hands.

"We'll find them," I said. "We'll go back to Pong Tuk, and if they're not there, we'll know which way they went." I nodded my head, slowly. "And where they'll have ended up."

"With *hundreds* of *thousands* of other evacuees trying to get back into the city? How will we find them, Nyah. *How?"*

"We'll find them, Older Brother. We'll find them somehow."

Day Eight - The Smell of Water

"Nyah. Wake up."

I opened my eyes to blackness.

"Wake up." Puamaak caught the end of my hammock, and shook it.

"Did you hear something?" I whispered.

"No, but we have to get up and get going. Because we have to get to Highway Two *today.*"

I was instantly awake. "Today? Why?"

"Because once the Vietnamese get their minesweepers onto it, we're blocked. *Completely.* Two runs all the way down to Vietnam. I remembered in the middle of the night, and it woke me up. I've been awake since then."

"But they can only sweep one area at a time," I said. "We'll get around them."

"No. They'll start from *both ends.* From the Phnom Penh end in the north, and from the Delta end in the south. Just like they would with 101. And as soon as the south end's clear, they'll start bringing their troops in. The troops that will occupy Takeo."

"How far away is it, do you think?" I asked.

"About halfway across the province."

"Halfway across the province?"

"Yeah. And we'll have to go even further than *that.* Even if the Vietnamese aren't there when we get there, we can't make camp anywhere near the highway – they could move in overnight. From the north, *or* from the south. Or from both ways – we'd wake up surrounded again. And we have to be in our hammocks, with all our gear tied up, before the moon rises. Because it will be full tonight."

"OK," I said, "I'm awake. Let's go."

We climbed out of the tree together, packed up and headed out.

"How well can you see?" I asked, tugging on his shirt to guide him.

"I can see the silhouette of the kapok pretty clearly. And now I can see a rise ahead of us – that must be a levee." We got up onto the path, and I took the lead. Just like we'd done in the army.

I fished some cold roasted cassava out of my pack, turned back and handed it to him. "There's water straight ahead of you. Drink all you can."

He looked down the path, straining his eyes. "Nyah, what is it in your ninja-like brain that tells you there's water there? I'm willing to bet that you can't see it any better than I can."

I didn't answer, but ran ahead to the waterhole instead. "In front of you, forty paces," I whispered back to him. "Don't fall in. We don't have time."

We drank as much as we could and started for the kapok again.

"You didn't answer my question, Nyah. How do you know there's water around? There's *something* that clues you in. What is it?"

"If you want me to tell you, you have to promise that you won't argue with me and insist it's not possible."

"Little brother, is this discussion going to be anything like the one we had about the water dragon? Where the *mythological* suddenly becomes the *completely logical?*"

"Yeah... I have a very powerful sense of smell, so I can smell a waterhole. Even from half a kilometer away. I've never met anyone else who could do it."

"I've never even heard of anyone else who could do it," he said. "So it's the smell of the water."

"No, it's the smell of the damp earth around it."

"OK... that's logical... I believe you, Nyah. I do."

"And if the water's bad I can taste it, when other people can't. You've never noticed that my tongue is half again as long as anyone else's? I have more taste receptors."

"Taste and smell are connected somehow," he said. "So maybe those extra receptors help you to find water, too."

"Oh, but there's more. We Khmer are a very old race, and we were isolated, until we started to trade with India, and China, and the Indonesian kingdoms. We were isolated for so many thousands of years that we became genetically distinct. I have some *sixth sense* left over from my Khmer ancestors – whenever I get near water the tip of my nose starts to sweat, and I get a funny feeling in it. So you see, either way, using my sense of smell and taste, or using that other sense, I can always find water."

"So you can't teach me how to do it," he said.

"Well the next time I smell water, I'll see if your nose starts to sweat. Maybe you have the sixth sense, but just don't know it."

"Probably not, Nyah – I'm half Chinese."

"Well I'll bet there are lots of things you can do that I can't just *because* you're Chinese... I'll bet you can light firecrackers and get six meters away before the fuse even burns down."

"Of course I can. All Chinese kids can."

"And you can eat those disgusting fermented Chinese eggs?"

"Yeah – love 'em. Used to eat 'em all the time."

No wonder his growth had been stunted.

"Told you you can do things I can't."

"But you have more ancient genes than your ability to smell water, Nyah. I've watched you climb every tree you've climbed since the day we got away from our unit. Your toes are much longer than they should be, for the size of your feet. And your arches are higher than anyone else's. And your *hands*... they're too big for the rest of you. They're almost like front feet. When you climb a tree you wrap your hands and your feet around the trunk as though you've been doing it for a million years. I've never seen anything like it. Except in the zoo."

"Now that's not funny."

"Really, Nyah. And you have more upper-body strength than you should have, for your size. That's what enables you to shinny up a palm, or pull yourself up into a tamarind . Or pull *me* up into a tamarind. And then there are your eyes... Hey, if I had eyes that big I'd be able to see in the dark, too. I wish I could show you to the critics of the man who proposed the theory of evolution –

you're exactly what he was trying to describe. But you're the 'before'. Not the 'after'."

"Oh, but there's even more," I said. "When I haven't been out in the sun for awhile – like the year I had to live in Phnom Penh – when I first get back outside my skin changes color in just a couple of hours. My family used to remark on it. When I'd leave the house my eyes would be darker than my skin, but when I'd come back again my skin would be darker than my eyes. I'm a human chameleon."

"So that's why *you* didn't burn when we crossed the lakes. So many generations of your ancestors lived in Cambodia that they actually began to evolve. To be able to tolerate the tropical sun." He laughed. "Well it's no wonder they call you 'Gecko', with your big eyes, your long tongue and your gecko-like feet and hands. And all that other stuff. But I wonder why those traits evolved out of the rest of the Khmer population?"

"Because in a civilized world," I said, "they're of no use. Finding water, for example. Before the takeover you'd get water from a tap. Or a reservoir. Or a well. All man-made things. The Khmer haven't had to find their own water since before the time of Funan. And if a person can't get up a tree, he just... makes a ladder."

"Or buys one," he said.

"Yeah."

He paused for a moment. "I wonder if that's why you're so... *small.* Because you're... primordial. Primeval. Primitive. Prehistoric."

"You're not much bigger yourself."

"Oh. Yeah."

"But I'm not done *yet,*" I said. "I have a third way of finding water. If the fish are the kind with slime on their scales, I can smell them."

"Well anyone can smell fish. That's why the better stores are located *away* from the fishmongers."

"No, not the dead fish. The *live* ones. Swimming – *under water.*"

"Nyah. You're kidding."

"I told you you wouldn't believe me."

"Oh no, I *do*. But maybe it's not just genetics. Maybe you're more attuned to your surroundings than the rest of us, because you grew up on a farm."

"Most Cambodians grew up on a farm," I said.

"Yes, but they had to work. You grew up on a farm, but you didn't have to work. So you had time to observe the natural world around you, and develop a keener awareness of it. Like the man who proposed the theory of evolution."

"And I know to pay attention all the time," I said. "Yeah, six years of war will do it. But you've had four. Next time we find water *pay attention,* and see if you can smell it."

The going got easier for my friend as soon as the sun came over the horizon, and we set a steady pace. We fished out some of our jerky and ate it as we walked, then started walking faster. But this was all rice country – there was no cover for us here. We picked up our pace *again,* and began to close the distance between ourselves and the kapok tree quickly.

"What are we going to do," I asked, "when we get to the village underneath the kapok? There could be 'clean-up' cadres there. What are we, and which one of us is doing the talking?"

"Infantrymen, and, me. We got separated from our unit when the Vietnamese routed it. We're trying to get to Highway Two so we can get back to army headquarters to report for duty."

"Were *is* army headquarters?" I asked.

"Hell if I know. And no one else does, either. So we're fine."

"OK... but let me show you more ways to hide, so no one sees us in the first place. Much easier than trying to lie."

"I thought you'd already shown me everything you know."

"Are you kidding?" I said. "There's enough other stuff to fill a *book*. To start with, take your 'kramaa' off your head – there will be less of you to see. You'll be better camouflaged, too. A flash of brown and black can be mistaken for a calf, or a dog, or a baby water buffalo. But a flash of brown and black wearing a 'kramaa'? Well I think you can figure that out..."

He took his 'kramaa' off and made a pack out of it again. "Now," I said, "I'll show you where to hide when there's nowhere to hide at all. OK – to do this, you have to know which direction your enemy is coming from. Let's say he's coming from the kapok in front of us. You look for an irrigation ditch that runs perpendicular to his path. You walk to it slowly and flatten yourself out on his side of the ditch. If you don't have a ditch you use the back of a levee. As he's walking toward you he'll look right over you, and never see you. Then you just wait for him to turn around and go back where he came from. Guards are what you usually have to worry about, and that's what guards do – always. I had to hide like that when I was stealing sweet potatoes, and melons and squash. They're all planted in raised rows."

"You hid behind those *little tiny rows?*" he asked. "You're *kidding*."

"No. But remember, I was *always* very small. OK – do you know how to hide under water?"

"If I don't know how to hide in a ditch, Nyah, you think I know how to hide under water?"

"OK – you wade right into the thick of the reeds, snap one off, slide under water face up, start breathing through the reed, and stuff some mud up the back of your shirt so it doesn't float. I never had to do it after the takeover, but I had to do it in Prai Anchaan plenty of times. The bully was always after me, and the more he couldn't find me, the madder he'd get and the harder he'd look."

"So you snap off a big papyrus reed," he said.

"*No,* not papyrus. They're not hollow."

"Well how would I know that?"

"Did you have papyrus mats in your house in Phnom Penh?" I asked.

"Yeah – everyone did."

"Why do you think papyrus make such good mats?"

He rolled his eyes. "Because they're not hollow. So what kind of reed do you use?"

"I'll show you when we hit the next pond. But there is one thing you have to watch out for, when you hide under water like that."

"Water snakes?"

"Well yeah," I said, "but I was thinking of water *buffalo*. Those reeds are their favorite thing to eat, and you don't want them to step on you. So you slide out of the way if you sense one coming. You can't see them of course – the water's too muddy."

He shook his head. "I wonder how long it will be before the Vietnamese can solidify their control, and I can live in Phnom Penh again... No, I'm serious. If I had to hide that way I'd end up trampled and drowned together."

"But if I were *with* you, you'd be OK. That's why neither one of us would make it without the other. I could get both of us through hiding under water, but I wouldn't have *heard* whoever it was that was coming. So I wouldn't have tried to hide."

We reached the kapok and found that there was a good solid ladder tied to it. "So someone still picks the pods from this tree," said Puamaak.

I climbed up and looked out over the landscape, and climbed back down again with a pocketful of kapok. I'd use it for tinder if my kerosene gave out, and I had to start a fire without a lighter.

"The village is completely empty," I said. "No 'clean-up' cadres, and no one hiding in any of the houses."

"So now you have X-ray vision?"

"*No* I don't have X-ray vision. It's just common sense. There are coconuts lying on the *ground*. It's just like when we went through the abandoned Vietnamese village – if there had been anyone there they would have had the coconut trees all staked out, waiting for the nuts to drop as soon as they'd ripened. And then they would have *picked them up*. Come on, we have to take another mark." And I lay down on the ground up against the kapok, with the top of my head pointed toward Phnom Da behind us. I looked over my toes.

"The big Bodhi tree on the horizon," I said. "That's our next mark."

"It's probably at another burned-out temple, but that's OK – the temple will be deserted. Let's get some coconuts before we leave this place, in case we can't find water."

We got to the Bodhi midmorning. I climbed it, didn't see a road, climbed down again and made a compass using the kapok and the Bodhi. "That's our next mark," I said, pointing. "The ebony, way over there. And there will be a ladder tied to it so people can get up it to get the fruit – that's what they make their black dye from. Are you sure this will work, just going forty-five degrees southwest? What if we never hit a landmark?"

"Nyah, it would be *impossible* to miss Highway Two. It runs south down the entire length of the province – that's our *problem*. But actually, the road we're looking for will lead us right to it. When you climb your next tree, look for a road running forty-five degrees southwest."

I shook my head. "There's no way I could have found my way back to Prai Anchaan from where we escaped, that's for sure. Because I don't know any of the roads. If I'd been by myself when I hit Highway *One* I wouldn't have known what it was."

"But you knew the army had taken you across the Mekong, and so you knew you had to go back to it. West. And that's the only way you could have gone, because the Vietnamese were shelling us from the east. You would have gone up One northwest, and you would have hit the Mekong."

"And then had to decide," I said, "whether to go north or south."

"You would have known that Prai Anchaan was north because the Khmer Rouge moved you so far south when they relocated you to Pong Tuk. And you would have figured out that, when they moved you from camp to camp, they never moved you further north than they'd moved you south in '75. You would have known which way to go, Nyah. But supposing you and I had never met – what you would have done when our commanding officer gave the order to retreat? You couldn't have escaped alone. Well, you *could* have, but you wouldn't have."

"I would have stayed close to our squad leader,' I said. "If anyone else could have gotten out of there alive, it would have been he." I paused. "What would you have done?"

"I could have stayed close to our commanding officer and gotten some protection from him, for awhile anyway. But no, I think I would have done what you would have. I would have stuck with our squad leader. He was the lowest-ranking officer – he had no connections, because he was from a poor family. But he was the smartest of all of them."

"His people," I said, "were the kind the Communist philosophy tells us should be idealized. And promoted. But he was never promoted."

"The Khmer Rouge had everything upside down, little brother. The *smartest* officer in our platoon was the one at the bottom, while the *commanding* officer couldn't even think for himself. All he could do was follow orders. That's why our platoon ended up on the top of that mountain – because he couldn't think what else to do, and there was no one higher in rank there to tell him."

"Our squad leader would have known that by running up that mountain our platoon would be treed."

"Nyah, I wonder if he *went* up the mountain. I'll bet he tried to escape. And if *we* made it, I'll bet he did, too."

"It would have been harder for him, though. I mean, he couldn't pass himself off as a lost kid."

"He wouldn't have had to pass himself off as *anything* – if *we* haven't run into any people, he hasn't either!"

We reached the ebony at midday. I climbed it and saw a road in the distance, running forty-five degrees southwest. But there was a small grove of coconut palms right where we would hit it. Which meant that there was a village there; coconut trees don't plant themselves.

"The only problem with using our human compass in Takeo," I said, "is that tall trees are always the best marks here. But they were all planted by humans, so there's always a village at the bottom of them. Oh – I found your road."

He closed his eyes and let out a sigh. But both of us knew that shadowing that road would take us through villages, just as using my compass had. We couldn't avoid them any longer.

We hit the road an hour later, checked for coconuts on the ground, picked up a couple and drank the water, then pried out all the meat. "Let's rest a few minutes, Nyah. But just a few. I don't know how much further we have to go to get to Two."

We hit the highway just before sundown. Puamaak had been right – it wasn't paved.

"Listen for buffalo," I said. "They may not be bellowing, but they'll be making all sorts of other noises."

We zeroed in on the village wallow and stopped when we were right across the road from it. "I'll go first," he said. "You stay one city block behind me."

"And if you can't handle the buffalo on the other side?"

He stepped out of the way and gallantly motioned for me to go ahead. "*I'll* stay a block behind."

We got across the road quickly and headed southwest again. "There weren't any mines," said Puamaak.

"There were no buffalo dead in the road. I think whoever mined here purposely skipped their crossing. So there are a few people left in the army who haven't forgotten our Buddhist ways."

We walked on another couple of kilometers, ducked into a stand of trees, and I started to make a fire.

"Don't," whispered Puamaak. "We'll just eat cold food tonight. We have no idea how far over the 'gkeeah' went. Be sure you hang my hammock right next to yours, but let's not talk tonight. And when you wake up in the morning, figure out if there's anyone around before you get out of the tree. Or say anything to me."

"OK," I said. "But for as far as I can see, there's no light from oil lamps."

"That means *nothing*. The cadres might have ordered a blackout because of the Vietnamese invasion. Or people might be trying to make the cadres think they've left, when they haven't. Or they might have run out of oil years ago."

"I understand."

He exhaled very slowly. "We should be about half way across Takeo, so I think tomorrow we'll come up on the fringes of the 'gkeeah'. We'll begin to run into evacuees – and we may have to deal with cadres. Eat all you can tonight, do the same tomorrow morning, then hide whatever food you have left underneath your shirt. Hide your lighter, too – because we *have* to be able to cook."

He put his face in his hands, and then raised it to look at me. "If we can just make it through tomorrow, Nyah, we'll make it."

Day Nine – *Fish and Lies*

"Are you awake?" I whispered.

"Yeah."

"I climbed higher up the tree. Complete 'gkeeah'. There's no one out there."

"I heard you go up."

"I'll get the fire started."

"Nyah – could you see Phnom Treil?"

"No. Not yet."

We climbed down, gathered firewood and kindling and built our fire. "We're on a lake," I said. "My grandfather is still looking out for us."

I went down to the shoreline for water and quickly returned to my friend. He took our cups from my hands and put them on the fire.

"What are you doing?" I asked.

"If you couldn't see Phnom Treil it's either hiding in the mist, or Highway Two is not halfway across the province – I wasn't sure. We may have another half to go until we even get into Kampot, and that means covering even more ground than we did yesterday. If our feet don't swell, it will be easier for us. So I'm going to make tamarind tea. Isn't that what your grandfather used to do? Make teas out of things?"

"Yeah, but I never saw him do it with tamarind."

"He didn't have to walk like we do. Not until we were all marched out of Phnom Penh, anyway. Thought I'd try it. See if it works."

I leaned forward and put more wood on the fire. "Not a bad idea."

He was quiet for a minute. "Little brother, by the time we make camp tonight I want us to be as close to Pong Tuk as we can get without being discovered. We'll go in in the morning, as soon as there's enough light so that no one will mistake us for Vietnamese. As for today, we need to just keep shadowing the road, looking for Phnom Treil. Once we can see it we'll have some idea of how much further we have to go."

"But we *have* to get more food today, because there will be none for *us* in Pong Tuk. If the 'gkeeah' didn't go over that far there will be food there, but no extra rations. And if the 'gkeeah' *did* go over that far, all the food stores will be mined. How far do you think we're going to get without food? As for our families, we can't come home without food for them. Your father may have been Chinese, but your mother's Khmer, and that's the Khmer way – especially in bad times. But we don't know how many people there will be to feed. Your sisters may be in a work camp, or they may be in Pong Tuk. So will we need to bring food for one person, or for three? We don't know. We don't know anything. So we have to catch as much as we can today. And we're in the perfect place to do it. That's what I meant when I said that my grandfather is still looking out for us."

He nodded. "You're right, little brother – we'll have to bring them food. I wasn't thinking."

A cold mist had moved in from the lake, and we moved closer in to our fire.

When the water came to a boil he opened a tamarind pod, dropped some of the fruit into the water, and sat back to let it steep. When he thought it was ready he picked up my cup with my 'kramaa' and handed it to me. "OK, let's give my tea a try."

We wrapped our 'kramaas' around our cups and our fingers around our 'kramaas'. We stared into the fire as we waited for it to burn down.

"I wonder," I said, "if my *mother* knows any of my grandfather's medicine."

"What happened to him, little brother?" He paused. "Tell me if you want to. If you don't, that's OK."

I looked down into the flames. "By the time we ended up in Pong Tuk we'd been driven out of Prai Anchaan, driven out of Phnom Penh, and relocated three times. He had to walk each time we had to move – everyone did. And he did all right. But when they began to starve us, he was the first to decline – he was all muscle, and had no fat on his body at all. Not like the city people around us."

I shivered, and took a sip of the drink my friend had made for me. "About a month after we got to Pong Tuk, his whole body began to swell. We couldn't get any salt."

"And the sea was not far away... The 'old people' had salt. But they wouldn't give it to you..." He sighed. "I'm sorry, little brother – I'm just making you feel worse. Go on."

"One night, a little yellow owl landed on his windowsill. I always slept next to him, so we both saw it. Of course, I tried to pretend it wasn't there. But he told me to look at it – that it had come as a sign to him. I told him he'd get better."

"But you knew the owl meant otherwise."

I looked down into the fire again, and nodded. "But there was nothing I could do. One morning, a few days later, he told me he'd had a dream. He'd seen his friends, all dressed in white, calling to him. They were the friends who'd already died. The friends who'd sat on his balcony in the afternoons in Prai Anchaan, discussing remedies and spells. Oh yes – my grandfather was a true shaman – he used healing spells as well as medicines. And they worked, too. Well anyway, my grandfather said that in his dream his friends had called to him. 'Come with us! Come with us! Don't be afraid – we'll all be together again!'

That night the swelling in his body went down, and I could see how thin he was. When I woke up in the morning I found him cold and stiff beside me; he must have died just after we'd fallen asleep. I was the one who had to tell my mother." I shrugged my shoulders. "And then I had to go to work, or they would have killed *me*... I guess that's the end of the story."

Puamaak slid our food into the coals and we sat there without speaking, just staring into the glowing embers.

Suddenly, he turned to me excitedly. "You know what the dream means? That the aunt who raised you, and your grandmother, were alive when he had the dream. Or *they* would have been in it, too. They at least made it through the march out of Phnom Penh and into a resettlement village. And your grandmother was old – they wouldn't have made her work hard. So she should still be alive. When it's safe, you and your mother can go back to Prai Anchaan to find her."

"Yeah, you're right. My aunt and my grandmother *would* have been in the dream, if they were already dead. And if they're still alive, they might be making their way back to Prai Anchaan right now. My cousins, too – there were seven of us. Surely some of them survived."

"Don't worry. If your mother isn't in Pong Tuk, my mother will take you in as though you were her own son. And help you to find your family. Especially when I tell her how you taught me to find food, and use a fish trap, and float down the rivers so I wouldn't have to walk. And how to paddle a boat. Ha! Wait until I tell her how to *find* a boat. I wouldn't have made it without you."

And then he was quiet for a minute. "Do you know how I survived the camps?"

"You told me. You weren't in them very long."

"I lied to you, Nyah. I was in two and a half years before they put me in the army. I told you I wasn't in very long because I didn't want you to know what I did to survive." He shook his head as he remembered. "I was *lost*. Oh, I'm not stupid – I knew I wouldn't last very long. I knew the other boys weren't going to teach me how to find food, because then we'd be competing for it."

"So what did you do?"

"I started *kissing up* to the guards. Mending their uniforms, cleaning their guns, fixing their shoes. Playing lookout, and covering for them. *Anything,* so they'd give me more food. I even rolled the bodies of the kids who didn't make it in papyrus mats for them. Yeah, that's how I survived. And when I got into the army, I had to do the same thing. I must be almost fifteen, you know. I should have been sent into combat months ago." He paused. "But I never hurt anyone, Nyah. Oh, no – I would never do their dirty work for them. I would never be *one* of them."

"You don't have to tell me all this."

"But I'm sure you suspected *something*. You knew I wasn't... like you. But I did do one good thing. When I rolled each body up in a mat, I made sure the boy was really dead. I knew the Khmer Rouge had buried lots of people alive, so I'd stall until rigor mortis began to set in. It only takes a few hours, and I was always able to stall that long. I did a good thing – I know I did."

"You did a *very* good thing. I wasn't that smart. I had to volunteer to help bury boys when I was in the infirmary so they wouldn't send me back to the camp. So, you see, you and I did the same thing, with the same purpose. But I never thought to check for myself to be sure each boy was really dead. I just wrapped him up quickly, so I wouldn't have to see his face anymore."

He nodded. "I always turned the face away from me, while I was waiting... But all those things I did. I did them for my mother. So that, someday, I could get back to her and help her."

"I understand. Did you know any of the dead boys?"

"*No.* I was always too afraid to talk to anyone. You were *brave,* when you came up to me at muster your first day in my unit."

"What did I have to lose? I knew if I couldn't buddy up with someone I wouldn't make it. That's not bravery – it's quite the opposite."

"What was the closest you ever came to… not making it."

"Well… each time I got an infection in my toe, I had to stay away from everyone. That cut me off from my support line – the group of boys I always shared my rats with, and who, in turn, did things for me."

"The cadres separated you from them?"

"No. I stayed away on my own. Because my foot smelled like a dead body. And then there were the *flies*… They would land on the infected toe, and bite me – they were eating me alive! And it *hurt* – they bit me *so hard*. I figured it wouldn't be long before I had maggots crawling in my toe. I didn't want anyone to see me like that – so I stayed away. But then they put me in the infirmary."

He shuddered. "I never had anything like that happen to me."

"Oh, and our work camp ran out of food once – for *two days*. Ran out completely. But they made us work anyway. Oh, yeah, I thought I was going to die. But then I got a big rat in my trap. And then there was the time they worked us forty-eight hours straight because the commune was behind schedule. That's when I saw boys fall asleep on the levee, roll into the rice paddy and drown in fifteen centimeters of water. And there was one other time, when they had us digging canals. It wasn't the sixteen-hour days, it was the weight they had me carrying. More than what I weighed myself. I thought my bones would split, and went to bed one night thinking I would never wake up again. But I did. If I hadn't been drafted when I was, I'm sure I wouldn't have lasted much longer."

"And then they were going to send you into combat. So you would have died anyway. You know what I worried about the most? That I'd be killed, and my mother would never know what happened to me. And then when you landed in my unit, I worried that you'd be killed, too – so neither of our mothers would ever know if we were still alive."

"And they would never give up hope that we'd come back some day. They'd always be looking for us. In every face that passed them on the street, in every face in the crowd at Bun Ōm Touk, in every face in the market. For the rest of their lives."

We sat quietly for a moment, staring into the last of our fire.

"Nyah?"

"Yeah?"

"That first day, on the mountain…"

"Yeah?"

"If you'd had an AK-47, and someone had come at us… Would you have used it?"

"Yes."

We finished our tea in silence.

"Puamaak?"

"Yeah?"

"Our escape… You didn't plan it in a second and a half, did you?"

"No."

"You planned it when our squad leader came to you and told you they were going to put you into combat."

He nodded.

"And you were *just waiting...*"

He nodded again.

"Puamaak?"

"Yeah?"

"Thank you for taking me with you."

He smiled. "Neither one of us would have made it without the other. But I wouldn't have left you, little brother."

He started to get up, stopped, and sat down again. "How did you figure me out?"

"It was just too clever, the way you did it. And right in front of everyone. Just too clever."

His eyes met mine in the mist. "I didn't want to die."

I nodded. "And I understand why you couldn't tell me, until it was time to go."

"What if there'd been no opportunity?" He shuddered.

"I know you a lot better now than I did nine days ago, my friend. I think you would have *made* one... But what was the worst thing that happened to you in the last four years? Tell me if you want to. If you don't, that's OK."

"Seeing them take my father away. And then wondering if they'd come back, for my mother. Or my sisters. I was always on edge after that, except when I was asleep – and then I had nightmares. You're never the same, after they take your father away."

"Don't think about it."

"I *try* not to. But I can never forget my mother's face, when she realized why the soldiers had come. She wasn't supposed to be unhappy that they were going to execute her husband because he was considered an enemy of the state. So she couldn't even cry."

"If she had, they would have punished her. Or taken *her* away with *him*, leaving you and your sisters completely alone. Yes, your mother would have known what was at stake... What a brave woman. You must be very proud, to have a mother like that. She must be a very fine lady."

He nodded. "She is... Was your mother home when they took your father away?"

"No. She had already been assigned to work in the fields, and had left the house at dawn. There was a knock on the door. I opened it, to see a single soldier on the other side. And one more waiting at the foot of the ladder-stairs. The first instructed my father to come out.

He knew what they wanted with him, and that he would not be back. He turned to me and said, 'Keep an eye on your brother and sister, and take care of your mother.'

And then he turned around again, and walked away with the soldiers. He never looked back.

When I'd heard my father's words I hadn't realized that that was the last I would ever see of him. The soldier had said they needed him for a special project. But when my mother came home and asked where he was, and I told her about the soldiers, she understood. And when I saw the tears begin to roll down her cheeks, suddenly, *I* understood."

I paused for a moment. "I saw him once after that, by chance. In a chain gang. So I was at least able to tell her that they hadn't executed him yet. But they must have, later – I mean, we never saw anyone who'd been taken away come back. He was an officer in the Lon Nol army."

"Ahhh…"

I looked down into my empty cup. "But a lot of my memories are gone. I learned very quickly that if I were to survive I'd need to remember *anything* that would help me. And there just wasn't enough room in my brain. So I started pushing things out. Or, should I say, just… letting them go. To make more room. So, you see, now I only remember the things I need to know to stay alive."

"Yeah, I do the same thing. But what was it that *most* helped you to stay alive? The *one* thing."

"That I could always find water... But there was one other thing. The other boys – they were paralyzed with fear at night. Too afraid to sneak out to look for food."

He nodded. "Ghosts."

"But my grandfather had taught me not to be afraid of them. 'The fish you ate last night,' he would say, 'did it come back to haunt you? The ghosts that swirl around a temple at night – do they ever come to disturb you? And all the people in this village who have died in the generations before you – do you dream about them? There are always ghosts around, Nyah, but they won't hurt you. Chose your fears wisely – it is the *living* you must be afraid of.'"

I turned to my friend. "But the camp guards were just as afraid of ghosts as the boys were. Remember you asked me how I hacked open my stolen coconuts without them hearing me? I told you I just found a deep woods. I didn't want to tell you where I really went. To the burial ground outside the camp. Yes, I sat on the graves to eat my food. And if the guards heard a noise coming from that direction, they would just assume... But I knew they went there in the daytime. So I would bury the husks, and leave no trace that I had ever been there… But what was it that most helped you to stay alive? The one thing. Except for helping the camp guards and the officers, of course."

"I kept a picture of my mother in my head. Like a photograph. And I'll see her tomorrow – I know I will."

"We'll get more food, and hide it. We can tie it up in a tree outside Pong Tuk, where we can get to it easily. But what are we going to do about the cadres? If we outrank them now, like you say we do, they can't send us back to the army. Or send us out to the fields. Or send us anywhere. But it's a catch-22 – if we tell them we're in the army, we can't stay in Pong Tuk. What's your plan?"

"We'll tell them we're leaving the following morning to go find our unit. And then, as soon as the sun's down, we'll sneak out – taking our families with us. By the time they miss our mothers in the morning, we'll all be *long* gone… Come on, let's eat. When we're finished, show me how to get fish from the lake."

Now, you know my problem here. Just as my comrade was the only living

Cambodian who couldn't climb a tree, I was the only living Khmer who couldn't catch a fish. Without a trap, anyway. But Puamaak was *not* going to find that out. Not today, anyway.

"OK," I said, "I'll show you."

We finished our food and walked down to the shoreline. I pointed to a bridge on the road we'd been shadowing. "The fish are under there. It's cooler, and darker – they think they're hiding under a log. But we'll be doing the same thing they are – hiding. No one will see us if we're underneath the bridge."

We made our way along the bank, sending mudskippers sliding into the water ahead of us. Then we ducked into the shadows beneath the bridge.

"OK, little brother. What do we do now?"

"Watch."

I looked for the shallowest spot, and started to build a dam around it with sticks and mud. "We used to do this in the paddies when we were kids. But we were just playing then... You start on the other side."

Within half an hour the shallow spot was almost fully enclosed by the dam. I found a low-growing palm with wide fronds and made a couple of scoops, as I'd done on the east bank of the Mekong. My friend closed the gap in the dam and I handed him a scoop. "Start bailing," I said, "just like you did the boat."

We bailed for almost an hour. And then the largest of our catch began to surface – the mudskippers. My friend started to chase them.

"Don't waste your energy," I said. "Let them waste theirs. They'll slow down in a few minutes. Keep bailing."

In a few more minutes the next largest of our catch began to surface – the mud crabs. I started to grab them by their hind legs, so they couldn't pinch me. "These I have to catch, or they'll burrow down into the mud. *Now* you can get the mudskippers. Remember, get as many as you can, because we don't know how many people they'll have to feed."

Puamaak caught all the mudskippers enclosed by the walls of our dam and put them in his 'kramaa'.

"Keep bailing," I said, "until we get down to the snails." And within half an hour, we had enough snails for the next couple of days. Then we dug clams out of the mud.

"OK," I said, "I'll rebuild the fire while you clean the mudskippers. We'll make jerky out of those and save it for our families. I'll cook everything else with tamarind; it will last at least until tomorrow night."

We returned to our campsite and got everything cooking, but because our cups were so small we had to cook in batches. As each batch finished we picked the meat out of the shells and spread it on a strip of banana leaf. When the last batch had cooled I folded the banana leaf into an envelope that I could hide underneath my shirt. I made another envelope for Puamaak, and, when the mudskippers were done, put them into it. Then I took off my shirt, turned it inside out and put it back on again; that would keep my lighter safe. Puamaak was right – we had to be able to cook.

We broke camp and walked until dark, eating our catch as we shadowed the road. And my friend never noticed that we had caught no *fish*.

Day Ten – *The Last Wave*

"Nyah – can you see Phnom Treil?"

It was just dawn. Puamaak was several branches below me, trying to get up to where I was.

"Yes. I can see it."

I could see, too, that the 'gkeeah' had extended over here. But I wasn't going to tell him anything until I could get more information.

He started again to make his way up to where I was.

But I was already coming down. "Come on, let's head out. Save an hour by eating our shellfish cold. I'll untie our hammocks, you untie the food."

We got out of the tree quickly and headed for the western edge of the grove. Puamaak hurried ahead of me, anxious to get a better look at the landscape. And estimate the distance to Phnom Treil.

I came up behind him and caught his arm. "*Comrade!* We have to be just as cautious here as on that first day, when the Vietnamese were below us and our platoon was above us. Just as cautious – if not *more*."

We looked out across the plain that stretched between us and the mountain. "No smoke," he said. "But that doesn't mean there's no one in the villages. It means that no one's cooking. Or that they know how to hide their smoke; my mother had a way of doing it. How far to the mountain, do you think?"

I shook my head, slowly. "Couple of hours?" I held out a piece of jerky. "Couple of hours if you *eat* – more, if you don't. You know, it's not a very big mountain. Not nearly as big a I remember it."

"You're almost four years older now, " he said. "And you're just *looking* at it – you're not *climbing* it. Like we had to do to get the god damn bamboo shoots for the god damn cadres. But do you remember how they got us there? They marched us down a road that runs into this one, right at the foot of the mountain. That's Thirty-one. That's the road to Pong Tuk."

He took the jerky, looked out over the landscape again and shook his head. "We won't have much cover... we'll meet up with cadres, sooner or later. Nyah, you're going to hear me lie today like you've *never* heard me lie before. 'We got separated from our unit when the Vietnamese routed it. They have tanks, and they're *right behind us!*'" He rolled his eyes. "Come on – let's go." And without another word, we started our last push for Pong Tuk.

We came upon a village within half an hour. Empty. We picked up a couple of coconuts and drank the water as we walked.

We came upon another village. Empty. And another...

Now, as I've said about a hundred times, I'd worried ever since our first day that Puamaak just wouldn't make it. It wasn't just that he was so thin, it was that he always had to struggle to keep up with me. And it never seemed to get any easier for him.

But now, the more villages we came upon that had been abandoned, the more he picked up his pace. *I* was having trouble keeping up with *him*. I wondered how he would react when we found Pong Tuk empty. I knew him better now than I did when we'd escaped, ten days ago – but I still didn't know him very well. Would he have a complete breakdown? He'd obviously been very close to his mother. And she was the one thing that had kept him going the last four years – he'd said so. I thought again of the chances that she'd survived. Much poorer than my mother's.

Or were they? He'd talked about his cousins in the village on the Mekong. His mother had probably grown up in that village. And moved to Phnom Penh when she got married, like *my* mother had. Well if she was originally a village girl, that would improve her chances. That would improve them a *lot.* I would be sure to tell him that later today, when we didn't find her.

I could tell from what I'd seen from the tree that the 'gkeeah' hadn't happened in the last few days – if it had, I would have seen evacuees. Whether there were any cadres left, I'd only been able to guess. But now, we'd been through several villages that were completely abandoned. If Puamaak hadn't figured out that the 'gkeeah' hadn't happened in the last few days, he was figuring it out now.

"Maybe the cadres will be gone, but our mothers won't," he said.

I was not going to lie to him – that would just make everything worse. "That's not how a 'gkeeah' works, and I explained that to you before. If the *cadres* are gone, *everyone* is gone. The cadres are always the last ones out."

"Nyah, what do you really think we'll find when we get home today?"

"It's not 'home' – it's the relocation village we're going back to because there's nowhere the hell else we can go, until we know if our families are still there. Don't call it 'home'. As to what I think we'll find... *I* don't know. Turn your brain off for awhile. I'll tell you when to turn it back on again."

"My mother will be in Pong Tuk, Nyah. I'm the only son, and the youngest child. My mother will be waiting for me."

"I'm not the only boy, and I'm the oldest. And my family will believe that if I survived the last four years, I can fend for myself now."

My friend turned to me, slowly. "You mean, all this way, you thought there would be no one waiting for you?"

"Only once we'd crossed the Bassac, and I could see that there'd been a 'gkeeah'. My mother wouldn't risk the lives of her other children to wait for me. And my uncles wouldn't try to talk her out of leaving. They're not like my oldest uncle. The youngest one had the accident when I was young, and was distant after that. The older one went away to school, so I never got to know him very well. And then there's the fact that I was always so *small*... None of them would ever believe that *I* survived. No, there will be no one waiting for me."

"Nyah, my mother will take you in. We'll all go back to Phnom Penh together, and we'll find your family – both halves of it."

Let's just get to Pong Tuk, I thought, *and get this over with. NO ONE will be there.*

"Do you remember," I asked, "when they first told all of us Pong Tuk boys that they were going to put us in a camp? They made it sound like one of those summer camps you see in the American movies. We were *excited.* Something new. Something different. And just us boys. We thought we'd be back again in a week."

He nodded. "I remember."

"And then it started. They had us clear forest for paddies first. Cut down the trees, dig out the roots and pull up the scrub, all by hand. This wasn't fun – and we certainly weren't learning anything. The first week went by, and it looked like they were going to keep us a little longer. Then the first month went by, and we started to wonder what was going on. When *six* months went by and there was still no talk of us going back to our families, and we'd learned what it was to be beaten and starved, I finally understood. But do you remember that moment, when it all crystallized? The moment you realized that they were *never* going to let you go back to your family. That moment helped to prepare you for today."

We walked five hours that morning, to get back to Pong Tuk. To look for people who wouldn't be there. And we walked in silence – for the first time on our journey, there was simply nothing to say.

I climbed a tamarind outside the perimeter of the village and climbed back down to my friend. "I didn't see anyone, but there are no coconuts lying on the ground. So there's a 'clean-up' detail here." I motioned for him to go ahead. "We'll go to your house first."

I knew that if his mother wasn't there, mine wouldn't be, either – so we could just leave without wasting any more time. I didn't want to run into cadres. Desperate men backed into a corner, who had both machine guns and bayonets.

We moved quickly around the perimeter of the village. 'New people' were segregated – they had to live on the outer edge, in huts built expressly for them. I didn't know how he was going to find his mother's – they all looked the same to me. Each had a single room in the front, and a kitchen in the back behind a half wall. Why they'd built a kitchen in each hut had always been a mystery to me – we'd have been shot if we'd used it for anything more than boiling water.

"The old loquat tree, up ahead," whispered Puamaak. "The house at the foot of it . That's my mother's."

I caught his arm. "Remember – you must be more cautious now than ever. And if your mother isn't there, I'll stick with you until we find her."

We crept forward and reached the hut, only to find the door hanging open. He pushed through the door anyway, and I didn't have the heart to stop him. It creaked like the bones of the dead.

We walked into the front room and looked over the half wall, into the kitchen in the back.

The scene that he so desperately wanted to unfold suddenly filled my brain. His sisters running forward to greet him, and his mother hugging him to be sure that he was real. His father standing back to take everything in, waiting his turn to hug his only son.

But now... the house was empty.

I was behind my friend, but I could hear the tears in his voice. "She's gone. *"*

"But someone's cooked here this morning," I said. "I can smell the fire."

He began to walk toward the kitchen. "Mother?"

I grabbed his arm and pulled him back. "She won't recognize your voice. You were ten when you left, and now you're almost fifteen. She'll think it's a trap. Say her maiden name, and the name of the village she grew up in."

"Soriya Vaang of Rhoneah Village. I'm your son, and I've come home."

And suddenly, she was there. She'd been hiding behind the half wall, having heard our footsteps. And she'd stood up when she'd heard a stranger say the name of her village.

She ran forward and grabbed him, and wouldn't let him go. She was taller than he was, and suddenly, he didn't look like an infantryman any more. The cool-headed soldier who'd gotten us through the minefield on Highway One was suddenly... just a kid.

But not for long. "We don't have much time, Mother. The cadres."

"I know, I know," she said, putting him at arm's length. "Just give me *one minute* to look at you. Not much taller than four years ago, but certainly a different color!" She laughed, and tried to smooth his matted hair. And then she remembered. "Your sisters are safe – don't worry!" And that's how we knew his father had never come home.

The tears were streaming down his face now, but he brushed them away. "Mother, is there anyone else left in the village? We didn't see anyone."

"There's only one family left. They disobeyed the evacuation order, like I did. If the cadres find them, they'll shoot all of them. But the mother – she won't leave. She has one boy who hasn't come home yet. But... who is this with you? I'm sorry, I didn't see you come in behind my son."

I moved forward, into the light.

"Nyah?"

I knew she didn't recognize me – she had never known me. "Madame, how do you know my name?"

"Your mother. She told me all about you. *She's* the one still waiting for her son. She said you were very small – when I saw you, I thought, that must be the Little Gecko."

And suddenly, she was all logistics. "Son, you take the kerosene. Nyah, you take the rice pot. I'll take the rice. Yes – *rice* – I got it from the village headman just before he left. I was the one with a piece of gold, so I got what his family couldn't carry. Let's get over to Nyah's house quickly, so we can get out of Pong Tuk."

"And away from the village cadres," said Puamaak.

"Are you *kidding?*" she said. "They were the first to leave. *Terrified* of the Vietnamese. They assembled everyone and asked each mother if all her children were here. Then they separated us into two groups – the families whose mothers had said, 'yes', and the families whose mothers had said, 'no' – just a few of us. Then they took the first group as *hostages* and started marching them toward Phnom Sanhaan. Said they were going to hole up there, and if the Vietnamese discovered them, they were going to threaten to mow down all the mothers and their children with their AK-47s. Oh yes – they still have bullets. Then there are the rogue cadres, moving in packs. Looking for anyone *they* can take hostage. We've been hiding ever since we heard."

"You mean…" Puamaak started.

"*Yes.* If you'd come home four days earlier – if you'd been closer to Pong Tuk – all of us would have been taken hostage and marched up Phnom Sanhaan. Even your sisters. *All* of us." She started for the door. "Nyah's house is in the middle of paddies; we'll have no cover at all. Follow me. Don't talk – don't say a word. Just *follow* me."

We made our way over to my mother's house, and saw the door hanging open. "No, they're in there," Puamaak's mother whispered to me. "That's the way we agreed to leave our doors, so it would look like we were gone. And like the house had been booby-trapped."

I hesitated. Puamaak pushed ahead of me and through the door.

And there they were – or what was left of them. Through all the skin and bone I could make out the faces of my youngest sister, my younger brother, my mother and her two youngest brothers. And that's how I knew my father had never come home.

"Nyah's back," my mother said to the rest of them – as if they couldn't see me for themselves. "Let's go." They each got up, and picked up a pack.

It was as though I'd just come back from the market or something. Like I'd only been gone an hour. I'd been gone *three and a half years*. Not one person so much as gave me a hug, or asked me if I was OK.

Puamaak's mother whispered in my ear, "My son got the warmer welcome, but *your* mother – she risked the lives of her other children, and her brothers, to wait for you. She must love you most of all." And she put her arm around me.

I knew I wasn't my mother's favorite, but *something* had made her wait for me. And as for the absence of any kind of a greeting, well, what did I expect? I'd been gone almost one third of my lifetime. My brother wouldn't even have recognized me – I'd been gone half of his. And my sister had been a baby when I'd left.

My mother motioned to her brothers to lead the way, and the next thing I knew, we were moving out. I wouldn't have a chance to visit my grandfather's grave, to thank him for sending me the owl that had sent us down the Mekong – south of the worst of the marshes. That's what really saved our lives, you know. That owl my grandfather sent me.

Puamaak and his mother and I fell in behind my uncles, and my mother and her two youngest children fell in behind us. We moved quickly out of the village, but not in the direction of the road. I had no *idea* where we were going.

And suddenly, Puamaak and I found ourselves on a levee whose path was not well worn. This area had been thick forest when he and I had lived in Pong Tuk, but now, it was all paddies. There was no cover for our families anywhere. But there was none for anyone else, either – Puamaak's mother felt it safe to talk, if only in a whisper.

"You must have been in the army," she said to the two of us, "not in a work camp, or you would have been home by now." We nodded, and she lowered her voice still further. "We heard all the units were routed by the Vietnamese. Well I'm glad – that's the only way they would ever have let you come home."

"Oh, our unit was routed, Mother, but they weren't going to let us come home. We *escaped*."

"*Escaped?*" she exclaimed. "But... how did the two of you end up together in the first place? You were sent off to a work camp in June of 1975, and Nyah was sent off a few weeks later. So we figured you weren't sent to the same camp – especially as you weren't the same age."

"Well, Mother, a few months later, we ended up in the same camp. And we recognized each other from Pong Tuk. And then we got sent off to different camps again, and I got drafted, then Nyah got drafted, and then they put him in my unit. He recognized me right away, the very first day. We just stuck together after that."

Puamaak's mother lowered her voice still further. "But you can't tell *anyone* you're deserters. *How did you get away?*"

"This is what happened," said Puamaak. "We were in a combat zone, but we were well behind the front lines. Then, with no warning at all, our commanding officer ordered all of us to retreat up a mountain. I figured that was our one chance to make a break for it, and I looked at Nyah, and he looked at me, and I told him to just... *follow me*. I told the guys behind us that we were going to pull out of line to take a leak. So we did. Except we *didn't* take a leak – we just pretended to, and dropped back further in the line. And then we did it again, telling a different set of guys the same story, and we came back into the line almost at the end. And then we did it *again,* so there would be no one behind us to see us take off. And then the Vietnamese started shelling us, so we ran into the jungle – and just kept right on running. I ditched my AK-47, and Nyah ditched his – we were infantrymen, Mother – and then we ditched our uniforms. In case anyone caught us. We were just going to pose as two lost kids, trying to find their families. But no one ever *did* catch us. We swam two rivers and crossed two minefields to get out of the combat zone, then stole a boat, then took the boat almost all the way over to the Bassac. Then we swam the Bassac, saw Phnom Da so finally knew where the hell... heck... we were, and just walked toward Phnom Treil from there."

"No *wonder* it took you so long to get home," she said. "All the children suddenly started coming back in waves. The first wave was the younger children, in their first work camp; the camp guards told them how to get back to Pong Tuk. The second wave was the older children, in work camps further away; your two sisters were in that wave. We have no idea how they found their way back. The third wave was the men who'd been sent off to work camps; your uncles were in that wave, Nyah. The fourth was the boys from the army – we have no idea how they found their way back, either. When you didn't come back in the second wave, we thought there was a *chance* you were still alive. But then the third wave came in, and you weren't in it. When the fourth wave came in everyone said that that was it – that anyone who had survived the last four years had made it back, and there was no one left to come home. We went to bed that night thinking you must have died in the camps, years ago. The families that hadn't been taken hostage left the village when the last of their children returned, or when they finally gave up hope. But your mother and I, Nyah – we wouldn't leave. I sent my girls to safety with another family three days ago, after the fourth wave came in and you weren't in it. You must have been further away than anyone else – you're the *last wave*. Where *were* you?"

"On a mountain near the Mekong Crossing," said Puamaak. "In Prey Veng Province."

"Ba Phnom. Oh my *god* – Ba Phnom! You've come from across the Mekong! I can't *believe* you made it back alive." And she started crying again.

"But there was another reason we were so late," I said. "Our unit was one of the last to retreat. We think some of the others retreated as much as a day and a half before our commanding officer gave us the order. It looked as though the villages had been burned the day *before* we escaped."

"And then we fell asleep the first night," said Puamaak. "That put us another half day behind."

"But your feet – both of you – what happened to your shoes?"

"We had to ditch them, Mother. They were Ho Chi Minh sandals – army issue. Would have given us away if anyone had caught us." He turned to look at me. "Ha! We could have kept them after all. Our AK-47s too."

"But the other boys from the army," she said, shaking her head, "they told everyone that the army had just told them to go home… But they had no shoes, either. Or uniforms. They came back looking just like the two of *you.* "

Puamaak and I looked at each other, and then back at his mother. "They *all* deserted!" she laughed.

"But there's been a complete 'gkeeah', hasn't there," I said. "We haven't seen a single person all the way across four provinces."

"Yes," she said. "We think the Vietnamese took Phnom Penh about a week ago. They got across the Mekong at *night* – one of the boys coming back from the army told us. He said it was the night of the first-quarter moon."

Puamaak said nothing for a minute, and then he turned to me. "That must have been the night we fell asleep on the mountain. Yeah… that would make sense… The artillery fire we heard just before we fell asleep – the Vietnamese were fighting their way to the Crossing. And then, sometime during the night, the shelling stopped. That's when they got across. No wonder they never came up the highway when we were trying to cross it – they were already well on their way to Phnom Penh. Pushing the army and all the villagers in front of them. That's why the villages looked like they'd been evacuated so far ahead of when we got to them."

"And that explains why we saw no stragglers," I said. "And why the 'clean-up' cadres had already left."

And then Puamaak got that funny look on his face again. "Nyah, when we were trying to get out of the war zone… all that time… we were running from an enemy that wasn't even there. And our squad leader is *still alive* – even if he *did* go up the mountain with our commanding officer. Yeah, he's out there. He's out there somewhere."

"That's why," I said, "we didn't hit any mines when we walked up the grade on the farm road. The Vietnamese had already been through, with their minesweepers and their…"

I was interrupted by my youngest uncle. "But they would have sent in a 'clean-up' detail. Very quickly. To look for holdouts, surveillance, wounded and deserters. Anyone who might get in their way. Because they'd send more infantry up One just as soon as they could." He clicked his tongue. "'Running from an enemy that wasn't even there…'. Their 'clean-up' detail would have *shot* you if they'd found you. But what would you boys know…"

Puamaak's mother opened her mouth to speak, but quickly thought better of it. *I can't cross him,* she thought. *I can't cross anyone in Nyah's family. Because without them, my son and I will never make it to Pochentong.*

But Puamaak had seen his mother's reaction. He turned to her, rolled his eyes toward my uncle and mouthed the words, *"I'll explain tonight."* She raised her eyebrows, and nodded.

She put her hand on his shoulder. "But how did you survive, all these years? The city was all you knew."

"I did just what you told me to do, Mother. I learned to lie."

"And how to find food," I said. "He has quite a unique method of catching snakes. I'm sure he'll tell you all about it."

"But I didn't really think I'd make it, Mother. Nyah only thought he was going to die *four times* since we left Pong Tuk, but I thought I was going to die every *day.* When I woke up each morning I'd ask myself if I was really still alive. But then the hunger would set in again, and I'd know I was." And his mother started crying again.

"Do you know," she said, "that in another three hours you would have missed us? We just couldn't wait any longer – not with the rogue cadres around. If you two had come home tomorrow, or tonight, or *this afternoon,* you wouldn't have found us here. And you wouldn't have known where we'd gone. There's nothing to write with any more, to leave a message. And if the cadres had caught us writing – *anything* – they would have killed us. Firstly, for lying about being educated the last four years, and secondly, for collaborating with the Vietnamese. They can't read – they wouldn't have been able to *read* what we *wrote,* and would have just assumed…"

I looked at Puamaak. "Three hours. The time it would have taken us to get to Phnom Da, climb it, and decide to go to Prai Anchaan instead of to Pong Tuk. We found our mothers because of a mangy pack of *dogs.*" And I suddenly wondered about those dogs. I looked back at the grove of trees on the south side of the village.

"But where are we going now?" Puamaak asked his mother. "We're headed west. We should be going north, up Thirty-one – the road we came here on in '75. That's how you get to Three."

"Thirty-one's been mined." She hesitated for a moment, and turned to look at her son. "And you crossed it just a few minutes ago, didn't you? Coming in from the east, there would have been no way around it."

Puamaak nodded, and looked at me; in his desperation to find out if his mother was still alive, he'd just walked right across it. And I'd followed, in his footprints. Because he was my elder, I had trusted him.

Now he looked back at his mother. "So we're going to try to get to Thailand?"

"No, to Pochentong," she said. "That's where I sent the girls. And your mother, Nyah, is going to try to get through to Prai Anchaan, to see who else in your family survived. We have to go west, through the pass between Phnom Brauphnom and the Phnom Sanhaan range, to pick up Highway Three further west in Kampot. But the Vietnamese may already have minesweepers on it – we don't know. No one knows *anything*. We heard the Vietnamese bombing the provincial capital, and then the army sent soldiers down here on foot to tell the cadres we all had to get out. So they could station troops here. But then the troops never came... The people who left after the fourth wave came in are from Takeo. They don't know *where* they're going to go, because the cadres told them they can't go east. That the Vietnamese already have minesweepers on Highway Two. The population is just swirling around from one place to another, like ghosts in the wind."

"So," Puamaak said to me, "the Vietnamese had been and gone by the time we got to Two."

"You know," said his mother, "you two made it through because you never ran into anyone else – no Vietnamese, no Khmer Rouge, no evacuees. But that won't be what it's like, from here to Pochentong."

"And how far is it," I asked her, "going this way."

"More than one hundred and thirty kilometers."

Puamaak and I just looked at each other – we hadn't even had a chance to sit down. But this is what war is. We were the lucky ones – we'd found our mothers. And we knew where we were going. We didn't know what we'd find once we got there, but at least we knew where we were going.

"We'll have to walk the whole way, little brother," said Puamaak. "There'll be no rivers we can use. Or fish trap, to get food easily."

His mother looked into his face. "Oh... so *that's* how you got so burned. Coming over water."

"Yeah. I got sunstroke, too. Like in '75."

"Then you must learn to be very careful," she said. "A lot of the people you saw dead on the road in '75 – that's how they died. But we'll be able to go at our own pace this time, and it's cool season."

"What year is it, Mother?" he asked.

"It's 1979. I've been counting the rice harvests since the takeover, and there have been four of them. You're fourteen. And Nyah, your mother told me you're twelve. None of the kids know how old they are anymore."

Puamaak looked at me. "So you were right, little brother. There's only two years' difference between us."

I turned back to take my mother's pack, only to find that we were being followed by... a cow. "Your brother's job in the work camp," said Puamaak's mother, "was to take care of that little Brahma. So when he was told to go home, he brought it with him. He didn't know what else to do with it – it's not even a year old."

"Nyah," asked Puamaak, "how are we going to hide all the way from here to Pochentong with a *cow*?"

"I don't know," I said, "but I'm sure my mother has it all figured out. You don't know her yet, my friend." I took her pack, then handed her our food and turned back to my friend. "She can ration it out. She's good at that."

"Nyah," he said, "you promised you'd tell me when we got back to Pong Tuk – what was in the antidote that saved her life?"

I tossed my head back over my shoulder. "*Ask* her."

"Madame," he said to my mother, "the time you brushed up against the poisonous frog. Your father mixed an antidote. What was in it?"

"I don't know," she said. "He gave me some kind of a… tea. He mixed it up very quickly and poured it down my throat. I just remember… trying to *spit it out*. It tasted terrible. He never did tell me what was in it."

"Where did you run into this frog, Naum?" asked Puamaak's mother.

"Highway Three," she replied. "I'll show you the place when we get to it. We can't go around it."

"Then we should all know the antidote," said Puamaak's mother, "and be sure we have the ingredients with us."

It was then that I realized that *none of us* had shoes.

Puamaak turned to me. "Well?"

My youngest uncle had stopped, and now he whipped around.

"*Shut up!*" he rasped, as loudly as he dared. "*All* of you. You're making us a target with your noise. There will be rogue cadres around, hunting for people they can use as hostages. Anyone who knows this area knows that this pass is the only way out of here, and that they can use it as a trap. *If they catch us,* they'll drag us up Phnom Sanhaan with the other hostages. And our lives will be *over*. There will be no food for us – they'll take what we have, and we'll starve in a week. We'll watch each other die." He looked at me and tossed his head. "You two boys – get behind your mothers and the children, and let them get fifteen meters ahead of you. Then no one can ambush them from the rear. Naum, Soriya, you and the children hang back fifteen meters behind *us*. Watch for my signal – if I see anyone coming I'll put my hand in the air. You let go of the Brahma's tether and whack him on the rump, then duck into the scrub with the children. Boys, you duck into the scrub when you see the Brahma take off. I'll tell the cadres that the two of us are Army. *Officers*. Our unit was routed by the Vietnamese, and we're trying to get back to it. We heard they're headed up Three to fight the Vietnamese in the north. And I'll tell them that, if they hurry, they can catch the Brahma and eat it. And that there are still *people* in Pong Tuk – once they've got the yearling they'll keep going, to hunt for hostages. We two will go on our way and circle back for all of you when the coast is clear. It will take us a day and a half to get past Phnom Sanhaan and over to Highway Three, so for a day and a half, you'll all shut up. Does everyone understand?"

We all nodded, without a word. "*And watch for mines!*" he rasped.

He turned around, and we started through the pass.

*It's been more than thirty years now,
since my friend and I started through that pass.
The war between the Vietnamese and the Khmer Rouge dragged on,
and eventually, our families went different ways.*

*I've made ten trips back to Cambodia, and have tried to find my friend.
But I can't. Because I can't <u>ask</u> about him.
I cannot remember his name.*

Solid line – the boys' journey to where they'd last seen their mothers,
three and a half years before (Ba Phnom to Pong Tuk)
January 6th to 15th, 1979   9.5 days, 120 kilometers (75 miles)

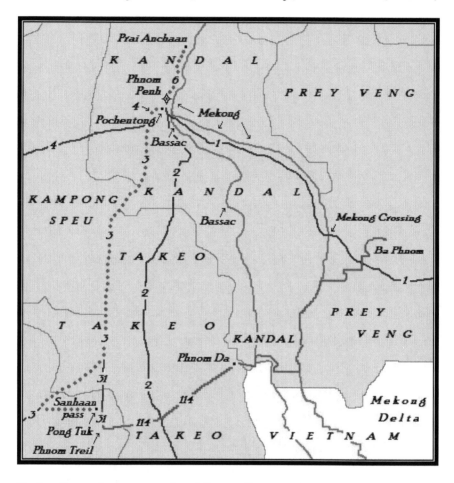

Broken line – the journey ahead, begun January 15th, 1979
137 kilometers (85 miles) to Pochentong (southwest Phnom Penh)
169 kilometers (105 miles) to Prai Anchaan

Nyah's story continues in the sequel to this book,
<u>No Front Line</u>

What Really Happened (and How we Figured it Out)

Photographic restoration by FotoTechnika Fine Art Imaging, Inc.

Lang (on his mother's right) a year after his escape,
in Khao-I-Dang refugee camp in Thailand.

Look at his aggressive stance, and the determination in his eyes.
The day he and his comrade walked back into Pong Tuk,
they would have been even thinner than his brother is here.

As we said in the foreword, when we began to write Lang's story down we were missing most of the pieces. As it turned out, the detective work we had to do is almost as good a story as the one of the boys' journey. The narratives that follow relate how we did our research, how we used the information we had to get more, and what triggers brought back Lang's memories.

We also want to clearly separate fact from fiction. We wrote his experience as a story because we wanted to take you into the world he knew in 1979, but to do so, we had to bridge gaps in his journey. We don't want our book to be added to the ever-growing pile of "Based on a True Story" novels, where the reader has to *guess* what is real and what is not. We want our readers to know.

But to begin at the beginning, it's important to understand why we were missing so many pieces of the puzzle when we started. Before Lang came to the United States, no one ever *asked* him how he had escaped from the army or gotten back to his mother – not his family, or neighbors in Prai Anchaan who'd survived the war, or the people he met in Khao-I-Dang. When he was resettled in Florida his new classmates asked him how he'd ended up there, but he couldn't speak English well enough to tell them. And once he got into the workforce, well, it seemed like everyone was just too busy. You're getting the picture here – he never *recounted* his story. So it began to slip away.

Jump to 2014, when we finished the book. In the end, we found it's far easier to get information than we'd ever thought possible – determination and imagination are the keys. We used the Internet for everything from how cold it was at night to what phase the moon was in. We used satellite photographs to determine the boys' route, and look at areas we couldn't get in to. We read history books, and articles on the Web, to try to understand the centuries of conflict that had landed two children in a war zone. It was by luck that we so quickly located the survivors who had the information we needed, but, with tenacity, we would have found them eventually.

But I should tell you here how Lang and I talked about the most painful events in his life without triggering nightmares. Disney. There's a sunny Parisian café in the French section of the EPCOT park in Florida, where you're enveloped by the smell of French coffee and baguettes. And surrounded by *families* – children who will never be taken from their parents, mothers who will never have to watch their children starve, and fathers who will never disappear. I would ask him the worst of the questions there, and then we'd finish our coffee and move on to the Moroccan section. And the pain would be forgotten.

We hope this book will encourage others with incredible experiences – especially refugees, whose stories are so seldom told – to write their stories down. If you're one of those people and would like to tell your story, get started. Don't worry about your English; your children will find it exciting to get involved and help you. And you don't have to write a book – you can write a short story, or an account, or a collection of notes to pass down to your children. You don't have to start at the beginning, either – you can start at the most interesting part of your story and work backward and forward. Or you can do what we did – tell only a *part* of your story. We chose to write about the end of Lang's four-year ordeal, when he could begin to put his life back together and dream of the future, because I didn't want to write about the horrors of the work camps. I did have to lay the background for his escape, but was able to confine the worst of what he'd seen to one paragraph ("By this time we'd seen all the ugly faces of war..." in "The Turning Point") and short stories scattered throughout the book.

So just get your story down. We have confidence in you, because you *survived*. We know that you can do it.

When we finished the first draft of this book we were still left with a complete mystery – why Lang hadn't run into the Vietnamese army on Highway One. Comparing his position on January 6th, 1979 to the position of the Vietnamese infantry as documented in the historical record, he should have. The narrative that follows describes how we found out *why* Lang saw what he saw – an empty highway.

The Missing Army

You can see the ravages of war in burned-out buildings, half-empty schoolyards, and burial grounds that shouldn't be there. But you can see it most clearly in the eyes of its survivors.

We were standing in the office of the Municipal Administrator of Ba Phnom District, on a warm afternoon in 2011. It was lunchtime, and we'd walked in, unannounced, looking for information about what the Vietnamese infantry was doing on January 6th, 1979. The day after Lang escaped. Because the key to his story lay in those first 24 hours. The boys had met no other *people* – and that's why they'd survived.

The man obviously in charge introduced himself as the Assistant to the Municipal Administrator, and asked us what we wanted. There was not a uniform in the place – the man stood there in front of us in no more than a 'kramaa' wrapped around his waist. We told him we were looking for information from the Khmer Rouge era – from the battle for the Mekong Crossing. "Please," we said, "finish your lunch. We'll wait outside."

We went out into the courtyard, and waited. I was nervous – if we couldn't get the information we needed, I really didn't want to publish our book. Why had Lang never run into the Vietnamese? What were they *doing?* The historical record said they took the Crossing on the 5th, and were waiting on Highway One for their bridging equipment to catch up to them on the 6th (so they could get across the Mekong to take Phnom Penh, which they did on the 7th). There was no one left for them to shoot at – the Khmer Rouge army had made a complete retreat. And so, according to the historical record, they just sat there. January 6th, 1979 – the one-day break in the artillery fire. The single clue that had made it possible for us to place Lang at Ba Phnom with certainty. The single clue that had made it possible for us to write the book, because we finally had "Nyah's" starting point.

But it wasn't just that the boys hadn't seen anyone – they hadn't heard anything, either. The anti-tank mines as the Vietnamese minesweepers ran over them, and the anti-personnel mines as the infantrymen hit them. The bridging equipment as it was put into place, and the trucks, the tanks, and the big guns, as they clattered onto it. Instinctively the boys had run to the north side of Ba Phnom on the 5th, to put the mountain between themselves and the artillery fire. But they'd spent the whole day of the 6th coming *around* it, and when they'd finally gotten a clear view of the south... there was no one there. The boys concluded that the Vietnamese were further east, having never advanced from the position from which they'd been shelling the day before. But the historical record said the Vietnamese were sitting on Highway One at the Crossing, all backed up on each other – the boys should have been looking *right at them.* Even if they couldn't see them, they should have been able to hear them. What had *really* happened?

We'd never get the information from the Cambodian side. The Khmer Rouge army had retreated and the civilians had fled; there were no Cambodians there to see *anything.* As we sat there, waiting for the Assistant to finish his lunch, we asked ourselves why we were there at all.

Oh, I'd tried to get the information from the Vietnamese side, in the United States. I'd located one veteran of the Cambodia takeover, but he didn't know what had happened on January 6th because he hadn't been sent into Cambodia until three weeks later. And I'd been lucky to find *him* – almost all veterans of the 1979 invasion still live in Vietnam (most American Vietnamese left Vietnam before 1976).

So we'd decided to come through Saigon, on our way to Cambodia to take the photographs for the book. We planned to ask at the war museums if anyone could help us. We'd boarded our plane, settled in, and had found ourselves seated next to a pleasant Vietnamese engineer. We told him why we were headed to Saigon. As he took our drinks from the stewardess and passed them over to us he said, as gently as he could, "They're not going to talk to you."

When we arrived in Saigon we immediately booked a flight to Cambodia, because the engineer had told us something *else*. We'd never get through customs with the 50 kilos of medicine we were carrying for the victims of the 2011 Cambodian flood without being heavily taxed. Worse yet, the medicine might be confiscated. We slept on a bench in the airport waiting for our flight the next morning, to avoid the customs agents.

When we arrived in Phnom Penh we headed straight for the mapseller in the New Market, and got a map of Ba Phnom District. We started to plan the route we'd take to get a shot of the mountain as the boys would have seen it, as they ran toward it. That's when I saw the Municipal Administrator's headquarters marked on the map. Well, it was on the way... And so, here we sat, in front of his office. The last of our last resources.

The Assistant summoned us in. When we re-entered the office we saw that he had dismissed all the other officers; he stood there alone. He sat down on a plastic chair, motioned to us to do the same, and asked us again what we wanted. He leaned back in his chair, wearing only his red-and-white-checked 'kramaa' – the picture of complacence. But his eyes darted about, nervously – constantly – looking around to be sure there was no one listening. Yes, you can see war most clearly in the eyes of its survivors.

We told him again that we were looking for information about the battle for the Mekong Crossing in 1979. "*Oh,*" he said, sitting up a little straighter, "if you'd just come a few years earlier. My *father* – he could have given you *so* much information... But he died." And he slouched back in his chair again.

My heart sank. The man either didn't have information, or wasn't going to give it to us. We'd *never* be able to get it – and, as I've said, I didn't want to publish our book without it. I imagined the first few lines of the foreword... 'I *tried* to find out where the Vietnamese were on January 6th, and what they were actually doing. I tried finding Cambodian survivors, I tried American Vietnamese, I even tried going to Vietnam. But I... just couldn't get the information.' I didn't like how that sounded. I didn't like it at all.

The man looked around again – but only by moving his eyes. First from one window to another, and then from the side door to the front door. He suddenly straightened up again. "I was in a work camp just north of Highway One. I was ten at the time – *and I saw it all!*"

"When the cadres in my camp heard the Vietnamese were coming," he said, "they told us boys to go – to just *get out,* and go home. My village was east of Ba Phnom – so if I'd fled west, across the Mekong with everyone else, I wouldn't have been able to get home to see if my mother and father were still alive. So as the Vietnamese advanced up the highway on the afternoon of the 5th, I just kept backing off – north – just enough to be out of the way. Waiting to circle back behind them. I watched them, as I waited – and I saw it all."

"As their army came up the highway," he continued, "their infantry fanned out to flush out any remaining Khmer Rouge. Both anti-tank mines and anti-personnel mines had been laid, but they still advanced very quickly."

"When did they get across the Mekong?" I asked – because that was the key to the whole thing.

"Oh, it was all very quick. They got across that night – the night of the 5th."

No wonder the boys had never run into the Vietnamese on the 6th – *they weren't there.* And they hadn't heard them preparing to cross the Mekong on the night of the 5th because they'd put the mountain between themselves and the invading infantry, and had then fallen deep asleep from exhaustion. The artillery fire they heard on the 7th was the Vietnamese taking Phnom Penh.

"Did they use the old car ferries to get across?" I asked.

"No, they had their own bridging equipment. The ferries ran throughout the Khmer Rouge years, but the Vietnamese didn't use them to get across that night."

We told him that's all we needed to know, and asked if we could use his name in the book. He said yes, that was no problem – he wrote it down, with his telephone number. Yes, that was no problem – but his eyes never stopped moving.

So it was not as we had thought, when we wrote the first draft of the book. Lang had been convinced that all the civilians had fled the war zone – that's what he'd seen when he'd climbed the big tamarind that first morning. In fact there had been a few people who had simply hidden, waiting to go back home. Like the man in front of me, slouched back in his plastic chair. You know, he didn't *have* to tell us anything. He could have just said, "What would *I* know? I was just a kid." Our next trip back to Cambodia, he's getting one hell of a present.

How We Used the Clues We Had

We had so little information in the beginning that we squeezed everything we could out of every shred we had. For example, when the Vietnamese veteran we interviewed described the terror of night-blindness, I put this together with Lang's assertion that his comrade had been malnourished to the point that his growth had been stunted. When I asked Lang if the boy had been night blind, he said, yes. But *Lang* had not. Why?

I remembered reading somewhere that if you're put on a desert island and can ask for only one food, you should ask for sweet potatoes. I asked Lang if he'd been able to get them. He said yes, he'd been able to steal them at night. I looked up night blindness – lack of Vitamin A. Then I looked up the nutritional value of sweet potatoes – 700% of the daily requirement for Vitamin A. Bazinga.

Lang then said he'd learned from his grandfather how the sweet potato plant grows, and that you can steal one from each plant without killing the plant. Then he explained how he hid between the rows of potatoes if he thought the guard was coming, that he could eat as many potatoes as he could steal raw, and that he could cache them (which he could *not* do with rats).

But sweet potatoes contain all *kinds* of nutrients. The knowledge that he'd been eating sweet potatoes and jungle rats (an excellent source of lean protein) enabled us to understand why his growth hadn't been stunted, as his friend's had. And why he hadn't had to eat so much raw cassava that his nervous system had been damaged.

Then we asked, who *else* might have been night blind? The guards? Would this partially explain why Lang never got caught? He doesn't remember any of them becoming very thin, so assumes they were getting the vitamins needed to prevent night blindness, but of course we'll never know. But how about the other boys in his work camps? Certainly most of them would have gone night blind. But Lang said that night-blindness wouldn't have been the only reason they wouldn't have gone out at night to search for food. Firstly, they were afraid of being caught and severely caned. Secondly, they were terribly afraid of ghosts. And then Lang told me how his grandfather had sat him down and had a rational discussion with him about whether or not ghosts could hurt you.

All this information, derived from *one line* in *one interview* – that the Vietnamese soldier had been night blind. And this gave me three key reasons why Lang survived, when so many others didn't – he didn't go night blind, he wasn't afraid to go out at night, and he wasn't as malnourished as the other boys because he could steal food at night.

"How ineffectual the human mind can be – I wondered what else I was missing."

I first heard Lang's story on a hike in Florida in 2001; it was the first thing he ever told me about himself. As we walked through the jungle on a cool, spring morning, it reminded him of Ba Phnom. He told me how he'd escaped with the older boy, how they'd hidden, how he'd found food for them, and how they'd found their way back to their relocation village. But it was the ending that got me – that their mothers were the only ones left in the village, still waiting for their children. And that's why I decided that, someday, I would write his story down.

We started the book eight years later. Now, this was my *husband* I was writing about – I thought I knew him when I put down those first few lines. But I quickly learned that I did not.

I'd originally thought that he *had* run into the Vietnamese, although he'd insisted he hadn't. That, even if he hadn't run into them on Highway One, he'd run into them somewhere else. I mean, they'd blitzkrieged Cambodia in a five-pronged land and air attack, and had taken control in less than three weeks. They were *everywhere.*

Lang told me that he remembered clearly escaping mid afternoon, running for the mountain, ditching their uniforms and then falling asleep right next to them, waking up sitting up against the tree, climbing his first reconnaissance tree, seeing the farm road, the burned-out villages and the wandering plow animals, and getting back down into the lowlands late that afternoon. And finding their mothers in Pong Tuk. But he couldn't remember much in between.

So I figured the journey must have been so traumatic that he'd blocked out everything. *Especially* running into the Vietnamese. Well, the ending of the story was the most important thing, and I had that. And I had the escape itself. I figured I could fill in with stories he'd told me of events before the escape.

I wrote the first chapter, and then got onto Google Maps to see if I could figure out the route they would have taken to get down into the lowlands. Looking at the satellite photos, I found I could determine it easily. I wrote the next few chapters without having to ask Lang anything more than what they'd been able to find to eat. I figured I'd just write the whole book that way – determining the route they would have chosen with the information they had, and then asking Lang how they'd gotten across the terrain and found food in each different geographical area.

When they finally got to Highway One I wrote a *gripping* chapter about the two boys running into the Vietnamese infantry, and then running for their lives. Because I thought that must have been what happened.

After I'd finished Book One I asked Lang to read it to be sure it was accurate – except for my addition of his running into the invasion forces, of course. I quickly realized that he was having trouble picking up the nuances in the written language. So I started reading the text to him, adding the nuances with the tone of my voice. And that's when he started to remember more. I'd read a chapter, and he'd say, "Oh no. That's not how we did it. *This* is how we did it." Or, "Are you completely out of your mind? I would never have crossed the Mekong where it was two miles across holding onto the trunk of a banana tree. I would have stolen a boat!" (Most of the other deserters got across around Neak Luong, where the river is much narrower, holding onto banana trees.)

I wrote, and *re*-wrote, as Lang remembered more. And re-wrote again, when he remembered something else. And then I remembered what it was that he'd remembered in the first place – before we'd started the book. And I felt like such a fool.

His most vivid memories were of the most traumatic events in his life. Sitting in the bomb shelter waiting to die and seeing bodies when he came out again, the death of his two friends in the UXO explosion, becoming separated from his grandfather in the march out of Phnom Penh, the death of his grandfather, the horrors of the work camps, his first day in the army, trying to escape from his platoon in broad daylight, the Vietnamese shelling, waking up totally lost underneath the tree... His memories of all of these things had been crystal clear, right from the beginning. But his memories of the middle of their journey had faded because nothing had *happened* to either boy. And the reason he didn't remember running into the Vietnamese was because he didn't.

So I took out the "gripping" chapter and wrote *The Seventh Scenario* to put in its place. And I continued to write, and read back to him what I'd written.

I asked him what diseases he'd had as a child. In the list he rattled off, he included smallpox. I told him he couldn't *possibly* have had smallpox – he had no pockmarks. He insisted he did. I insisted he didn't – he must have had chicken pox. "If you had pockmarks, I'd see them. And I don't see them. Besides, you were vaccinated for smallpox – there's the scar, on your arm."

"I was vaccinated by the Red Cross," he replied, "*after* I'd had smallpox. And you can't see the pockmarks because they're on my scalp, *underneath my hair!*" And then I remembered how many times he'd talked about his aunt trying to clean the pocks on his scalp.

I wondered, at that point, how I could have been married to someone for seven years yet know so little about him. But we see our husbands or our wives in the same circumstances every day – getting the kids off to school, going to work, paying the bills... Think of how very small that window is that we see them through. Do we ever stop to ask ourselves what they are, outside of it? Before we started the book I didn't know that Lang knew anything about traditional medicine. I didn't even know that his grandfather was a shaman. Or that he keeps track of what phase the moon is in, and, on a sunny day, can tell the time without a watch. Or how infallibility he believes in karma – that your good deeds can later save your life. *Or* that he'd had smallpox. And now I finally understand why he can manage anything, from tying off a leaking hose in the engine of our car with a tee shirt, to scraping around in the kitchen and making a really nice meal out of leftover lunchmeat, to building a successful career as a PC/LAN Systems Analyst by "watching the older boys".

Ask your life partner about things outside of that tiny window you see them through. You may find another person underneath the one you know.

"Puamaak"

As Lang says at the end of his story, we can't locate his comrade because we don't know his name.

Lang wouldn't have used his first name because the boy was his elder; he would have called him 'Puamaak' (friend) or 'Bong' (older brother). And Lang would probably never have known his last name. People from well-to-do families stopped using their surnames so that they couldn't be traced back to their families.

Lang's mother remembered calling him "Teea", but Lang said that didn't sound familiar. She didn't know his last name, probably because "Teea" and his mother never told her.

And so, because we had no way to locate him, we were left with what Lang remembered about him. But because the two of them could never talk freely until they'd escaped, Lang had never known much about him in the first place. He remembered that the boy was very intelligent, and just seemed to *know* a lot (he was much more capable than I made him out to be in the story because I wanted "Nyah" to explain things to him, so the reader would get the explanation). He was part Chinese, was from a merchant family in Phnom Penh, had two older sisters, had adored his mother and had also been close to his father, knew his father must already be dead, had had three years of French in school, could cook, could swim very well but couldn't climb a tree to save his life, had 20/20 vision but was night blind, had been in the army for about a year, was an infantryman but had started out as a porter, was effeminate but not homosexual, had survived by "kissing up" to the camp guards and the officers, and could lie his way out of just about anything. Lang thought he was fourteen, but said he might have been older (certainly not younger). And he remembered what he looked like – especially his height.

When he talked about this boy I sensed that they were not best friends. I asked him if they'd teamed up just to stay alive, and he said that that was pretty much the way it was. "You had to lie to stay alive back then," he said. "I understood that – I had to do it, too. But I was always afraid that he would lie to *me* – we were only in the same unit three months, and I never got to know him well enough to know if he would, or he wouldn't. I didn't think it safe to trust him completely. But I know he did care about me. He helped me more than once when we were in the army, and on our journey, he never tried to take more than his half of our food – although he needed it more than I did. If anything had happened to me, I know he would have been devastated."

So I began to build the character of the older boy from Lang's description. He'd remembered him carving chopsticks on their journey and said that he *looked* Chinese, so I made him half Chinese, gave him a Chinese father and a Khmer mother, and sent him to Chinese school. Based on the fact that his mother had survived the years in Pong Tuk, and that *someone* had taught him how to swim, I made her a village girl.

But I needed a lot more than what I had – I needed to know what was in his *head*.

Firstly, how did he know so *much?* I thought he would have known more about the world outside of Cambodia than his younger comrade because he'd grown up in Phnom Penh during the Lon Nol years. I had an advantage here – I'd studied in Manila on scholarship in 1970 and had visited Kuala Lumpur and Bangkok on the way home, so understood how very cosmopolitan and Westernized most Southeast Asian capitals were at that time. Lang's comrade would have grown up in a period in which all the foreign embassies were still open, the American military was there to support Lon Nol, French expatriates still lived in the capital, and people could speak relatively freely. His parents would have had access to daily newspapers and magazines, and he would have heard them talk about current events. He would have grown up with American television and seen foreign movies (especially American action films, which he would probably have talked about with his father). If in fact he'd gone to Chinese school he would probably have been ahead of his grade level, especially in mathematics. And Lang believes that his parents didn't exclude him from adult conversation, just as Lang's grandfather had not excluded him; this was unusual in Cambodia.

Secondly, how much did he know about mines? When the boys had to cross Highway One, I had to know how much training the army would have given him in how to lay and detect them. And when they got to their first village, I had to know if the army would have taught him the pattern to use for a village. I consulted a man who had been an officer in the Lon Nol army, who knew how the Khmer Rouge army had operated. He said that anyone who'd been in the army a year would have been taught how to lay and detect mines, and the pattern to use for both a road and a village.

Thirdly, why did he choose to go back to Pong Tuk? Prai Anchaan would have been the boys' best option. It was only eighty kilometers upriver, they couldn't possibly have gotten lost getting there, they could simply have walked along the riverbank the whole way (which they knew wouldn't have been mined), they would have been able to get all the fresh water and food they'd need, they would have been able to get *around* Phnom Penh, and, once they'd reached their destination, they would have been able to hide on Lang's grandfather's land and catch food in the paddies. In the end Lang decided that the boy had simply wanted to get back to his mother, and had thought she was in Pong Tuk. He was the one navigating, so that's where they headed.

And fourthly, how did he know how to get back to Pong Tuk? *This* was the million-dollar question.

The route they took, as I've said, was easy to figure out. I identified thirteen points at which the boys would have had to make a decision which way to go, and at the first twelve, there was no decision to make – there was only one logical option. Lang had told me that they'd never disagreed on a decision, and now I could clearly see why.

Decision Twelve would have landed them at the south-to-east bend of the Bassac, near Phnom Da, where they had to make Decision 13. But I think the bend in the Bassac was where he was trying to get to anyway. It's the best landmark in all of Southern Cambodia, and *someone* had told him how to get back to Pong Tuk from there. He couldn't have figured it out himself.

But who could have given him directions? We went back to the escape itself, to see if we could figure it out.

As their unit was retreating he'd turned to Lang and told him that they should try to escape. He'd turned back a second time to say, "Don't worry. I can get us home." So we know he had *some* information at this point, if only how to get back to Pong Tuk once he'd crossed the Bassac.

We don't think he got it from their squad leader; if *he'd* known that they would all have an opportunity to desert, he would have had the two boys marching near him. In other words, we don't think he knew that the boys would need to know how to get back to their relocation village. He wouldn't have known how to get to Pong Tuk anyway.

We don't think Lang's comrade got the information from the scout or the senior officers, or he would have known where they were; they could have told him he was near the Mekong Crossing. But Lang said that, when the two of them woke up the next morning underneath the tree, his comrade was just as lost as he was. And neither the scout nor the officers would have risked being overheard revealing their position or giving directions.

Certainly no one told him how to get around the marshes, or they would have gotten back to Pong Tuk sooner.

The boy's parents would never have imagined that he would end up so far away. And they probably wouldn't have known how to get back to Pong Tuk themselves – not from as far away as Phnom Da.

He probably wouldn't have remembered the map of Takeo and Kampot from school because neither was his home province. And he'd never heard of Pong Tuk before he was relocated there with his family.

So we were *still* stuck – who gave him the information?

As the Khmer Rouge moved him from work camp to work camp, each time further east, he would probably have ended up in a camp near the Bassac – just as Lang had. We know that he spent a lot of time with the camp cadres; that's how he'd survived. They were adults – they knew where they were. And *he* knew they knew where they were. We believe he would have tried to get directions before he was drafted, thinking that, someday, he'd need them.

But no one in his right mind would have risked being overheard giving directions to an inmate.

I asked Lang if the boy could have bought the information. If his mother might have been able to send gold with him, sewn into his work clothes. And if he might have been able to find someone so tempted by the gold that he would risk giving directions. Lang said that giving or taking a bribe was an even greater risk than giving or asking for directions; both parties would probably have been killed, and they might have been tortured first. He said the boy wouldn't have risked it.

So all we can do is guess. Having observed first hand this boy's remarkable ability to get people to trust him, Lang thinks he may have found a camp guard too stupid to realize that he was being pumped for information. And made sure there was no one else around to hear them talking.

The Search for Pong Tuk

Lang's mother told me where the village of Pong Tuk was when I first began writing the book. And when I bought a map of Kampot on our 2010 trip, sure enough, there it was – just south of a market town called Took Meas. "Pong Tuk" was written out clearly, in English (I couldn't read Khmer at the time).

I was in no hurry to go there; I knew what had happened in 1975 and 1979, and didn't really need to see the place. And Lang didn't want to go because his grandfather had died there. *I'll look at Pong Tuk with Google Maps,* I thought, *just as I looked at Ba Phnom, and all the places the boys passed through.*

When I began Book Three I got out the map I'd bought in 2010, pulled up Google Maps, and zeroed in on Pong Tuk. But there was nothing there. I then looked back at my provincial map and saw that there was no road to Pong Tuk, although Lang's mother had said you could drive to it. *OK,* I thought, *my map's a little off. Pong Tuk's in this general area – somewhere.*

In 2011 we went to Ba Phnom and Phnom Da. We'd seen when we'd flown in from Saigon that all of Southern Cambodia was flooded – the monsoon rains had been exceptionally heavy, and water levels were the highest they'd been in thirty years. The view of the flooding from Phnom Da further convinced us that we shouldn't try to get to Pong Tuk; it would mean a trip of 100 miles (160 km., much of it on back roads), there would be no towing facilities or place to stay if we got stuck, and there would be no medical facilities if we had an emergency. Lang still didn't want to go, anyway.

2012 brought another flood, so, once again, I didn't try to get to Pong Tuk.

We moved to California that year, and began to hike every chance we got. Each trail was marked with its destination and length, and, as our confidence increased, we began to take longer hikes. But soon the whisper of a question arose in the back of my brain – and the more hikes we took, the louder it got.

According to Lang's mother, Pong Tuk was just north of the Vietnamese border. I'd calculated that the boys had covered 100 miles (161 km.) in 9.5 days, which meant that they'd averaged 10.5 miles (16.9 km.) per day. Lang and I were now taking 10-mile hikes quite often, pulling out bottled water and packed sandwiches when it was time to eat. The question was, how had the boys averaged 10.5 miles a day when they'd had to look for food and water, cook, climb trees and figure out in which direction they should go next – especially considering the shape they were in, and that they couldn't move at night. Well, there was only one way to do the math. But the more we hiked, the louder the question nagged at me. I dismissed it. They'd used the rivers– that must be it.

But an even larger question still loomed over the whole book – how had the older boy found their way back to a place as tiny and remote as Pong Tuk? Yes, at their first 12 decision points there was only one way they could go, but once they were across the Bassac, they had choices. And the older boy had made the *right* choice – because someone had told him what to do. But *who?* And *what* had that person told him?

Lang kept saying, "We used my human compass to go 45 degrees southwest, and just kept looking for Phnom Treil." But at what point would they

have been able to see it? When we'd climbed Ba Phnom and looked for the
Mekong less than 7 miles (11 kilometers) away, we couldn't see it – and we
were 480 feet (147 meters) up. And I had never been able to find Phnom Treil on
a map – it couldn't be all that big a mountain. Had the boys really just done as
Lang had said – gone 45 degrees southwest and looked for Phnom Treil – and
gotten lucky? But again, I dismissed the question – if it was more complicated
than that, wouldn't Lang have remembered? And when I looked at where Pong
Tuk was in relation to Phnom Da, yep, 45 degrees southwest. So they *could* have
gotten lucky.

I finished the book and began to write the sequel. But I really needed to see
the pass they'd had to walk through to get out of Pong Tuk. I told Lang that, as I
hadn't been able to find Pong Tuk with Google Maps, I'd go down to the village
with his mother. I wanted some photos of the pass, anyway – I wanted our
readers to be able to see it.

This time, Lang said he thought he should go. I tried to talk him out of it,
ever afraid he'd begin to have nightmares again. But he said, "No, I want to go.
When I see it again I might remember something important to our first book."

And so, in 2014, we headed out of Phnom Penh early on a cool January
morning, determined to be back by nightfall. I pulled out three provincial maps
– Kandal, Takeo and Kampot – and began to trace our route as we drove along.
The route the family would have been forced to take in April of 1975.

Once on Highway Four Lang's mother gave directions to our driver, Lang's
cousin. "After the airport, take the highway that splits off from this one." OK,
the new highway was Three. Easy enough. And, according to where Pong Tuk
was on my Kampot map, that's the way we should have been going.

We got onto Three and passed through town after town, but couldn't find
signs to tell us their names; within half an hour, Lang and I had no idea where
we were. "Take the left fork up ahead," Lang's mother instructed his cousin.
Lang leaned over and whispered to me, "I recognize this place – this is where
we lost my sister in 1975." So he knew we were still going the right way, but he
didn't know where we were.

"Can you tell me," I asked his cousin, "when we cross the border into
Kampot?" A little while later he turned back to me and said, "We're in Kampot
now." But when I looked at my map I saw *four roads* that split off from Three
and go over the border. Lang and I couldn't figure out which one we were on.

A short while later Lang's mother said to his cousin, "Turn in at the temple
over there. We're going to the village next to Pong Tuk first."

"We're *here?*" I said. "We *can't* be. We haven't been driving long enough."

By this time I had been doing research for this book for five years. I had
long since learned how very difficult it is to do research in Cambodia, and that
you must be prepared for anything. And so, I was. I had brought with me the
map of *every single district* in Kampot Province. *And* a compass. Really.

"What 'srōk' are we in?" I asked our host. "Angkor Chey," he replied. I
took out my sheaf of maps, found the one for Angkor Chey, and began to pour
over it as Lang's mother pulled gifts out of her bag. The man's wife had served
as headman of this village when Lang's mother had lived in Pong Tuk, and the

couple had helped her to keep what was left of her family alive. She'd kept in touch with them for thirty-five years.

As I've said, when I found Pong Tuk on my map in 2010, I couldn't read Khmer. But, in 2013, I'd learned. "I *found it*," I said to Lang. "Right here. We just came off 31 – here. And the mountains you see over *here* on the map – they should be southwest of us." I pulled out my compass and verified our position.

"But Phnom Treil isn't there," he said, looking at the mountains. "None of those peaks is the right shape."

"It's around here somewhere." And I began to pour over the map again. "Here it is! Five miles south of us. At the junction of 31 and 114."

And suddenly, I understood how the older boy had found their way back to Pong Tuk. Once he'd gotten them over to Takeo, he had shadowed the roads. He'd had the two of them go 45 degrees southwest so that they would run into Road 114, and then he'd used Phnom Treil to locate 31. And that's why he'd kept telling Lang to look for Phnom Treil; Phnom Sanhaan (the highest peak in the range southwest of us) is actually closer to Pong Tuk, and ten times higher.

I'd originally thought that he knew nothing about the roads (except highways One, Two and Three) because Lang didn't, and because he was only ten when he left Pong Tuk. This is what I think happened. As they marched him away from his mother in the summer of 1975, he was absolutely desperate to find out how to get back to her. Once out of the village they turned him south on 31 (the road he'd first come to Pong Tuk on, in April), and he made a mental note of the road number. This was shortly after the takeover, and the road signs may not yet have been taken down. When they turned him west on 114, he again made note of the road number. He already knew Phnom Treil by sight and name because he'd been sent down there to collect bamboo shoots, and he realized that he could find the junction again by looking for Phnom Treil. If the road signs had already been taken down, he would have asked what the two roads were – what did he have to lose? So he learned that he had to know how to get to 114 if he was ever to see his mother again. And later on, when he asked for directions, those are the directions he asked for.

I had long since come to the conclusion that, without the older boy to talk to, we would never know how he had navigated; this was the one mystery that we had not been able to solve. Now, Phnom Treil had solved it for us.

I recalculated the distance the boys would have come – 75 miles (120 km.), not 100. And then I recalculated the average distance they would have covered each day – 7.9 miles (11.36 km.). This made a *lot* more sense than 10.5 (16.9 km.). It was still a lot of ground to cover in 12 hours considering all the things they had to accomplish each day, but I felt that, by using the waterways, they could have done it.

I looked at the provincial map again and saw another Pong Tuk northwest of us, in a different district. "So there are at least three Pong Tuks in Kampot Province," I said to Lang. "Your mother originally told me that Pong Tuk was south of Took Meas, and that's the first Pong Tuk I found on a map. We're north of Took Meas here – she got 'south' and 'north' mixed up!"

We took our leave and drove to our final destination. And the minute we rounded the corner into the village, Lang did remember more. He pointed to the temple grounds. "That was the killing field. That's why we were never allowed near the temple. But we knew – we used to see the lights at night."

We passed the temple quickly, and I pointed to the Phnom Sanhaan range. "No wonder you kept saying that Phnom Treil was blue. All these mountains look blue. It's the mist." And we drove into the village.

In the five long years it took us to write this book, I'd often felt as though someone were looking over my shoulder. We'd found out where Lang and his comrade had escaped, and when, too easily. We'd been able to trace their route up to the point where they'd crossed the Bassac too easily. We'd found a Vietnamese veteran of the invasion too easily. And we'd located an eyewitness to the Vietnamese infantry's movements at the Crossing... too easily. Now, as we pulled into a lane that ran between rice fields, Lang was suddenly quiet. His eyes had fixed on something. When his cousin stopped the car he pointed to a shed ahead of us. "That's the house we lived in."

"Who would *ever* have believed the thing survived?" he said. "Look – they've used the original frame, rebuilt it, and put an addition on the right and the left. When we lived here the walls were palm fronds hung vertically from the eve – like on the addition on the right. They've put woven-reed walls on it now. And a decent roof. And look at the *trees* around it – there was *nothing* when we came here. Can you imagine being driven out of your home, marched to the middle of nowhere, and put in a shed in the middle of rice paddies with no tree cover for the sun and the rain? All alone, so everyone could see your comings and goings. Can you believe all seven of us lived in that one room, before they split us up?"

We walked up to the shed, and he put his hand on the sheet of woven reeds that now served as its front. "This is where my grandfather died – his bed was on the other side of this wall."

We did not ask to go in.

The house in Pong Tuk, as it looks today. Compare it to the one on page 270, which is typical of the houses "old people" lived in.

The Euphoria of Freedom

Lang said that he and his comrade were absolutely euphoric on their journey – that they told jokes and stories and played tricks on each other all the way across Southern Cambodia. Because they were *free.* Every aspect of their lives had been controlled for four years, but now, they were their own masters.

I didn't write their story with their jokes and their tricks because I felt that I didn't have the skill to do this without causing offense to other survivors. But I did try to understand why the boys were euphoric, because it made no sense to me that they were – they were hungry and weak, the older boy was sick from malnutrition, they were afraid of running into people, mines and rabid dogs, and they didn't know if their families were still alive.

Lang said that the reason for their euphoria was psychological – they had been empowered overnight, and found themselves able to use their empowerment to save their own lives. He was particularly proud of the fact that he could find enough food for them, and make it taste more like what they'd had before the takeover.

But I felt that this was only part of the equation – that there must have been physiological factors. They had been continuously deprived of sleep for four years but were able to get almost twelve hours their first night, and all they needed once they were out of the war zone. They had been starved for four years, but were able to find enough of the foods that contained the protein and vitamins they needed once they were across the Mekong. They had had little access to clean water, and had often not had enough water, but were now able to take advantage of the rivers and the canals. I reasoned that some of their euphoria would have been the result of the beginning of their physical recovery.

But it's also important to understand that the boys did not yet know how many of their relatives had not survived. It's reasonable to assume that they thought that most of their cousins had, simply because *they* had. Lang had been the most sickly of all the cousins in his clan, and as a result the most coddled, yet *he'd* made it. But the boys really didn't understand how extraordinary they were – Lang had picked up survival skills faster than the boys around him, and the older boy had learned to survive without ever having to find his own food!

As for whether or not their mothers were still alive, they didn't want to think about it, so they didn't – they were children, not adults. ('Nyah' discovers who in his family has survived in the sequel to this book.)

Education, Observation, Determination, Endurance, Intelligence, Adaptability and Luck – The Many Reasons that Lang Survived

At least one third of the Cambodian people died between 1975 and 1980. We think it's important to list the reasons that Lang did not, all in one place.

He was ambidextrous – he could do any task with either hand, and could often see an alternative solution to a problem. He'd acquired tremendous immunity by the age of four from a long succession of tropical diseases. He didn't contract malaria in the camps – our Vietnamese source told us that many of his comrades did. He'd learned to hide by the time he entered school, thanks to the village bully. And he was always very small, which made it that much easier. He'd learned to climb trees very well; he had long fingers and toes and high arches in his feet, and had watched adults climb to get fruit and coconuts. Because he weighed less than everyone else he could get further up into fruit trees without snapping the branches. He knew where to look for nests and hives, and wasn't afraid of getting bitten or stung. He knew to avoid rabid animals at any cost. He'd learned how to handle a boat from his uncle, how to cook from his aunt, and how to build a fire, handle livestock and use a machete from his grandfather. He'd made a pact with himself to survive when his family had been driven out of Prai Anchaan – when he was only seven. He'd already had mathematics and science by the time his school was closed, which meant that he'd learned to reason and had developed basic problem-solving skills. He'd learned to *learn* in three different ways – by processing formal presentation of material, by memorization, and by observation, and had learned to watch older boys to pick up skills he didn't have. He'd even taught himself how to ride a horse. When he was put in his first work camp the cadres didn't separate the Pong Tuk boys; he believes this is why they couldn't brainwash him. He made friends with other boys, and they formed alliances to help each other. His grandfather had taught him the difference between proteins and carbohydrates, and that he needed both; he was able to get a rat trap and, when he could no longer get enough rice, knew to try to get cassava and taro root. His grandfather had also taught him how to recognize all the common crops, in any stage of maturity; he even understood how each grows. Which was what enabled him to steal sweet potatoes – he never went night blind when almost everyone around him did, and could cache the potatoes so he'd have something to eat if he couldn't get enough food the next day. His grandfather had taught him not to fear ghosts, so he was able to venture out at night when other boys were afraid to – and eat his stolen food in the burial ground. He knew when he couldn't be seen because he could predict the moonrise. He was able to steal foods that can be eaten raw, so was less dependent on raw cassava (which contains cyanide). He never lost his 20/20 vision, which helped him to find food and do reconnaissance on their journey. And he *did* learn to lie. That's how he was able to stay in the infirmary so long, and get more food while he was there.

He'd also learned to recognize people by "the things that never change –

their gait, their voice, their dialect, how they move their eyes..." Had he not developed this skill he wouldn't have recognized the other Pong Tuk boy at muster his first day in his new platoon; he hadn't seen him for almost three years. If the two boys had not "buddied up", Lang would probably have been caught up in the mass desertion and died trying to cross the marshes.

But no one who survived this period did so without a *tremendous* measure of luck. Had Lang's mother brushed up against the poisonous frog *after* her father had died, *she* would have died; without her, Lang and his brother and sister would certainly not have survived. Lang had been handed the 'kwaiw' to clear a place to sleep when being marched to a new work camp, and the cadre who gave it to him simply forgot to take it back; without it he couldn't have husked coconuts, cleaned fish, skinned jungle rats, cut vine to make rope or bamboo to make ladders, and the hundred other things he did with it to survive. The boys were already out of the work camps at the time the Vietnamese invaded – they were getting more food, *better* food, and were not assigned to hard labor. Their squad leader had been successful in keeping both of them out of combat. The Vietnamese invaded in the dry season, right after the harvest – the boys had been getting extra rations for about a month. They fell asleep after they got away – they got twelve hours of complete rest before they tried to get out of the war zone. They didn't get caught up in either the retreat or the mass desertion, and so ended up on a different trajectory than the rest of the army. The villages had all been evacuated by the time they got to them, and they didn't get caught up in the Phnom Sanhaan hostage situation. The older boy had been drafted before Lang had, and so had been taught (in theory, anyway) how to get through a road or a village without hitting a mine. The villages in southwestern Takeo and northeastern Kampot hadn't been mined because there had been no time, but Road 31 had – yet the boys never hit anything. They found tamarinds all the way along on their journey, to sleep in, to hide in, to do their reconnaissance from, and to get food and medicine from. They didn't run out of kerosene. And they never ran into a Vietnamese "clean-up" unit.

But what greater luck did they have than ending up in the same unit? Both boys were very, very smart, but neither knew, until they "buddied up", how smart the other was. Once they figured it out, however, they pooled their brainpower very successfully. And if Lang's comrade hadn't been older than he was, they probably wouldn't have survived – Lang had had world geography in school but not Cambodian geography, and believes he wouldn't have been able to find his way back to either Pong Tuk or Prai Anchaan. And the older boy could *swim,* although he was Chinese; if he'd never learned, the outcome of their story might have been very different.

I asked Lang how he went on each day, especially in the camps. He was in them more than three years. He said he didn't think about it – that it was his *nature* to try to survive. Just as a sapling doesn't break when you bend it, but springs back instead – because that's its nature. But if you ask *him* how he survived, he'll tell you that he just kept pushing himself to adapt. He forced himself to learn to do things he never *imagined* he could do. He says the hardest of these was to learn to kill for food.

Binding the Pieces of the Story Together

Because I had so little information from the middle of the boys' journey, I filled in with things Lang remembered from before the escape – the childhood illnesses, the village bully, the boy who crushed his shoulder, the French sunbathers, being told at five who his mother was, jumping off trees into the water after school, the fishing trips with his oldest uncle, the talk with his grandfather about ghosts, the Holiday of the Rowing of the Boats, the bomb shelter, his mother proposing that he be sent to France, the Lon Nol troops firing at the Khmer Rouge insurgents from his schoolyard, the UXO accident, the skirmishes in his village, the Water Monitor eating bodies, the move into Phnom Penh, his new school, watching American television and movies, the relocation to Pong Tuk (becoming separated from his family on Highway 3, the loss of the older of his sisters, the poisonous frog and the relocations that preceded Pong Tuk), how his father was taken away, the owl and his grandfather's dream, finding the beehive, watching boys bring in a King Cobra in Pong Tuk and in one of his work camps, catching and stealing food (climbing coconut trees in the dark, hiding between rows in the vegetable gardens, trading sandals he'd found for a rat trap, and catching the giant rat), the theft of the older boy's hammock (which left him without one until he was drafted), getting trench foot and injuring his toes, the infirmary and finding the boy who had hung himself, the boys who drowned in 16 cm. of water (and the other incidents in the "all the ugly faces of war" paragraph), the boy who died from overeating, crossing the Mekong with the army in a tiny fishing boat, his first day in his platoon and how he recognized the other boy from Pong Tuk, his commanding officer flaunting his American gear, his squad leader trying to keep him out of combat, and his comrade surviving by "kissing up", lying, and eavesdropping on the officers.

I also used things Lang's mother remembered – her maid, the frog, stealing rawhide and then boiling it to have something to feed her children, the children coming back in waves in 1979, Lang's eight-year-old brother returning with a young Brahma because he didn't know what to do with it, the rogue cadres and the hostage crisis, and walking in the footsteps of others to keep from hitting a mine. And she explained why she couldn't leave a note, or any other written communication, to tell Lang that she was still alive and where she was headed.

I had to supply things I thought the boys would have encountered, such as the temple and the fish traps, using what I saw with Google Maps. I also switched a monsoon-season rainstorm for a dry-season one so the boys would get stuck on the bank of the Mekong – I needed a way to illustrate that Lang could hide where there was nowhere to hide, and escape where there was nowhere to go. And I added the other boy's getting sunstroke to reinforce that Lang was not sure, all the way along, if his comrade was going to make it.

To complete the story's ending I gave the boys and their mothers knowledge they simply didn't have. All the two women had been told when ordered out of Pong Tuk was that they must go west because the Vietnamese had invaded Cambodia from the east, the Vietnamese already had minesweepers on Highway Two, and Road 31 had been mined. (They'd heard the bombing of the provincial capital themselves.) They didn't know that the Vietnamese had come up Highway One, that they'd managed to ford the Mekong, or even that they'd taken Phnom Penh. No one asked the boys where they'd come from or how many days they'd walked – they were all literally running for their lives, and there was no time for questions. They knew the boys must have been in the army because they were in "the last wave", but no one figured out that there had been a mass desertion at the Mekong Crossing. And, as I've said, the boys believed that the Vietnamese invasion force had been behind them in the combat zone; it was only when Lang and I interviewed the Assistant to the Municipal Administrator of Ba Phnom District that we learned what had really happened.

"We still have your lighter to start our fires with, and we can use our water cups for cooking pots. We still have our waterproof hammocks, and can use them as ponchos when it rains. And we still have our machetes."

These were the boys' only possessions.

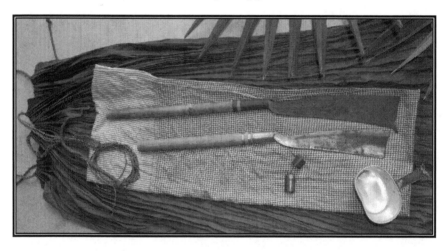

The checked fabric is a "kramaa" folded to a quarter of its size.

Chapter Notes

Out!

"We could still hear them below us – a relentless boom… boom… pssssssss… BOOM! It was almost dark, and they were still shelling. We didn't know how long we'd been running – we just ran."

Ba Phnom, as it would have looked to the boys as they ran toward it.

We climbed the mountain on the north side, the area the boys had run to to get away from the shelling. As we left the plain I saw a burned-out building from the war – it was so *eerie* to see it there, after more than thirty years. Then I remembered that the boys' uniforms must still be out there – somewhere – buried under a tangle of vines. And when we reached the top of the mountain I looked west to see if I could see the Mekong, and saw the remains of the canal the Funanese (we presume) had built to get to Ba Phnom from the river. I'd read about these ancient canals, but I'd never *seen* one. It was all very surreal.

The "X" pattern the black straps of Ho Chi Minh sandals make across the instep and ankle is the reason the boys had to ditch their shoes. Lang and I happened upon *The Iron Triangle* while watching TV one evening. In the scene where Ho, a North Vietnamese soldier, is seen stealing through the jungle, Lang immediately pointed to his feet. *"That's* why we had to ditch our shoes! Look how easy it is to spot the soldier, even though he's back in the jungle. And the pattern is easiest to spot when he's moving."

Lang never did figure out that they were going to put him into combat. I asked him what they had him carrying the day of his escape, to be sure the boys really had no food with them. When he told me that they'd switched him *that morning* from carrying fish and rice to carrying ammunition... So who *was* carrying the food? Probably the officers who were planning to desert.

As for their unit running up the mountain, now he doubts they ever did. Before we met the man who gave us his brother's eye-witness account of the battle for the Mekong Crossing, Lang and his comrade had thought that they were the only deserters. The Assistant to the Municipal Administrator estimated the desertion rate at 95 percent. Lang had assumed that his squad leader had been killed, but now he thinks he got away.

He remembered very clearly he and his comrade coming up with a strategy together to try to get out of the war zone – look too insignificant for any soldier, on either side, to bother with, so that no one would question them. But it would not have worked. Firstly, the boys were just too many days behind the evacuees to claim to be evacuees themselves. Secondly, by the time they woke up under the tree, both armies knew what the desertion rate had been the day before; there would have been no doubt who the boys were. Thirdly, the Vietnamese knew that the Khmer Rouge were using child soldiers; our Vietnamese source told us that his unit, a "clean-up" detail, had been shown pictures of them and told to shoot them. The boys didn't get to Highway One until a day after the Vietnamese infantry had come through, and then got away from it quickly, but it was just by chance that they never ran into any "clean-up" units.

Their plan to pose as "old people" once they got out of the war zone would probably not have worked, either. As Nyah says, "... they'd know we're 'new people'. We're just too thin. We look like we just walked out of a death camp." And the older boy looked Chinese; most "old people" were Khmer (not mixed).

When they surmised that some of the Vietnamese coming up Highway One were Khmer Kraum, they were right. The Vietnamese army had selected the men for the Highway One assault force purposefully – one third were Khmer Kraum.

Of the U.S.-South Vietnamese invasion of Cambodia in 1970, Dr. David Chandler wrote in <u>The Tragedy of Cambodian History</u>:

"The principal effect of the operation – beyond the casualties incurred and the intensified U.S. alliance with Lon Nol – was to push mainforce Vietnamese Communist units deeper into Cambodia, where they soon began to take apart Lon Nol's poorly-trained forces." (Chandler, 1991, p. 204)

Of the carpet bombing in which Lang and his family found themselves caught up, Dr. Chandler wrote in <u>A History of Cambodia</u>:

"In the first half of 1973, the United States postponed a Communist victory by conducting a bombing campaign on Cambodia that, in its intensity, was as brutal as any conducted during World War II. Over a hundred thousand tons of bombs fell on the Cambodian countryside before the U.S Congress prohibited further bombing. No estimate of casualties has ever been made, but the campaign probably halted the Communist forces encircling Phnom Penh, even though some people have argued that it hardened the will of the surviving Communist forces." (Chandler, 2000, p. 207).

The comet sighted in 1970 was the Bennett Comet.

At the time the boys escaped they thought the chances their mothers, *if* they were still alive, were still in Pong Tuk were about 50/50. But the chances that they *were* still alive? In Lang's words, "We just didn't want to think about that."

***Lang (right) in a country store, buying the machetes
for the photo on page 260. The stores on Highway One
where the boys crossed the minefield would have been much like this one.***

The shopkeeper is Chinese/Khmer (note his sunburned skin); you can imagine how different the two boys must have looked from one another.

Day One – *Alive*

The idea for the opening of this chapter came from something many survivors have told me – that the first thing they did upon awakening each morning was to ask themselves if they were really still alive.

Cambodia was cooler in 1979 than it is today, and the boys escaped in the coolest season. The temperature on their first night, when they slept underneath the tree in short-sleeved shirts and shorts with their hammocks still in their packs, wouldn't have been more than 60 degrees Fahrenheit (15.6 degrees Centigrade). When Lang first told me of the conditions in the work camps, he said that the worst thing after the hunger was the cold. When the boys had to work the paddies in monsoon season, they had to work in the rain. And sometimes it rained all day. He remembers being chilled to the bone, and dreaming of the soft, warm blankets he'd had in Prai Anchaan.

"I was only paying attention to all the places I wanted to go, and the things I wanted to see. The great temples of Angkor in the north..."

The crushing silence Lang remembers from the jungle on Ba Phnom is something I've heard other survivors talk about – the total absence of any sound of life. But the decimation of the bird population was partially due to the use of DDT before the war. When Lang and I began going to Cambodia in 2003, we would ask ourselves the same question everywhere we went – "Where are the *birds?*". We've read that the decimation of the human population by the Khmer Rouge, and their relocation of people away from key habitats, resulted in an increase in the number of birds in some areas. And that numbers began to rise throughout the country sometime after the war. But Lang and I only began to see birds in numbers around 2010 – 35 years after the takeover.

When trying to convince his comrade that it was safe to look for food, Nyah says, "... no one could make a move up here without being heard. Not even Viet Cong." The boys called all Vietnamese Communists "Viet Cong" because they didn't know there were different factions; here, he was referring to their reputation as masters of stealth. The Viet Cong had been absorbed into other Vietnamese Communist factions by this time.

Neither boy knew what year it was, or how old he was. Some people had been counting the rice harvests, but the boys hadn't thought to do that. And their mothers hadn't thought to tell them to.

It was odd how I learned of Lang's ability to recognize people that he shouldn't have been able to – by "the things that never change –their gait, their voice, their dialect, how they move their eyes..." We watch a lot of BBC movies, and BBC "recycles" their actors. I realized that Lang could recognize actors he'd only seen before in different costume and makeup, when they were younger or older. It was absolutely incredible – *I* couldn't do it. When I remarked on this ability, he told me how he did it. "Did you learn that in the work camps?" I asked. "Yes," he said, "I guess I did."

The arsenic-for-dysentery cure is from my own experience, when I studied in India. I was given a tablet by my host family, swallowed it, and was *then* told what was in it!

One of the first questions I asked when we started the book was what the boys had talked about on their journey. Lang said, "Food!" Even when they were able to get enough, they couldn't stop talking about it. This is why I had them compare recipes and talk about their mothers' cooking throughout the story.

Lang tried to explain to me how his commanding officer had navigated without maps, but I just couldn't understand how this could be done. After several tries he packed me up in the car and took me to the home of a man who'd been an officer in the Lon Nol army. When *he* explained it to me, I understood – they just put local boys in each platoon, so they could tell the commanding officer where they were and how to get to their next destination.

The original line about the bombers approaching Prai Anchaan read, "When we heard the B-52s coming, we scurried for our hole in the ground like rabbits when a big hawk flies over." I had researched what type of plane the U.S. had used, and had read that it was the B-52. Lang and I were walking just south of a naval base one day, heard a plane above us, and looked up. He said, "*That's* the plane that bombed us – not a B-52." I mentioned it here not because I think it important what type of plane was used, but because, in 1973, Lang *saw the plane at very close range* shortly before it dropped its payload. There was no air raid warning system of any kind, and people literally ran for their homemade bomb shelters when they saw the planes coming. I changed the line to, "When we saw the bombers coming..." Prai Anchaan never took a direct hit (although Lang lost relatives in other villages), but Lang still remembers the horrific shock waves – he was afraid he would die of internal bleeding.

The United States dropped 2,756,941 tons of bombs on Cambodia between 1965 and 1973 – more than the Allies dropped in all of World War II. (*Bombs Over Cambodia* at *www.yale.edu/gsp/publications/Walrus_CambodiaBombing_*

OCT06.pdf.) Cambodia is the size of Oklahoma. The authors of *Bombs Over Cambodia* analyzed the Air Force data on the American bombing of Indo-China between 1964 and 1975, released by former-president Bill Clinton in the Fall of 2000:

"The impact of this bombing, the subject of much debate for the past three decades, is now clearer than ever. Civilian casualties in Cambodia drove an enraged populace into the arms of an insurgency that had enjoyed relatively little support until the bombing began, setting in motion the expansion of the Vietnam War deeper into Cambodia, a coup d'état in 1970, the rapid rise of the Khmer Rouge, and ultimately the Cambodian genocide."

Pin Yathay, a highly-placed Western-educated engineer in a position to see what was happening first-hand, later wrote:

"The effects of the raids were exactly the opposite of those intended – they drove the communists deeper into Cambodia." (Yathay, 2000, p.15)

The Khmer Rouge used the memory of the carpet bombing to get people to leave Phnom Penh quickly in April of 1975 – they told the populace that the U.S. was going to bomb the capital.

A monster vine of wild rambutans

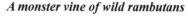

Day One – *All the Degrees of Dead*

The idea for this chapter came from an incident that happened when the boys were in the same work camp. Lang was swimming, and rolled over on his back. The older boy started laughing. He told Lang that he looked like a floating skeleton because his ribs stuck out. Lang, incredulous that the older boy didn't realize that he was just as thin, told him so. The older boy didn't believe him, and Lang didn't have a mirror to prove it.

The boys' method of getting to their feet was a practice born of the camps. They worked in crews of about half a dozen boys. They were so weak that, after sitting down for their break, they'd find themselves unable to get up again. One would take it upon himself to get to his feet, extend his hand to the crewmate sitting next to him, and pull him to his feet. The boy would then continue on down the line until the whole crew was up. They all rotated in this role; someone else would get the crew on its feet after the next break.

We estimated Lang's height from the photo taken in Khao-I-Dang (he was standing next to his mother, whose height we knew). We had no way to estimate his weight.

When Lang's squad leader joked that the recoil of an AK-47 would knock him over, he always did it in front of his lieutenant. Lang interpreted this to mean that the man was trying to keep him out of combat. And he remembers one other cadre who showed him kindness. An official in one of his work camps gave him his own shorts, because Lang's were torn all the way down the front (they no longer covered his testicles). Lang traded for a pair of shorts that fit as soon as he could, but kept the larger pair to make bandages.

You can see the kind of jungle rat he trapped in the classic movie, *Heaven Knows, Mr. Allison.* Very different than a city rat.

"Slaing" turned out to be Strychnos nux vomica Loganiaceae – the Strychnine Tree. Little wonder Lang's grandfather warned him about it!

Day One – *Recon*

Both boys would have been keenly aware of the centuries of territorial disputes between Cambodia and Vietnam and Cambodia and Thailand. They would have learned about them in school, and have heard their elders talk about them at home. Pol Pot's raids into the Delta had actually started early in 1977, and by the end of the following year the Vietnamese had already launched several retaliatory attacks. When the Vietnamese launched the December, 1978/ January 1979 invasion, they planned to stop at the eastern bank of the Mekong. But as Cambodian troops melted ahead of them, they changed their plans and decided to take the whole country.

Not all teachers were executed. Some lied about their work before the takeover, and were not discovered. Some had actually joined the Communist movement before 1975, disillusioned with the corruption of the Lon Nol regime.

Day One – *Hunted*

Lang insists that the army didn't tell them what the Vietnamese uniform looked like. He thought they'd be using the black Viet Cong uniform, which looked like his. In fact, they were using a modern green one.

Day One – *The Road* and *The Seventh Scenario*

"So how big is a super highway?"
"Maybe twice as wide as this – two lanes instead of one.
About the width of Highway Six
where it passes through your grandfather's village."

Two farmers crossing Bridge Thirteen in Prai Anchaan.

He hurried up the grade and onto the new road.
"A paved road. You call it a paved road, Nyah."

The intersection of the farm road (left) and Highway One.
Notice the height of the trees – all planted after 1979.

Lang remembered his comrade saying, when they woke up under the tree that morning, that they should have started moving at night the night before. But after their first day, he never suggested it. We think Highway One was where he realized that anyone who might have seen them in the dark would have shot them; that they were actually better off moving in the daytime.

Lang has no memory of crossing the minefield. They may have simply walked across the intersection, too tired to realize that they weren't still on the farm road until there *was* no road (i.e. until they'd walked off the south shoulder of One, and so were already through the minefield).

Readers have asked me why I assumed that what I saw with Google Maps in 2009 was in fact what had been there in 1979. My reply is that rural Cambodia changes very little from one year to the next. When we went to Ba Phnom in 2011 we found that there was still no bridge at the Mekong Crossing – we had to cross by ferry. The farm road was still unpaved. At the first tributary the boys swam a new bridge had been constructed, but it had been built right next to the old one and was much like it. Some of the buildings that had been damaged had not been rebuilt at all. Many of Prey Veng's bomb craters had been filled, but many had not; I could see them clearly with Google Maps. I reasoned that the main difference between what I saw with Google Maps and what would have been there in 1979 would be the amount of tree cover and the number of buildings standing – the years of carpet bombing, the civil war, and the destruction of the Khmer Rouge as they retreated would have left the plains of Prey Veng largely deforested and many of its buildings destroyed. The intersection of the farm road and Highway One is nine kilometers from Neak Luong, one of the most heavily carpet-bombed areas in all of Cambodia.

Day Two – *Stripped* and *The Sound of Water*

Our Vietnamese source told us that his reconnaissance unit was not issued enough food. Depending upon how short they were, they might have had to kill someone they'd taken prisoner and never report that they'd found him because they couldn't share their own rations with him. Lang later learned first-hand that the Vietnamese infantrymen ate dog meat if they could get it.

There was, in fact, a famine in 1980, for the reasons the two boys talked about.

We happened upon the story of the officer who taught himself how to fly a helicopter on the Internet.

On the following page is a photo of a typical Khmer home. Try to pick out (left to right) the Brahma, the fruit trees, the stairs up to the family's living quarters, the grate built across the lower story so livestock can be kept there, the terracotta rain barrel in front of the tarpaulin right of the grate, the cylindrical fish trap on the ground to the right of the banana tree, the clothes hanging on the line, the haystack... and *no fence* against the neighbors. ☺

Day Two – *Between Hell and High Water*

"I'd never known anyone who hadn't learned how to handle a boat before
he'd learned to ride a bike – if my classmates in Phnom Penh
didn't know how to do it, well, they'd never let on."

Children paddling home from swimming. This is monsoon season – this lake
covers paddies that are dry in the winter. It's much like the lakes the boys
paddled across in "The Omen"; the lakes would have shrunk to a canal by May.

"You're going to find a <u>boat</u>?
Nyah, you've never been here in your life –
how would you even know where to look for one?"

Prai Anchaan children playing on a fishing boat submerged in the silt of the
Mekong. This boat is like the one the two boys would have 'borrowed',
and has been buried in the same way (note the stake and the rope).

Day Three – *The Turning Point*

Dragon boats at The Holiday of the Rowing of the Boats

The boats are actually paddled, not rowed; there's a row of paddlers along each gunwale. The number of boats varies from year to year and, these days, some are manned by women.

Note the offering of bananas on the bow – a carry-over from when Cambodia was Hindu, before Jayavarman VII declared Buddhism the state religion in the twelfth century.

"Ten thousand rowers race a hundred and fifty dragon boats through the stretch of river where the Tonle Sap and the Mekong collide – straight through to the Royal Palace!"

"Yes, the riverfront in Phnom Penh is the place to be.
Fortune tellers vie with one another to look the most exotic –
and therefore the most clairvoyant."

A fortune teller on the boardwalk reading the cards under a banyan.
The pins on her sweater are Buddhist charms.

The 'chaidey' at Wat Phnom that holds the ashes
of the king who moved the capital to Phnom Penh

Saambō was retired in 2012 in response to pressure from animal rights groups – the city is no place for an elephant, and the pavement was too hard on her feet.

Day Four – *Swamped* and *The Map*

These are the chapters that I referred to in the foreword, where my brain would start grinding away at two in the morning trying to figure out how the boys had crossed the marshes. The man who gave us his brother's eye-witness account of the battle for the Mekong Crossing said that his brother had ended up in Kampong Speu province. The boy had had to go without food for two weeks, and later died from the trauma. Because of where he'd started and where he'd ended up, and because he hadn't been able to find food, we reasoned that he had crossed the marshes. And at the point where we think he would have crossed them, they were about 25 kilometers wide. So I went through every scenario I had the two boys go through, trying to figure out how they did it. Then, after two weeks, I woke up one morning knowing just what they must have done. Because I remembered that Kandal Province was the *home province* of *both boys*. I thought of how much I remember of the map of my home state, compared to how little I remember of the states next to it. I reasoned that the older boy, if not both boys, would have remembered the distinctive pattern the Mekong and the Bassac make on the map as they flow closer and closer together. Lang had already told me they would have dug a boat out of the silt on the bank of the Mekong, so I knew they could go as far south on the river as they wanted to.

The Vietnamese did in fact bring some of their reinforcements in on

Highway 101. They transported them across the Mekong in the Delta, then bussed them up 101 at night.

Lang's mother went back to Cambodia as soon as she felt the country was relatively stable again, in the late 1990's. She began to go once a year after that. I met her in 2000, and thought she was simply going back to visit her family. When we started this book, Lang told me that she had been going back to try to find the daughter who had become separated from the family during the march out of Phnom Penh. In 2004 she finally located someone who was able to tell her that her daughter had not survived. *Twenty-nine years* after the girl had taken the "other" road. And thus the dedication of this book; had Lang's mother not learned her daughter's fate, she would still be looking for her.

The African Queen was actually made by a British company, Horizon Pictures (the boys would have thought it was a Hollywood film).

Day Four – *The Snake*

When Lang saw the boys in Pong Tuk bring in a four-meter-long cobra, he became even more determined to keep his family alive. But he found the beehive quite by chance. He'd been given the job of taking care of a water buffalo and was riding it back into Pong Tuk one morning, just looking up at the sky. And that's when he saw the hive. He climbed the tree, smoked the bees out, snapped off the branch the hive was on so it wouldn't fall to the ground, climbed down the tree with the hive, and took it to his mother. And, yes, he got several stings in the process, but says he hardly noticed – he was intent on getting food. This was just after his grandfather's death.

Lang saw a boy in one of his work camps bring in a cobra, too. Which meant that the boy was able to provide for his friends (as Lang did, with his jungle rats) and receive life-sustaining favors from them in turn. The boys were moved into one wooded area after another to clear for paddies, and wooded areas are the King Cobra's habitat.

I wrote this chapter because I wanted the reader to understand how desperately hungry 'new people' in many (if not most) areas of the country were, even right after the takeover. Lang's grandfather had been in prime physical condition before being forced out of Phnom Penh, but he starved to death in just a few months. But I wrote this chapter in a light-hearted vein because I wanted the reader to understand that the boys who were catching these snakes were far too young to understand the risk they were taking; one bite from a King Cobra will kill a small boy in less than thirty minutes. Boys were thrust into the role of provider by the takeover, and the sudden removal of their fathers made them even more desperate to keep their mothers alive. They simply caught anything they thought their families could eat, too young to understand that if they died in the process they would have actually *diminished* their family's chances of survival.

I included the story about the UXO accident because it underscores the fact that children do not always have the capability to weigh the risk of their actions. Lang saw boys as old as fifteen playing with live ammunition.

Day Five – *The Messenger*

Lang didn't understand what his grandmother was trying to explain to him about the French sunbathers – that they were simply trying to get a tan. He'd honestly thought they were trying to preserve *themselves* like his aunts preserved their fish!

The area where I had the boys see the electric light may have been evacuated at that time, and the border may have been marked – we couldn't get into the area to ask.

Day Five – *The Ruined Temple*

"The walkway led into the temple compound between two 'chaidey' – miniature pagodas, one for each of the temple's patron families, used to keep the ashes of all the generations of their dead together."

'Chaideys' at Wat Koh in Phnom Penh

In 1975 there was, typically, one Buddhist temple per village and its surrounds. It was centrally located, and its buildings were the largest around. By closing the temple and killing its occupants the Khmer Rouge could, in a single stroke, wipe out the area's center of worship, all its monks and an important educational institution, cut off access to most families' gravesites, and demoralize the local population in the process. They could then use the grounds and buildings as killing fields, prisons and torture centers – further desecrating the temple and demoralizing the population. In some areas they simply used them for storage. In the chapter entitled, "The Map", the older boy *assumes* that the Khmer Rouge had demolished all temple buildings. The boys had not been allowed anywhere near the temple in Pong Tuk, but believed that the buildings had been destroyed because they couldn't see them sticking up above the trees. They may also have seen temples that had been destroyed on their way to Pong Tuk from Phnom Penh. They didn't see any temples after 1975 because they were in work camps, and then the army.

The temple I had the boys stop at was the only one in the area where they would have been looking for one. I could see with Google Maps the double line of old trees running out from it to the river. They were *huge*; the temple obviously predated the takeover, and had been built in a time when people still came to the temple by boat.

- - - - - - -

We were sitting at a wedding banquet one evening, in the United States, waiting for the event to begin. Lang's mother began to look around for her friends, and every time she saw one of them she waved, and laughed, and smiled.

Then she turned around.

When she turned back to us, her expression had completely changed. She whispered something to Lang. I was sitting on the other side of him, and asked him what was wrong.

"My mother recognizes that man – the stranger at the table behind us." I turned and saw a middle-aged Chinese man I'd never seen before, dressed in an expensive suit.

"My mother says he was a high-ranking Khmer Rouge official," Lang continued. "That he sent his children away to school in Beijing during the Khmer Rouge years, so they would be safe. While her children starved. Apparently he's just moved into town, so we'll be seeing him again."

I looked at the man at length. The most remarkable thing about him was that he seemed to be doing so much better than all the refugees around him. Many Cambodians have recurring health problems from the Khmer Rouge period, and from living in poverty after they came to the United States (remember – many have little or no education – that's why the Khmer Rouge spared them). But he looked healthy. And he obviously had money.

Much publicity has been given to the fact that virtually no Khmer Rouge have been punished for their crimes. Only five were ever indicted. The rest were never even arrested, including Pol Pot. Some actually get through the U. S. immigration process and live here among us, as United States citizens; this man was not the only one we've met.

It should also be noted here that three quarters of the cadres at the top were Chinese/Khmer, including Pol Pot.

We did see the stranger a few times after that. But instead of sitting at a table in the center of the room, as he had the first time we saw him, he'd choose a table in the corner – away from the main activity, where the light was lower. He would sit down when he first came in, quietly, and not get up again until he left the party. As though he knew he'd been recognized the first night he'd turned up.

- - - - - - -

Lang was watching <u>Band of Brothers</u> one evening. The scene was the liberation of a Nazi concentration camp. The commanding officer told his men to unlock the inmates' doors, but suddenly reversed his order. He told his men to keep them locked in so that they couldn't get to a food source and die from overeating; the Allied troops would ration their food until they could safely eat a full meal again.

The minute the officer explained his action Lang cried out, "I remember! They used to bring in tons of food after the harvest, once a year. And then tell us we could eat all we wanted. I stopped eating when I began to have trouble breathing, but there was a boy sitting near me who couldn't stop. Suddenly, he said he couldn't breathe. He fell over, and the cadres later told us he was dead."

Day Five – *The Omen*

The Indianization of Cambodia is written in the current chart of South Asia. The earth's major shallow ocean current systems are produced by winds that blow steadily, in a persistent direction (the winds set the surface water in motion, and this results in slow-moving currents). The currents are deflected by the west-to-east rotation of the earth on its axis, clockwise in the Northern Hemisphere and counter-clockwise in the Southern Hemisphere.

So where in these wind and current systems was Oc-Eo? At 10 degrees north latitude and 105 degrees longitude – in the Northeast Trades wind belt, east of India.

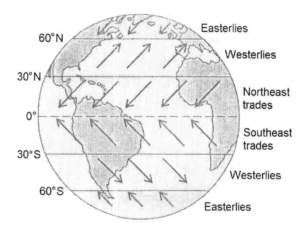

from <u>Marine Biology – an Ecological Approach</u>, by J. Nybakken and M. Bertness (p. 13)

And where is India? Look at the chart, and *look at the currents*.

The ancient traders could use both the Equatorial Countercurrent and the Northeast Trades to get to Oc-Eo and back. The *history* is in the *science*.

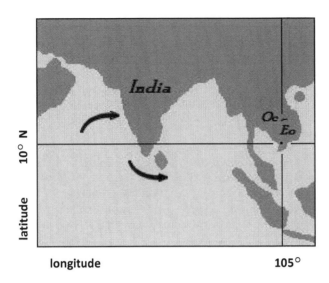

Equatorial Countercurrent

based on a chart from <u>Marine Biology – an Ecological Approach</u> (p. 14)

Not all scholars are in agreement on whether Oc-Eo was the seaport for the principality (or collection of chiefdoms) identified by Chinese sources as "Funan" (i.e., it may have been the seaport for another political entity).

Day Five – *The Trap*

The conglomerate trap I described is what I saw with Google Maps, except that the one I saw looked like it was made of aluminum. I showed the photograph to Lang and he said that, in 1979, the trap would have been made of bamboo. There was one in Prai Anchaan, but it didn't survive the war.

Now, if I could have seen that trap in a satellite photograph, you can imagine how big it is. I assumed it wasn't a power station because it's in a remote area and because it wasn't on the Bassac (a much larger river). And it does make sense that there would be fish traps there – the river drains a vast expanse of marshes to the north of it.

I wanted to get into this area in 2011 to ask what had been in the river in 1979, but we couldn't. The problem was the record flooding. Looking at the Bassac from the top of Phnom Da I could see that we wouldn't be able to drive into that area to hire a boat. I tried to hire the boatman who had brought us to Phnom Da to take us over to the Bassac, but he wouldn't – he said it was too far. When I pulled out my maps to see how far it *was*, I found they didn't agree with one another on where the *border* was. None of us could risk crossing over into Vietnam by mistake.

And Lang decided that the area was too remote to be safe, especially as we would be asking questions about the Khmer Rouge period. I'd asked at Phnom Da if the residents had been relocated because there are two Hindu temples on the mountain, and had been told they hadn't. More conversation revealed that the source of the information was pro-Khmer Rouge. "You just never know who you're talking to," Lang said, "– not out here. It's not worth taking the risk."

Day Six – *Four Hours*

Preah Maha Vimaladhamma Pin-Sem Sirisuvanno, a living treasure of information about the traditional Khmer arts and the abbot of Wat Bo in Siem Reap, told us of the dinosaur carving – and that it *is* a dinosaur. It's in Ta Prohm temple, near Angkor Wat, and was carved in the twelfth century. (If you rent the movie *Lara Croft: Tomb Raider* you can see this temple – watch the scene just before Lara falls through the floor.)

Some scholars believe that the Stegosaurus was not yet extinct in Cambodia when Ta Prōhm was built because the people of that time didn't have the paleontological skills to determine what a dinosaur would have looked like from finding a skeleton. There are many websites out there with more information on the famous Ta Prohm stego – just Google it!

Day Six – *The Body in the Water*

Lang's grandfather gave him the live-worms-in-coconut-water potion many times – it's a commonly-used remedy for fever. But Lang asked me to tell you that you must steep the worms in the coconut water for at least an hour before the medicine will work.

All Lang remembers of this part of their journey is what they were able to find to eat. He knew that insects are particularly nutritious, and caught them whenever he could. You can see a nest of Cambodian weaver ants in the May, 2011 edition of *National Geographic*. He remembered catching diving beetles when he saw them at Disney's Animal Kingdom, and we found ourselves going from display to display – centipedes, turtles, bats – with Lang saying, "Yeah, I ate that. Here's how I caught it, here's how I cooked it, and here's how I got it out of the shell." He had completely forgotten about the Water Monitor; when he saw the Komodo Dragon he pointed to it and exclaimed, "I remember a lizard like that in Prai Anchaan!" And then he proceeded to tell me how it had suddenly appeared after a firefight.

Why the boys never came upon a body is still a mystery. It was probably because they avoided villages. As for the war zone itself, as we've said, most Khmer Rouge units retreated before the Vietnamese even got to them; Lang's commanding officer gave the order as soon as he learned that the Vietnamese had tanks. And boys in other units may have taken off before their commanding officers even gave the order to retreat.

Lang and his comrade thought of bodies as like the shed exoskeletons of dragonflies – the dragonflies were somewhere else now, and didn't need them anymore. The boys were happy for the people who had died because they'd escaped from the endless fear and suffering of life under the Khmer Rouge.

Day Seven – *The Bassac*

When Lang's family came to the U. S. as refugees the only way his mother could make ends meet was to work two full-time jobs, then buy a house, and then turn the house into a boarding house for other refugees. The story of the forced marriage came from one of her boarders (the groom himself). Ah, but you wondered how they showed a movie without electricity, didn't you? They simply hooked the projector up to a car battery.

Day Seven – *The Temple on the Mountain*

We took a canal built by the French to the area of Phnom Da, but, once we were out there, many of the canals we travelled on were constructed by the people of Funan and Chenla.

The temple on the top of Phnom Da is visible for miles, and can't be mistaken for anything else. It dates to the early Angkorian period and is made of brick. The photograph below was taken in the flood of 2011; the boys would have been able to walk to the mountain in January of 1979.

There's also a stone Chenla-era temple on Phnom Da – don't miss it.

Day Eight – *The Smell of Water*

Lang really does have the crazy genetic traits described in this chapter. He even says the smell of a pond changes throughout the day as the water warms.

Day Ten – *The Last Wave*

The fact that the two boys' families were the only ones left in Pong Tuk waiting for their children is what compelled me to write this book. Once I understood that Lang and his comrade were the last wave – because they were the furthest away, their unit was one of the last to retreat, and they'd fallen asleep their first night – it made a *little* more sense. But that doesn't alter the fact that the two mothers shouldn't have been there, because of the risk. But they were.

Lang thinks he understands why his comrade's mother waited. Firstly, her son was the baby of the family. Secondly, she knew another family with whom she could send her girls to safety, and, if her son did not come back, she knew she could make the journey to Phnom Penh with Lang's family. Thirdly, her son could help the family to survive in ways that his sisters couldn't because he was physically stronger than they were. She would have anticipated that he would have to build a semi-permanent shelter for them if their house in Pochentong had been destroyed or commandeered.

But we've spent many an hour trying to figure out why Lang's mother waited for him. It may have been because he reminded her so much of her remarkable father, and her duty to him. Or because she knew that Lang had learned from him how to find food and survive in the "new" Cambodia more than had anyone else in the family. But it may have been Lang's *compassion*, gained from watching his gentle Buddhist grandfather heal the sick and comfort the dying, that made her wait for him. She knew he would help her to keep the rest of her family alive.

Each hut built for "new people" included a kitchen so that the family could cook until the communal mess hall had been set up (in Pong Tuk, this was shortly after Lang's family arrived and before he was sent to his first work camp). After that, they were only allowed to boil water. Lang's mother once stole and boiled rawhide so as to have something to feed her children. He says it smelled horrible, but they were so desperate that they ate it. Pin Yathay describes in Stay Alive, My Son the conditions under which "new people" in the communes were forced to live (see Recommended Reading).

It was the pattern of Phnom Treil against the mountain behind it that Puamaak was looking for. The Khmer Rouge stripped Phnom Treil down to the bedrock, but by 2015, the jungle had overtaken it again.

Had Lang's uncles been caught by the Khmer Rouge, they might have been executed so that they could not ally with the Vietnamese (they were 'new people', men, and in their prime years). Posing as army officers would probably not have saved them, and they knew it. They had been in work camps for three and a half years, and looked it.

The hostages were never marched up Phnom Sanhaan, presumably because the cadres were afraid of being trapped there by the Vietnamese. Instead the cadres drove their captives west, almost to the Thai border, and executed them there.

Between two and three million people were marched out of Phnom Penh in 1975, which would have meant that more than a million would have been trying to return in 1979.

Please see the last paragraph of "Binding the Pieces of the Story Together" (page 259) for additional information about the boys' return to Pong Tuk.

A Word from Lang

I have heard the policies of the Khmer Rouge described as a "social experiment", intended to increase agricultural production. But I do not believe that anyone who lived through this period would describe them as such. The men and women of the Khmer Rouge leadership were like Adolf Hitler and his henchmen – murderous, and sadistic. My family lived through the civil war, the takeover, the three-year-and-nine-month regime, and the year following the Vietnamese invasion (in which atrocities by the Khmer Rouge continued), and that is what we saw.

If in fact their policies were intended to increase agricultural production, they would have tried to keep "new people" in the communes and work camps *alive*. Instead, they worked and starved us to death. We were not even allowed to eat what we ourselves had produced – not the fruit, not the vegetables, not the root crops, not even the rice:

"… the 1975 (rice) crop was harvested and villagers saw most of it hauled away in government trucks to undisclosed destinations. In fact, in a contorted stab at self-reliance, the regime exported several thousand tons to China to pay for Chinese aid. The rice harvest of 1976 was exported also, but by then government demands on the population were even greater, and starvation occurred on a national scale." (Chandler, 1993, p. 260) "The rice harvest of 1977 was siphoned off to feed the army, to be stockpiled in forest hideouts, or to earn hard currency abroad." (Chandler, 1993, p. 302) The Vietnamese invaded Cambodia just after the rice harvest of 1978.

I will tell you what it was like in the work camps – Lord of the Flies. Small cliques of boys pitted against each other, all competing for the same resources, desperate to stay alive. The cadres watched us, and showed no interest in keeping us alive – even when the camp couldn't meet its quotas.

And I will tell you what happened to the half of my family not relocated to Pong Tuk. They walked back to Prai Anchaan, where they were known, and were labeled 'new people'. Most were executed, or starved, within a year – even though my family had been renowned as the most progressive farmers in the area. The Khmer Rouge didn't consult them on a single agricultural issue.

And if the Khmer Rouge's policies were intended to increase agricultural production, they would have found a way to rationalize the use of engineers in their colossal irrigation projects – if only those men who had opposed Lon Nol. And they would have used available machinery. Pin Yathay, a Canadian-educated engineer who had opposed Lon Nol, describes the building of a critical irrigation canal and how he was treated:

"…the four-mile canal was to be dug with no machinery at all… No one had surveyed the site, there were no plans, and no one kept records… thousands of men and women dug… without anybody even checking that the canal that we were building ran downhill away from the lake… Occasionally, some… brave... technician would try to tell the Khmer Rouge how the work should be done… The reply was always the same: 'Why do you try to tell us what to do?'" (Yathay, 2000, pp. 75-77) "Meanwhile, the rains had begun. We slept in the open on mats, near the work site, so urgent had it become that we complete our task.

We had no tents. We just lay out on our mats beneath the trees, soaked. The place swarmed with mosquitoes. We shivered the nights away, huddling around fires built both for warmth and to keep away the insects." (Yathay, 2000, p. 76)

As for the mass executions, the Khmer Rouge justified them as the elimination of collaborators against the state. But they killed *babies* – often by holding their feet and swinging them against a tree to smash their skulls. What kind of "experiment" was this?

Calling the policies of the Khmer Rouge a "social experiment" is like calling the ethnic cleansing of the Nazis a "social experiment". The Khmer Rouge themselves crafted the "experiment" lie. But those of us who were *there* – in the communes, in the work camps, and in the labor brigades – heard the cadres whispering among themselves,

ពួកថ្មីត្រូវលុត្ត ។

("The 'new people' must be eliminated.")

The key is the last word, លុត្ត ("leutt" – "to eliminate"). But it is the origin of this word that makes its use by the cadres so very ironic. It comes from the Pali word, "lutta" ("broken"). This word would have come to Cambodia with Buddhism, whose first precept forbids the killing of any living being.

But what happened in Cambodia can happen again – anywhere.

I've lived in the United States since 1981, and see an alarming increase in the number of elected officials who don't appear to be qualified for the positions they hold. They don't have the education, the experience, the dedication, or even the common sense required. And what does anyone's religion have to do with his qualifications?

These officials play a part in determining our domestic and foreign policies. But they're the ones *who can be most easily controlled.* And *you* can't know who's controlling them.-

Education is the keystone of democracy. Stay well informed, support your sources of unbiased, accurate and comprehensive news, prepare diligently to cast your vote, and discuss the issues and the candidates openly. Ensure that your children receive the very best education, both in school and at home, and that they learn to *think.* Know how incredibly fortunate you are to live in peace, and do everything in your power to perpetuate it.

Lang Srey
August, 2014

The Water Dragon ~ *Is... It... Real?*

A modern-day "neak" on the roof of a municipal building

Now, if I'd been twelve-year-old Nyah, I would certainly have been looking for a "neak" in the deep hole at the head of the fish trap river. He believed it was a real animal, and thought it might not be extinct. What started me thinking that perhaps it *is* a real animal is the consistency of its depiction, and the fact that it doesn't have anatomical features that don't make sense (such as wings that wouldn't support its weight). And what made me think that it might not be extinct was a photograph I'd seen of one, on a poster in a Lao temple. And then there was that U-Tube clip... So Lang and I decided to do some research.

First, we had to define what constitutes a "neak" – what anatomical parts it has. We looked at the rooves of several temples and came up with ten definitive features:

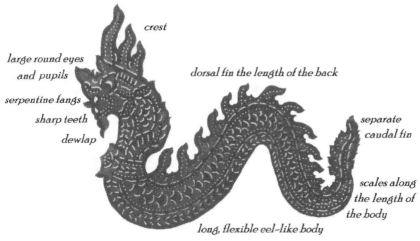

crest

large round eyes and pupils

serpentine fangs

sharp teeth

dewlap

dorsal fin the length of the back

separate caudal fin

scales along the length of the body

long, flexible eel-like body

Then, we had to determine what's *missing:*

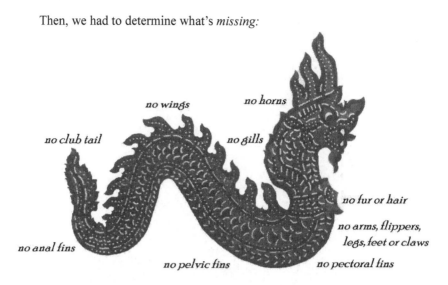

no wings   no horns

no club tail   no gills

no fur or hair

no arms, flippers,
legs, feet or claws

no anal fins

no pelvic fins   no pectoral fins

At this point we came to the same conclusion as Nyah's comrade: "It's the fins that have got me thinking… So a 'neak's not some kind of giant water snake – a reptile. Or something like the Water Monitor – that's a reptile, too. Or a dinosaur-like creature, like the Loch Ness Monster – they say he swims with flippers. And a separate caudal fin? I used to go with my mother to buy eels in the market – I remember very well what an eel looks like. Their dorsal fins are joined to their caudal fins. So the 'neak' isn't some kind of giant eel. That leaves… *fish.*"

But it is *not* a fish. *There are never any gills.*

So now we didn't know what it *was,* but we thought we knew what it *wasn't:*

~   a bird (no wings, legs, feet or claws)
~   a mammal (no fur or hair)
~   a plesiosaur (no flippers)
~   an eel (the dorsal fin and caudal fin aren't joined) or other fish (no gills)
~   a snake (snakes don't have fins)

Well, this left us pretty much stuck. So we decided to stop looking at the animal and start looking for linguistic clues.

To do this we went to Wat Bo in Siem Reap in search of its abbot, Preah Maha Vimaladhamma Pin-Sem Sirisuvanno. He is a living treasure of information about the traditional Khmer arts, and has founded a school at Wat Bo so that masters can pass on their skills. He told us that the modern Khmer word *"neak"* comes from the Sanskrit word *"naga".* I've mapped the progression for you on the next page (I *knew* there was a reason I saved my college textbooks…). He said the "neak" is a snake.

Sanskrit →	Old Khmer →	Modern Khmer
नाग *nāga** "snake"	नाः (Pou, 2013, p. 286) *nāăk* "a serpent gifted with miraculous powers and great strength" in Buddhist mythology,	នាគ *nēăk* "water dragon"
Please note: नाग is not related to *nagara* ("city"), the word from which **Angkor** was derived (Pou, 2013, p. 282; Monier-Williams, 1976, pp. 525, 532) or to *nāgara* ("town-born") (Monier-Williams, 1976, pp. 533, 532) *ə sounds like ŭ in the English word, "but"	Please note: Sanskrit **nā** (ना) has changed to Khmer **nēa** (នា) because ន instead of ណ was used to transliterate ना. The Sanskrit unaspirated consonant **g** (ग) has changed to Khmer **lă** (ះ) as follows: The Sanskrit unaspirated consonant **g** changed to the Khmer unaspirated consonant **k** because there is no **g** in Khmer. ះ (**lŏ**) instead of क (**lau**) was used in place of **g**, but neither inherent vowel (**ŏ** or **au**) sounds like the Sanskrit inherent vowel **ə**. **ă** (ៈ) was added to ះ to substitute **ă** for the inherent vowel **ŏ**, presumably to closer imitate the sound of the Sanskrit inherent vowel **ə**.	the final **ă** has dropped
	Please note: I used the Devanagari script here only for convenience, to illustrate how the consonant and vowel sounds changed. Sanskrit would most probably have first reached the Khmer in a different script.	

So now we had a snake with dorsal and caudal fins, a dewlap, and a crest on the top of its head. We were thoroughly confused. But Preah Maha Pin-Sem is the expert, so we continued to listen.

He said the "neak" is an artistic progression of the Indian "naga" seen on temples of the Angkorian era.

A three-headed naga on the lintel of Preah Einkosei

And just as the image of the Indian "naga" was based on real Indian snakes (the Indian, King, Caspian or Monocled cobras, or a species now extinct), the image of the Cambodian "neak" was based on real Cambodian snakes. He explained that the "neak" can be either of two snakes, which are probably found only in Indo-China.

So just as the Khmer adopted an Indian architectural form and then rendered it in a Khmer style (Angkor Wat the best-known example), they adopted the form of the "naga" and then rendered it as one of their own indigenous snakes. This is consistent with what they did with other Indian forms, such as the "apsaraa" – in Cambodia these celestial beauties are always carved with Khmer faces and coiffures.

One of the snakes Preah Maha Pin-Sem told us of is a *huge* animal, solid brown in color (slightly lighter than mahogany). There's an old story about hunters who ventured deep into the jungle and sat down to rest on what they thought was a log – until it moved.

A man in the room while we were talking to Preah Maha Pin-Sem told us another story. A group of men sent by Khmer Rouge cadres into the jungle in Battambang Province to do some task or another stepped over a log on their way. But, on their return, all that remained of the "log" was an indentation in the grass. The man who told the story had heard it from one of the men who had stepped over the "log".

Note that neither of these stories associates this snake with water – only with jungle.

Preah Maha Pin-Sem told us that the two stone statues of a gargantuan serpent in front of the South Gate to Jayavarman VII's royal city of Angkor Thom (pulled by gods on one side of the road and demons on the other) depict this snake. It has the head of a cobra and no crest, fins or dewlap. The "naga" in the photograph on page 288 has been rendered as this huge snake.

The other snake is a smaller snake, the "Pooah Krai". It has a black body with ivory bands. It injects venom into its prey through fangs, and also sprays venom from its fangs (like the Indo-Chinese Spitting Cobra). And it has a protruding, hard ridge running down the length of its back (suggestive of a dorsal fin). A "neak" railing at Wat Lao Buddharangsy in Modesto, California shows the ridge.

Although difficult to see in this photograph, the tip of the tail looks more like a rattle than a caudal fin. But also note that the body flattens out at the bottom – this animal is moving over land.

We looked again at the shadow puppet, and realized that it depicts the "neak" with the same short, stout body as the Pooah Krai temple railing. As you can see, this animal isn't slithering through water, either – note the three bushes.

Preah Maha Pin-Sem told us that the Pooah Krai is, in fact, *not* a water snake – that it lives in the jungle. But it's associated with water because it hibernates in ponds (with other Pooah Krai) to increase the potency of its venom. And, like most snakes, it can swim.

Another reason the "neak" would be associated with water is that, in both India and Southeast Asia, snakes are associated with water. Illustrative of this is that some statues of the Buddha include a many-headed "naga" spreading its hoods over the Buddha to protect him from the rain. And legends suggest that, at Angkor, snakes were associated with the water used for agriculture. So even land snakes were associated with water, both in the original Indian form and in the Khmer rendering of it.

And so the elusive "water dragon" is not an aquatic animal at all – it's a terrestrial animal.

OK, we now had two terrestrial Cambodian snakes, each with a head crest, dewlap and fins. We were still confused.

Preah Maha Pin-Sem explained that the crest, dewlap and fins that are part of the anatomy of the "neak" seen in modern-day Cambodian architecture and popular culture are the result of relatively-recent Chinese influence. It seems today's Khmer like the fancy Chinese dragon better than the more subdued Indian "naga". He pointed out that Angkorian "neak" do not have these three anatomical features.

So now we had the answer to the twenty-five-thousand-dollar question – is the "neak" a real animal? Yes – it can be either of two Cambodian snakes. On to the million-dollar question – are these snakes extinct?

Preah Maha Pin-Sem said that the last sighting of a Pooah Krai was during the French colonial period (1863 – 1953). Both Khmer and French reported seeing them. (There must be a record of this gigantic snake in some French scientific journal *somewhere* – if only a photo of a dead one, or an artist's rendering. If you know of such a record, please contact us.) The man who described the "log" in Battambang Province believed that that was the last sighting of the mahogany-colored snake.

There are several wildlife refuges in Indo-China that offer the habitat these two snakes need to live and hide (vast tracts of dense, wet jungle). We all came to the conclusion that there may be a few left out there. The Pooah Krai should look like the railing in the photo on page 289, *plus* black and white stripes and possibly a rattle at the end of the tail, and *minus* the dewlap, crest and caudal fin. (Oh, and the ears – the Lao sculptor got a little carried away...)

The other snake should be solid brown in color and as big as a log. It seems the people who told the stories about it didn't see its head or its tail, but, if you saw a snake as big as a log, would you stick around?

And the photo we'd seen of a "neak"? It's a picture of U.S. seamen holding a dead oarfish found off the California coast. But it was *passed off* as a photo of American GIs on the Mekong during the Vietnam War holding a "neak". Wikipedia exposed the hoax *(http://en.wikipedia.org/wiki/File:Mekongnaga.jpg)*. The oarfish is a deep-water ocean (salt-water) fish – there would be no habitat for it in Cambodia or in the Mekong Delta. And its head looks nothing like that of the "neak" (it appears the photo was photo-shopped for the hoax). But, as we've said, the "neak" can't be a fish because it's never depicted with gills.

And the U-tube clip of something BIG swimming in the Mekong? *(www.youtube.com/watch?v=ZArv10aBP88)* If you view it in "full screen" mode and look at the footage where the crowd *'ooh*'s and *'aah*'s, you'll see that the second head that comes up out of the water is attached to a different animal than the first head that came up. And that both animals are very short, and are being followed by animals like them. Fish, probably migratory fish, swimming one after the other in a long, thin line that may have looked like a water dragon from the shoreline. Not a "neak". Sorry.

Bibliography

British Broadcasting Corporation. (September 14, 2011). *Thailand – Cambodia Temple Dispute*. Retrieved March 2, 2012 from *www.bbc.co.uk/news/world-Asia-Pacific-123780001*.

Cambodia Tribunal Monitor. (2012). Retrieved 2012 from *www.cambodiatribunal. org*.

Center for Khmer Studies. Wooden Architecture of Cambodia – A Disappearing Heritage. Phnom Penh: Center for Khmer Studies, 2006.

Chadwick, Douglas. (2011, May). Why Weaver Ants Rule the Forest. National Geographic Society, 88 - 97.

Chandler, David P. A History of Cambodia. 3rd ed. Boulder: Westview Press, 2000.

Chandler, David P. The Tragedy of Cambodian History: Politics, War, and Revolution since 1945. New Haven: Yale University Press, 1993.

Fitzgerald, W. V. (May 6, 2009). Phnom Penh Post - *Cambodia: One Dead and Six Ill after Eating Poisonous Frogs*. Retrieved 2010 from *digitaljournal.com/article/272230*.

GAISMA. (2010). Retrieved July 6, 2010 from *www. gaisma.com/en/location/prey-veaeng.html*.

Google Maps. (2012). Satellite photographs of Cambodia and the Mekong Delta. Retrieved 2010, 2011, 2012 from *www.nationsonline.org/oneworld/map/google_map_cambodia.htm*.

Hand of Help. (2012). Retrieved 2010 from *www.ngo-handofhelp.org*.

Headley, Robert Kirk, Jr. Khmer-English English-Khmer Dictionary. Washington, D.C.: Catholic University Press, 1977 (and the SEAlang Library Khmer Dictionary at *www.sealang.net/khmer*).

Joffé, Rolland (Director), & Clark, Jim (Editor) (1984). *The Killing Fields* [Motion picture]. London: Goldcrest Films.

Khmer440. (2012). Retrieved February 26, 2012 from *www.Khmer440.com/k/ 2012/02/the-poor-are-losing-their-homes-but-its-OK-an-elephant-has-been-saved.*

Landmine and Cluster Munition Monitor. (2012). Retrieved 2010 from *www.the-monitor.org*.

Mekong River Commission. (2012). Retrieved 2010 - 2012 from *www.MRCMekong.org.*

Monier-Williams, Sir Monier. A Sanskrit-English Dictionary. Berkeley: Shambhala Booksellers, 1976.

Morimoto, Kikuo. Silk Production and Marketing in Cambodia – Research Report for UNESCO Cambodia. Phnom Penh: Institute for Khmer Traditional Textiles, 1995.

Nybakken, James W. and Bertness, Mark D. Marine Biology – an Ecological Approach. 6th ed. San Francisco: Benjamin Cummings, 2005.

Owen, Taylor & Kiernan, Ben (October 2006). *Bombs Over Cambodia.* Retrieved February 28, 2012 from *www.yale.edu/gsp/publications/Walrus_Cambodia_Bombing_ OCT06.pdf.*

Pou, Saveros. Lexique de Sanskrit-Khmer-Français (Sanskrit Utilise au Cambodge). Phnom Penh: Editions Angkor, 2013.

Reyum Publishing. Kbach – A Study of Khmer Ornament. Phnom Penh: Reyum Publishing, 2005.

Robson, Craig. Birds of Southeast Asia. Princeton University Press, 2005.

Schanberg, Sydney. Beyond the Killing Fields. Washington, D.C.: Potomac Books, Inc., 2010.

Schanberg, Sydney. The Killing Fields: The Facts Behind The Film. London: Weidenfeld and Nicolson, 1984.

Smith, Francis. Khmer Faces – A Beginning Khmer Language Textbook and A Khmer Heritage Language Textbook. Bangkok: Francis Smith, 2007.

Stone, Richard. (2009, July). Answers from Angkor. National Geographic Society, 26 - 55.

Ung, Loung. First They Killed My Father: A Daughter of Cambodia Remembers. New York: Harper Collins Publishers, Inc., 2000.

Weisel, Elie. Night. New York: Bantam Books, 1986.

World-Timedate.com. (2013). Retrieved June 18, 2013 from *www.world-timedate.com/astronomy/moonrise_moonset/moonphase_data. php?year=1979&city_id=421.*

Yathay, Pin (with John Man). Stay Alive, My Son. Ithaca: Cornell University Press, 2000.

MAPS

Administrative Map of Angkor Borei District, Ta Kaev Province 2008 - 2010. No city of publication or publisher listed.

Administrative Map of Angkor Chey District, Kampot Province 2008 - 2010. No city of publication or publisher listed.

Administrative Map of Ba Phnum District, Prey Veng Province 2008 - 2010. No city of publication or publisher listed.

Administrative Map of Treang District, Ta Kaev Province 2012. No city of publication or publisher listed.

Cambodia. Map. Singapore: Periplus Editions [HK] Ltd., 2011.

Geographical and Road Network – Kampot Province. No city of publication, publisher or year published listed.

Geographical and Road Network – Kandal Province 2007 - 2010. No city of publication or publisher listed.

Geographical and Road Network – Prey Veng Province 2010 - 2011. No city of publication or publisher listed.

Geographical and Road Network – Ta Kaev Province 2010 - 2011. No city of publication or publisher listed.

Google Maps. (2012). Maps of Southern Cambodia and the Mekong Delta. Retrieved 2010, 2011, 2012 from *www.nationsonline.org/oneworld/map/google_map_cambodia.htm.*

Kampot. No city of publication listed: Japan International Cooperation Agency (JICA) and Ministry of Public Works and Transport (MPWT), no year of publication listed.

Southeast Asia Monsoon Latitudes. No city of publication listed: National Geographic Society, 2009.

Vietnam Laos Cambodia. Munich: Nelles Verlag GmbH, 2006.

INTERVIEWS

Preah Maha Vimaladhamma Pin-Sem Sirisuvanno, Abbot, Wat Bo (Wat Rajabo), Siem Reap (for Khmer traditional medicine and the origins of the Cambodian water dragon)

Mr. Vanny Hin, Assistant to the Municipal Administrator of Ba Phnom District, Prey Veng Province (for the movements of the Vietnamese army at Neak Luong on January 5, 1979)

Mr. Chun Pel, Lieutenant, Lon Nol army (for how the Khmer Rouge army navigated without maps, the pattern used to mine villages, the hostage-taking as the cadres retreated from Pong Tuk, how much information the general populace would have had about the U.S. withdrawal from Vietnam and the fall of Saigon, and how much Lang's comrade would have known about demining)

Mr. Pho Nau, husband of the woman who served as headman of the village next to Pong Tuk in 1979 (for how the residents of Pong Tuk learned of the Vietnamese invasion, which areas were mined, and the fate of the Phnom Sanhaan hostages)

Mr. Retthy Reach (for his brother's eye-witness account of the battle for the Mekong Crossing on January 5, 1979)

Mr. Pyara Bagg Sandhu, B.S., Marine Biology, University of California at Santa Cruz (for the science behind the trade winds and currents that brought Indian traders to Cambodia, for identifying the lizard that ate the bodies in Prai Anchaan as the Water Monitor, and for finding the scientific article about the oarfish that was passed off as a "neak")

Hong Tek, M.D. (for Khmer traditional medicine)

The name of our Vietnamese source has been withheld at his request.

All survivors were interviewed in person. We selected our sources purposefully so as to interview as few people as possible to obtain the information we needed, in respect for their losses during the Khmer Rouge period. No one declined an interview.

MOTION PICTURES REFERENCED

Lean, David (Director) and Coates, Anne V. (Editor) (1962). *Lawrence of Arabia*. London: Horizon Pictures.

Huston, John (Director) and Kemplen, Ralph (Editor) (1951). *The African Queen*. London: Horizon Pictures.

Huston, John (Director) and Russell, Lloyd (Editor) (1957). *Heaven Knows, Mr. Allison*. Los Angeles: Twentieth Century Fox Film Corporation.

Salomon, Mikael (Director) and Fox, Billy; Ottey, Oral Norrie; Parker, Frances & Richards, John (Editors). (2002). *Band of Brothers, Episode 9 (Why We Fight)*. New York: HBO.

Sturges, John (Director) and Webster, Ferris (Editor) (1963). *The Great Escape*. United Kingdom: Mirisch Studios.

West, Simon (Director) and Puett, Dallas & Scantlebury, Glen (Editors) (2001). *Lara Croft: Tomb Raider*. Mutual Film Company.

Weston, Eric (Director) and Watts, Roy (Editor) (1989). *The Iron Triangle*. Scotti Brothers Pictures (I).

Recommended Reading

Yathay, Pin (with John Man). Stay Alive, My Son.

This intrepid survivor was the first to write a book-length account of life under the Khmer Rouge, and his story is more compelling than any work of fiction. A Canadian-educated engineer, he was exceptionally observant and perceptive. He explains how the Khmer Rouge gained a following by deceit, how their refusal to use engineering principles (as the Angkorian people had) ensured their failure, the realities of life in the communes, and what it took to escape to Thailand. His is the most compelling story I've ever read; it should be part of every home library.

Owen, Taylor and Kiernan, Ben (October 2006). *Bombs Over Cambodia.* from *www. Yale.edu/cgp/walrus_Cambodiabombing_Oct06.pdf.*

This must-read article discusses the carpet bombing of Cambodia and its consequences.

Stone, Richard. (2009, July). Answers from Angkor. National Geographic Society, 26 - 55.

This article describes the foundation upon which the great wealth of Angkor was built – a massive irrigation network that made possible the cultivation of more than one rice crop per year. It was this agricultural model that the Khmer Rouge drove the Cambodian populace to emulate, while taking from them the tools to do it.

Chandler, David P. A History of Cambodia.

Dr. Chandler's book imparts perspective on the depth of the 2000-year-old civilization that the Khmer Rouge destroyed. Of particular interest is "Sihanouk's Rule: A Balance Sheet" (pp. 198 - 200).

Chandler, David. The Tragedy of Cambodian History: Politics, War, and Revolution since 1945.

This book identifies the many players on the stage of Cambodian history after World War II, and the complex roles they played.

Schanberg, Sydney. The Killing Fields: The Facts Behind The Film.

Schanberg's book contains stunning photographs that drive home what war does to children.

Traveling to Angkor Wat?
You can drop off badly-needed reading glasses in Siem Reap (new or used)

This recipient is a landmine victim, a double amputee.

A person's ability to see his work determines when he must retire.
One pair of reading glasses can perpetuate the income of an entire family, and give an artisan with a skill that's dying out more years to pass his knowledge on. We've prearranged two drop-off points for you:

Wat Bo – This Buddhist monastery runs a school for underprivileged boys and teaches the traditional Khmer arts. They'll distribute your contribution to instructors, monks and farmers. They also need clothing for the boys in the school. From Wat Bo Street turn east on Achar Mean Street; the temple gate is at the end. Ask for the abbot, Preah Maha Pin-Sem. Don't miss the museum and the 19th century paintings inside the older temple building.

Institute for Khmer Traditional Textiles – This teaching organization will distribute your contribution to instructors and weavers. Go south on *Road to Lake* to House #472 (look for the IKTT sign on the right). Ask for Mr. Morimoto's assistant in the gift shop (second floor).

Wherever you go in the world, you can make a difference.

*You can collect reading glasses
from your friends and officemates before you leave,
and drop them off
at a religious institution or library at your destination.
Explain that you'd like them to distribute the glasses
to those who can't afford them.*

It will be the best part of your journey.

48437546R00184

Made in the USA
San Bernardino, CA
25 April 2017